THE ECONOMIC DEVELOPMENT OF *Tanganyika*

Report of a Mission organized by the International Bank for Reconstruction and Development at the request of the Governments of Tanganyika and the United Kingdom

THE
ECONOMIC
DEVELOPMENT
OF *Tanganyika*

PUBLISHED FOR

The International Bank for Reconstruction and Development

BY The Johns Hopkins Press, Baltimore

© 1961, The Johns Hopkins Press, Baltimore 18, Md.

Distributed in Great Britain by Oxford University Press, London

Printed in the United States of America

Library of Congress Catalog Card Number 61–9915

Second Printing, 1963

THE MISSION

William E. Stevenson, Chief of Mission
Walter A. Chudson, Adviser on Commerce and Industry
J. P. Hayes, Economist
F. Hellinga, Adviser on Water Resources
E. R. Hondelink, Adviser on Transport and
              Communications
Svend Laursen, Chief Economist
George W. Tower, Adviser on Mineral Resources
Egbert de Vries, Agricultural Economist
C. C. Webster, Adviser on Agricultural Production

PREFACE

This is the report of an Economic Survey Mission to Tanganyika, organized by the International Bank for Reconstruction and Development at the request of the Governments of Tanganyika and of the United Kingdom as the Administering Authority under the United Nations Trusteeship. The task of the Mission, as agreed upon by the two Governments and the Bank, was to assess the resources available for future development, to consider how these might best contribute to a balanced program of social and economic development, to make recommendations for practical measures to further such development, and to indicate the financial implications of such recommendations.

There were nine members of the Mission. With the exception of one economist from the staff of the International Bank, the members were recruited from outside the Bank's staff.

After conferences in London, en route, the Mission arrived in Tanganyika early in June 1959, and most members remained there until late August. During their stay, members of the Mission travelled extensively throughout the territory, visiting all the principal agricultural areas, mines and many of the manufacturing and processing enterprises, as well as other areas which remain undeveloped up to the present. Each of the nine Provincial Headquarters was visited, and conferences held with the various members of all the Provincial Teams and several of the District Teams.

The Mission received the fullest cooperation from the Government of Tanganyika. His Excellency the Governor met with Mission members on several occasions, and the Ministers and their staffs made themselves freely available for conferences and were unfailingly helpful in providing reports and data.

With the untiring help of the Liaison Officer provided by the Government of Tanganyika, Mr. F. J. Riddell, the Mission had the benefit of meetings with many representative groups and with a large number of individuals of varying interests. It had valuable conversations, both formal and informal, with the Chairman of the Tanganyika Elected Members' Organization and with many of the Members of the Legislative Council, both elected and appointed.

Organizations with which Mission members met included the Town Councils in nearly all the larger towns of the territory, officials and leaders of the principal cooperative unions and societies, representative Native Authorities and Chiefs' Councils, Chambers of Commerce and various other private bodies.

While in East Africa, members of the Mission visited the East Africa High Commission in Nairobi, Kenya, and conferred with various of its departments and services, notably the East African Railways and Harbours Administration, the East African Statistical Department and the East African Income Tax Department. Help was received from the regional headquarters of various of the commercial banks. Members of the Mission also visited the Royal Technical College in Nairobi, and Makerere College in Kampala, Uganda.

In London, the Mission had conversations at the Colonial Office, the Bank of England, the Colonial Development Corporation, the Commonwealth Development Finance Corporation and elsewhere.

The Mission wishes to express its appreciation for the whole-hearted cooperation and friendly hospitality received by its members from officials and private citizens alike in Tanganyika and in Nairobi, Kampala and London.

Thanks are also due to the United Nations and the Food and Agriculture Organization of the United Nations for participating in the initial briefing of the Mission, to the former for making available a staff member to participate in the Mission, and to the latter for examining and commenting on a draft of this report. A special acknowledgement must be made to the experts of the FAO taking part in the Pangani, Ruvu and Rufiji basin surveys. The Mission is greatly indebted to these experts for their generosity in discussing their findings, which were for the most part still unpublished at the time.

In September 1959 the Mission members reassembled at the Bank's headquarters in Washington for the purpose of preparing this report. In June 1960 the Chief of Mission and the Bank economist revisited Tanganyika for discussions based on a draft of the report and to inform themselves of more recent developments.

In the report which follows, the first three chapters are designed as an introduction to the rest, and cover the outlines of the Mission's view of the development task, a description of the territory's present state of economic development, and a rather detailed examination of budgetary aspects of development. Chapters 4-11 deal with agricultural and livestock development. Development of manufacturing, power, mining, transport and communications and of the tourist trade are considered in Chapters 12-14. Chapter 15 is devoted to questions of educational expansion and policy. The last two chapters deal with the machinery of planning, the question of maintaining the present high competence of the civil service, the future of the monetary system and possible modifications of the fiscal system.

The Mission's recommendations are made throughout the report; for convenience, they have been summarized in an appendix at the end. An effort has been made to cover the ground in the chapters without going into unnecessary details and technicalities. Certain background information and discussion of points of a rather technical nature have been put into a number of annexes, which may be regarded as extended footnotes to the main text. Supplementary statistical tables have been set out at the end of the volume.

It will be noticed that the Mission has not discussed problems of the social services, other than education, although it has made allowance for them in its budgetary discussion. The Mission was equipped specifically to examine the directly productive sectors of the economy, and its aim has been to confine this report to subjects about which it felt it had something to say which would be useful either to readers inside Tanganyika or to others outside who are helping or could help Tanganyika's development.

In transmitting the report to the Government of Tanganyika, the President of the Bank noted that since the Executive Directors and management customarily do not review the recommendations of economic survey Missions in detail, the report as transmitted represented the views of the Mission rather than positive recommendations of the Bank. The letter added, however, that the Bank believed that the findings of the report deserved the most careful consideration and discussion. Similarly, while other international agencies were given an opportunity to comment on the portions of the report of particular interest to them, responsibility for the recommendations of the report is to be regarded as that of the Mission alone.

Finally, the Mission records with sorrow the death of its Chief Economist, Svend Laursen, in February 1960. This sad event, which inevitably delayed the completion of the report, was felt as a severe personal loss by the other members of the Mission, and, we are assured, by the many people who became his friends during our stay in Tanganyika. Mr. Philip Hayes assumed the role of Chief Economist upon Dr. Laursen's death and upon him devolved the major burden of drafting the final report.

CURRENCY, WEIGHTS,
STATISTICAL CONVENTIONS

Currency

The currency in circulation is the East African shilling, which is maintained at par with the United Kingdom shilling (= 14 U.S. cents).

The East African shilling is divided into 100 cents.

Shs. 2/40 means 2 shillings and 40 cents.

The pound (£), equal to 20 shillings, is used as a unit of account.

Thus:

Shs. 20/- = £ 1 = $ 2.80
 £ 1 million = $ 2.8 million
 $ 1 million = £ 357,000 (approximately)

Weights

Avoirdupois weights are generally used in this report.

1 pound (lb.) = 0.454 kilograms
1 hundredweight (cwt). = 112 lbs. = one-twentieth of a long ton
The ton used is the long ton
1 ton = 20 cwt. = 2,240 lbs. = 1,016 kilograms

Statistical Conventions

— nil, or less than half the last significant figure shown in other figures of the same series.

n.a. not available.

Figures in square brackets [ ] are rough estimates.

Figures are generally rounded to the last significant figure shown. For this reason, components in a table may not necessarily add to exactly the total indicated.

GLOSSARY

The following glossary gives definitions of:

i. African words, e.g. mbuga, miombo;
ii. technical words, e.g. catena, cusec;
iii. words with a special sense in the context of this report, e.g. African, natural resources.

ACRE-FOOT—a measure of volume: the amount required to cover one acre to the depth of one foot, i.e. 43,560 cubic feet or approximately 1,233 cubic meters.

AFRICAN—as applied to people in this report, usually refers to the indigenous population of Tanganyika alone—i.e. the African population as opposed to the Indians, Pakistanis, Goans, Arabs or Europeans.

ALIENATED (land)—land made available for use by non-Africans, as agricultural estates, urban land, trading centers.

AQUIFER—water-bearing stratum with clearly defined upper and lower limits.

BALE—unit of measurement of cotton, 400 lbs.

BOMA—(i) a ring fence, as in "cattle boma"; (ii) an administrative center, e.g. the offices occupied by a District Commissioner and his District Team.

BUNDS—embankments to hold out floodwater.

CALVING RATE—number of calves born in each year expressed as a percentage of the number of adult cows.

CATENA—a succession of geological strata reappearing in regular sequence on the slopes in undulating country.

CD&W—Colonial Development and Welfare. Under a series of Colonial Development and Welfare Acts, the United Kingdom Parliament has provided funds to finance projects of development in or on behalf of the British overseas territories. The bulk of these funds is disbursed in the form of grants.

CUSEC—a measure of rate of flow: one cubic foot per second.

DOMESTIC EXPORTS—the expression is used in this report to denote *all* exports of goods produced in Tanganyika. (In Tanganyikan nomenclature, domestic exports are exports of home-produced goods to destinations other than Kenya and Uganda.)

EAST AFRICA(N)—this term is used in the report in the special sense of relating to the three territories, Tanganyika, Kenya and Uganda.

EXPATRIATE—person who is not a permanent resident of Tanganyika —e.g. a British government servant who may be expected to leave the territory on retirement.

GHEE—clarified butter.

HAFIR—excavated water storage tank, the excavated soil being used to form a dam on the lower side, thus increasing capacity.

INVISIBLES—external transactions other than merchandise trade and capital movements; e.g. payments for insurance and other commercial services, payment of interest and dividends.

JAGGERY—coarse, unrefined sugar.

kWh (KILOWATT HOURS)—thousands of watt-hours; measure of the amount of electricity generated or used over a period of time.

LOCAL GOVERNMENT AUTHORITIES—this term is used in particular to denote the bodies known in the past as NATIVE AUTHORITIES (q.v.)

MAKERERE—Makerere College, the East African University College, located in Kampala, Uganda.

MBUGA—dark clay alluvial clay with very gradual slope, often liable to flooding during the rains.

MIOMBO—an open canopy type of woodland characteristic of the drier areas between 1,000 and 4,000 feet above sea level. The predominant trees are species of *Brachystegia, Isoberlinia, Julbernardia* and *Pterocarpus*.

MW (megawatts)—millions of watts; measure of electric capacity.

NATIVE AUTHORITIES—the local authorities, particularly in rural areas, developed from the traditional tribal or sub-tribal authority. The way in which, and the extent to which, these authorities have evolved from the traditional form varies from place to place. With reference to the future functions of rural local authorities, it has been thought appropriate to use the term LOCAL GOVERNMENT AUTHORITIES.

NATURAL RESOURCES—The Tanganyikan appellation for anything to do with agriculture and animal husbandry. Although the term is an odd one, suggesting as it does that minerals are either unnatural or not a resource, nevertheless it is difficult to think of a suitable replacement.

PADDY—rice in husk.

pH—measure of acidity or alkalinity. pH = 7.0 is the neutral value; a lower value denotes acidity, a higher value alkalinity.

POMBE—African beer. The ingredients vary in different parts of the territory.

ROYAL COMMISSION (EAST AFRICA)—a commission appointed by Royal Warrant in the United Kingdom in 1953 ". . . to examine the measures necessary to be taken to achieve an improved standard of living . . ." in the three East African territories of Kenya, Uganda and Tanganyika. The Commission's Report was published in 1955 (Cmd 9475). (The Royal Commission should not be confused with the East Africa High Commission—see pp. 33-34).

SFERICS—a method of establishing the location of thunder storms at a distance by radio direction finding.

SHAMBA—agricultural holding.

SWAHILI—the lingua franca of East Africa. It is a Bantu language, modified by Arabic influences. It is the habitual language of many Africans along the coast, but is a second language, taught in primary schools, in the inland areas.

TRACE ELEMENT—any element of which small quantities are required in the soil for the proper growth of plants or the well-being of animals.

U (Uchagga, Ugogo, Usakuma)—prefix of locality: Uchagga is a synonym for "Chaggaland".

Wa (Wahehe)—plural prefix, used to denote the people of a tribe. The alternative prefix, Ba-, is also found in Tanganyika, as in Bahaya.

CONTENTS

xviii

Education

Fiscal Policy, Financial Institutions, Planning and Staffing

xxii

Tables

Maps

Diagrams

INTRODUCTION AND PROGRAM OUTLINES

CHAPTER 1 *THE DEVELOPMENT TASK*

This report has been written at a challenging point in the history of Tanganyika. Since September 1960 there has been for the first time a majority of elected ministers. This change should make it clear to the people of Tanganyika, as never before, that their future is in their own hands. Development depends on greater and more effective effort by those who produce. That the people should come increasingly to realize the connection between their own efforts and the improvement of their conditions of life is the main hope for rapid and satisfactory development in Tanganyika.

The role of leadership, of careful planning, of skillful management of the public finances is none the less essential. In an economy like that of Tanganyika, dominated by peasant agriculture, the Government and the administrative machinery have a vital part to play in promoting and shaping development. And the difficulties facing the new Government, while by no means insuperable, demand the most careful forethought.

The recent development of Tanganyika has been highly satisfactory in many respects. Agricultural, mining and industrial production have all been increasing rather rapidly. The volume of exports has continued to grow, even after the Korean boom, at an average annual rate of 6 percent, and the comparatively wide range of its exports has protected the territory from the worst effects of the decline in commodity prices in recent years. Thus export earnings in 1959 were nearly twice those of 1950. There is ample evidence of a widespread rise of living standards. Many other countries might envy this performance.

It appears that there should be little difficulty in maintaining a reasonably satisfactory rate of growth of production and exports over the next few years. The Mission's main concern has been with the problem of maintaining the growth of production in the longer run.

Tanganyika will progressively exhaust certain comparatively easy development possibilities which were opened up by past development efforts and by the booming commodity markets of the earlier postwar years. With the passage of time, easy possibilities of taking more land into use inevitably diminish. Moreover, existing African methods of agriculture and pastoralism lead increasingly to depletion of soil fertility and, in places, to erosion.

While it is the physical problems which are fundamental, their solution is made more difficult by the smallness of government financial resources. Government expenditures play a key role in stimulating and making possible increase in production. This is true not only of government investments in tangible assets such as roads and dams, but also of government current expenditures on, for example, agricultural extension work, surveys and planning, or the education of the people.

The current revenues of the Central Government have reached a level of about £ 22 million a year (gross). Total taxation, central and local, appears to absorb rather more than 20 percent of total monetary incomes, and it is hardly possible to envisage any substantial increase in this proportion. These revenues are at present supplemented by certain grants from the outside world, principally United Kingdom Colonial Development and Welfare grants. These two sources allow the Government of Tanganyika to spend, without further borrowing, only about £ 2.7 a year for each man, woman and child in the territory. This is a very low figure in relation to the size of the development task.

Development in Tanganyika could benefit greatly from increased grants from the outside world and from external loans bearing low rates of interest, long repayment periods or liberal periods of grace before service becomes due. This report will indicate several directions in which government expenditures could be usefully increased if the necessary finance is in fact available. However, in any circumstances the rate of economic advance will depend to a major degree on the skill and efficiency of the Government in making the most effective use of the resources at its disposal. Consequently, a considerable part of this report is concerned with questions of planning and method. It may be hoped, indeed, that the greater Tanganyika's success in making effective use of the limited resources at its disposal, the more it will appear to merit financial and technical assistance from the outside world.

ELEMENTS OF A PROGRAM

The main development task in Tanganyika is to improve the methods of peasant agriculture and cattle keeping, or to transform present methods and organization into systems making more productive use of the land. Peasant farmers and pastoralists form the bulk of the population. Tanganyika should have no difficulty in finding markets for increased agricultural exports on terms which are satisfactory, given the territory's generally low costs of production.

Many other aspects of development are closely related to the improvement and transformation of agriculture and animal husbandry. One of the main tasks in transport development is to construct and improve feeder roads serving areas of agricultural production, actual or potential. The growth of manufacturing depends on the size of the internal market, and so to a great degree on the growth of agricultural production.

Agricultural Improvement and Transformation

The Mission's proposals for agricultural and livestock development may be regarded as falling into two categories, "improvement" and "transformation."

In the next few years, the main increase of production will have to be looked for in improvement within the general framework of existing methods. The key to the "improvement" program is effective extension work, and the Mission makes recommendations for certain changes in extension methods and organization. There seems also to be a great opportunity, in the new political climate, to turn the energies of the people towards productive achievement, in part by adopting community development methods.

By continuation of existing programs, with the modifications suggested in this report, it should be possible to secure a continued increase of the volume of agricultural exports over the next few years of the order of 5 percent a year. However, this report argues that limited improvements are not enough. Present African methods over much of the territory differ little from the traditional pattern of shifting cultivation and extensive grazing of cattle. In most areas, these methods give only a low level of productivity, incapable of being increased rapidly so as to provide an appreciable improvement in the standard of living of the people, incapable of making an adequate contribution to the economy of the country, and incapable of yielding satisfactory returns on capital investment. At the same time, these methods cause cumulative deterioration of the soil and of the hydrological regime.

The growth of African agricultural production has been achieved more by increasing the area under cultivation than by raising yields. While productive and accessible land was abundant, wasteful use of land seemed unimportant. Now, however, it is becoming impossible to solve all problems simply by taking more land into use. Although in the territory as a whole there are many lightly populated areas of considerable productive potential, there are other areas where growth of population, coupled with increased demand for land in order to grow cash crops side by side with subsistence crops, is causing serious deterioration. Resettlement of people from overcrowded or deteriorated areas, even when feasible, usually involves high costs for provision of access roads, water supplies and possibly bush clearing. These costs are only justified if a fairly high level of production is attained in the newly settled areas. Moreover, unregulated settlement of new areas is likely to extend the risk of soil deterioration, and so eventually to lead to a decrease in the total productive capacity of the land.

With these considerations in mind, the Mission recommends, side by side with the continuation of the "improvement" approach, the adoption on an increasing scale of "transformation" programs aimed at the creation of markedly more efficient agricultural systems. The joint aims of these "transformation" programs should be: to make more productive use of the land of Tanganyika, while at the same time protecting or even building up the fertility of the soil; and to institute types of farming which will justify the injection of capital. This involves the creation of farming systems based on more intensive and permanent use of the land by efficiently run, planned farms of economic size.

In some areas, it may be possible to bring such farming systems into existence by a gradual system of change, improvement shading imperceptibly into transformation. In many populated areas, however, transformation would involve reorganization of land tenure and some redistribution of holdings; present resistance to such changes, coupled with reluctance to adopt the methods required for conservation farming, will make progress slow, so that returns to capital and effort would be low and delayed.

Consequently, the transformation program should rely to a considerable degree on securing quicker and higher returns on investment and effort by using selected, sparsely populated areas for planned settlement schemes and cattle ranches. In some places it is in any case already desirable to move people from overcrowded and deteriorating areas into others which are at present little used, and such action will become increasingly necessary in the future. Many of the larger schemes would be best organized on a partnership basis, in which individual Africans farm the land but a public authority provides capital works, productive services and an element of skilled management.

Given the inadequacies of rainfall over much of Tanganyika, irrigation schemes may be looked on as "transformation" operations of particular promise. On the one hand, the success of the schemes depends on the adoption of good cultivation methods. On the other hand, the superior yields to be achieved by suitable cultivation methods under conditions of irrigation give an incentive to cultivators to submit themselves to the necessary degree of regulation. In order that the full promise of these schemes may be realized, the most careful preparation is obviously required. Consequently, the Mission proposes that the next five years or so in irrigation and flood control work should be predominantly a period of investigation, planning and building up of staff. Thereafter a rather considerable program of investment in irrigation works should be undertaken, as soon as the necessary preparations are completed and financial considerations allow.

It now appears possible to undertake with some confidence the expansion of partnership cattle ranching. Successful adoption of other types of large-scale agricultural schemes depends on further research and experiment covering not only technical questions but also matters of organization.

The preliminary investigations, trials and experiments on which a successful "transformation" approach must depend will, of course, place an additional burden on the public finances in the initial phase. The return on the expenditures will inevitably be delayed and, indeed, of uncertain size. Nevertheless, the Mission believes that immediate action is desirable in order both to avoid a check at some future date in the pace of development and to reduce as soon as possible the dependence on methods which destroy the fertility of the soil.

The fact that the "transformation" program will at first impose a net burden on public finances reinforces the need so to organize "improvement" activities that they shall bring about the greatest possible increase of marketable production and hence of revenue. A major part of the "improvement" effort in the near future should be concentrated on crops and areas which promise the greatest returns to public expenditure in terms of increase of marketed production. Such a policy will not only increase production and incomes, but will also raise government revenues and so ease the restraint of the fiscal strait jacket.

Mining and Manufacturing

Development of agriculture and cattle keeping, because of its central importance and the difficulty of the problems it involves, takes up the greater part of this report. However, attention is also given to the contributions to development which may be expected from mining, manufacturing and the tourist trade.

While it is impossible to count, with any degree of certainty, on greatly increased output of minerals, geological indications are favorable. It is desirable to find the means of accelerating progress in basic geological mapping. Government mining policy should be modified as is necessary to increase the attraction and encouragement to further prospecting by private interests. Expansion of the Government's own reconnaissance prospecting activities seems justified to bridge the gap between basic geological mapping and the prospecting efforts of private concerns.

To promote further development of manufacturing, the Mission endorses the idea of setting up a small investigatory company, preferably calling on outside experience. As a second stage, it may well be desirable to set up a development company with money to invest. However, in promotion of manufacturing development as in agricultural programs, it is necessary to keep in mind the relationship between costs and prospective returns: efforts to encourage growth of manufacturing must be kept in scale with the results which can be realistically expected.

Tanganyika is fortunate in possessing sites allowing progressive expansion of hydroelectric capacity in stages.

Expansion of Education

A major and immediate call on the limited resources available to the Government of Tanganyika is for the expansion of secondary and higher education. The needs of a country which is moving into independence and of a developing economy demand a major effort to increase the number of Africans receiving more than four or at most eight years of schooling.

PLANNING AND ADMINISTRATION

In the circumstances of Tanganyika, it appears essential to take a long view of the development problem. Even though it should prove possible to secure a continuing growth of total money incomes over the next few years by around 5 percent a year, what can be achieved next year or the year after is still strictly limited in relation to the size of the development task. Really substantial changes in methods and organization are required, and such changes are inevitably an affair of many years. On this long view, the developments of the next few years have to be looked at not only as ends in themselves, but as foundations for further development in the future. The necessity for a long view has implications for budgetary policy which are set out in Chapter 3.

The Mission welcomes the recent establishment of a Development Committee at ministerial level, under the chairmanship of the Minister for Finance. It recommends the further strengthening of the central planning staff in the Treasury: expenditure on qualified personnel to provide the Development Committee with the facts and analysis on which its decisions should be based appears to us to be a sound use of part of Tanganyika's scarce budgetary resources.

The Administrative Machinery

Tanganyika is fortunate in possessing an efficient civil service. It is possible in this report to assume that complex programs will be carried through in an orderly and systematic manner. If it were not possible to make this assumption, the report would have to be written in a very different way, and it would be necessary to make a more guarded estimate of Tanganyika's development over the coming years.

The Mission welcomes the proposal that there should be an official in the Office of the Chief Minister responsible for the program of "localization" of the civil service. It is obviously highly desirable that as many posts as possible should be filled by properly qualified Africans. However, it has to be accepted that the number of Africans of the requisite educational standards will remain small for several years to come, even after the most rapid possible expansion of educational facilities, and that there are many claims on young people emerging from the medium and higher levels of the educational system, outside the civil service as well as in it. The hard fact, therefore, is that for many years to come an efficient civil service will be a service highly dependent on expatriate officers.

In July 1960 the Government of the United Kingdom announced its decision to take over for a period of ten years the cost of inducement pay and allowances of overseas staff in all British territories which were not independent at that date. This offer appears likely to be of very great value to Tanganyika. Statements on record show that responsible African leaders accept the necessity for Tanganyika on its side to offer to expatriates terms and conditions of service which will induce them to stay in the territory. This policy, which accords well with the ideal of a multiracial society, is in any case no more than the course of "cool self-love" for Tanganyikans who desire the continuing development of their country.

CHAPTER 2 *CHARACTERISTICS*
OF THE ECONOMY

Before passing to a discussion of the problems of finance, of planning and of priorities suggested in the last chapter, it is necessary to outline the conditions which assist or impede development in the territory, the course of development to date and the present state of the economy.

SIZE AND POPULATION

Tanganyika is a large territory, having a land area of 341,150 sq. miles—roughly the same size as Nigeria, almost as large as the whole of Pakistan or as Venezuela, and nearly 30 percent larger than Texas. Further, much of the center of the territory is arid bush country, and a considerable part of population and economic activity is concentrated in various areas around the periphery (see Maps 2 and 4). Although roads and railways link the main populated areas (Map 8) distances and dispersion are themselves obstacles to development, making transport costly and complicating administration.

While many important problems of finance and planning can and should be considered on a territory-wide basis, at another level the development problems of Tanganyika are extremely heterogeneous, differing widely from one area to another. The case of the relatively prosperous Wachagga, with their bananas and coffee grown on the slopes of Mount Kilimanjaro, in no way resembles that of their neighbors the Masai, nomadic cattle herders of the arid plains. The problems of the Wasukuma, peasant cotton growers to the south of Lake Victoria, are very different from those of the Wagogo in the center of the territory, a people under the constant threat of famine caused by failure of the rains. Some 120 main tribal groupings are recognized (see Map 5). Different tribes have different customs and habits, adapted to the widely varying conditions in which they live. It is difficult and often misleading to generalize about a territory so large and so diversified.

Peasant cultivators and nomadic or semi-nomadic cattle keepers form by far the largest part of the population. Out of an African population of 8.7 million in 1957, less than 0.5 million were listed as being in paid employment. Trade (together with some small-scale manufacturing) is largely in the hands of the Indians, Pakistanis, Goans and Arabs, who number rather over 100,000 in total. The 20,000 Europeans are administrators and technicians, together with a small number of owners or managers of agricultural estates and persons engaged in commerce and industry.

The over-all population density is low, 26 per sq. mile in 1957. The natural increase of the African population is believed to be fairly slow, in the neighborhood of 1.6 percent a year. Not only are death rates high, but the birth rate is comparatively low. The Asian groups have a higher rate of natural increase, perhaps 2.5 percent a year. The size of the European population depends for the most part on net immigration. The annual rate of increase for the population as a whole may be put at about 1.75 percent. By 1970, over-all population density may have increased to about 32 per sq. mile. It is a fair generalization that Tanganyika has no problem of population pressure analogous to that of many Asian countries. Less than 10 percent of the land is cultivated, though a considerably larger proportion is grazed. However, the figures of population density and land use must be seen in relation to the low productive potential of much of the land. In some parts of Tanganyika, particularly in various highland areas, there is already land hunger. Tribal boundaries and personal attachment to the native environment hinder movements of population, and so tend to freeze the present uneven distribution and to prevent people from moving from unproductive or overcrowded areas to more favored places. Chapter 4 shows that land can no longer be considered an abundantly plentiful asset, so that measures to prevent deterioration of land in use and to increase production per acre are becoming increasingly urgent.

THE CENTRAL IMPORTANCE OF AGRICULTURE

Although, as will be seen, much of the territory provides difficult conditions for agriculture and even for livestock, nevertheless agricultural and livestock development will in any circumstances remain a principal preoccupation of public authorities. At present agricultural and livestock products together contribute about 80 percent of export earnings against 13 percent for minerals, and the agricultural and livestock sectors account for over 70 percent of the physical product of the territory, including subsistence (see Table 1). Even if mineral production were to increase very greatly in the coming years, the bulk of the population would continue to be engaged in agriculture and pastoralism, and the task of securing widespread income increase would still be one of agricultural and livestock development.

Minerals still make a somewhat limited, if important, contribution to the economy. However, the geological indications are promising, and efforts to promote increased mineral exploration are highly justified. While the results of such exploration are very uncertain, and it would be impossible to rely upon increase of mineral production, this is a possibility which can be hoped for.

Manufacturing development has been proceeding rapidly in recent years, and may be expected to continue a high rate of expansion, though without becoming a major employer of labor. Only about 20,000 persons now work in manufacturing establishments employing five or more persons (excluding service trades and early processing of agricultural products). Tanganyika's immediate comparative advantage appears to lie in agricultural production. Although unemployment among Africans who move into the towns creates local social problems, there is no over-all problem of lack of opportunity to work for a living, such as is found in many countries of higher population density. Consequently, efforts to accelerate further the growth of manufacturing by means of protection or other special expedients do not seem appropriate, and industrial development in Tanganyika should continue to depend on the growth of the internal market, and thus, to a great degree, on the development of agriculture.

Tanganyika is one of those economies which have developed primarily through the growth of exports of primary products. Forty percent of money incomes is derived from exports, and 80 percent of export earnings is contributed by agricultural and livestock products. There should be no serious problem in finding markets for increased agricultural exports. Among major exports, coffee presents a special case because of an international agreement limiting exports. Only in the case of sisal does the output of the territory constitute an important percentage of world supply. For practically all other products,

TABLE 1   Tanganyika Gross Domestic Product at Factor Cost, 1958

	Monetary Activities	Subsistence Activities	Total	(As percentage of total product)		Monetary Product as Percentage of Total for Sector	As Percentage of Total Production of Goods, Monetary Plus Subsistence
				Monetary Activities	Monetary plus Subsistence		
	(£'000)	(£'000)	(£'000)				
Agriculture	36,273	44,900	81,173	35	47	45	61
Livestock	3,502	11,525	15,027	3	9	23	11
Forestry	3,135	2,150	5,285	3	3	59	4
Hunting and fishing	347	2,581	2,928	—	2	12	2
Mining	6,186	—	6,186	6	4	100	5
Manufacturing	6,750	—	6,750	6	4	100	5
Handicraft	1,500	4,698	6,198	1	4	24	5
Construction	6,089	4,381	10,470	6	6	58	8
Public utilities	955	n.a.	955	1	1	n.a.	
Transport and distribution	19,251	n.a.	19,251	19	11	n.a.	
Ownership of dwellings	3,334	n.a.	3,334	3	2	n.a.	
Public administration	11,326	n.a.	11,326	11	7	n.a.	
Miscellaneous services	5,334	n.a.	5,334	5	3	n.a.	
Total	103,982	70,235	174,217	100	100	60 [a]	100

[a] This proportion should be somewhat smaller, since it takes no account of the value of services in the subsistence sector.

SOURCE: See Annex VI.

Tanganyika's share of the world market is negligible. Thus Tanganyika should in general have no difficulty in exporting increased agricultural production at the going prices.

The Mission does not expect the general level of prices for Tanganyika's agricultural exports to fall in the next few years seriously below the 1958 level, leaving aside the possible important exception of coffee. In any case, prices of most of Tanganyika's export crops could probably fall considerably without causing any serious check to the expansion of production. From the peak of the Korean price boom in 1951, export prices have on the average declined to about 60 percent of the previous maximum, but the volume of exports has almost doubled. The apparent insensitiveness of peasant agricultural production to decline in price is probably related in part to the fact that basic food requirements are satisfied by subsistence production, and that most cultivators still look upon production of cash crops as a supplementary activity costing little in terms either of money outlay or of alternative income foregone.

TABLE 2   Commodity Composition of Tanganyika's Total Domestic Exports to Destinations outside East Africa [a]

(percent of total by value)

Commodity	1923 & 1924	1936 & 1937	1948 & 1949	1952 & 1953	1957 & 1958
Sisal	23.7	41.7	57.3	42.7	24.4
Coffee	13.1	8.1	6.7	14.1	18.1
Cotton	12.9	13.1	9.7	11.8	17.0
Total	49.7	62.9	73.7	68.6	59.6
Diamonds	—	0.1	7.8	7.2	9.4
Gold	n.a.	15.8 [b]	3.4	2.3	2.0 [c]
Hides and skins	7.2	5.5	3.1	3.4	3.0
Cashew nuts	—	0.1 [b]	0.5	1.2	3.2
Groundnuts	14.6	5.6	0.4	0.9	2.3
Castor seed	—	—	0.4	1.9	2.1
Other	n.a.	[10.0]	10.8	14.6	18.4
Total	100.0	100.0	100.0	100.0	100.0

[a] Prewar figures apply to exports to all destinations.

[b] 1938.

[c] Based on production figures of Mines Department. Export figures appear to include under lead ore and concentrates the gold which is obtained as a by-product of lead.

SOURCE: Annual trade reports.

There must be limits below which prices could not fall without making cultivators unwilling to incur the money costs or effort of increasing production; but it is generally considered that these limits are unlikely to be reached in practice, although the supply of certain minor crops such as castor seed and chick peas is said to be sensitive to price. For plantation production, which at present contributes roughly one third of total exports by value, price is rather more crucial, however, because of the more considerable element of some-what inflexible money costs.

Importance of African Agriculture

The main development effort has to be concentrated on African agriculture. Estates owned and managed by Europeans or Indians are at present major producers of export crops, producing virtually all the sisal and tea, the greater part of tobacco, wheat, pyrethrum and seed beans and peas, and some of the coffee. But the estates occupy only one percent of the land area of Tanganyika, and latterly the alienation of land for non-African agricultural use has been on a very limited scale.

African peasant producers account for around 55 percent of Tanganyika's exports of crops and about 65 percent of the value of all marketed crops. Of total crop production, including a fair valuation of subsistence, African peasant producers contribute over 80 percent. Livestock are almost entirely African owned.

THE PHYSICAL ENVIRONMENT

Rainfall and Water Resources

The chief factor limiting and shaping the agricultural and live-stock potential of the territory is rainfall.

a. Rainfall is low in annual total amount over much of the country.

b. Rainfall is everywhere seasonal, thus limiting the production of annual crops to only part of the year. In some areas, where there are two good rainy seasons a year, or one long rainy season, perennial crops can be grown and good yields of annuals are possible. Over much of the country, however, there is only a short rainy season followed by a long, severe dry season, with the result that perennial crops cannot be grown, annual crops must be restricted to quick-maturing, drought-resistant species, and yields are low. In these areas pasturage for stock is very meager during the dry season.

c. Much of the rainfall occurs in storms of high intensity during which a large part of the precipitation runs off the soil surface, and is thus lost to the crops. This is especially important in areas where there is a low total rainfall in a short wet season.

d. Rainfall over most of the country is unreliable, varying greatly in total amount from year to year and in its distribution between months within the rainy season.

The rainfall pattern is summarized by Map 2. The areas shaded in green have a good or fair expectation of receiving 30 inches of rain during the year, and it is within these areas, rather under one third of the total area, that favorable conditions are to be found for the economic production of arable crops. At the other extreme, the areas shaded in gray have a poor expectation of receiving even 20 inches of rainfall. These areas, again almost one third of the total area, give unfavorable conditions for crop production, and are mainly suitable for extensive ranching or pastoralism. The unshaded (white) areas are intermediate, but are for the most part somewhat marginal for economic arable farming except so far as irrigation is feasible.

Over much of the country the low total amount and seasonal character of the rainfall result in many rivers and streams drying out completely during the dry season. Only 30-40 percent of the territory is reasonably well supplied with water by nature throughout the year. Much of the remainder is virtually uninhabitable unless artificial water supplies can be provided during the dry season.

It appears that in most areas it would be technically possible to provide water for humans and cattle, though in many places the cost would be prohibitively high. Development of rural water supplies is required not only to open up for use certain areas which are at present uninhabited or only thinly inhabited, but also to improve conditions of life in some inhabited areas. In many places, existing water supplies do not meet even minimum hygienic requirements, and water-borne diseases are prevalent. In some places, much time and effort has to be spent in bringing water from distant sources. Examples are known where it takes one day to go to the watering point, another day to bring the water back to the village. It is interesting to note that nowhere in their extensive travels did members of the Mission see animals used to transport water.

A rough calculation suggests that around 4 million acres could be opened up for crop production by irrigation or flood control (cf. Annex III). This is less than 2 percent of the total area of the territory, but the addition it would make to the area cultivated by Africans is of the order of 20 percent.

Soils

Soil survey or reconnaissance has only been done over limited areas in Tanganyika. There are therefore inadequate data on which to base any assessment of the proportions of total land area occupied by good and bad soils; but it is very evident that agricultural potential is limited over large areas by soils of inherently low nutrient status.

This limitation applies, for example, in an extensive, though relatively narrow, coastal strip where poor sandy soils over sedimentary rocks predominate, in a large area of sandy soils in the eastern part of the Southern Province, inland of the coastal strip, and in extensive areas in the neighborhood of Sao Hill and in the Njombe district of the Southern Highlands Province, where the soils are highly leached red or brown sandy types. In none of these areas does it seem likely that fertilizers or manure could be economically used to improve fertility. On the other hand, for the inherently poor, highly leached lakeshore sands of Bukoba District in West Lake Province, and the very large areas of poor upper-level soils of the Usukuma catena in Lake Province and in the northern part of Western Province, it has been shown that crop yields can be appreciably raised by fertilizers and manures, although the economy of the use of these materials has not been proven except with cotton, and the use of either material by African farmers is so far negligible.

Apart from these large areas of poor soils, there are extensive regions of reddish brown and yellowish sandy loams on basement complex rocks which constitute relatively old soils in an advanced stage of weathering, and are therefore at best of only moderate fertility. Although not very fertile, these soils are capable of giving good yields of crops if they are properly handled and if fertilizers are used.

Associated with these soils, and also with the Usukuma catena, there are in the bottoms of valleys the dark heavy clays, or *mbugas,* which are more fertile. These are widespread in Tanganyika and must in total amount represent a very considerable area of fertile soils; but hitherto they have not by any means been fully utilized, mainly because of the difficulty of cultivating them with hand tools. It seems desirable that in many areas a greater use should be made of these mbugas, which are capable of giving better returns than the red soils, if means of handling them suitable for African use can be found.

Apart from the mbugas, extensive areas of really fertile soils are confined to the volcanic soils of parts of the highlands in the Northern, Southern and Southern Highlands Provinces, and to alluvial soils in the larger river valleys. The latter soils, the use of which is likely to depend largely on the development of irrigation, suffer in many places from two limitations: firstly that a considerable proportion of such soils are saline or alkaline; and secondly that they are often rather variable in texture, fertile heavy clays being interspersed with patches and strips of less fertile sandy soils of high water requirement. Both these features will increase the difficulties and the cost of their utilization under irrigation.

It can thus be seen that, although Tanganyika has vast, thinly populated areas, nevertheless good soils, particularly in conjunction with adequate and reliable rainfall or with favorable irrigation possibilities, are a somewhat scarce asset which should be developed efficiently and protected against deterioration.

Vegetation and Tsetse Flies

About 65-75 percent of the country is under open woodland (*miombo*) or bushland and thicket, together with the man-induced savannas and grasslands derived from them. These vegetation types form suitable habitats for tsetse flies. Consequently, tsetse fly infests about 60 percent of the total land, and prevents its use unless measures are taken to eliminate the fly or control the diseases which it carries. These measures are costly in relation to the return which may be expected from much of the land, which is of low potential.

THE HISTORICAL SETTING

To understand Tanganyika's present development problems, it is necessary to appreciate that the history of modern economic development in Tanganyika is extremely short, having begun, it may be said, in 1884, when Karl Peters founded the Union for German Colonization. Before that date, the principal contact of the inland parts of

TABLE 3   Growth of Tanganyika's Exports [a]

Year	Sisal[b] ('000 tons)	Coffee ('000 tons)	Cotton ('000 tons)	Ground-nuts ('000 tons)	Cashew Nuts ('000 tons)	Tea ('000 tons)	Hides and Calf Skins ('000 tons)	Skins and Fur Skins ('000 tons)	Skins and Fur Skins (nos. '000)	Diamonds ('000 carats)	Total Value (£ million)
1913	21	1.1	2.2								
1919	17										
1920	17										
1921	8	3.8	1.1	12.5			1.4	.14			1.3
1922	10	4.3	1.5	16.5			1.9	.17			1.7
1923	13	4.0	1.5	18.7			2.4	.19			2.6
1924	18	5.3	2.5	9.1			2.4	.29			2.9
1925	18	6.0	4.5	15.9			1.3	.30			3.0
1926	25	6.5	4.9	14.1			2.4	.36			3.3
1927	33	6.6	3.9	10.6			2.8	.48			3.9
1928	36	10.4	4.9	7.8			2.1	.47		23.3	3.7
1929	46	8.9	4.9	17.3			1.7	.36		13.3	2.6
1930	50	11.5	3.7	3.1			2.0	.17		7.8	1.6
1931	56	9.3	2.4	15.9			2.6	.10		1.4	2.2
1932	61	11.4	3.2	19.2		—	3.9	.26		1.4	2.5
1933	70	12.7	5.1	8.0		—	3.1	.31		1.2	2.6
1934	73	14.8	5.6	16.4		—	3.1			1.4	3.4
1935	83	18.6	10.0	22.8		—	3.1		959	2.7	4.5
1936	81	12.1	11.3	22.3		—	3.2		1,571	3.2	5.0
1937	91	13.6	11.5	3.8		.1	3.0		1,572	3.6	3.7
1938	101	13.7	8.9	3.8		.1	3.5		1,157	3.4	4.3
1939	93	16.6	11.6	4.5	.9	.2			1,151		
1946	112	10.0	4.0	.5	3.2	.6	2.6		1,408	119	11.1
1947	96	13.9	7.0	3.5	1.3	.4	3.4		1,790	92	16.2
1948	117	11.3	9.9	3.1	5.6	.5	2.6	.78		148	20.9
1949	133	12.0	10.8	.8	3.6	.4	3.3	.73		131	24.0
1950	120	15.0	7.0	.1	6.5	.5	4.1	1.41		131	40.5
1951	142	16.6	8.3	3.5	8.2	.8	2.5	1.51		9	47.4
1952	158	18.6	11.1	9.4	11.5	1.0	3.1	.83		332	35.4
1953	171	15.2	14.8	1.1	11.4	1.1	4.4	1.09		171	37.3
1954	168	19.4	12.1	2.5	16.3	1.6	4.5	1.22		330	37.9
1955	174	18.5	20.4	5.6	18.2	1.7	3.8	1.12		323	47.0
1956	186	21.6	27.9	15.1	16.7	2.0	3.5	1.07		358	47.0
1957	182	18.5	27.2	16.1	33.7	2.2	3.6	1.08		373	41.4
1958	198	22.2	32.1	12.6	31.3	2.3	3.6	1.23		515	44.3
1959	209	19.6	30.7	12.1	33.2	2.7	4.5	1.35		555	47.9

[a] The quantity figures are for domestically produced exports to all destinations up to 1948, but from 1949 exclude exports to Kenya and Uganda. The total value figures apply to domestic exports to all destinations, including Kenya and Uganda, throughout the period shown.
[b] Exports of sisal were less than one ton in 1898 and 1899, reached 15 tons in 1901, jumped to 225 tons in 1902, and thereafter increased very rapidly to the nearly 21,000 tons shown for 1913.
SOURCE: East African Statistical Department.

the territory with the non-African world was with Arab trading caravans and slave raiders, and the main exports of the territory were ivory and slaves. In another sense, the present phase of development is of even more recent origin. Up to the end of the Second World War economic development was, for a number of reasons, somewhat sporadic. Economic development as an overriding preoccupation of Government may be said to date effectively from about 1946.

The German Period

In the 30 years preceding the outbreak of the First World War, the Germans devoted much money and energy to the development of plantation agriculture, introducing not only sisal but also coffee, tea, cotton, rubber and cinchona, and experimenting with many other crops. These crops were grown on alienated land, and no attempts were made to induce the Africans to turn to the production of cash crops. Some mining activities were also begun during this period and, more important, two railways were built, one from Tanga to Moshi in the north and the other from Dar es Salaam to Kigoma in the central part of the territory.

This development was abruptly ended by the outbreak of the First World War, during which a campaign was fought in the territory. After the end of the war, in January 1920, a League of Nations mandate was given to the United Kingdom to administer the territory.

The Interwar Years

A period of postwar reorganization was succeeded, in about 1925-29, by a period of rapid expansion during which public expenditures increased and there was considerable private investment. This spell was brought to an end first by the depression and subsequently by political uncertainties as to the future of the territory.

Nevertheless, the interwar period was by no means entirely one of stagnation. Exports of domestic produce increased in value from about £1 million in 1921 to nearly £4 million in 1928, and then, after a setback during the depression, to £5 million in 1937. Efforts were made for the first time to induce African production of cash crops. In the '20's, these efforts were concentrated on the encouragement of cotton growing, particularly in the Lake Victoria basin and the eastern districts of the territory. At the same time the Wachagga rapidly increased their numbers of Arabica coffee trees, and a similar expansion of Robusta took place in Bukoba District.

During this period, the transport system was gradually improved. The mileage of roads "passable to light motor traffic in the dry season" increased from 2,650 miles in 1921 to nearly 12,000 miles in 1938. The latter figure, however, included some 4,000 miles of roads maintained by native authorities, generally to a poor standard. Railway construction between the wars was limited. A new line was built from Tabora to Mwanza on Lake Victoria. The extension of the Tanga line from Moshi to Arusha was completed in 1929. A branch line from Manyoni on the Central Line to Kinyangiri, opened in 1934, was an economic failure, and after the Second World War the track was taken up and used for the new line to Mpanda. (Ironically, the economic viability of this new line is now somewhat uncertain because of the closing down of the mine at Mpanda.)

Although there was no fighting in the territory during the Second World War, serious dislocations did of necessity occur. The normal channels of external trade were disturbed, and the domestic transport system was subjected to great pressure because of military movements of supplies and personnel. Most important of all, the mobilization created a general problem of manpower shortages; in particular, the mobilization interfered with efficient administration and with management of the big estates producing for export markets. None the less, after a few years of declining production many of these difficulties were overcome, and the volume of exports again increased, especially in fields important to the allied war effort.

The Postwar Period

In 1946 Tanganyika became a United Nations Trust Territory under British administration, and its political status was thus clarified. The territory has benefited from the United Kingdom postwar colonial development policy, and from 1948 to 1958/59 has received over £ 10 million in U. K. and foreign grants, largely grants under the U. K. Colonial Development and Welfare Acts. It has also enjoyed certain borrowing facilities in the United Kingdom.

For the sake of completeness, it must be mentioned that Tanganyika was the scene of the Groundnut Scheme, adopted in 1947, an effort by the United Kingdom to convert empty stretches of the territory into a large-scale producer of vegetable oil by the application of mechanical methods. The failure of this scheme gave an expensive, but in the long run salutary, demonstration of the need for thorough research and experimentation before attempting radical innovations in tropical agriculture. The scheme left behind physical capital in the form of the port of Mtwara, the Southern Railway and a number of roads. These have contributed to the development of the Southern Province, but at the same time the railway and Mtwara port have incurred operating losses which have been a charge on the Tanganyika budget. Land cleared at Kongwa, Urambo and Nachingwea was handed over to the Tanganyika Agricultural Corporation, which has built up valuable experience in running planned settlement schemes and in cattle ranching. Finally, the injection of purchasing power by way of the expenditures of those engaged in the scheme appears to have given a certain stimulus to the economy of Tanganyika.

Another feature of the postwar period has been the increase of systematic government attention to the promotion of development. In 1946 the Government of Tanganyika published a development program for the period 1947-56, envisaging total public development expenditure of £18 million. The initial plan has subsequently been revised on several occasions or replaced by new plans, and as a rule expenditures have fallen short of the plan targets. But, although attempts at planning on a longer than year-to-year basis have had little real significance up to the present, it remains the case that the role of Government in promoting economic development has increased, so that the government budget has become increasingly important as an instrument of economic change.

While development has been aided by capital inflow, Tanganyika has itself made substantial contributions to the finance of its development effort from its own resources. This has been made possible by the growth of export earnings in the expanding commodity markets of the postwar years. While the value of exports has fluctuated considerably during the period, with the Korean War as the major disturbing factor, the underlying trend has been sharply upward (see Diagram 1). Although the main export staples, sisal, coffee and cotton, still contribute about 60 percent of export earnings, it is noteworthy that various new crops fairly recently introduced into African farming in Tanganyika are now also making an appreciable contribution, notably cashew nuts and castor seed. The upward trend of agricultural exports has been reinforced by increased production and export of diamonds.

TANGANYIKA: VALUE OF EXTERNAL TRADE AND INDICES OF VOLUME AND AVERAGE VALUE OF EXPORTS

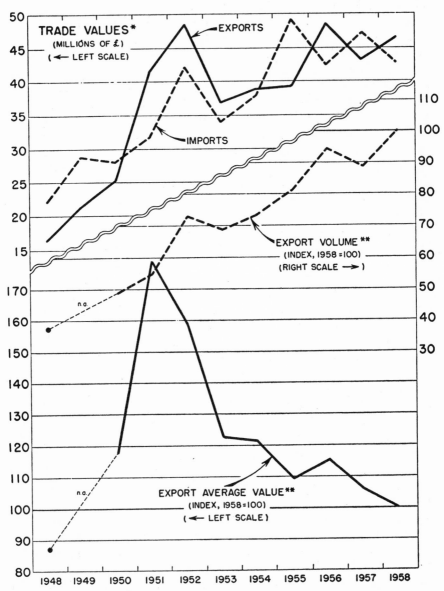

*Include trade with Kenya and Uganda. Exports include re-exports.
**Cover only exports to final destinations outside East Africa.

Diagram 1

The Recent Rate of Growth

The rate of growth of exports gives a fair indication of the rate of growth of the economy as a whole. Exports take about a quarter of all the goods and services produced in Tanganyika, and generate about 40 percent of money incomes in the territory. Thus, although national income statistics are only available from 1954 on, it seems possible to assert that from 1948 to 1958 the economy as a whole grew at an annual rate of at least 5 percent. From 1952 the volume of exports has been growing at around 6 percent a year; in the years immediately preceding 1952 it was growing considerably faster. As between 1948 and 1958, both volume and value increased about 2.7 times, or at an average annual rate of just over 10 percent. During the same period, commerce and industry grew at a high rate, though the product of these sectors is still quite small in absolute terms. By contrast, production of African food crops and other subsistence activities probably advanced at only a slightly faster rate than the population increase: say, by 2½ percent a year. Combining these growth rates, and keeping in mind that the subsistence sector produces somewhat less than half of total output, it appears that an estimate of 5 percent for the average, over-all growth rate in recent years may even be somewhat conservative. Since the annual population increase is estimated to be about 1.7 percent, it is clear that there has been a very real gain in per capita income.

PRESENT STATE OF THE ECONOMY

Income and Living Standards

In spite of this high rate of growth, Tanganyika remains a low productivity economy, at the low end of the international income scale. The approximate per capita income level seems to be about the same as in India or Pakistan, though average nutritional standards are probably somewhat higher in Tanganyika than in India and Pakistan.[1] The total value of marketed goods and services, officially esti-

---

[1] Some detailed estimates of production of African food crops are given in Annex V.

mated at £ 98 million in 1958, is thought by the Mission to be somewhat higher, probably a little over £ 100 million (see Annex VI).

As may be seen from Table 1, the importance of the subsistence sector is still considerable. Of course, the impression of the relative importance of subsistence and monetary activities depends to a great extent on the basis of valuation used for subsistence products. On the basis of valuation of subsistence used in Annex V, it is estimated that the proportion of total output which does not enter the market economy is as high as 40 percent. In many parts of the territory, particularly in the south, subsistence activities on this valuation appear to outweigh monetary activities. In certain northern areas, by contrast, monetary activity greatly predominates. Many Africans in Tanganyika have only minimal contacts with the monetary economy. The great majority of Africans are in an intermediate position, depending upon subsistence production for many of their staple wants, but selling some cash crops and buying some goods and services for money, so that in varying degrees they are partly in the "subsistence economy" and partly in the "monetary economy." Some rely entirely on monetary income and are thus wholly in the "monetary economy."

Production of cash crops is very generally looked on as an activity taking second place to production of food for the family. Even most African coffee growers regard coffee as subsidiary to their bananas. Chagga families not only grow coffee and bananas on the slopes of Kilimanjaro, but also grow food crops in plots lower down, possibly several miles distant. In such circumstances, increased specialization and exchange would appear to have clear advantages, but it is considered to be out of the question at the present. The general policy of giving first emphasis to self-sufficiency in food was in fact rational in a situation where crops were uncertain, the terms of trade between food and cash crops highly variable and the margin above starvation dangerously narrow.[2] Even today, advantageous specialization would depend in many areas not only on improved transport facilities and increased storage, but also on increased efficiency in food production. Nevertheless, preoccupation with self-sufficiency is breaking down in many places. Both the Wasukuma of Lake Province and the Bahaya of West Lake Province now rely to an increasing extent on food imported from other areas. The degree of specialization may be expected to increase, if only very slowly. At the same time, money transactions will continue to encroach upon subsistence. Even African beer

[2] See John R. Raeburn, "Some Economic Aspects of African Agriculture," *The East African Economics Review*, January 1959.

(*pombe*) is a major object of monetary transactions in many parts of the country.

African money incomes appear to average very roughly £6 per caput. Incomes on this level are of course usually supplemented to a substantial degree by subsistence production. Some African agriculturalists secure considerably higher money incomes. For example, the average payment from cooperatives to African coffee producers on both Kilimanjaro and Meru in 1957/58 was estimated at £47.

As a generalization, the nutritional status of Africans in Tanganyika is considered to be fair, but it is known that the diet is commonly deficient in protein, calcium and certain vitamins. The principal defect is the absence of a suitable weaning diet. In places there is a constant threat of famine following on a failure of the rains. The Wagogo of the Central Province suffered serious famines in 1953 and 1954. In 1958 there was a severe food shortage over much of the Kilwa District in the Southern Province and local food shortages in parts of Newala, Masasi and Mtwara Districts. While the Mission was in the territory, food scarcity was threatening in Nzega District in the Western Province, though here the situation was not particularly acute because of the comparative ease of bringing in food supplies from the outside. Endemic debilitating diseases such as malaria and bilharzia are widely prevalent.

Capital Formation and Government Expenditures

The rate of capital formation in Tanganyika appears to be rather high for a country of very low per capita income. In 1958 (a year in which total capital formation was in fact somewhat depressed), total gross capital formation, public and private, constituted some 16 percent of gross domestic product. If capital formation in the subsistence sector is excluded and gross capital formation in the monetary sector is related to incomes generated in the market economy, the ratio has been substantially over 20 percent. This comparatively high ratio can, of course, be explained in part by the fact that much of the basic demand for food is satisfied in the subsistence sector and that, as a consequence, a higher proportion of monetary income can be devoted to capital formation than in an economy where monetary income covers the bulk of consumption needs. Further, a part of the gross investment was financed by grants and loans from the outside world rather than by domestic saving. In the absence of reliable balance of payments data or surveys of sources of finance for private capital for-

TABLE 4 Gross Fixed Capital Formation in Tanganyika by Industrial Use, 1957

(£'000)

Industrial Use	Private Monetary	Private Subsistence	Central Government	Local Government	Government Corporations[d]	All Sectors
Agriculture, livestock and forestry	2,314[a]	—	149	46	—	2,509
Hunting and fishing	223	—	—	—	—	223
Mining and quarrying	1,193	—	68	—	—	1,261
Manufacturing	1,714	—	—	—	—	1,714
Construction	1,541	—	—	—	—	1,541
Public utilities	749[b]	—	1,417[c]	79[c]	—	2,245
Transport and communications	1,224	—	966	153	2,585	4,928
Distribution	2,002	—	—	—	—	2,002
Ownership of dwellings	2,579	5,397	718	181	225	9,100
Public administration	—	—	101	186	—	287
Social services:						
Education	—	—	1,025	294	—	1,319
Medical	—	—	359	128	—	487
Other	763	—	14	64	—	841
Unallocated	—	—	951	125	—	1,076
Total	14,302	5,397	5,768	1,256	2,810	29,533

[a] Including capital formation of the Tanganyika Agricultural Corporation.
[b] Capital formation by Tanganyika Electric Supply Co., Ltd.
[c] Including irrigation development and rural water supplies.
[d] Notably the East African Railways and Harbours Administration and the East African Posts and Telecommunications Administration.

SOURCE: East African Statistical Department.

TABLE 5   Supply and Use of Resources in Tanganyika, 1958 (including subsistence)

	(£'000)
Gross domestic product at factor cost	174,217
Commodity imports	42,606
Invisibles (net)	[4,000]
Taxes on expenditure	8,452
Less subsidies	210
Available resources at market prices	229,065
Exports	46,408
General government consumption expenditure	17,869
Gross capital expenditure of general government } Gross capital expenditure of government enterprises }	8,483
Gross capital formation of private enterprises	18,918
Private consumption	137,387
Use of resources	229,065

SOURCE: See Annex VI.

mation, the importance of private capital inflow and of reinvestment of profits of externally owned enterprises cannot be assessed. The role of grants and loans to the Government from external sources will be described in Chapter 3.

About one third of total domestic capital formation is made by the public sector (including services of the East Africa High Commission) and the remaining two thirds by the private sector. If investment in the subsistence sector is excluded, the importance of public investment is greater: the approximate proportions for the period 1954-58 were: central and local government, rather over 25 percent; the East African Railways and Harbours Administration and the East African Posts and Telecommunications Administration, about 15 percent; and private, rather under 60 percent.

Table 5 shows the breakdown of gross domestic fixed capital formation in 1957 by sector and by industrial use. The pattern appears to be fairly typical of that throughout the last few years (cf. Table 64).

Of private monetary capital formation in recent years, nearly 30 percent has been in the service sectors—transport, distribution and miscellaneous service trades—and about 20 percent in the construction of dwellings. About 20 percent has gone into manufacturing and mining, rather over 10 percent into the construction industry and

TABLE 6   Functional Analysis of Government Expenditures in Tanganyika, 1957

(£'000)

Category	Central Government			Local Government			General Government			As Percentage of Total General Govt. Expenditures
	Current	Capital	Total	Current	Capital	Total	Current	Capital	Total	
Economic Services										
Agriculture, forestry, veterinary	1,845	149	1,994	194	46	240	2,039	195	2,234	8
Water development (irrigation, rural and urban)	452	1,417	1,869	30	79	109	482	1,496	1,978	7
Roads	873	933	1,806	315	153	468	1,188	1,086	2,274	9
Other	1,153	114	1,267	97	50	147	1,250	164	1,414	5
Total Economic Services	4,323	2,613	6,936	636	328	964	4,959	2,941	7,900	30
Social Services										
Education	3,169	1,025	4,194	405	294	699	3,574	1,319	4,893	18
Medical	1,766	359	2,125	396	128	524	2,162	487	2,649	10
Other	201	327	528	103	64	167	304	391	695	3
Total Social Services	5,136	1,711	6,847	904	486	1,390	6,040	2,197	8,237	31
Administration, Law and Order	5,004[a]	101	5,105[a]	1,115	186	1,301	6,119	287	6,406	24
Public Works	650	1,081	1,731	41	248	289	691	1,329	2,020	8
Other	2,106	−270	1,836	123	78	201	2,229	−192	2,037	8
Total	17,219	5,236	22,455	2,819	1,326	4,145	20,038	6,562	26,600	100

[a] Net of transfers to local government bodies.

SOURCE: East African Statistical Department.

rather over 15 percent into agriculture. The remainder of some 5 percent is accounted for by the capital formation of the Tanganyika Electric Supply Company.

Of public capital formation, including that carried out by East Africa High Commission services, the largest items have been transport and communications, notably road and railway building; irrigation, rural water development and urban water supplies; and school building. These forms of capital formation have accounted for roughly two thirds of the total for the public sector in recent years. Public investment has already done much to build up the "infrastructure" of the economy. In particular, the main transport network may be regarded as approaching completion in relation to the present transport needs of the territory, though some sections have still to be brought up to adequate all-weather standards.

To understand the vital role of public expenditures in the promotion of economic development in Tanganyika, it is necessary to take into account not only capital expenditures but also many of the current expenditures of central and local government. Table 6 shows a functional analysis of general government expenditures in the year 1957, which here again is selected as having been fairly typical of the pattern in recent years. It will be seen that, in relation to the centrally important sectors of agriculture and animal husbandry, government current expenditures have been considerably larger than government capital expenditures (including irrigation works and development of rural water supplies). Certain current government expenditures, those on agricultural research and extension work being a leading example, appear likely to have a greater impact, pound for pound, on the growth of production than do many government capital expenditures. It would be highly misleading to equate "developmental" with capital expenditures and "non-developmental" with current expenditures. The functions of central government expenditure, current and capital combined, are suggested by the following analysis of the budget estimates for the fiscal year 1960/61:

a. Administration, police, tax collection: about 35 percent of total budgeted expenditures, predominantly current. It is inevitable that in a large country with a small budget these essential central government functions, on which the development of a modern economy depends, should form a large part of total expenditure.

b. "Investment in people"—largely education and health: about 30 percent of the total, again predominantly current. Such expenditures may be expected to have a considerable, if indirect, effect on productive ability.

c. Infrastructure, largely expenditure on roads: 10 percent of the total, half capital and half current (the current part being the large item of road maintenance). In considering this type of expenditure as a proportion of the total, it has to be remembered that the considerable expenditures on railways, ports, posts and telegraphs are the responsibility of East Africa High Commission services, and do not enter into the Tanganyika budget.

d. Expenditures aimed at the development of particular productive sectors—agricultural extension work, services to mining, industry and commerce, irrigation and rural water development and so on: just under 20 percent of total budgeted expenditures. About 70 percent of this category is in the current budget and about 30 percent in the capital budget.

e. Expenditures on what may be loosely termed consumer services, including such items as urban water supplies and African urban housing: well under 10 percent of total budgeted expenditures. About 60 percent of these expenditures is current and 40 percent capital.

Local government expenditures, current and capital, have been rather less than one fifth as great as those of central government, reaching an estimated total of £ 5.8 million in 1959 for all local authorities, rural and urban. Local government bodies raising revenue and incurring expenditures are the Dar es Salaam Municipality, Town Councils, Township Authorities and Local Treasuries. Of these, the bodies of greatest interest to this report are the Local Treasuries, operating in rural areas.

The Local Treasuries now spend about £ 4 million a year, one third on local administration, nearly a quarter on education, medical facilities and sanitation, and only about 6 percent on agricultural, forestry and veterinary activities. To some extent, the pattern of expenditures by local government bodies is shaped by arrangements for matching of central and local funds. Thus it has been laid down that Local Treasuries should meet 50 percent of the recurrent costs of primary education; but very few are considered able to do so in practice.

It is desirable that Local Treasuries should have a larger financial stake in development projects and programs of local importance. The present sources of Local Treasuries' funds, and a possible reform of their finances, will be discussed in Chapter 16.

TANGANYIKA AND EAST AFRICA

The economy of Tanganyika has certain close links with those of Kenya and Uganda; the three territories are joined in a *de facto* customs union; the East Africa High Commission, with headquarters in Nairobi, is responsible for East African Railways and Harbours and East African Posts and Telecommunications, both of which cover all three territories, and also for certain common research and other services; there are formal arrangements for exchange of information between the three territories and, as seems desirable, coordination of policy. The Mission considers that this "East African" approach to common problems is valuable and should be maintained.

The northern and southern boundaries of Tanganyika by no means conform with the economic geography of British East and Central Africa. For important parts of Tanganyika the natural transport routes lie outside the territory: the Lake and West Lake Provinces communicate with the outside world to a considerable extent by way of Lake Victoria and the Kenya Railway; much of the trade of the Kilimanjaro area passes by way of Nairobi and Mombasa, also in Kenya. The north and south of Tanganyika are divided by the arid, empty wastes in the middle; the Southern Province is somewhat cut off from the rest of the territory by the Rufiji River. To date, the frontiers have not been allowed seriously to distort the natural pattern of economic development, thanks, to a great degree, to the East African customs union. It is highly desirable that future development should follow rather than struggle against the pattern set by economic geography.

However, it has to be recognized that the customs union arrangements are not without disadvantages for Tanganyika, disadvantages which are further discussed in Chapter 12. Nevertheless, the Mission believes that it is in the long-term interests of Tanganyika to seek the solution of particular difficulties by negotiations with the other two East African territories rather than to abandon the essentials of the customs union.

The functions of the East Africa High Commission are conveniently divided into the "self-contained services," East African Railways and Harbours and East African Posts and Telecommunications, and the various "non-self-contained services" (listed at the end of Annex I).

It has been seen that the two "self-contained services" of the High Commission have been responsible for about 15 percent of monetary fixed capital formation in Tanganyika over the past few years. Such capital formation does not directly enter into the public finances of Tanganyika. However, borrowing by the East African Railways and Harbours Administration or by the East African Posts and Telecommunications Administration is covered by the joint and several guarantee of the three territorial governments, and is apt to affect market sentiment concerning the credit standing of East Africa as a whole, and hence to influence the terms on which the Government of Tanganyika can borrow. The "self-contained services" in general meet their current expenditures from the proceeds of charges and fees. However, there are provisions whereby the Government of Tanganyika may have to undertake to cover any losses according to an agreed formula. The 1960/61 budget estimates contain the not inconsiderable figure of £ 187,000 for payment in respect of the losses of the Southern Province railway and the port of Mtwara, and make token allowance for the prospective need to cover losses on the Mpanda line.

The "non-self-contained services" of the High Commission (research, statistics, customs and excise collection, income tax collection, civil aviation, meteorology, etc.) are financed in part by contributions from the three territorial governments, in part by the United Kingdom. Tanganyika's annual contribution is just over £ 1 million.

In 1960, an expert commission (the Raisman Commission) was in East Africa with the following terms of reference:

"a. To examine the arrangements at present in force in East Africa for a common market area, for economic coordination between the territories and for fiscal uniformity with regard to the measures now taken:

"i. to facilitate inter-territorial trade in the products of local agriculture and manufacturing industries, and to develop such industries in East Africa;

"ii. to secure uniformity in fiscal and financial matters, including the methods used to allocate the yields from customs, excise and income taxes between the territories;

"iii. to provide the East Africa High Commission with revenue necessary to meet the costs of the services administered by the Commission for the benefit of the territories and to apportion the cost of such services between the territories.

"b. To consider the advantages and disadvantages generally of present arrangements and whether or not those arrangements are economic and are fair to the interests of each of the individual territories and to make recommendations for any necessary adjustments, additions or modifications to them."

The findings of the Raisman Commission may be expected to form a valuable complement to the present report.

THE MONETARY SYSTEM AND ITS CONSEQUENCES

A final feature of the institutional arrangements in East Africa, of some significance for this report, is the currency system at present in force.

The currency in circulation, the East African shilling, is issued by the East African Currency Board. The Board's operations cover not only Tanganyika, but also Kenya, Uganda, Zanzibar, British Somaliland and the Aden Protectorate. The function of the Board is to make available on demand East African currency against deposits of sterling and sterling in exchange for East African currency.

This currency board system has certain economic consequences which it is important to appreciate. The Board is obliged to keep sterling assets equivalent to a high proportion of the currency in circulation in East Africa, and thus in effect the territories have foreign exchange reserves more than sufficient to meet any call on them which can be expected in practice. Moreover, depletion of the sterling holdings of the Currency Board, except by any depreciation which may occur of the value of the securities in which they are held, is automatically accompanied by a corresponding reduction of East African currency in circulation, so that drafts on reserves tend to be self-correcting.

Further, the opportunities for Tanganyika to impose a strain on the balance of payments through internal inflation are so limited as to be virtually negligible. In the first place, there is at present no threat of balance of payments difficulties due to increase of credit by the commercial banks. The commercial banks are all expatriate institutions, and their liabilities are backed by external assets.

More important in the present context, the Government cannot finance deficits by money creation or by borrowing from a local central bank, there being no central bank in Tanganyika. Thus, under the present system, the Government cannot attempt to escape from its financial limitations by tempting but dangerous inflationary devices. Government expenditures have to be financed from revenue, from the proceeds of borrowing, from grants received from the outside world or by drawing down accumulated reserves, and so these outlays have to be kept down to the level which these sources of finance allow.

A benefit of this system is that the balance of external payments can be regarded, for all practical purposes, as looking after itself. The financial stringencies of development show up in immediate, clear and inexorable form in the budget, and not in the less immediate form of balance of payments difficulties. It must be admitted that the currency board system introduces certain rigidities and deficiencies in monetary control which may become seriously inconvenient at a certain stage of development. However, the Mission considers, for reasons set out in Chapter 16, that the East African Currency Board should be retained for the immediate future in its present form. We believe that the element of safety and automatism which will thus be maintained in Tanganyika's monetary relations with the outside world are on balance salutary at the present stage of the territory's development.

CHAPTER 3 *BUDGETING FOR DEVELOPMENT*

It will be apparent from what has been said above that the pace and shape of future development in Tanganyika are highly dependent on public action, notably in the central task of improvement and transformation of African agriculture, in providing, improving and maintaining communications over the large distances of the territory, and in "investment in people," notably by education. But public action is restricted, first and foremost, by the very limited taxable capacity of this low-income economy. Even taking into account the grants which Tanganyika receives at present, chiefly from the United Kingdom, and the sums which the Government of Tanganyika can afford to borrow, limitation of financial resources remains the main restriction on the public development effort and hence, to a major degree, on the development of the economy as a whole.

It has been pointed out in the last chapter that, under the currency board system, the strains of development appear in the budget rather than in the balance of external payments. The budget is where the shoe pinches. Therefore, while the Mission has been concerned with the promotion of economic development in all its aspects, it has had to pay particular attention to the budgetary implications of its proposals. It would be useless to suggest policies and programs which are out of touch with the hard budgetary realities. It is, indeed, easy to draw up a list of projects and activities all of which would make useful contributions to the development of the territory. The planning problem is to prune this list to the size dictated by available financial means, to balance one valuable public expenditure against another, when both have to be kept within rather narrow limits.

Tanganyika's present development problem is one of financial stringency rather than of "limited absorptive capacity"; the present administrative machinery could handle a larger development effort if it had larger funds at its disposal; and insofar as present development efforts or an expanded effort are hindered by certain shortages of skilled personnel, these shortages could be overcome to a considerable degree if the money were available—money to hire experts and to assure them of favorable financial terms.

Two conclusions are evident. On the one hand, development in Tanganyika could greatly benefit from continued and expanded inflow of grants and technical assistance and from the availability of loans on soft terms. On the other hand, the Government of Tanganyika, which has to take the financial resources available to it as a datum, must plan efficiently in order to make the most effective use of resources which at best must be expected to remain small in relation to the size of the development task.

The Problem of Planning Ahead

Because it is in major degree concerned with the means of sustaining a fairly high rate of growth in the longer run, the Mission would wish to examine the budgetary feasibility of its proposals for a fairly long period ahead. In relation to irrigation and flood control works, in particular, the Mission has felt obliged to look as much as ten years ahead: on the one hand, such works demand a preliminary period of investigation, planning and building up of staff; and, on the other hand, immediate preparation and recruitment and training of staff need to be related to the scale of works which it is intended to carry out in due course.

However, it is in fact very difficult to judge what level of government developmental expenditures will be feasible in Tanganyika beyond the next two or three years. A number of important financial uncertainties have greatly complicated the Mission's task, as, of course, they similarly complicate the task of the planning authorities in Tanganyika.

The first and major uncertainty concerns the amount of grants and free technical assistance which Tanganyika may hope to receive from the outside world in the coming years. In recent years, Colonial Development and Welfare (CD&W) grants from the United Kingdom have financed some 20 percent of Tanganyika's central government capital budget. The present CD&W allocation is for a period up to March 1964, and provides the relatively substantial sum of about £ 1.7 million a year up to that date. The question arises of what grant assistance Tanganyika will receive when the present CD&W allocation is exhausted. Tanganyika may well appear a worthy candidate for external contributions to its development effort above and beyond those which have already been promised: its needs, as a low income country with certain major physical problems, are indisputably great; and, at the same time, it has the capacity to make effective use of external contributions so long as it maintains the efficiency of its public administrative and technical staff. The Mission thinks it realistic to assume that Tanganyika will in fact receive continued grants and technical assistance; but the prospective amounts cannot be predicted. In the context of total central government expenditures of the order of £ 30 million, £ 1 million or £ 2 million more or less in the financial resources available to the Government in each year makes a considerable proportionate difference in the scale of the development effort which it is possible to envisage.

A central problem of Tanganyikan budgetary policy is how much the territory can and should borrow. This depends to a major degree on the terms on which loans will be available. Tanganyika could benefit substantially from opportunities to borrow on "soft" terms. Here again, it is hardly possible to predict what facilities will in fact be available to Tanganyika.

Another element at present unknown is the amount of money Tanganyika will receive pursuant to the undertaking of the United Kingdom Government to meet the cost of inducement pay and allowances for expatriate government servants (see p. 10).

The feasible scale of future expenditures of particular importance to development is also affected by various uncertainties concerning other categories of expenditure. There are, for example, various uncertainties connected with the timing and budgetary implications of full political independence. These include the question of compensation to expatriate civil servants for interruption of their agreed terms of service: the extent of this burden, and the degree to which it will be Tanganyika's sole responsibility, are not at present clear. Then there is the question of the costs of external representation after independence. At present, services of external representation are provided to Tanganyika by the United Kingdom without charge. This arrangement will still be available after independence, provided that Tanganyika remains within the Commonwealth. However, no doubt an independent Tanganyika will wish to establish its own embassies or high commissions in at least a few key centers. Another point which has to be remembered is that, starting in 1960/61, the United Kingdom Government has relieved the East African governments of the cost of the maintenance of military forces in the territory, a saving to Tanganyika of £ 620,000 a year. On attaining independence, Tanganyika will have to accept once more the financial burden of such military forces as it requires.

Other expenditure items are even less predictable, even to the authorities in Tanganyika. There are, notably, a number of substantial contingent liabilities of the Government, some of which may well have to be discharged.

In the face of the many financial uncertainties, the task of budgetary planning is to combine flexibility in adapting to changing circumstances with a greater degree of continuity than has been achieved in the past. The Mission considers that the recent decision in Tanganyika to draw up development plans looking three years ahead, but with annual revisions, is an appropriate approach to this problem.

The aim of this chapter is not only to discuss the broad problems of budgetary policy, but also to review the general shape of the Mission's proposals in their relation to the financial possibilities. To this end, fairly detailed figures will be presented below, extending to 1965/66, or for five years after the financial year in course during the final revision of this report. This period goes a further two years beyond that to be covered in the initial three-year plan to be drawn up by the ministerial Development Committee in Tanganyika. Thus an effort is made to establish a slightly longer context for the first of the new three-year plans, even though it is precisely for the two years following the first three-year plan period that the financial uncertainties become particularly acute.

The foundation for the Mission's expenditure projections is the reckoning that the expansion of production which may be expected over the next few years should make possible continued annual increases of central government current revenue of the order of 4.5 percent, or of roughly £1 million a year. The possession of reserve funds, totalling about £ 4 million, will enable the Government to plan for increases of current expenditures (including debt service) on the scale indicated, even though disappointing revenue returns must be expected in some years. Thus it is possible to reckon on at least a continued gradual increase of the possible scale of total government expenditures.

In practice, the Mission assumes a somewhat greater expansion of total central government expenditures than is justified by the prospective development of those financial resources which can be counted on with a fairly high degree of certainty. That is to say, the Mission makes some allowance, inevitably rather arbitrary, for the fact that Tanganyika can hope to receive grants, technical assistance and possibly soft loans over and above those which have already been specifically promised.

Because this allowance is inescapably somewhat arbitrary, it follows that the expenditure projections given must be regarded as indications of the general shape of the measures recommended, rather than as exact blueprints intended to be followed in detail. Changes in the appreciation of financial resources, refinement and revision of costings, revised assessments of technical feasibility and of returns may all give the Development Committee reason to make adjustments to the size and pattern of expenditures shown. In fact, the Mission considers that the Development Committee will be fully able to tackle the function of year-to-year planning, especially if the machinery of planning is strengthened as suggested in Chapters 11 and 17. Given existing standards of competence in Tanganyika, the Mission has thought it appropriate to suggest guidelines rather than to attempt the task, in any case impossible in the circumstances, of laying down a hard and fast development plan.

RECENT BUDGETARY DEVELOPMENTS

The Mission does not in fact propose any radical break with the budgetary policies of the last few years, but rather certain changes of balance in the context of expanding outlays made possible by a continued rise of revenue, and certain improvements in planning. It is therefore convenient to lay the foundations for the projections to follow by means of a brief sketch of recent budgetary history. The general shape and effects of government expenditures in recent years have been described in Chapter 2. The following paragraphs are mainly concerned with the course of expansion of the budget over the postwar period.

The scale of government activity, though small in absolute terms, has increased very rapidly in the postwar period. Current expenditures made by the Central Government rose from £ 5.4 million in 1947[1] to almost £ 20 million during the fiscal year 1958/59. The estimates for 1960/61 call for expenditure of £ 22 million.[2] Central

[1] Up to 1953, the fiscal year coincided with the calendar year. From 1954/55, the fiscal year has run from July 1 to June 30.

[2] On the basis of presentation used for the budgets of the immediately preceding years.

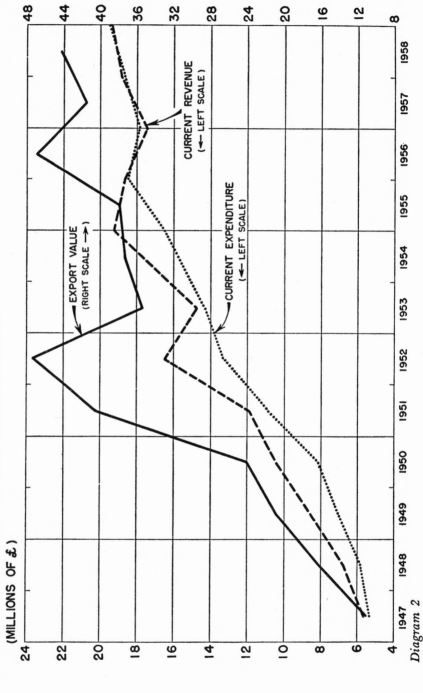

TANGANYIKA: VALUE OF EXPORTS AND CENTRAL GOVERNMENT CURRENT REVENUE AND EXPENDITURE

(MILLIONS OF £)

Diagram 2

government capital expenditures rose sharply from £ 0.4 million in 1947 to about £ 5 million in 1952, and thereafter have fluctuated between £ 3.2 million and £ 5.5 million.

This increase of expenditures has been accompanied by certain stresses and strains, which illustrate the nature of the budgetary problems to be tackled in the future.

Development of the Current Budget

In the postwar years up to 1955/56, central government revenue was greater than current expenditure, thus leaving a margin for the financing of capital expenditures. Over the following few years, however, increase of expenditures tended to outstrip the growth of revenue. This gave rise to a feeling of acute budgetary difficulty, resulting in deliberate measures, sometimes even of an emergency nature, to hold current expenditures down to the approximate level of revenue: for example, in October 1958 the Government imposed a freeze on recruitment of staff.

The deterioration which occurred in the balance of the current budget cannot reasonably be attributed to sluggishness in the increase of revenue. Indeed, the buoyant rising trend of current revenues has been a notable feature of the postwar budgetary picture. Here it is necessary to take a fairly long view. The fact that revenue in 1958/59 was still little higher than in 1954/55 is attributable to exceptional circumstances. The hump in revenue in 1954/55 was a delayed effect of the Korean boom (see Diagram 2): the high export earnings of 1951 and 1952 gave rise to large income tax liabilities, notably by sisal estates, and there were administrative delays in collecting this tax. On a longer view, current revenue can be seen to have increased from £ 8.6 million in 1949 to £ 22.1 million in 1959/60, an average annual rate of increase of over nine percent. Diagram 2 suggests that revenue has tended to increase very nearly in the same proportion as export earnings.

A major part of the increase in revenue in recent years has come from import duties, excise duties and income tax (see Table 7). Africans are taxed largely through import and excise duties and the personal tax. While receipts from import and excise duties are responsive to increases in African incomes, the personal tax, though in principle levied according to a graduated scale, is not in fact very responsive to income changes. Very few Africans pay income tax, which is in major degree a tax on the sisal industry and other European estates, on commerce and on industry. Greater detail on tax structure and tax rates will be given in Chapter 16. Central government revenues now amount to about 17 percent of total monetary incomes in the territory.

Recent difficulties in maintaining balance in the current budget may be attributed to the fact that, from 1951 to 1954/55, current expenditures were allowed to parallel the rapid rise of revenue which

TABLE 7 Government of Tanganyika Current Revenues, 1948–50 and 1955/56–1958/59

(£'000)

Category	1948	1949	1950	1955/56	1956/57	1957/58	1958/59
Import duties	2,704	3,150	2,984	5,527	4,999	5,312	6,691
Excise duties	467	557	713	1,604	1,824	2,095	2,059
Income tax	652	1,097	1,884	4,507	4,066	4,283	3,525
Personal tax[a]	984	1,019	1,052	1,537	1,163	1,413	1,306
Other taxes	680	656	1,524	1,276	1,476	1,561	1,672
Provision of goods and services	294	338	402	995	1,104	1,303	1,324
Government property income	751	1,387	1,244	1,839	1,786	1,972	1,853
Miscellaneous revenue ..	179	383	595	1,397	1,074	894	981
Total	6,711	8,586	10,397	18,680	17,492	18,834	19,412

[a] For the years to 1950, native house and poll tax *plus* non-native poll tax. In the later years, the same *plus* personal tax. Personal tax alone was £ 902,000 in 1955/56, £ 1,096,000 in 1956/57, £ 1,381,479 in 1957/58 and £ 1,288,000 in 1958/59.

NOTE: A more detailed breakdown of sources of revenue in 1957/58 and 1958/59 is given in Table 77.

SOURCE: Tanganyika *Statistical Abstract*.

occurred during this period. The administrative delays in collecting income tax after the Korean boom obscured the exceptional nature, now sufficiently apparent, of this revenue increase. The expansion of current expenditure is, indeed, very understandable, given the low level of expenditure in the years up to 1951. However, the process, once begun, was inevitably difficult to check. Further, increasing current expenditures have also been entailed by the expansion, from 1950, of the capital budget. The striking increase in road and bridge maintenance can be seen in Table 8. There have been new schools

TABLE 8   Government of Tanganyika Current Expenditures,
1948–50 and 1955/56–1958/59

(£ '000)

Category	1948	1949	1950	1955/56	1956/57	1957/58	1958/59
General Administrative							
Services	1,513	1,987	2,432	5,095	5,634	5,847	6,499
Economic Services							
Agriculture	238	284	279	566	647	633	630
Veterinary	142	176	211	359	466	456	440
Road and Bridge							
Maintenance	185	202	281	785	826	908	970
Other	296	367	519	1,684	1,743	1,822	1,806
Local Government	457	529	574	939	657	647	626
Social Services							
Education	373	724	709	2,669	2,915	3,124	3,303
Medical	479	638	683	1,669	1,665	1,723	1,785
Other	39	66	130	200	194	202	218
Unallocated Public Works	336	527	701	1,447	1,201	903	1,470
Public Debt Service	237	130	131	543	715	1,005	1,251
Miscellaneous	1,547	1,432	1,477	2,537	1,182	1,424	529
Total	5,842	7,062	8,127	18,491	17,847	18,694	19,527

NOTE: A more detailed breakdown of expenditures in 1957/58 and 1958/59 is given
in Table 79. Figures in this table differ to some extent from those in Table 6,
where adjustments have been made in accordance with national accounting
definitions.

SOURCE: Tanganyika *Statistical Abstract*.

and hospitals to staff. In addition, borrowing to finance capital
expenditure increased debt service from the very small figure of
£ 131,000 in 1950 to over £ 1 million by 1957/58 and to an estimated
£ 1.7 million gross in 1960/61.

In spite of the efforts to check the continuing rise of current expenditures, small current deficits did in fact occur in 1956/57 and
1958/59, but they were kept to manageable size (see Table 9), and
could be covered without difficulty by drawing on reserve funds
accumulated in the earlier postwar years. In March 1959 the Government of the United Kingdom gave an undertaking in general terms
". . . to assist Tanganyika in meeting its financial difficulties." However, no special financial assistance under this guarantee has been
required. Whereas the estimates for 1959/60 predicted a current
budget deficit of £ 1.3 million, unexpectedly large revenues in the

TABLE 9 Financing of Capital Expenditures of the Government of Tanganyika, 1947-1958/59

(£ '000)

Year	Surplus on Current Budget	Development Plan Reserves	Agricultural Development Reserves	Miscellaneous Domestic Resources^a	External Grants^b	Loan Funds and Advances in Anticipation	Total
1947	256	157	101	—	165 (135)	—	424
1948	869	216	129	—	340 (267)	311	996
1949	1,524	319	194	—	511 (566)	663	1,687
1950	2,270	546	260	—	1,605 (1,093)	1,027	3,438
1951	1,123	781	322	—	657 (1,175)	2,070	3,830
1952	3,096	1,539	340	106	1,080 (1,016)	1,924	4,989
1953	410	1,500	363	44	1,293 (1,085)	526	3,726
1954 Jan.—June	1,652	181	176	50	453 (440)	741	1,601
1954/55	2,808	415	301	76	530 (850)	2,015	3,337
1955/56	189	423	246	467	677 (677)	2,271	4,084
1956/57	−355^c	149	^d	1,011	922 (922)	3,200	5,282
1957/58	140	612	^d	1,056	899 (899)	2,887	5,454
1958/59	−115^c	438	—	1,091	1,283 (1,283)	2,347	5,159

[a] The expansion of this item from 1956/57 is explained by the inclusion of the proceeds of "tap" issues of local development bonds. Other major items in recent years are capital contributions by Native Authorities towards the cost of primary schools and rural water supplies; donations; lump sum premia collected from residential, commercial or industrial plot holders in respect of their road frontage or rail sidings.

[b] Owing to differences in time between incurring expenses and recovering expenditure from Colonial Development and Welfare funds, expenditures financed from grant money (figures not in brackets) may differ in any year from grants becoming available (figures in brackets). The difference is carried to a suspense account.

[c] Deficit.

[d] Included with "miscellaneous domestic resources".

SOURCE: Tanganyika Statistical Abstract.

year, together with very considerable underexpenditure of the sums voted to various departments, resulted in a sizeable surplus in spite of the introduction of various supplementary expenditures. The 1960/61 budget shows an estimated current deficit of £ 441,000. However, revenue may well be somewhat higher than the original official estimate, and some continued underexpenditure must be expected, so that, unless considerable supplementaries are introduced during the course of the year, near balance or even another surplus can reasonably be expected.

Thus, contrary to the impression prevailing over the past few years, it may be concluded that there is at present no acute problem of preventing the development of unmanageable deficits in the current budget. The chronic problem, of course, remains: that the small absolute size of the financial resources available to the Government of Tanganyika necessitates very careful budgeting of expenditures.

A lesson of recent budgetary history is the need to make the best possible assessment of future financial resources, and particularly of the prospective development of current revenue. Underestimation of prospective finances may lead to unnecessary restriction of public activities, thus holding back the rate of development of the economy and hence the future increase of public revenues. Overestimation can lead to financial difficulties which can be remedied only at the cost of discontinuities in public programs.

The structure of current expenditures, excluding debt service payments, has remained fairly constant over the last decade, as is indicated by Table 8. The most rapid increases in expenditures from 1950 to 1958/59 were on education and on road and bridge maintenance and other economic services apart from agricultural and veterinary services. These latter have remained rather small in relation to total expenditures.

Development of the Capital Budget

From 1949 through 1954/55, there were surpluses on the current budget averaging slightly less than £ 2 million a year. These surpluses were used for the finance of capital expenditures and to build up reserve funds, some of which still remain unspent. From 1948 to 1953, while capital expenditures were increased from £ 1 million to the neighborhood of £ 4 million a year, an average of about one third of these expenditures was financed from revenue or accumulated

TABLE 10: Government of Tanganyika Capital Expenditures, 1948–50, 1955/56-1958/59 and Estimates for 1960/61

(£'000)

Category	1948	1949	1950	1955/56	1956/57	1957/58	1958/59	1960/61 (estimates)
Economic								
Agriculture and Animal Husbandry	169	229	359	90	72	147	247	217
Water Supplies	140	162	168	311	470	492	634	715
Roads	112	180	1,094	1,172	939	906	849	1,386
Other	71	301	113	208	85	90	140	401
Social								
Education	47	227	292	674	1,026	1,196	1,135	677
Township Development	73	104	450	570	1,292	993	810	721
Public Health and Social Welfare	65	9	44	346	419	309	291	303
Public Buildings and Works	272	341	906	707	942	1,253	966	1,471
Other	47	134	13	6	38	68	87	289
Total	996	1,687	3,438	4,084	5,282	5,454	5,159	6,180

NOTE: Figures in this table differ to some extent from those in Table 6, where adjustments have been made in accordance with national accounting definitions.

SOURCE: Tanganyika *Statistical Abstract*.

reserves. Such financing nevertheless remained less than the current surpluses over the period, so that reserve funds were augmented. During the same period, slightly less than one third of capital expenditures was financed by grants from the outside world, and just over one third by borrowing, which averaged just over £ 1 million a year over the six years, and was in the neighborhood of £ 2 million in only two years (see Table 9).

The situation in the three most recent years for which final figures are available, 1956/57-1958/59, was markedly different. While total capital expenditures had increased only from the neighborhood of £ 4 million in 1951-1953 to an average of £ 5.3 million in 1956/57-1958/59, borrowing had increased by a larger proportion, and averaged £ 2.8 million a year in the later period, financing between 45 and 61 percent of capital expenditures. (These figures do not include the proceeds of "tap" issues of local development bonds.) This increase of borrowing was largely in compensation for the disappearance of current surpluses and a reduction in the use of reserve funds to finance capital expenditures. Grants, at around £ 1 million a year, were about as great in 1956/57-1958/59 as in 1950-1953, but financed a smaller proportion of the somewhat increased capital expenditures.

The rising trend of borrowing has, of course, involved rising debt service obligations as noted above. However, debt service still absorbs substantially under 10 percent of current revenue.

The recent level of borrowing has been to some extent a matter of choice, even given the level of capital expenditures, since there existed the alternative of devoting to capital expenditures a part of the accumulated reserve funds to which allusions have been made above. These reserve funds are not to be confused with the reserves of the Currency Board, which are separate and distinct, and which are not available to the Government except through the device of Currency Board loans against the "fiduciary issue" (see p. 332). Their nature and amount in mid-1960 is shown in Table 11. The reserve funds are invested in interest-bearing securities, and it may on occasion appear advantageous to incur new borrowing to finance capital expenditures, rather than to sell securities. In periods of financial stringency, the Government of Tanganyika has received advances from the Crown Agents for Overseas Governments and Administrations on the security of the reserves, and has thus been able to avoid selling assets on disadvantageous terms. The existence of these reserve funds has been, and remains, an element of flexibility in the budgetary situation.

TABLE 11: General Reserves of the Government of Tanganyika
at June 30, 1960

	(£ '000)
Reserve Fund	2,000
General Revenue Balance	2,508
Agricultural Development Reserve	32
Development Fund	414
Balance of fund set aside to meet losses on former government monopoly export of maize and rice	128
Less advances from the Crown Agents	1,072ᵃ
Net balance of general reserves	4,010

ᵃ The securities in which the stated reserves are held are deposited with the Crown Agents for Overseas Governments and Administrations in London. Against these securities the Crown Agents make advances to the Government of Tanganyika. The figure shown is the amount of such advances outstanding at June 21, 1960.

SOURCE: Government of Tanganyika.

In spite of the existence of these reserves, the recent feeling of budgetary crisis led to cuts in the capital budget. The capital budget for 1959/60 was reduced to barely over £ 4 million, and this figure was in fact considerably underspent. Expenditures provided for in the budget reached only about £ 3.6 million. Even after a supplementary vote of £ 350,000 to increase the permanent capital of the Land Bank, the level of expenditure was the lowest since 1954/55. The 1960/61 budget, by contrast, aims to raise capital expenditures above the level of the years 1956/57-1958/59.

The composition of government capital expenditures has been discussed in Chapter 2. Their development over time is illustrated by Table 10.

A PATTERN FOR FUTURE BUDGETS

The Mission's proposals, the general nature of which has been sketched in Chapter 1, affect a broad range of budgetary expenditure items, both capital and current. It is consequently impossible to describe their budgetary implications at all adequately without going into a certain degree of detail. A major point which has already been mentioned is the recommendation to undertake without delay the preparatory stages of an agricultural "transformation" program, even though this involves expenditures the return on which is inevitably delayed and often rather uncertain.

Expenditure Recommendations in Outline

Before a more detailed account is given of the way in which the current and capital budgets might develop according to the Mission's recommendations, the following notes sketch the budgetary effects of the Mission's main proposals.

Agricultural "Improvement".
a. Improvement of quality and increase of size of the agricultural extension staff. This accounts for a considerable part of the increase of current expenditures shown for agriculture and veterinary services.

b. A more active program of agrarian lending including lending for the establishment of processing facilities. Monies to be lent are provided in the capital budget projections. The establishment of regional loan officers is reckoned as a charge on the current budget.

c. Provision, both current and capital, is made for the adoption of pilot community development schemes.

Agricultural "Transformation".
a. Increase of agricultural and livestock research, investigations and trials is partially allowed for in the current budget projections. It is recommended that Tanganyika should also seek additional technical assistance to expand and widen this type of activity.

b. Provision is made for an almost threefold increase of water development staff over the next few years (current) and for continued surveys and investigations (capital), in preparation for a greatly increased program of irrigation and flood control works.

c. While increased allowance is made for capital expenditures on irrigation and flood control in the years up to 1965/66, it is envisaged that the major increase of such expenditures would occur over the following five years, after the interim period of preparation and planning. The Mission proposes that from about 1968/69 such activities should become a major part of an expanded capital budget.

d. Allowance is made for some planned settlement schemes to be undertaken directly by the Government, and also for government loans to the Tanganyika Agricultural Corporation to finance supervised ranching schemes and planned settlement schemes.

Mineral Surveys. Financial provision is made for:

a. Acceleration of basic geological mapping.

b. Government mineral reconnaissance work, to bridge the gap which exists between basic geological mapping and private prospecting.

c. Acceleration of topographical mapping. Such mapping, needed as a preparation for geological mapping, is also desirable in connection with water development, planning of agricultural development, road building, and a variety of other developmental activities.

Development of Commerce and Industry.

a. Provision is made for the financing of a company to investigate and publicize opportunities for industrial development.

b. Sums are set aside in the capital budget for a small industrial financing institution.

c. Provision is made for the establishment of courses to train Africans in small-scale industry and commerce, and to improve the local administration of loans for these activities.

Transport and Communications. Since railways, ports, posts and telegraphs are the responsibility of East Africa High Commission services, the main responsibility of the Government of Tanganyika in the field of transport and communications is for construction, improvement and maintenance of roads.

a. The Mission makes financial provision for continued construction and improvement of main roads. However, it considers that with certain exceptions roads, railways and water transport now provide main transport routes which are reasonably adequate in relation to the economic activity to be foreseen in the near future. It therefore proposes a gradual reduction of expenditure on construction and improvement of main roads, to be offset by an increase of expenditure on construction and improvement of feeder roads in rural areas.

b. In the current budget projections, provision is made for a considerable increase of expenditure on road and bridge maintenance. This reflects not only the increased maintenance requirements of new or improved roads, but also an allowance for some raising of present standards of maintenance.

Educational Expansion. The Mission endorses the idea of an educational "crash program" with the principal aims of sharply increasing the number of secondary school places available to Africans and of expanding technical training facilities.

a. The capital costs of this program are not particularly great by comparison with the large capital expenditures which have been incurred in recent years in building primary schools.

b. By contrast, the current costs of an educational program such as appears desirable are very heavy. The Mission envisages that the Government of Tanganyika will seek external assistance to meet a part of these costs.

Planning. The Mission makes various proposals for the improvement of planning methods and the strengthening of government planning staff. However, these recommendations do not necessitate any great increases of budgetary expenditures.

Current Expenditure Projections

The way in which budgetary expenditures might be expected to develop in accordance with these recommendations is shown in Tables 12 and 13.

In considering the impact of the Mission's proposals on the prospective development of the central government budget it is convenient to begin with the current budget. As has been pointed out, many current expenditures are as important in their effects on development as any capital expenditure. And, while there are difficulties in estimating the funds likely to be available for the finance of future capital budgets, current budget projections can be based on the somewhat firmer foundation of estimates of the prospective development of current revenue. Finally, examination of the potential development of the current budget shows the impact of increases of debt service obligations, and so throws light on an important element in the finance of capital expenditures.

Table 12 is founded on the reckoning that current expenditures can be allowed to increase in line with the estimated increase of current revenue, from just under £ 21 million ("net" basis) in 1960/61, by 4.5 percent or roughly £ 1 million annually, to nearly £ 26 million in 1965/66. The basis of this revenue projection is explained in Annex IX.

TABLE 12   Current Expenditures of the Government of Tanganyika, Development Envisaged to 1965/66

(£ '000)

	1960/61	1961/62	1962/63	1963/64	1964/65	1965/66
General Administrative						
Services	6,720	6,955	7,165	7,300	7,455	7,610
Economic Services						
Agriculture	832	890	955	1,020	1,090	1,165
Veterinary	502	520	540	560	580	600
Rural Water Supplies .	359	400	555	720	860	1,020
Forests	333	350	365	380	400	420
Mines, Industry and						
Commerce	130	165	175	185	195	205
Lands and Surveys ...	301	315	320	325	330	330
Geological Surveys ...	135	135	140	140	145	145
Road and Bridge						
Maintenance	1,091	1,250	1,350	1,460	1,575	1,700
Aviation	174	180	185	185	190	190
Other	382	390	400	410	420	430
Social Services						
Education	3,279	3,445	3,615	3,795	3,985	4,185
Medical	1,931	2,100	2,200	2,250	2,300	2,350
Other	271	285	305	320	335	350
Unallocated Public Works[a]	1,052	1,060	1,070	1,080	1,090	1,100
Local Government	688	710	735	760	785	810
Public Debt Service	1,594	1,735	2,010	2,295	2,520	2,760
Miscellaneous	696	670	620	550	550	550
Contribution to Develop-						
ment	250	180	10	—	—	—
Total	20,718	21,735	22,715	23,735	24,805	25,920

[a] Including urban water supplies.

SOURCE: *Estimates of Expenditure, 1960/61*; Mission estimates.

Table 12 takes as its starting point the budget estimates presented for the year 1960/61, and is based on a comparable degree of "net-ness".[3] Expenditures are classified according to their economic significance rather than according to their place in the administrative framework, as in the budget. The classification used follows in

[3] Comparison of the current revenue and expenditure estimates for 1960/61 with the figures for previous years is complicated by a change in the method of presentation used. In the estimates for 1959/60 and the immediately preceding years, receipts for specific services, such as school and medical fees, were treated as reve-

general that of the Tanganyika Unit of the East African Statistical Department, as in Table 8, though with certain modifications. These modifications, and the comparison with the presentation used in the budget, are explained in Annex VIII.

The figures assume the continuance of the salary scales in force in mid-1960. In fact, a commission has been appointed which is to inquire into conditions of service, including remuneration, of expatriate government officers in Tanganyika. It may be expected that increases of salary scales will follow. However, while the total effect of the recent undertaking of the Government of the United Kingdom to take over the cost of inducement pay and allowances of overseas staff is not yet known, it may be assumed that it will considerably more than offset such increases of expatriate officers' pay as are to be expected in the near future.

Within the general framework of a 4½ percent annual increase of total current expenditures, the figures in Table 12 show some change in the pattern of expenditures over the next few years. Leaving out of account for the moment public debt service, the Mission recommends considerably greater than average rates of increase for current expenditures classified under: Rural Water Supplies; Mines, Industry and Commerce; Road and Bridge Maintenance; Agriculture; and Other Social Services, a heading which includes, notably, community development. In absolute terms (leaving out of account for the moment public debt service and expenditure on general administrative services) the greatest increases of expenditure indicated are for: Education; Rural Water Supplies; Road and Bridge Maintenance; Medical Services; and Agriculture (in that order).

The prominent place given to increase in expenditures for *rural water supplies* is in line with the Mission's recommendation that staff should be built up over the next five years or so to a size capable of handling 25,000 acres a year of irrigation and flood control development by about 1969/70. The cost to the current budget of such staff would be at about its maximum under the proposed program in 1965/66. Subsequently, as capital works in irrigation and flood control increased, staff costs would, under current accounting procedures,

---

nue. In the 1960/61 budget, by contrast, they are shown as appropriations in aid of expenditure, and both total budgetary expenditures and revenues are set out net of these sums. Budgeted expenditures for 1960/61 amount to £ 20.7 million on the new net basis, but to £ 22.2 million on the basis of presentation used in the budgets of the preceding years. The 1960/61 budget provides for increases of gross current expenditures over those of 1958/59 in most categories (see p. 449).

be increasingly charged to capital works, and the burden on the current budget (4 percent of the total in 1965/66) would decrease absolutely as well as relatively. The arithmetic of this proposition is set out in Annex VIII.

A 7 percent annual increase has been allowed for current expenditures on *agriculture*. About half of this increase is an allowance for the program, already in hand, for the training and employment of an improved grade of agricultural extension worker. The additional increase is intended in part to cover the cost of some additional staff to carry out investigations and trials needed for the "transformation" program. It may be hoped that some such staff may be secured under various technical assistance programs. In this case, the cost of the staff itself would not appear as a charge against current revenue, although certain associated costs would. Another item which needs to be taken into account is subsidies to the Tanganyika Agricultural Corporation to enable it to bear losses arising out of certain projects of an experimental nature (cf. Chapter 11, p. 235).

Elsewhere we recommend the adoption on an increasing scale of two different types of *community development* approach to rural development, one intensive and the other extensive. Increased expenditures, particularly for the intensive type of program, are shown under Other Social Services, and account for the comparatively large proportionate increase of this item.

The reasons for the considerable increase, both proportionate and absolute, in the expenditure allowed for *road and bridge maintenance,* and the purpose of the considerable proportionate increase for *industry and commerce,* have been explained above (p. 52).

The increase of current expenditure shown for *education* is, in absolute terms, second only to that for public debt service. It has been pointed out above that this increase still does not cover the total cost of the "crash program" at present under consideration in Tanganyika. Since education accounts for nearly 16 percent of budgeted current expenditures (net basis) for 1960/61, it is not possible to project an increase of education expenditures markedly more rapid than the forecast rate of revenue increase without very seriously limiting the feasible expansion of other current expenditures. Table 12 shows a 5 percent annual increase for current education expenditures as against a 4½ percent increase for current expenditures as a whole. This does not mean that the Mission considers that the expansion of educational facilities will necessarily have to proceed more slowly than present plans contemplate. The Mission judges that Tanganyika's educational program may well attract grants and technical assistance from the outside world.

Even though the allowance made for increase of current *medical* expenditures is only of the order of 4 percent a year on the average for the period shown, it is still fairly large in absolute terms, at about £ 420,000 over the five years.

Attention must now be given to the increases in expenditures allowed for *general administrative services.* Except for relatively small sums for additional planning staff, the increases in this item are generally for types of expenditure outside the field of the Mission's most immediate concerns. However, it has been necessary to pay attention to the potential development of these expenditures, since they affect the sums likely to be available for the purposes in which the Mission is more directly interested. The increase allowed in Table 12 against general administrative expenditures is in fact the third largest in absolute terms (after public debt service and education). However, it is relatively small in percentage terms, and a serious question arises whether the increases shown will in fact prove adequate, and hence whether the sums regarded as available for other categories of expenditure may not be somewhat overestimated, given the assumptions made concerning the development of current revenue and of debt service liabilities.

A considerable part of the increase shown is required for the planned increase in police expenditures under a program which has already been put into action. Another rising expenditure item included is civil service pensions.

Additional expenditures associated with the achievement of independence have been referred to above. It may be noted that minimum diplomatic establishments in London, Washington and to the United Nations alone could easily cost, together, more than £ 200,000 a year, or a large part of the total increase allowed against general administrative services for any two years after 1962/63. It has been seen that resumption of Tanganyikan responsibility for land forces on the scale of recent years would cost over £ 600,000 a year. On the other side of the coin, it may realistically be expected that the bill for expatriate salaries will be somewhat decreased on independence, for a time at least, by the resignation of some expatriate civil servants; but this is a relief to the budget of a not entirely beneficial nature, since it would be accompanied by a reduction in the performance of the government machine.

While several of the major uncertainties on the expenditure side affect the item for general administrative services, in relation to Table 12 the essential point is very clear. The larger the increase for this item, the less there will be, other things being equal, to spend for other purposes with a greater or more immediate impact on economic and social development. This is not to say that there may not be a case for a greater expansion of expenditures on general administrative services than is shown by the table. Many expenditures in this category are themselves of the greatest importance to the healthy development of the territory. The point is, as always, that one expenditure must be regarded as being at the expense of another. It is necessary to strike a careful balance between expenditures, and to make sure that items of lesser benefit are not favored at the cost of other items of greater importance.

The general implication of the development of current expenditure shown in Table 12 is to concentrate the increases, made possible by the growth to be expected in current revenue, on certain activities believed by the Mission to be of key importance at the present stage of development—notably agriculture, water development and education. Certain other activities are allowed only a smaller proportionate increase. Virtually all, however, are allowed some increase. The small size of the increase shown against *geological surveys* is accounted for by the inclusion of additional expenditures for this type of activity in the capital budget. The *miscellaneous* item covers, notably, payments to cover operating losses on railways and contributions to the cost of the various common services performed by the East Africa High Commission. It is assumed that means will be found of reducing the loss liability for the Southern Province railway, so that the item of £ 187,000 for losses on this railway and the port of Mtwara will be reduced in subsequent years. On the other hand, there is likely to be a loss to be met on the Mpanda line, following the closing down of Uruwira Minerals. As to the High Commission services, it is possible that these costs may be readjusted following the report of the Raisman Commission (see pp. 34-35).

Detailed discussion of the increase shown against *public debt service* and of the diminution and disappearance of the projected figures for *contributions to development* is best held over for a full consideration of the finance of future capital budgets. At these points the current and capital budgets interact. It may be noted here, however, that the increase of debt service obligations over the next few years may perhaps be overstated, depending on the terms on which Tanganyika will in practice be able to borrow and on the extent to which grants may be available to finance capital expenditures. This possible overstatement of debt service liabilities may be set against the possible understatement of the sums which may be required in practice for general administrative expenditures.

The Capital Budget—Future Size and Balance

In framing the above illustrations of the development of the current budget, a principal starting point has been the expected rate of growth of current revenue. In giving a similar picture of the future development of the capital budget, no such foundation exists. The total of financial resources available for the finance of capital expenditures cannot be foreseen at all exactly. How much Tanganyika can afford to borrow depends to a major degree on the terms on which loans are to be had: Tanganyika could benefit substantially from opportunities to borrow on "soft" terms. The uncertainty concerning the future availability of grants from the outside world is also of considerable importance in relation to the size of the capital budget.

The picture of the development of central government capital expenditures over the next few years, given by Table 13, is dominated in quantitative terms by the Mission's recommendations for an increase in *water development* works—irrigation and flood control in particular. According to the figures shown, water development expenditures would increase from less than 12 percent of the capital budget in 1960/61 to over 25 percent in 1965/66.

The figures in Table 13 are, indeed, more influenced by considerations of the desirable future expansion of water development works than appears from the table itself. While the expansion of such works must depend both on the successful completion of preliminary investigations, planning and trials and on the availability of finance, the Mission suggests that such expenditures might well increase not merely from £ 0.7 million in 1960/61 to £ 1.7 million in 1965/66, but up to a level of about £ 4.3 million to be reached by about 1969/70 and to be sustained in the succeeding years. The Mission considers that with proper preparation and organization, this form of investment should be capable of making a very substantial contribution to the development of the territory, and will justify fairly heavy borrowing. It therefore considers that Tanganyika must ensure that it is in good financial condition in order to be able to undertake this borrowing. It is partly for this reason that no very great expansion of total capital expenditures is envisaged for the next few years. To put it in

TABLE 13   Capital Expenditures of the Government of Tanganyika, Development Envisaged to 1965/66

(£ '000)

	1960/61	1961/62	1962/63	1963/64	1964/65	1965/66
Water Development						
Irrigation }	176	150	250	400	600	900
Flood control }		90	110	130	150	170
Small water supplies	358	370	385	400	420	435
Surveys and investigations	108	150	150	150	150	150
Miscellaneous equipment	73	75	75	75	75	75
	715	835	970	1,155	1,395	1,780
Other Natural Resources						
Agriculture	144	150	150	150	150	150
Planned settlement schemes	2	25	50	75	100	100
Veterinary	80	100	100	100	100	100
Afforestation	137	180	180	160	160	140
Ngorongoro	38	—	—	—	—	—
Loans to TAC	401	455	480	485	510	490
	—	100	50	50	50	50
Social and Community Development	40	45	55	60	70	70
Transport						
Trunk roads	1,082	1,000	1,000	900	800	675
Feeder roads	304	340	380	475	575	700
Airports	72	25	25	25	25	25
	1,458	1,365	1,405	1,400	1,400	1,400
Mining						
Geological mapping	100	75	75	75	75	75
Other mining surveys	—	50	35	35	35	35
Small Loans	100	125	110	110	110	110
Development Corporation	14	500	500	500	500	500
Lands and Surveys	200	100	100	100	—	—
	45	10	10	10	10	10
Education	677	630	585	600	600	600
Health	263	275	275	350	375	400
Township Development	721	365	365	460	515	600
African Urban Housing	141	100	100	120	130	140
Security	887	700	600	200	150	100
Government Buildings	250	200	200	175	150	150
Government Housing	150	75	75	75	75	75
Miscellaneous	118	120	120	150	160	175
Total	6,180	6,000	6,000	6,000	6,200	6,600

SOURCES: *Estimates of Expenditure, 1960/61;* Mission estimates.

other words, the Mission considers that an expansion in a few years' time of well-prepared irrigation and flood control projects (and probably also of some planned settlement schemes) is more important than any great expansion of capital expenditures in the immediate future, insofar as the two courses have to be regarded as alternatives.

Such expansion of water development works as appears technically feasible over the next few years can be provided for without any great allowances for increase of total capital expenditures. This is because various other capital expenditures can reasonably be expected to decline from their 1960/61 levels over the following few years. For example, the present level of expenditure on police accommodation (*security*) is of the nature of a "crash program", and will not need to be continued into the future. The present program of erection of *government buildings* will increasingly meet the needs of the administration for adequate office space, and the level of expenditure on this item can be reduced in future years.

Similarly, as has been mentioned above, the *education* "crash program" does not appear to necessitate particularly high capital expenditures, and thus capital expenditures for education are put at a lower level than those of recent years, when there has been widespread building of primary schools.

The figures for *road development,* nearly a quarter of the capital budget for 1960/61, have been held fairly constant over the period shown. However, as noted above, within this total there is a progressive change of emphasis as between trunk roads and feeder roads.

To turn to various smaller items: an allowance has been made for increased investment directly by the Government in *planned settlement schemes.* It is envisaged that other planned settlement schemes and also cattle ranching schemes will be undertaken by the Tanganyika Agricultural Corporation (TAC), and that the Government will have to make *loans to the TAC,* on suitable terms, at first for the further development of existing cattle ranches and for the expansion of operations at Nachingewea, if this proves feasible, and subsequently for further planned settlement and ranching schemes. As against these loans, the Government will in due course receive service payments from the TAC. The question of the future financial relationships between the Government of Tanganyika and the TAC is further discussed in Chapter 11.

While "transformation" activities will in due course call for fairly large direct investments by government and public authorities, no very great increase of direct public investments appears to be called for by agricultural "improvement" programs. Allowance is made for a slightly higher rate of public investment in livestock facilities (*veterinary*), and for expanding capital outlays in connection with *community development* activities. A more considerable new provision is allowed for *small loans*. This provision is largely for a more vigorous program of agricultural lending and for the finance of agricultural processing facilities where loans are not available from commercial sources; but the sums are also intended to cover loans for small-scale commercial and handicraft ventures.

The allowance made for *afforestation* is explained in Chapter 9, and is subject to revision following the completion of an FAO study of Tanganyika's prospective timber requirements.

Provision is made for the acceleration of *geological mapping* above the pace of recent years and for the adoption of an expanded *minerals reconnaissance* program.

In the capital budget of 1960/61, £ 200,000 was put aside towards the initial capital of a *development corporation* to assist industrial development. The intention was to provide a further £ 200,000 in 1961/62 and £ 100,000 in 1962/63. The spread of the total provision of £ 500,000 over four years instead of three, in Table 13, is merely for the sake of holding down the total of capital expenditures shown for 1961/62.

It will be noticed that Table 13 shows reductions from the levels of 1960/61 in the allowances made for *township development* and *African urban housing*. These reductions spring from the conviction that the limited funds available must be concentrated so far as possible on activities giving high returns in the growth of economic activity.

In interpreting the small absolute size of the total capital expenditures shown in Table 13, it is necessary to recall that capital expenditures on railways, ports, mails and telecommunications are made by East Africa High Commission services, and hence are not included in the table. The two projects of railway extension at present being carried out by the East African Railways and Harbours Administration (see Chapter 14, p. 286), have an estimated total capital cost of some £ 3 million. Capital expenditure in Tanganyika by the East African Posts and Telecommunications Administration might well average about £ 150,000 a year in the next few years. Further, as has been pointed out above, it is misleading to concentrate too exclusively on the capital budget, since various current expenditures are just as important to development as are capital expenditures.

It remains the fact that the capital expenditures indicated for 1965/66 are only 25 percent higher than the average level attained in the years 1956/57-1958/59, an average rate of increase over eight years of less than 3 percent a year. The projection of a rather gradual increase of capital expenditures over the next few years is founded on the following considerations:

a. The lack of any assured source of grants to replace the present Colonial Development and Welfare allocation when it is exhausted.

b. The desirability of keeping a margin of borrowing capacity in hand, in anticipation of an increase, after proper preparation, of water development works and of other projects related to an agricultural "transformation" approach.

Financing of Capital Expenditures

In considering how capital expenditures of the size indicated are to be financed, it is convenient to begin with those financial resources which are in greater or less degree predictable, thus arriving at a residual to be met by new external borrowing or from other sources which cannot at present be firmly relied on. A rough sketch map of sources of funds to finance government capital expenditures up to 1965/66 is given in Table 14.

Tanganyika's allocation of United Kingdom Colonial Development and Welfare (CD&W) grants is sufficient to cover over a quarter of the capital expenditures shown for the period up to 1963/64.

At the beginning of the fiscal year 1960/61, roughly £ 5.2 million of Tanganyika's allocation remained uncommitted, and the total amount not yet issued was some £ 6.9 million. On the expectation that not more than about £ 120,000 of these sums will be used to finance current expenditures, there remains about £ 6.75 million to finance capital expenditures. Although CD&W grants will cease to be available when Tanganyika becomes independent, sums already committed at that time for approved purposes will, according to existing precedents, be provided under the Commonwealth Services Vote.

Some continued underspending of the sums voted for capital expenditures may reasonably be expected in 1960/61, and it is assumed that capital expenditures will in fact be of the order of £ 5.5 million, instead of £ 6.18 million as provided for in the budget; and consequently that drawing on Colonial Development and Welfare grants

TABLE 14   Sources of Finance for Future Capital Budgets

(£ '000)

	1960/61	1961/62	1962/63	1963/64	1964/65	1965/66
Colonial Development and Welfare	2,200	1,700	1,700	1,150	—	—
Local Government Authority capital contributions, etc. .	150	150	150	150	150	150
"Tap" issues of Local Development Bonds	100	105	110	110	115	120
Internal long-term borrowing	350	365	380	395	410	425
Transfers from revenue	250	180	10	—	—	—
Total	3,050	2,500	2,350	1,805	675	695
Capital expenditures as in Table 13	5,500ª	6,000	6,000	6,000	6,200	6,600
Balance to be met from external borrowing, etc.	2,450	3,500	3,650	4,195	5,525	5,905

ª On the assumption of some underexpenditure.
SOURCE: Mission estimates.

will be less than the £ 2.7 million allowed for in the budget estimates —say £ 2.2 million. It is assumed that drawings of the remaining CD&W funds will be distributed over the years 1961/62-1963/64 as shown in Table 14.

Certain limited sums can be counted on from internal sources. In the first place, there are the capital contributions made by local government authorities towards the cost of primary schools and rural water supplies, donations, and lump sum premia collected from residential, commercial or industrial site holders in respect of their road frontage or rail sidings. These items are estimated as contributing a total of £ 150,000 a year.

Past experience suggests that the Government of Tanganyika can raise about £ 350,000 a year by local sale of medium- or long-term securities.

Under present arrangements, the East African Currency Board is authorized to invest £ 20 million of its assets in securities of the governments of the territories in which the Board operates, Tanganyika's share being about one-third. In September 1959 the Currency Board subscribed just under £ 1 million to a local loan raised at 6.5 percent, and the total of such holdings is £ 1.2 million. It must not be supposed, however, that the whole of the remainder is available for investment in long-term securities. In addition to the necessity to preserve an adequate degree of liquidity, it is also the policy of the Board to support the development of Treasury Bill markets in the territories. The Permanent Secretaries of the Treasuries of the territories are now members of the Board, and so will be in a position to assess the proper balance between long- and short-term investment of the sums available.

Since October 1956 the Government of Tanganyika has made "tap" issues of local development bonds, encashable at par on six months' notice, or sooner subject to penalty. Provided further issues are announced from time to time, it is considered practicable to raise around £ 100,000 a year by this means. The highly successful issue of May 1958 carried interest at 5.75 percent.

To make an allowance, possibly conservative, for the effects of the continuing growth of the monetary economy, it is assumed in Table 14 that both forms of internal borrowing may be expected to increase by 4 percent a year.

A final internal item is the transfers from revenue, corresponding to the "contributions to development" shown in Table 12.

The residual item in Table 14 is the balance to be met from other sources. The balance has to be met from: grants over and above the CD&W grants shown in the table; external borrowing; and drawings on government reserve funds.

The growth of this residual item from £ 3.7 million in 1962/63 to £ 5.5 million in 1964/65 and £ 5.9 million in 1965/66 is largely due to the assumed exhaustion, by 1963/64, of CD&W monies. It seems fair to say that the growth of the residual item after 1962/63 to some extent reflects the increased budgetary uncertainties involved in looking so far ahead, rather than any necessary increase in the difficulty of financing capital expenditures of the size assumed.

The debt service figures from 1961/62 to 1964/65 shown in the current budget projections (Table 12) allow for increases in each year equivalent to 7 percent of the previous year's residual item, as shown in Table 14.[4] In other words, if the residual item in the finance of capital expenditures had to be met entirely by external borrowing, the Mission's projections for debt service up to 1964/65 would allow of such borrowing being serviced at an average rate of 7 percent, service becoming due in the year following receipt of a loan. However, by 1965/66 the increase of debt service which would be required on this

[4] See Annex VIII.

same basis rises to £ 420,000, or nearly 40 percent of the assumed increase in current revenue, as against the sum of £ 240,000 allowed in Table 12.

The extent to which the Mission's estimates can be considered realistic depends on the amount of grants which Tanganyika will in fact receive above and beyond the existing CD&W commitment, and the terms on which the Government of Tanganyika will be able to borrow.

Sources and Terms of External Borrowing. The traditional source of external borrowing for British territories is the London market. This source of borrowing had the advantage that the annual service charge involved was relatively low. The practice has been to put aside, in addition to the interest charge, "sinking funds" at 1 percent or 1¼ percent of the principal sum. However, East Africa has borrowed rather heavily in the London market in the past, and it is felt that this market would not be very receptive to any considerable volume of issues by the Government of Tanganyika. In borrowing in the London market, Tanganyika finds itself in direct competition with the Governments of Kenya and Uganda, and also with East African Railways and Harbours and East African Posts and Telecommunications.

It therefore appears that Tanganyika may have to meet a substantial part of its future borrowing requirements from sources involving rather heavier service obligations. Because of the risk that many territories will find it difficult to borrow further amounts in the London market, the United Kingdom Government has now made provision for Exchequer Loans to such territories. These loans will carry interest at ¼ percent above the rate at which the U.K. Government provides finance to domestic public corporations, a rate which is in turn based on the terms on which the Government can itself borrow for comparable periods. They will have to be serviced (interest and repayment) in equal annuities over the length of the loan. Tanganyika has recently raised its first Exchequer Loan, which is expected to have a total annual service cost of about 7.8 percent (6 percent interest, repayment over 25 years). Loans from the International Bank for Reconstruction and Development carry rather similar terms. They are conditional on the Bank's satisfying itself that the borrowing country is not likely to run into serious difficulties in servicing its external debt.

Loans of these types may for convenience be referred to as "hard" loans, as opposed to loans carrying smaller or more delayed service obligations, which will be referred to as "soft" loans.

In considering possible sources of borrowing, there remains the possibility that Tanganyika may be able to secure certain loans on "soft" terms. For soft loans as for grants, the quantities which will in fact be available are impossible to predict at the present juncture.

Borrowing Policy

While capital expenditures remain at a level of about £ 6 million a year, and CD&W grants continue to be available on a substantial scale, the amount of borrowing required presents no particular problem. However, the Mission's projections envisage a rise of capital expenditures just at the time when the CD&W allocation may be expected to be exhausted. In accordance with the Mission's recommendation of an expanding program of irrigation and flood control works and of other projects involved in an agricultural "transformation" program, the capital budget may be roughly envisaged as rising from the £ 6.2 million shown for 1964/65 to about £ 10 million in 1969/70 and subsequent years. The question arises whether Tanganyika will be able to borrow the sums required to finance such a rise of capital expenditures.

The Mission considers that the Government of Tanganyika would be justified in borrowing the sums required to support expenditures on the scale suggested in this chapter, provided that loans are available on reasonably favorable terms; and that it should shape its present policies on the assumption that such loans will in fact be available. We conclude that a considerably increased rate of borrowing would be fully justified by the increase of both production and government revenues to be expected from a well-executed program of expenditures of the types suggested. A major part of the additional borrowing would be for the expansion of irrigation works. Calculations in Annex VII suggest that these works should probably be capable of yielding a net return to the public finances, direct and indirect, roughly sufficient to cover the service charges involved even if they have to be financed by borrowing on "hard" terms. In other words, it should be possible to borrow, even on "hard" terms, to meet the cost of the proposed irrigation and flood control works, without imposing a net burden on the remainder of the budgetary situation. It will, of course, be necessary for the Economic Section in the

Treasury to investigate whether this preliminary conclusion is borne out in practice.

The fact must be faced that the program suggested presents an element of risk in face of the financial uncertainties which have been stressed throughout this chapter. It is important, though, not to exaggerate the practical importance of this risk. In relation to the policies to be followed in the next three or five years, the risk is that expenditures may be incurred in this period in preparing future "transformation" activities on a scale which it may conceivably prove impossible to finance. These expenditures would, of course, be at the expense of other activities which might give more immediate returns in terms of production and revenue. However, in view of the importance which it attaches to irrigation, flood control and other "transformation" projects, the Mission considers that this is a risk which the Government of Tanganyika ought to accept. The conclusion is that the preparatory surveys, investigations and trials to be carried out over the next few years should be geared to the assumption that capital expenditures will in fact increase from £6 million over the next few years to £10 million in 1969/70 and subsequent years.

In a build-up of capital expenditures of this order, the availability of "soft" loans, while they would not give the same degree of assistance to development in Tanganyika as grants, would be of great value. The types of softness of particular value to Tanganyika would be low interest rates, long repayment periods or generous periods of grace before interest or repayment becomes due.[5] Soft loans would reduce the burden of service payments associated with particular expenditures, and so help to preserve Tanganyika's creditworthiness as assessed by potential lenders.

Budgetary Flexibility

As was emphasized at the beginning of this chapter, any expenditure program looking more than two or three years ahead inevitably remains subject to revision, either upwards or downwards, according

[5] The device of repayment in local currency, as applied on loans from the United States Development Loan Fund, would not be of particular interest to Tanganyika, except insofar as the local currency payments might be re-lent to Tanganyika or as the Currency Board might make special arrangements to put sums equivalent to the local currency payments back into circulation, for example by means of an increase of the "fiduciary issue." Except on these conditions, the surrender of a claim over local currency is, under the currency board system, the surrender of a claim over real resources equivalent to payment in foreign exchange.

to the appreciation of financial means, which will certainly change with the passage of time.

Particularly in agricultural and livestock development in the conditions of Tanganyika, rates of return are highly uncertain: some projects or programs will be hits, many will be misses. Beyond a certain point, it is impossible to arrange proposed government expenditures in an order according to the rate of return to be expected or the degree of expectation of success. Moreover, the Mission's recommendations are based on a balance between activities designed to give a quick return in expanded production and increased government revenues and others—"transformation" activities—required to maintain increase of production in the longer run, but offering returns which are at best delayed and at worst highly uncertain. In such a program, the balance between various types of activity is inevitably to some degree a matter of judgment, and, similarly, adjustments to the program must depend on judgment.

If it becomes necessary to hold expenditures below the levels indicated in Tables 12 and 13, the Mission would of course urge that the shortfalls should so far as possible take the form of postponement of expenditures which have only a small effect on the growth of production. In Table 13, for example, the Mission allows for some increase of capital expenditures on township development and African urban housing in the later years shown, on the assumption that some increase of the total of capital expenditures will be feasible. If it is necessary to hold down the total of expenditures, then expenditures on these items will have to be regarded very critically.

If, on the other hand, it proves possible to increase expenditures more rapidly than the Mission's projections assume, then two leading claimants for additional expenditures would be construction and improvement of feeder roads and medical services.

In general, necessary adjustments of expenditure levels should be made in accordance with the principles set out in the final section of this chapter. Other considerations to· be borne in mind are the avoidance of discontinuities and imbalances such as are caused by discharging or failing to hire personnel whose absence will subsequently hold up government activities of high priority, by abandoning activities which are on the verge of producing good returns, or by cutting down capital works to the point that staff on the payroll are considerably underemployed. The authorities in Tanganyika are, of course, well aware of these considerations. However, adequate attention to them is only possible in the context of an effort to plan for a reasonably long period ahead.

ENDS AND MEANS IN BUDGETARY POLICY

It has been seen that government expenditures play a crucial role in the development of Tanganyika, and that these expenditures are limited, first and foremost, by the limited taxable capacity of the economy. Increase of government revenues is strongly needed in Tanganyika both to make possible increased expenditure from domestic resources on public developmental and social activities and to cover the service on additional borrowing.

Increase of revenue should be secured not by any substantial increase of the proportion of total money incomes taken by tax, but by the expansion of revenue-yielding activity. Current revenues of central and local government already amount to slightly over 20 percent of estimated total money incomes in Tanganyika; in the Mission's opinion, the tax burden of the territory is comparatively high and leaves little room for further increase. The desired increase of revenue should come from expansion of production and incomes, leading notably to increased collection of income tax from traders and to increased yield of import and excise duties. It will also be desirable to establish close links between payment of taxes, levies, dues, cesses, etc., and services rendered by the Government.

Thus the Mission recommends, as a central principle of budgetary policy, that a considerable proportion of public expenditures should be so directed as to secure the maximum feasible increase of revenue-yielding economic activity. This cannot be an exclusive or overriding aim, but it must be a very important aim.

The importance attached in this report to the revenue-generating aspect of public expenditures does not necessarily conflict with the conventional aim of development—to secure the greatest increase of the income of the population, with due regard for the claims of the present as against the future. In the short run, increase of revenue-bearing activity means increases of private incomes, only a part of which will be taken in tax. However, the Mission's principal concern is with the longer run. On a long view, the developments of the next few years have to be looked at not only as ends in themselves, but as foundations for further development in the future. Increase of government revenue, though not, of course, an ultimate objective, is a very important intermediate aim. Increase of revenue is required as a "feedback," whereby present development is made to provide the resources needed to maintain the pace of development in the future.

Feedback—A Practical Illustration

It is particularly in planning the agricultural "improvement" program that it is important to consider how to secure the maximum feasible increase of revenue-generating activity. The relevance of the feedback criterion can be seen in relation to an important problem of choice which inescapably faces the public authorities of Tanganyika.

Improvement of standards of living and conditions of life is particularly urgent in the many parts of the territory where food supplies are inadequate in quantity and quality, and where famine is a constant threat. It is necessary to continue existing programs of increasing and variegating food production in these areas, of introducing crops or strains particularly suited to land conditions, of building up famine reserves and of progressively improving communications with other parts of the territory. Such activity is of the greatest importance from the point of view of welfare. However, increase of subsistence production has no automatic effect on revenue, since it does not increase the amount of cash transactions on which direct and indirect taxes are levied. Even increased production of cash crops may have little automatic effect on revenue when it occurs in areas where the habits of mind of the money economy are not far developed. To cite an example, the Provincial Commissioner's Annual Report for the Central Province in 1958 states that: "the development of cash crops has only recently come into being and while it has resulted in increased cash in hand for the African population, a considerable proportion of that cash, particularly in Ugogo, has gone towards the purchase of stock. Increased African prosperity has not, therefore, been reflected in any large measure by a general increase in trade."[6]

The Mission concludes that the program for "improvement" of African agriculture over the next few years should be concentrated to a considerable degree on areas which give promise of the greatest possible return in terms of increased value of cash crops, and where the habits of the monetary economy are fairly well developed. Concrete proposals are made in Chapter 5.

[6] If more cattle are bought, so also more are sold, and so it might appear that the enlargement of the monetary economy comes about in this case merely by a more roundabout route. However, it may well be that the increase in Wagogo herds was achieved by the purchase of beasts which otherwise would have been sold for butchering, so that there was no net increase of money incomes and hence of tax-yielding expenditures.

Here, as in other matters to be discussed below, considerations of balance have to be borne in mind. Beyond a certain point, revenue might be obtained at too high a price in prolongation of unacceptable conditions of life for certain communities in the territory or of other adverse consequences, such as accelerated depletion of soil fertility. But it remains the case that expanded revenue is essential for the maintenance of a rapid pace of development.

Although public authorities cannot afford any very great expenditures for development of the least advanced parts of the territory and of areas of low productive potential, that is not to say that no development effort can be made in these areas. Although the traditional practice of communal construction or improvement through the tribal turnout has come to be widely resented as an archaic imposition, it cannot be accepted that the only alternative is the introduction of monetary capital investment. It is necessary to work out suitable adjustments of the old methods, involving as little expenditure of scarce government funds and as much local self-help as possible. The new political climate appears to give great opportunities to turn the energies of the people towards constructive achievement. It is with these considerations in mind that the Mission recommends adoption of the community development approach in rural development (see Chapter 5, pp. 109-11).

Questions of Balance

While the need to secure feedback by way of early expansion of revenue-generating activity should be a central principle in development policy in Tanganyika, it cannot, as already hinted, be an overriding principle. Quite apart from the need to relax the feedback criterion in order to relieve hardship in certain areas, it is necessary to give due weight to certain public activities which will give only slow or uncertain returns in the form of increase of public revenues.

This report stresses the need for "transformation" programs, aimed at making more productive use of the land of Tanganyika, while preventing the continued exhaustion of the fertility of the soil. The preparatory phase of such programs should be begun without delay, in order to avoid a future hiatus in the development process and to arrest the soil deterioration at present occurring in various parts of the territory. But the preparatory stage of a transformation program involves public expenditures on research, investigations and trials which will give no immediate return in increased production and revenue. In its early stages, the transformation program is an added net burden on the public finances. Even though it might prove possible to secure grants to cover part of the cost, it will be necessary to finance some of these activities from revenue or from additional borrowing.

Another claim on the public finances for an activity giving no early return in increased production and revenue is for expansion of post-primary education. The number of Africans completing 12 years of general education and sitting for the School Certificate examination in each year has only just passed the 300 mark. Thus Tanganyika produces in each year substantially less than 300 potential university graduates. This is not enough, especially for a country which is rapidly advancing towards political independence.

The need to increase expenditures of types which will give only small or delayed returns in terms of increase of public revenues reinforces the argument that other government expenditures should be directed to securing the greatest possible increase of revenue-generating activity. This applies particularly to the planning of an agricultural "improvement" program. The "feedback" principle applies not only to the balance between broad categories of government activity, but to the way in which particular types of government activity, and notably the "improvement" program, should be carried out. Further implications of this argument will appear in later chapters, and particularly in Chapter 5.

AGRICULTURAL AND LIVESTOCK
DEVELOPMENT

CHAPTER 4 *LAND USE AND TENURE*

The Mission's recommendations for agricultural and livestock development are based on its interpretation of the land use problems of the territory:

a. Traditional methods of African agriculture and stock keeping not only give very low yields, but have an inherent tendency to lead to loss of soil fertility and deterioration of the hydrological regime. The Mission considers that over much of the territory these defects can be overcome only by rather thoroughgoing changes in methods and organization.

b. Although over-all population density in Tanganyika is low, land of good productive potential is not so plentiful that erosion and deterioration of fertility can be treated as unimportant.

c. In certain areas, excessive demand for land is causing hardship or is leading to accelerated deterioration, and it is becoming increasingly desirable to relieve pressure by resettlement of population.

d. Settlement of empty areas often involves rather high public costs, and an adequate return on these costs will be secured only if settlement is accompanied by adoption of improved methods.

The examination of land use problems in this chapter is concerned largely with diagnosis leading to certain broad policy conclusions. More concrete recommendations for the development of agriculture, animal husbandry and forestry are set out in the succeeding chapters. The present chapter ends with certain recommendations on land tenure policy.

EXISTING METHODS AND THEIR DEFECTS

Crop Production

The traditional system of shifting cultivation, under which the land was only cropped to provide the food and subsistence requirements of the family, involved clearing an area from forest or regenerated bush, cultivating it for a period which usually varied from two to eight years, depending upon the nature of the land, and then moving elsewhere to repeat the process, leaving the land to recuperate under bush fallow for a prolonged period, usually not less than ten years and often considerably longer. Where stock were kept they were not integrated with crop husbandry, beyond being grazed on stubbles for short periods during which they would drop a little manure on the land. Normally they were grazed on bush pastures often at some distance from the arable land, and no manure was made or applied to the cultivated land. There was, therefore, a closed system which did not permit of any long-term improvement of the soil by the importation or transfer of fertility, but which inevitably led to a decline in fertility. Part of the initially high fertility of virgin forest soils was lost through erosion and oxidation and was never fully replaced, since the full regrowth of the natural vegetation was prevented by the limited duration of the fallow and by fire. Fire was used after rough clearing in order to free the land of debris for cultivation, and fires were also used to burn undergrowth and grass for hunting purposes and to stimulate a short-lived growth of green grass in the pasture areas during the dry season. These fires were commonly uncontrolled and swept fiercely across vast areas, destroying trees or checking their regeneration and burning up a great deal of vegetation and surface litter which would have added organic matter to the soil. The combination of shifting cultivation and fire has reduced huge areas of Africa, formerly under woodland, to mediocre scrub on soils of reduced fertility.

Despite its deficiencies, the system of shifting cultivation was a practicable one for people with only limited, primitive agricultural equipment, and it worked reasonably well so long as it had only to provide the food requirements of a sparse population. The present agricultural system over much of Tanganyika remains shifting cultivation, but with the important changes that cash crops have been added to subsistence production, while population has increased. Owing to the increased human and stock populations and to the cultivation of cash crops, there has developed increased pressure on the land. The bush fallow consequently tends to become reduced in duration, and is even eliminated altogether in areas where the population is particularly dense.

At the same time no alternative or supplementary measures for the maintenance of fertility have been introduced on any appreciable scale. Where beasts are kept they are still, as under the traditional system, not integrated with crop husbandry, nor is manure made and applied to the arable land. The use of fertilizers is so far negligible. Consequently there is a general tendency to soil exhaustion, soil erosion and declining yields.

These generalizations apply to African agriculture over much of the territory. Some areas where there are permanent crops, and notably the banana- and coffee-growing areas of Kilimanjaro, Meru and the west shore of Lake Victoria, present a rather different pattern. These are areas of population pressure rather than of soil deterioration.

Pastoralism

As with crops, so with livestock, existing African methods differ little in essentials from those practiced from time immemorial, and lead to a combination of low yields and deterioration of the land.

Extensive nomadic, or semi-nomadic, ranching of cattle, sheep and goats, sometimes combined with a limited shifting cultivation of food crops, is the main activity over large parts of the central, drier area of Tanganyika. In other areas, most of the tribes which depend primarily on crop production also keep cattle, as a separate and distinct activity. Comparison of Maps 2 and 3 shows that cattle are numerous in dry areas of the north and center of the territory where human population is sparse, but also in certain areas of relatively dense human population, notably Sukumaland to the south of Lake Victoria.

While Tanganyika is generally suitable for ranching, physical conditions are in many respects conducive to overgrazing. The alternation of a short rainy season with a long, severe dry season results in a relative abundance of grass for part of the year, followed by a period of shortage. Use of some pastures is restricted to certain times of the year, in many areas by lack of water and in some by seasonal flooding or waterlogging. Large areas cannot be used or can only be used for part of the year because of the presence of tsetse fly. Tsetse fly and lack of water hinder movement of stock in search of better grazing. When the rains fail, the carrying capacity of whole regions is drastically reduced.

While physical conditions restrict carrying capacity, each man is anxious to increase his herds and to possess as many beasts as possible. In the pastoral areas the land is owned and grazed communally but the herds are owned by individuals or families. No restriction is placed on the number of stock owned by an individual or a family. A family keeps large herds for its food supply and in excess of immediate needs in order to exchange stock for grain with cultivating communities. Large numbers of stock are commonly regarded as an insurance against drought years, on the assumption that the more stock an individual has, the more are likely to survive. In many areas there is reluctance to sell beasts, because it is numbers of stock rather than money or other possessions which give social prestige. Stock are also required as bride price. The head of a family may not be entirely at liberty to dispose of stock which appear to belong to him, because in fact he holds them in trusteeship for the family, and it may be incumbent upon him to retain them in order to be able to provide bride price for his younger brothers or his sons in due course.

The combination of communal ownership and grazing of the land with unrestricted individual, or family, ownership of stock results in both low productivity and deterioration of the land, because it immediately leads to disregard of two essentials of successful ranching, namely, adjustment of stock numbers to carrying capacity, and pasture management. Neither the individual nor the community exhibits any interest in these matters; what is everybody's business is nobody's business. There is no attempt to reduce total losses in dry years by the agreed limitation of the number of beasts held by each individual to the number which the land and water supplies could reasonably be expected to support. Little effort is made to organize rotational grazing and resting of pastures. The result is gross overstocking in relation to the pasturage available under the existing lack of management. In consequence the grass cover is largely destroyed, a process aided by the widespread setting of fires, which aid erosion by leaving the ground bare at the onset of the following rains. Erosion often begins at the watering places where animals congregate, and spreads and continues at an ever-accelerating rate. Springs and streams dry up or run for only brief periods in flash floods and the ultimate result may be the creation of near-desert conditions.

As in the arable farming areas, productivity is again low for other reasons in addition to the deterioration of the pastures and the land. As a consequence of the desire to possess as many animals as possible, there is little or no culling of heifers or castration of scrub bulls. Breeding is largely indiscriminate and uncontrolled and the stock are therefore of poor quality. Standards of animal husbandry are low and inadequate attention is given to disease control. As a result, calving rates and calf survival rates are low. These factors, combined with the general reluctance to sell stock except in times of drought, add up to the fact that the pastoral areas are contributing far less than their potential to the income of Tanganyika.

The Problem of Maintaining Fertility

Past experience shows the difficulty of promoting effective measures to maintain soil fertility and to prevent erosion within the framework of traditional African land usage. In the matter of maintaining soil fertility, the task is not merely to secure that appropriate methods are adopted: there is a need for further research and experiment to discover what methods are in fact required to protect or to build up fertility in the conditions found in many parts of Tanganyika. For many types of land, no effective alternative to the bush fallow is yet known—that is to say, no alternative which would effectively maintain soil fertility in the long term and which at the same time would be economic and practicable for the African farmer. Fertilizers, which would obviously be one means of maintaining fertility, are at present very little used. Information on the response of different soils to fertilizers and on the economics of their use with the majority of crops is very inadequate. With most crops, the use of fertilizers is only likely to be profitable if it is accompanied by selection of good crop varieties and by improved methods of cultivation. Further investigations are required before it can become possible to maintain fertility in many areas by use of fertilizers. Even if these investigations lead to satisfactory solutions for all or many of the cultivated areas, the problem remains of inducing African cultivators to adopt the practices required.

Prevention of Erosion

Effective means of preventing erosion on arable land, such as contour terraces and cut-off drains, contour planting, ridging and tie ridging, and restricting the cultivation of annual crops to the more moderate slopes, are well known and they have been urged upon the African farmers for years. In the pastoral areas, erosion control depends largely on preventing overstocking and ensuring elementary pasture management. The need for these has also long been urged upon the Africans. In many areas legislation was introduced with the agreement of the Native Authorities, requiring people to practice

TABLE 15 Use of Land in Tanganyika

(Areas in millions of acres)

Province	Total Land Area (1)	Acres Per Person (1957) (2)	Area of Forest Reserves (3)	Area of Game Reserves[a] (4)	Area Alienated (5)	Area Available for African Use (6)	Estimated Area Cultivated by Africans (7)	African Cattle Units ('000)[b] (8)	Acres Required Per Cattle Unit[c] (9)	Grazing Area Required (10)	Estimated Area Required for Cultivation and Grazing (11)	Area not Needed at Present (12)	Unneeded Area as Percent of Total Land Area (13)
Northern	21.18	27	1.07	2.00	0.41	17.7	0.76	1,691.6	10.0	16.9	17.7	—	—
Lake and West Lake	24.80	11	1.19	1.50	0.03	22.1	5.25	3,249.2	4.5	14.6	19.8	2.3	9
Central	22.53	25	0.27	—	0.14	22.1	3.14	1,482.5	10.0	14.8	17.9	4.2	19
Tanga	8.96	13	0.43	0.90	0.64	7.0	0.66	346.0	6.0	2.1	2.7	4.3	48
Southern Highlands	28.67	28	1.13	5.00	0.21	22.3	1.42	832.6	8.0	6.7	8.1	14.2	50
Western	50.08	47	15.32	0.46	0.06	34.2	2.70	1,013.5	6.0	6.1	8.8	25.4	51
Eastern	26.53	24	0.92	3.20	0.50	21.9	1.66	92.5	7.0	0.6	2.3	19.6	74
Southern	35.58	35	1.07	3.50	0.15	30.9	2.94	41.3	6.0	0.2	3.1	27.8	78
Total	218.33	25	21.40	16.56	2.14	178.2	18.53	8,749.2	7.0	62.0	80.5	97.7	45

[a] Areas of game reserve not included in forest reserve.
[b] Five sheep or goats or two donkeys = one cattle unit.
[c] I.e., the number of acres per cattle unit considered necessary if land deterioration is to be avoided.

SOURCES: Ministry of Land and Surveys; Veterinary Department; Mission estimates.

certain soil conservation measures and providing for them to be fined if they failed to do so.

Successful control of erosion, however, has been achieved only in limited areas, usually in places where legal enforcement of conservation measures was possible, and these legal powers have now for the most part been withdrawn because they became ineffective owing to the mass noncooperation of the people. The farmers have remained unconvinced of the need for anti-erosion measures and resentful of the work involved, while a certain number of African politicians have exploited the unpopularity of soil conservation rules for political purposes.

Over the greater part of the country there has been no effective development of conservation methods of agriculture, and there is, therefore, a cumulative deterioration of the soil and of the hydrological regime.

One of the reasons for lack of success in this, as in other matters of agricultural improvement, lies in the small size of the technical and administrative staff in a country as large as Tanganyika, and as indifferently provided with good access roads. Another reason may lie in the approach to extension work which has been followed in the past. Possible means of augmenting the staff and of changing the extension approach are discussed in Chapter 5.

LIMITATIONS TO EXTENSIVE LAND USE

It will be clear from the above discussion that present African methods depend on making use, over the years, of large areas of land: land which has been run down has to be left to a long period of bush fallow or may even be permanently abandoned. The rapid increase of agricultural production in recent years has been achieved, for the most part, through increase of the area in use.

The question arises why future development should not proceed by taking more and more land into use, and even to what extent production at the cost of soil deterioration is undesirable, if there is new land to be occupied as the old wears out. Over-all population density in Tanganyika is low, less than 30 persons per sq. mile; a rough calculation indicates that nearly half of the land area of the territory is not being used at present (see Table 15); from the air, vast stretches of the territory appear empty.

In practice, the Mission agrees with the East Africa Royal Commission that long-term economic advance in Tanganyika depends on the development and adoption of agricultural and livestock methods which allow more intensive land use while at the same time preserving, or even building up, the fertility of the soil. This conclusion is based on an examination of the costs of soil deterioration and of extending the area under use.

Availability of Empty Land

Closer examination shows Tanganyika to be by no means as empty as might at first appear. This is so, even though in any year the Africans are still cultivating only about 10 percent of the total land area available to them. In the first place, shifting cultivation requires several acres under bush fallow for every acre under cultivation. More important, the stock kept are so numerous, and the stock-carrying capacity of much of the land is so low, that some 35 percent of the land available to Africans would be required for stock if overgrazing were to be avoided.

Table 15 summarizes the position by province. Over the territory as a whole, roughly 17 percent of the land is reserved by the Government for forest and game reserves (see columns 3 and 4, and also Map 4). One percent is alienated for non-African agriculture, towns and trading centers (column 5). There remains a total of some 180 million acres available for African use (column 6).

No reliable statistics exist on the area of land in fact used by Africans for cultivation and grazing. The figures for areas cultivated by Africans, shown in column 7, were made available by the Ministry of Lands and Surveys. They include a certain amount of fallow. For grazing, an effort has been made to estimate the areas needed to carry the livestock population of the various provinces with existing grazing methods. Column 8 shows the number of African-owned animals, expressed as cattle units. Column 9 gives estimates of the number of acres required for each cattle unit, under the conditions of each province, if overgrazing is to be avoided. Column 10, the product of the two preceding columns, thus gives an estimate of the "required" grazing area. The actual area grazed is of course likely to be less, with consequent local overgrazing. Finally, the area not classified as cultivated or required for grazing is described as the "area not needed at present." It will be apparent that the term "unneeded" is used in this discussion in a rather special sense.

The table gives some very interesting results. The Northern Province appears as having no unneeded land, even though its population density is below the average for the territory, and although Africans cultivate a lower proportion of land available to them than in any other province. The Masai and other pastoral tribes keep very large numbers of beasts, while much of the land away from the mountain slopes is arid and has very low carrying capacity. The arid Central Province has a surprisingly large population considering the harshness of conditions there, and the Africans cultivate some 14 percent of the land available to them, a proportion surpassed only in the densely populated Lake Province. The cattle population of the Central Province is large, and the carrying capacity low. Consequently less than 20 percent of the total area can be considered unneeded, at least until cattle-carrying capacity is increased by water development and pasture improvement, and this 20 percent consists largely of a waterless and tsetse-infested tract in the south and east of the province. The Lake Province has the highest population density of all the provinces, by far the highest proportion of land under cultivation, and the largest livestock population. However, the stock-carrying capacity of the land is comparatively good. The figures used in Table 15 are for the Lake and West Lake Provinces together. The roughly 10 percent of unused land for the two provinces combined is largely in the West Lake Province, which is densely populated only in a strip along the west shore of Lake Victoria. The proportion of unused land would be smaller for the Lake Province alone, larger for the West Lake Province.

At the other end of the scale, the sparsely populated Southern Province is shown as having 78 percent of its total land in the unused category. In the Eastern Province, some 8 percent of the land available to Africans is at present under cultivation, but there is relatively little stock. The Western Province is more empty than the figures suggest, having over 15 million acres, mostly tsetse-infested miombo, classified as forest reserve, and so excluded from the area considered available for African use. The Southern Highlands Province is shown as having half its total area unused, but much of the unused part consists of grassland of low carrying capacity on poor soils.

From this general examination, it is evident that the availability of land for more extensive cultivation or grazing, or to replace worn-out land, differs widely in different parts of the territory. The beginnings of real land hunger are already evident in some parts of the country, for example among the Wachagga on Kilimanjaro and the

Bahaya, west of Lake Victoria. Population pressure resulting in land destruction in central Sukumaland has been temporarily relieved by movement of some of the people to lands lying to the east and west, following upon tsetse clearing and the provision of water in these areas; but this process cannot continue indefinitely.

OPENING UP OF NEW AREAS

In many places, obviously, the best land is already cultivated or grazed, and settlement of new land involves acceptance of lower yields, or else investments, often heavy, to make the new areas productive.

Bush Clearing and Elimination of Tsetse

Over much of the territory, opening up of new areas depends on clearing of bush, both to prepare the land for cultivation and also to eliminate tsetse fly. Miombo bush covers more than one third of the territory. This is an open canopy type of woodland characteristic of medium rainfall areas (30-40 inches) between 1,000 and 4,000 feet above sea level, in which the predominant trees are species of Brachystegia, Isoberlinia, Julbernardia and Pterocarpus. Miombo occurs in two huge main blocks, one to the west of the central plateau and the other to the southeast of the main area of mountains. Distribution by province is shown by Table 59, in the Supplementary Statistical Tables. Another type of vegetation presenting particular clearing problems is that described as bushland and thicket, commonly dry scrub with species of Acacia and Commiphora predominating. This, together with the associated types, woodland-thicket and thicket-grassland, probably occupies 15-20 percent of the land area (see again Table 59).

Both miombo and bushland and thicket are commonly infested by tsetse fly. Roughly 60 percent of the total land area of Tanganyika is tsetse-infested, and although in parts of this area the fly population is only slight, nevertheless over the whole area tsetse either prevents the use of the land or necessitates expenditure on bush clearing, insecticides, or the use of drugs to protect stock from disease.

In places, bush country can be cleared of tsetse and so opened up for cattle relatively cheaply, by discriminative clearing of only about 5 percent of the total area (see Chapter 7, p. 150). Clearing for cultivation, on the other hand, may well be very expensive. In some areas African settlers undertake their own clearing, with little or no cost to public authorities. This is happening, for example, in the westward spread of the Wasukuma into Geita and Biharamulo Districts. If an infested area is settled with people at a suitable density, and the bush is cleared for cultivation, then the habitat becomes unsuitable for tsetse flies, which are thus eliminated. But the extent to which settlement of this kind can be effected is somewhat limited. Many Africans are reluctant to move without their cattle, as is necessary in the first stage of opening up tsetse-infested bush. The traditional method of undertaking tasks by tribal turn-out has come, in many areas, to be associated with government compulsion and is resisted. A task for the new Government is to make such community effort once again acceptable, possibly by adoption of a community development approach. Where partnership schemes involving mechanization are contemplated, such as the tenant settlement schemes of the Tanganyika Agricultural Corporation, then the cost of the full clearing and stumping needed to permit the use of tractor-drawn implements would be heavy. Similarly, if Acacia-Commiphora thicket country is freed of fly for ranching purposes, additional expenditure is necessarily involved for further extensive clearing of the bush in order to permit the development of pasture. This will not, however, usually apply in miombo country, where grass is usually present under the fairly widely spread trees.

Finally, it should be noted that wherever land under Acacia-Commiphora and similar types of thicket is cleared for the purposes of establishing natural or sown pastures, there will always occur some degree of bush regeneration which, if left unchecked, will eventually result in the replacement of pasture by the original thicket vegetation and in return of tsetse fly. The rate of this regeneration will vary with local conditions and with the efficiency of pasture management, but it is inevitable in such country that some expenditure of money and effort will be required specifically for the control of bush regeneration.

Water Development

The greatest long-run prospect of increasing the economically useful area of Tanganyika is by way of water development. Water development is, however, expensive. Moreover, satisfactory exploitation of water development raises many complex organizational problems.

Rural Water Supplies. In most parts of Tanganyika it is technically possible to provide water for human consumption and for cattle. However, in many places it would be extremely expensive to do so. Provision of new watering points for cattle is desirable to eliminate the need for long treks in search of water, causing the beasts to lose weight, to protect against heavy mortality from starvation and thirst in especially dry years and to open new areas for grazing. However, it is necessary to guard against the danger that new watering points will merely enable more cattle to be kept, without a corresponding increase of the contribution of livestock to the economy and with extension or intensification of the danger of overgrazing.

Irrigation and Flood Control. Available data suggest that appropriate combinations of irrigation and flood control could add around 4 million acres to the cultivable land of the territory (see Annex III). This addition, while less than 2 percent of the total area of the territory, would make an addition of the order of 20 percent to the total area at present cultivated by Africans.

Irrigation works are costly. Successful irrigation farming involves the careful use of appropriate methods. Finally, certain of the areas which offer the best prospects for irrigation development are at present only very sparsely populated and are rather remote from the main areas of population.

The area giving the greatest *prima facie* scope for development by irrigation and flood control works is the Rufiji Basin, covering altogether nearly 20 percent of the total area of the territory and for the most part only thinly populated (see Map 7). In practice, this basin comprises three distinguishable regions, each with its own potentialities and problems. In the upper plain, between the Great Ruaha and the highlands from Mbeya to Iringa, available water would allow the irrigation of some 200,000 acres in the Bohoro and Pawaga Flats. This possibility is of great value, as a means of relieving overcrowding in the nearby highlands. A much larger developable area is found in the central section of the basin, the Kilombero Valley. Water control might make possible the development of 400,000-600,000 acres in this area. However, the Kilombero Valley is only very thinly populated at present, and any considerable development would depend on inducing the present inhabitants to accept settlers from other tribes and also on inducing people from elsewhere to move into a distant and unfamiliar place. A particular merit of the projected sugar plantation in the Kilombero Valley is that it provides the justification for a railway line into the valley, and so makes it accessible. Nevertheless, the development of the Kilombero Valley is clearly a rather long-term proposition. Finally, development in the Rufiji Valley at the eastern end of the basin is limited by the technical problem of flood control. (For an expanded account of development possibilities in the Rufiji Basin and the other river basins in the east of the territory, see Annex III.)

The Ruvu Basin also offers promising prospects for irrigation development. Some 300,000 acres in three flood plains appear capable of development once flooding has been checked. On the basis of the hydrological surveys so far completed, a stage-by-stage development seems to be feasible. Further soil and topographical surveys are necessary to complement the hydrological data.

The Pangani Basin is well situated to relieve population pressure in the Kilimanjaro-Meru area, but the water of the Pangani River is somewhat saline and a recent soil survey covering 230,000 acres below Nyumba ya Mungu showed most of the area to be definitely unsuitable or only doubtfully suitable for irrigation development. Similarly in the other river basins, available knowledge shows irrigation or flood control never to be an entirely straightforward or inexpensive matter (cf. Annex III). (The technicalities and economics of irrigation and flood control are further discussed in Chapter 8.)

Accessibility of Empty Areas

Since the transport network is for obvious reasons related to the present distribution of population, it follows that many of the underpopulated areas are remote from the main routes. Such areas could be opened up for cash crop production only after investment in road or railway construction.

Conditions of Opening Up New Areas

Further schemes to open up new areas for the relief of local overcrowding will be necessary in the years immediately ahead. In the longer run, there is considerable scope for development by resettlement of population in empty areas of good productive potential. However, it has been seen that the opening up of new areas for cultivation or grazing is frequently costly. It is necessary to ensure that levels of production in new areas will be sufficiently high to justify the cost of opening them up. Moreover, newly settled areas must be protected against the danger of destruction of fertility.

For both these reasons, the Mission recommends that settlement of new areas should, so far as possible, be undertaken on a planned basis, designed to give higher yields than are secured in traditional African agriculture while at the same time safeguarding or building up the fertility of the soil. Good land capable of being opened up for settlement at reasonable levels of cost is not so plentiful an asset that it can be squandered. At the same time, settlement of new areas gives opportunities of promoting improved methods to an extent which is seldom possible in areas already settled: compliance with rules of good husbandry should, where possible, be made a condition of settlement.

ELEMENTS OF LAND USE POLICY

The Mission recognizes that for the time being increased agricultural and livestock production must come mainly from land use on the present pattern. The "improvement" program outlined in subsequent chapters aims at increasing production by such methods as extension work and provision of credit. It is in fact largely a continuation of the present operations of the Ministry of Natural Resources, though certain changes of emphasis and of methods will be suggested.

There is still considerable scope for increasing production by further extension of the area under cultivation. However, extension of area brings dangers for the future, if new land is brought into cultivation under methods which deplete soil fertility and threaten erosion. Within the "improvement" program, preference should be given to promotion of methods allowing increased yields coupled with protection of the soil, as against extension of cultivated acreage under methods of cultivation which lead to depletion of fertility.

The customary methods of land use are unsatisfactory, and will become increasingly so. They result in cumulative deterioration of the soil and of the hydrological regime. They become untenable in overcrowded areas. They also tend to perpetuate low yields: neither shifting cultivation nor nomadic pastoralism is conducive to the use of improved methods capable of giving reasonably high yields. There are definite limits to the increase of the productivity of African agriculture and stock-keeping possible within the general framework of traditional African methods.

What is needed is to replace modified shifting cultivation and extensive pastoralism by methods making more intensive and more permanent use of the land. The aim must be to convert African agriculture from its present status of being little more than a traditional occupation, undertaken mainly for subsistence and resulting in land deterioration, to farming as a business activity on efficiently run, planned farms of economic size, justifying the injection of capital, achieving a much higher level of productivity and appreciably raising standards of living.

In places, extension work and related measures, aimed at improving African methods by progressive stages, may succeed in converting peasants into yeoman farmers using the land on a permanent basis and securing reasonably high and sustainable yields. This has indeed already occurred in a few areas, but on a very limited scale. The Mission considers that programs aiming at step-by-step improvement of methods, while essential to secure immediate increases of production, cannot by themselves make a sufficiently rapid and widespread impact on the land use problem.

It is for this reason that the Mission recommends, side by side with measures to secure continued increase of production by the most immediately feasible means, a "transformation" program, working towards more radical reform of methods and organization. It has already been suggested that the settlement of new areas gives an opportunity to introduce superior methods and organization, and that there is every reason why this opportunity should be seized to the greatest possible extent. This and other possibilities will be further discussed in Chapter 6. Irrigation schemes and many flood-control projects should be so planned and supervised as to assure sound methods, considerably different from those of traditional African agriculture (see Chapter 8). Irrigation and flood control thus fall into the "transformation" category. Another proposed type of transformation is planned cattle ranching with an element of skilled management (see Chapter 7).

LAND TENURE

Problems of land tenure affect all types of agricultural, livestock and forestry development—peasant production, efforts to organize African production on a larger scale, planned settlement, irrigation schemes, estate agriculture, and demarcation of forest and game reserves. The subject is therefore conveniently treated here, before the discussion of more specific matters.

Present Situation

Except in forest and game reserves or in areas alienated for towns and trading centers and for non-African agriculture, land tenure is in accordance with "native law and custom," which thus applies over more than 80 percent of the territory. All or virtually all land under native law and custom is regarded as "belonging" to some particular tribe or community. Although certain tribal boundaries are made somewhat indefinite by incursions of people from neighboring areas, in general such boundaries have tended to restrict movements of agricultural population on any substantial scale.

Rules of customary usage in matters of land tenure have never been by any means uniform over a large area. Nor are these rules static. All generalizations, therefore, are subject to regional exceptions and are liable to become outdated.

Among cultivating communities the most general custom was communal ownership of all land by the tribe or clan. Individuals did not, and for the most part still do not, own land, but have user rights in cultivated land, and commonly extending to fallow. In much of the territory, the right to occupy land is considered irrevocable; in many areas it is the fact of cultivation, the establishment of tree crops or the construction of a house which guarantees individual use for as long as the signs of individual activity persist; in certain places, occupancy may be terminated on grounds of misconduct. Inheritance of user rights is generally possible, by either matrilinear or patrilinear tribal rules.

When land was plentiful, the traditional system of land tenure was very informal. Land considered sufficient for subsistence needs would be allocated to members of the local community without question, and might be allocated to strangers at discretion. In these circumstances, the "local land authority" responsible for the allocation of land and the general supervision of land tenure was commonly a person or body of little importance, and in many areas the local land authorities still have no formal connection with the Native Authority.

In purely pastoral areas communal use, as well as ownership, of land was, and largely remains, the general rule. In many such areas individual ownership and tenure of land is likely to be impracticable because scarcity of water would make provision of watering points on individual holdings impossible or uneconomic, or because large areas of grazing can only be used for part of the year, necessitating seasonal migration of stock for effective use of land. Among the cultivating communities which also keep stock, there is generally communal use of grazing land, including land lying fallow and cultivated land from which the crops have been harvested.

Even in the traditional subsistence economy, there existed to some extent individual ownership of land, with certain restrictions. For example, there was virtually individual ownership by the Wachagga of their banana gardens (*Vihamba*), although land used for growing annual crops was communally owned and subject to annual reallocation of user rights. Some tribes, e.g., the Wabena, held that the clearing of land from bush made it a man's personal property. Normally, however, such ownership was subject to the restriction that a man might not finally dispose of his land to anyone outside the clan.

The penetration of the money economy, the increased pressure on the land, the decline in tribal authority, the planting of perennial cash crops and, in some cases, the erection of permanent houses, have all combined to bring about modification of the traditional systems of land tenure in various ways. There has been a strong tendency to development of individual tenure and ownership in land in places where the population is dense or where permanent crops have been extensively planted. In some areas this has occurred with the approval of the local land authorities, but in other places these authorities have prevented or opposed the acquisition of individual tenure. In many areas the traditional land authorities have made efforts to adjust native law and custom to meet changing circumstances, though often with only limited success; in other areas there has been evasion of customary law by people seeking individual ownership of land. The process of change and adjustment has thus in many places resulted in land tenure being in a confused and unsatisfactory state. The decisions of local land authorities have often become somewhat unpredictable. For example, under the old customs it was common practice for a man to pledge his user right in land to another in exchange for a loan, but he could always redeem his rights, however long the pledgee used the land, on repayment of the loan. In recent times, however, if a pledgee has occupied the land for a long period and has planted permanent crops, or effected other permanent improvements on it, it has often been held either that he has acquired permanent rights to the land which virtually amount to ownership, or that the pledger must pay compensation for the improvements before resuming occupation. These, and other, circumstances have led to much litigation. Reform is therefore desirable not only on account of the difficulties which communal tenure places in the way of agricultural improvement and development but also to restore order in land tenure arrangements.

Disadvantages of Existing Tenure Arrangements

Existing tenure arrangements have the following disadvantages from the point of view of economic development:

a. farmers have not the same interest in the care and development of their land as they would have if it were their own freehold property, and if they could not count on readily obtaining user rights in further land from the tribal area;

b. it is difficult to introduce more intensive, planned farming;

c. land use planning on an area basis is made very difficult;

d. there is no means of preventing unproductive or destructive use of land;

e. it is impracticable to move numbers of people from an over-crowded tribal land unit to one with land to spare;

f. land cannot be used as security for loans.

Considerations Affecting Land Tenure Policy

All questions of land tenure policy are of extreme delicacy because of the fears and anxieties of Africans, who see the land as the foundation of their existence. In recent years Africans have become very sensitive concerning the intervention of the central government in matters of land tenure. A phobia against "alienation" has developed, extending in some minds even to demarcation of forest and game reserves. The granting of "freehold" title to Africans on behalf of the Governor is by many considered alienation, or to threaten alienation, even if the sale to non-Africans is for the time being subject to government approval. Acquisition of individual title will bring a financial benefit to the title holder, but this desire of progressive farmers may be regarded by their neighbors with scorn and envy, and may be considered, rightly or wrongly, as "land-grabbing."

The economic issues involved are also of great complexity. For every economic advantage offered by increased individualization and negotiability of holdings, there is a corresponding danger to be avoided.

Increased security of tenure is desirable in order to remove the discouragement to improvements to the holding which springs from insecurity. ". . . individual tenure should lead to the release and encouragement of new genius and to new experiment in finding the most productive use of land" (Royal Commission, p. 323). But secure tenure ought not to give the right to ruin the land. The realization that land is not inexhaustible, has an economic value and in some areas is already in short supply indicates the need for concerted action with regard to land utilization as well as land tenure.

The establishment of negotiable property rights enables the land to be used as security for borrowing, and thus encourages and facilitates the provision of credit to farmers. But this raises the risk of excessive indebtedness, eventual concentration of ownership of land in the hands of those who have money to lend, and the creation of a destitute landless class.

The Need for New Land Tenure Legislation

Present land legislation offers little scope for much-needed changes in land tenure, general supervision of land usage and the establishment of new developmental schemes. In the Meru area it became necessary for the Native Local Authority to ask the Central Government for a 99-year leasehold in order to allow it to start a planned settlement scheme. People begin to resent asking for a permit to use land which they consider their own and which certainly is subject to some, however vague, rights of African groups which the Government has pledged itself to acknowledge and protect.

In its report, the Royal Commission (pp. 350 ff.) states the need for new land tenure legislation, and sets out a number of basic requirements, the most important being to ". . . establish grounds for confidence that existing property rights will not be arbitrarily disturbed." It rightly notes that: "A single legislative act converting all existing rights into full ownership in land would undoubtedly destroy more confidence than it would create and its implementation might well be quite impracticable." The Commission expresses the belief that the law should provide ". . . that government shall not exercise any right to dispose of land without an established legal process of adjudication and registration of all interests in the land in question first being carried out." To aid in reform, the Commission recommends the establishment of local land boards.

The Mission wishes to endorse these ideas, with some additional remarks regarding conditions in Tanganyika. If the process of adjudication of all existing interests in the land is to be carried out, the agrarian laws should recognize the following different rights and interests, falling into at least six main categories:

a. Forest and game reserves and other areas under (central) government control and use (*government lands*).

b. Forest reserves and other areas under local authority control and use (*local government lands*).

c. Land in freehold or leasehold granted by the central government or available for the granting of such leaseholds (*reserved lands*).

d. Land available for African agriculture and animal husbandry, to be subdivided into at least three categories:

i. Recognized *individual permanent holdings* (Vihamba, Muk, Malik, etc.: see p. 98).

ii. *Individual leaseholds* for definite or indefinite periods.

iii. *Communal lands* for temporary cropping and/or group grazing.

The latter sub-category would encompass, for the time being, all land not held under any of the other categories, but would be subject to more specific denomination if the need arises.

The Organization of Reform

The central problem in establishing administrative arrangements to carry through land tenure reforms is to reconcile initiative for change, which may well have to come largely from the center, with the due consultation of local interests and the securing of local consent, on which successful reform must depend.

In this process, the Mission believes, the establishment of local (area) land boards could play a useful part. Consequently the Mission endorses the adoption of enabling legislation to permit the establishment of such boards. They should be instituted gradually, as the need arises, covering carefully selected areas.

Composition and Status of Area Land Boards. The powers and responsibilities of the area land boards, and the ways in which they should be exercised, should be laid down by territorial legislation. As the Royal Commission suggests (p. 362), their composition might well vary to meet differing circumstances. They should be appointed rather than elected, and should contain effective representatives of the traditional land authorities, of progressive land users, and a limited number of officers of the technical departments most concerned.

The area covered by any single land board should be decided according to local circumstances. In some places, in order to preserve continuity with present practice and to make the land boards acceptable to local opinion, it would be advisable to make the jurisdiction of the land board coterminous with existing tribal or administrative boundaries. However, it is undesirable that the institution of these boards should perpetuate or strengthen the obstacles to well-designed land development presented by tribal boundaries. With the development of the sentiment of Tanganyikan nationality and in the process of economic change, a detribalization of land may in any case be expected in the course of time. It would be desirable that the geographical coverage of the various land boards should eventually come to correspond with ecological areas, which are often larger than the present tribal areas, sometimes smaller. To give an immediate example, it might well be desirable to have a single land board covering the whole of an area south of Lake Victoria including the areas of Biharamulo District which, while not part of Sukumaland proper, are being progressively settled by Wasukuma.

Functions of the Land Boards. The need to secure "confidence that existing property rights will not be arbitrarily disturbed" and for "adjudication and registration of all existing interests in the land in question" (cf. pp. 95-96) implies that the area land boards would have to be consulted if and when the central government wished to increase or decrease the area designated as "government lands" or "reserved land." The boards' main function, however, would lie with "local government lands" and with land available for African agriculture and animal husbandry. In many areas a major task of the area land boards would be the development of rules for the proper use of communal grazing grounds, designed to secure full advantage from provision of water, flood and tsetse control, etc. In performing these functions, the boards would have to consider the technical advice of the natural resources team (including the land utilization officer).

Where permanent improvements are proposed involving large public investments, it might well be made the responsibility of the land board to set rules for the use of the improved land or of water, under leasehold rights of tenure. The board might also be charged with drawing up financial arrangements designed to secure a return on the public investment directly from land and water users.

Fragmentation of holdings has so far only occurred in relatively limited areas in Tanganyika, so that few area land boards would for the time being need to occupy themselves with the task of consolidation.

The Form of Individual Title and Its Institution

The areas over which the need for individual tenure may now be felt may be assessed at perhaps a million acres in total. They will undoubtedly expand rapidly over the next generation. Although there is a consensus of opinion that individual holdings inheritable and saleable (within limits to be determined by law) are a prerequisite for agricultural development, considerable difference of opinion exists about the particular form which individual right to land should take. The term "freehold," even within quotation marks, has a flavor of European-type full ownership beyond any control of the community, and a flavor of having been introduced from the outside. Both features reduce its acceptability to Africans. The term "freehold" should be reserved for the existing land held in freehold, perhaps with the addition of land in urban areas used for business and residential purposes. However, it seems perfectly possible to devise a suitable term, in Swahili or with an acceptable Swahili counterpart. In English this might be "individual tenure." It would embrace various forms which have developed inside the African community (e.g., Kihamba in Uchagga), under Arab-Islam influence (Muk, Malik) and similar forms.

The right to confer this form of title need not necessarily continue to be vested in the Crown, Governor or Central Government. The recognition of the individual's right to permanent tenure must come from the smallest communal unit, first of all his neighbors. Registration of individual title by an area land board might well help to increase its acceptability.

While individual tenure can only be satisfactorily instituted where there is a fair measure of local consent, and to single out one or a few individual holdings in an otherwise communal area breeds trouble with neighbors and with the traditional land authorities, nevertheless this is a matter in which support for change will often have to come from the center. In certain areas it will be desirable for the central government to support the case of progressive individuals who desire, and would benefit from, individual tenure, and to bring about more rapid change than would occur solely on the basis of uninfluenced local public opinion.

The recognition of individual tenure could in many cases be usefully registered, with a simple situation map, by the area land board. In other countries in Asia and Africa, this form of land tenure has been found to offer sufficient security to the individual; land registration documents are accepted as evidence in case of litigation about inheritance or other civil procedures, and are often used extensively in establishing creditworthiness. Security for borrowing would be enhanced by a simple procedure for pledging of land and tree crops, with the requirement of making the pledge official by an annotation in the local ledger of registration. It would seem that a rather simple and inexpensive system of recognition and registration of individual holdings can be developed.

The institution of clear and negotiable title to land may not be sufficient in itself to enable land to be used as security for borrowing. If he is to advance money against the security of land, the lender needs to have some assurance as to the future market value of the land. In order to assure the institution of a reasonably stable market for land under individual tenure, it may be desirable to set up a government agency which will be willing on occasion to buy land and to hold it until a qualified private buyer is found who is willing to offer a fair price.

If, through the operations of area land boards, individual tenure is kept within the sphere of African land laws and customs, the problem of sale to non-Africans will be minimized.

Land for Reserves and Major Schemes

It may be hoped that the establishment of area land boards, which would have to be consulted if the Government were to put land in the "reserved" or "government-held" categories, would lead to increased flexibility in increasing the areas available for lease to non-Africans, for forest and game reserves and for such uses as agricultural research stations. On the merits of the case, local sentiment might favor placing land at the disposal of public authorities or even leasing it to non-African private occupants, provided local interests had a real say in the matter.

Where land is needed for irrigation projects, planned settlement schemes, partnership schemes and cattle ranches, it would be for the area land boards to concur in putting aside land for these uses, taking into account existing rights. The Mission believes that the formalization of area land bodies should in due course facilitate the necessary dispositions rather than make them more difficult. This belief is based on the desire usually found in African societies to accommodate individual and communal rights, and also upon the belief that local communities will be prepared to take the necessary steps to secure the clear economic advantages of government-subsidized or government-financed permanent improvements of the land.

CHAPTER 5 *IMPROVEMENT OF AFRICAN AGRICULTURE*

The diagnosis of the reasons for low productivity in African agriculture is of a kind familiar in underdeveloped areas. On the one hand, there are the difficulties of the environment. On the other hand, there are the shortcomings of peasant methods, organization and equipment:

   i. primitive methods, coupled with conservatism and resistance to change;
   ii. lack of managerial ability;
   iii. primitive and inadequate equipment; lack of capital;
   iv. limited influence of economic incentives;
   v. limitations imposed by customary land tenure.

Just as the diagnosis is familiar, so also are many of the remedies, at least in outline.

The "improvement" side of the proposed development program to a great extent continues the existing activities of the Ministry of Natural Resources. The following pages will concentrate on those points where the Mission wishes to make proposals for the modification of existing policies or programs. These include:

A. Increased concentration of effort on areas and crops in which the greatest increase of marketed production is to be expected, and improvement of planning techniques to ensure that public efforts are deployed in the most effective manner.

B. Reorganization of extension work on the basis of multipurpose extension workers, and adoption in some areas of a community development approach.

C. Reorganization of the administration of agricultural credit.

D. Measures to improve the market outlets for African crops and to increase cash incentives.

This chapter deals with crop production; discussion of livestock development is reserved for Chapter 7. Questions of research, some

101

of them affecting the improvement program, are for convenience grouped in Chapter 6. Finally, this chapter and those immediately following deal with questions of what should be done, rather than with who should do it and how the effort should be organized. Institutional aspects of agricultural development are held over for discussion in Chapter 11.

A. PLANNING

The Focal Point Approach

The Department of Agriculture has in recent years adopted a "focal point approach." In view of the limited staff and funds available, the aim has been to re-deploy staff so as to concentrate it in those areas and on those enterprises which are expected to yield the greatest increase in production and thus the maximum benefit to the territorial economy.

An example of focus of effort is provided by the concentration of a considerable part of the agricultural extension staff in the cotton-growing area of Sukumaland, Lake Province. It is to be hoped that collaboration between the Department of Agriculture and the Victoria Federation of Co-operative Unions in this area will lead to the increase of yields which is known to be technically feasible, and so will give a significant demonstration of what can be achieved by the policy of concentration.

Certain other operations do not appear to conform fully to the avowed purposes of the focal point approach. Production of certain crops, notably coffee, is being encouraged in some areas which are remote and have poor communications, so that returns to the effort and investment being made are reduced; and the staff available is probably being spread too thinly over too many projects of varying merit.

The Mission recommends that the efforts of the Department of Agriculture should be even more highly concentrated than at present on areas and crops likely to give high returns in terms of increased money income. Programs which seem to the Mission to justify a greater concentration of effort than is at present attempted are: improvement of the quality of coffee; the encouragement of increased

African cultivation of seed beans and peas; and extension effort to expand and improve African production of pyrethrum, of tobacco and of certain oilseeds. These proposals, and certain of the technical problems which they involve, are discussed in Annex II.

Although the greatest money returns will frequently be found in crops for export, the Mission does not intend to imply that all effort should be concentrated on the development of export crops. In the course of time, the development of Tanganyika will have to come about by the increasing growth of internal exchange, which implies a growth of specialization. As some farmers begin to specialize in producing export crops and rely on buying their food, and as non-agricultural activities grow, the scope will increase for profitable production of food crops for internal sale. However, such increased specialization depends on various requirements. In the first place, it depends on the reduction of the traditional preoccupation of the African cultivator with self-sufficiency in food. Further, certain forms of investment may be required before internal trade can develop, such as provision of storage facilities and roads connecting producing centers with internal markets. Development of internal commerce and specialization thus depends on a balance between changes in economic behavior and the construction of the appropriate facilities. The process is a complex one, and efforts to accelerate it may easily prove wasteful. While certain public efforts and works designed to encourage and facilitate the growth of internal trade may be thoroughly justified, it remains the case that favorable opportunities to bring about expansion of monetary activity will continue for several years to come to be largely in export production. Tanganyika is still at a stage where growth of export earnings is the main force in bringing about the development of internal exchange.

Improvement of Planning

A policy of bolder concentration of development effort raises the problem of selecting the areas and crops on which effort is to be concentrated. In its past judgments of where to concentrate its efforts, the Department of Agriculture and the ministry of which it is a part, the Ministry of Natural Resources, seem often to have fallen short of a thorough cost-benefit analysis.

The present machinery for the planning of agricultural development works is well designed in principle, although frictions sometimes arise in practice over operations involving two or more departments of the Ministry of Natural Resources. Projects are suggested in the Natural Resources Teams of the Districts and subsequently discussed in the Provincial Natural Resources Teams (see Annex I). There the objectives of the projects are established, costs are estimated and the feasibility of the projects is determined in general outline. After the projects have been rated according to local priority, they are brought forward to the Land Use Committee of the Ministry of Natural Resources. There the final decision on execution is taken in the light of territorial priorities and of availabilities of staff, funds and equipment.

The need is not to amend this procedure, but to secure that in its operation proper weight is given to the relevant economic considerations and to the collection of data on which adequate economic judgments can be based. To this end, the Mission proposes that an economist from the economic section in the Treasury (see Chapter 17) should be seconded to the Ministry of Natural Resources, to advise the Land Use Committee and to teach officers in the field how to evaluate projects and programs in terms of costs and returns, or at least how to collect the data on which such evaluation can be based.

Factors to be taken into account in planning include not only suitability of soil and rainfall, and interest and ability of the cultivators, but also market prospects of the crops under consideration, accessibility of markets or the cost of providing the requisite transport facilities, and the spending habits of those whose incomes will be increased. This last point affects both the "feedback" to be expected by way of increase of government revenue and also the effect of a particular development in leading to further growth of economic activity through increase of internal commerce.

B. EXTENSION WORK AND COMMUNITY DEVELOPMENT

Acceleration of the rate of increase of production and of the adoption of improved methods in African agriculture depends essentially on effective extension work. Effective extension work is the key to a successful agricultural improvement program.

There are many ways in which yields of African agriculture could be markedly increased even without radical changes in the system of farming. The agricultural extension service has already done much to promote the adoption of the changed methods involved, but the pace nevertheless remains slow. The following examination of the reasons for the limited results obtained under the present system leads to proposals for certain changes in approach and in organization.

Obstacles to Change

It is not lack of knowledge on the part of the agricultural extension service which is the primary obstacle to improvement and development. Although existing technical knowledge leaves certain important gaps, which need to be remedied by research, the knowledge now available is quite sufficient to effect very substantial increases in productivity, even within the present general system of land use and land tenure. For example, it has been clearly demonstrated in the Lake Province that the yield of cotton per acre can be at least doubled by a combination of timely planting and weeding, tie-ridging to conserve soil and water, and the use of manure or fertilizer (see Annex II). The difficulty lies in promoting the adoption of such quite simple but profitable improvements. On Kilimanjaro it has been shown that coffee yields can be greatly increased by reduction of shade, better pruning, mulching, and the use of improved strains (see Annex II). Yet the Wachagga of this area, though regarded as among the most industrious of the tribes, show little inclination to make the indicated improvements.

One major reason why the extension services have made such limited progress is undoubtedly the extreme conservatism of the farmers. Peasant farmers all over the world are notoriously suspicious of change. The African farmer might especially be expected to be so, if only because of his almost complete lack of education, and because his very survival depends on the production of food from his land, so that he is naturally very chary of risking partial or total failure of his crops by departing from his traditional methods. Suspicion of change is not necessarily irrational: regrettably, there have been numerous instances in various parts of Africa of insufficiently experienced expatriate officers recommending innovations which have proved unsatisfactory. Resistance to change also springs from the traditions of group or tribal life, with their accent on conformity to a pattern of behavior which militates strongly against the development of individual initiative.

Past Organization and Methods of Extension Work

In part the limited success of extension work is due to the ways in which it has been organized and the policies applied.

Originally the aim appears to have been to build up a cadre of qualified, expatriate technical officers assisted by a large number of locally recruited and trained instructors who had the apparent advantage of being available at comparatively low rates of pay. The object was to persuade the farmers in all the settled areas of the country to improve their methods.

This approach made little progress, partly because it spread available staff too thinly over the vast areas of the country, and partly because of the low standard of education and training of the lower grade of instructors.

Despite the deficiencies in extension staff, the attempt to enforce by law certain soil conservation measures and good husbandry practices, inherited from the period of German rule, was provided for specifically in an Ordinance of 1927 and increasingly applied and extended. Native Authorities were persuaded to pass rules and orders requiring people to carry out these practices. People who failed to do so were fined.

In the immediate postwar years, 1946-50, there was a tendency to apply the efforts to promote good husbandry by concentrated supervision and use of legal sanctions in limited areas, such as thickly populated highlands, where improvements in land use were urgently needed because existing methods were resulting in severe erosion and loss of fertility. There is no doubt that this concentration, coupled with legal sanctions, resulted in marked progress in a number of areas where special "improved land usage schemes" were operated. On the other hand, the majority of the people remained unconvinced of the need for soil conservation and other measures, and were resentful of the extra work involved in carrying them out. The extension workers were made responsible for reporting those who failed to observe the rules and so became liable to be fined. This naturally made the extension workers unpopular, and hampered them in their proper duty of being the friends, advisers and instructors of the farmers.

The unpopularity of this approach based on legal sanctions was in some areas exploited for political reasons. In places, the people seem to have been convinced that measures for improved land usage were unnecessary and were being imposed upon them by an expatriate

TABLE 16   Size of Staff of the Tanganyika Agricultural Department, 1950 to 1959/60

Year	Number of Persons[a]					
	Agric. Officers	Specialists	Field Officers	Assistant Agric. Officers	Field Assistants	Agric. Instructors[b]
1950	31	16	69	3	—	756
1952	42	20	84	3	—	971
1954/55	49	20	93	6	414	1,519
1955/56	48	22	100	6	526	1,520
1957/58	53	22	107	8	592	1,146
1959/60	58	28	120	12	731	1,282

[a] Figures include some headquarters staff. Also at any time a certain proportion of the expatriate officers must be expected to be on home leave. Figures for Field Assistants and Agricultural Instructors show number of persons for whom established posts existed. Figures for other categories show numbers appearing on the Staff List as being employed. The number employed in these categories invariably fell short of the number of established posts.

[b] The present policy is to build up the number of Field Assistants, who are better trained than Agricultural Instructors. No further recruitment of Agricultural Instructors is taking place, and this is consequently a wasting cadre.

SOURCE: Government of Tanganyika.

government largely for its own ends. At any rate in many areas they were readily persuaded to withdraw support.

By the end of 1958 it had become clear that the continued enforcement of regulations was impracticable without adequate cooperation of the people, and repeal of the regulations by the Native Authorities concerned followed. Some regulations backed by legal sanctions remain: for example, that ordering the burning of cotton stalks at the end of the picking season in the Lake Province, to avoid the survival of pests from one season to another. But such regulations are now the exception. As a consequence, in many areas where soil conservation measures and good husbandry practices had been making progress the people ceased for the time being to carry them out and exhibited a widespread reluctance, even in the absence of sanctions, to listen to any advice offered by the extension staff.

Meanwhile, however, in order to offset the effects of opposition to agricultural compulsion and the withdrawal of the land use rules, plans for concentrating extension work in the more receptive areas were being prepared. In September 1956, African representative members of the Legislative Council endorsed this approach by submitting to the Governor proposals for a five-year agricultural development plan. The stated object of the plan was to increase the African farmer's production and hence the territory's financial resources, so that the existing level of social services need not be curtailed because of financial stringency and could eventually be expanded. Accordingly, some 140 schemes were considered in consultation with local authorities. The majority of these schemes was based on expanding production of specified crops in specified areas by improvement of methods, introduction of higher-yielding strains and opening up of additional land if available.

Of the schemes reviewed and considered viable, 57 could be put into operation by use of the territory's existing resources. A further 29 agricultural schemes, 10 designed to increase the productivity of forests and two for freeing potentially productive areas from tsetse infestation were the subject of applications for Colonial Development and Welfare funds and in due course were undertaken with assistance from this source. A total of about 85 of these "increased productivity schemes" in the realm of agriculture has been maintained in areas where the response of the people has continued to be good. Together these schemes constitute the so-called "focal point approach" in agricultural extension work. It has been suggested above that the focus is still, perhaps, not sufficiently sharp.

Although very good progress is being made in increasing production of cash crops, this is being achieved much more by an expansion of acreage than by increased efficiency, better land use and higher yields per acre. In the meantime, elsewhere than in the areas covered by the "increased productivity schemes," new land is being opened up on the customary inefficient methods of land use, which will inevitably lead to soil erosion and exhaustion. An outstanding example of this is at Ismani near Iringa. Here something like 40,000 acres of virgin bush have been cleared in the last ten years, mainly for the production of maize for sale. The efforts of a field officer, stationed for two years in the area, to promote soil conservation measures were unsuccessful. Apart from limited fallows within the holdings, adequate measures to prevent erosion or maintain fertility have not been introduced.

Adoption of the Community Development Approach

The Mission agrees with the Royal Commission in advocating the replacement of the present, specialized extension workers by multi-purpose workers at the village level, a recommendation which will be further discussed below. The Mission also advocates the adoption in some areas of a community development approach to agricultural improvement and other aspects of economic and social development. In places it will be desirable to continue the present policy of concentrating extension effort on the few progressive African farmers who appear particularly willing to adopt new methods. However, in many areas it seems likely that more can be achieved by directing effort to the whole community in an attempt to convert the traditional African conformism from an obstacle to progress into a force for development.

The community development approach has a number of implications. In the first place it is based on the premise, hardly to be doubted, that all aspects of rural life are interrelated, and that an all-embracing approach to rural improvement is more likely to succeed than a number of piecemeal attacks on individual problems. At the stage of development reached in much of Tanganyika, agricultural improvement is often not merely a matter of changing techniques, but necessitates a revolutionary change in customs and way of life, requiring a process of education and guided social change. Secondly, community development aims at receiving the full approval and support of the people for the measures which it is desired to promote. The essence of the community development approach is to win the confidence of the people and to stimulate and organize their energies to work for the improvement of their conditions of life.

Community development may be regarded as "a method of giving back to African society the sense of community self-help which it used to have."[1] There are many valuable projects of construction and improvement which could be carried out in Tanganyika by voluntary effort, without the need for financing from scarce public funds. Formerly, such projects were accomplished by tribal turn-out organized

[1] UN Trusteeship Council, *Rural Economic Development of the Trust Territories, Report Submitted by the Food and Agriculture Organization Concerning Land Tenure and Land Use Problems in the Trust Territories of Tanganyika and Ruanda-Urundi,* United Nations, T/1438, February 19, 1959.

by the traditional authorities. In parts of the territory, anything resembling the traditional tribal turn-out is now resisted. It is a task for community development to make voluntary mobilization of effort acceptable. It is to be hoped that the dominant political party will give effective support to this aspect of community development.

Community development can also be regarded as a means of teaching to the farmers that the community has a right to ensure that individuals carry out certain duties, notably the duty to assist in the preservation of land and natural resources, both for the present generation and for generations to come.

At the present stage of Tanganyika's political development, there is a natural and commendable desire to turn the enthusiasm of the people, generated by the approach of independence, into constructive channels. It will indeed be desirable to work along these lines. However, there are certain very real dangers to be guarded against. For example, any idea of building up a new organization to carry community development within a short period to every district of the territory is likely to lead to a considerable expenditure of money on a body of insufficiently trained and often unsuitable men, incapable of doing much good and, indeed, able to do considerable harm. One very real risk is that initial enthusiasm, stirred up but not given skilled guidance, may rapidly give way to disillusionment after a number of abortive or disastrous enterprises. This report points out repeatedly that it is of the utmost importance that development efforts should be properly planned to assure that they do good and that they avoid doing damage, as, for example, by ruining land through the use of inappropriate methods. At best, there is the danger, pointed out by the Royal Commission, that "Vague projects of rural betterment . . . will simply lead to a dispersal of much well-meaning effort" (Royal Commission, p. 371).

In the present circumstances of Tanganyika, it seems appropriate to make a dual approach to community development.

a. The desire to make a widespread appeal to the energies and enthusiasm of the people should be organized not through the creation of a large new organization, but through existing bodies such as local authorities, cooperatives and the provincial administration, with the support and cooperation of the dominant political party. Technical guidance and specialized skills should be provided largely by officers of the existing departments of government. It will be necessary to organize this program with care, to ensure that all the bodies and persons concerned in a particular area pull in the same direction. Deliberate efforts should be made to steer activities under the program into useful projects, capable of being carried through without great risk of disappointment, and not involving dangers of serious damage due to inadequate technical planning. In order to maintain control and direction of this program, it would be desirable to build up a small body of skilled "trouble shooters," directly answerable to the Chief Minister but working in collaboration with technical staff of the Ministry of Natural Resources and other relevant departments.

b. At the same time, a parallel approach should be made by way of community development as a skilled operation carried out by carefully chosen and highly trained experts. In this second approach, quality should be stressed as against quantity. The temptation to spread wide and so to spread thin should be firmly resisted. This operation should begin on a pilot scale in one or two limited areas, and only after experience has been gained should the attempt be made to spread the effort to other areas. This program should incorporate efforts to secure objective measurement of achievement.[2]

The two approaches should be kept distinct. They would nevertheless cross-fertilize each other. Intensive, skilled community development work would perfect techniques which can be applied more widely over the territory; and experience gained in the less intensive but more widespread effort would reveal problems to be tackled by the specialist approach and would point to areas where intensive effort would be likely to secure large returns.

Reorganization of the Extension Services

The Mission recommends certain changes in the organization of agricultural extension work as well as in methods. Hitherto in Tanganyika, several departments concerned in the field of agriculture and animal husbandry have each maintained separate extension services. These are the Departments of Agriculture, Veterinary Serv-

---

[2] An interesting discussion of the aims, methods and problems of this second type of program is contained in Meyer, Marriott and Park, *Pilot Project India*, University of California Press, 1958.

For a description of the application of a community development approach in African circumstances, see Peter du Sautoy, *Community Development in Ghana*, Oxford University Press, 1958.

ices (which is concerned with animal husbandry as well as animal health) and, to some degree, Co-operative Development, and to these may be added the recently established Section of Community Development. These departments were for a time divided between the Ministry of Natural Resources and the Ministry of Co-operative and Social Development. The individual farmer may well be in direct contact with two or more officials, not very well trained, from different departments, each stressing the need for improvements and advances in his own particular field. Although efforts are made at coordinating extension work, it is felt that confrontation by a multiplicity of junior government officials must be somewhat confusing to an uneducated and rather primitive farmer. He is liable to have impressed on him at one and the same time the need for urgent action in several different directions, and may well find it difficult to understand the relation between the things recommended to him or the priorities to be accorded to them. The possibilities of spreading confusion are increased by the low level of education of the instructors themselves and the fact that each is only trained in one particular sector of agricultural or animal husbandry technique. Yet the "extension lines" which have to be put over to the farmer are all technically fairly simple, and instructors properly trained to an elementary level should be able to handle a comprehensive range of extension tasks.

A further disadvantage of the present system is that, to some extent, all the departmental instructors cover the same geographical ground and visit the same people. This not only results in duplication in the time and effort spent in traveling around and contacting a large number of scattered farmers, but also tends to prevent the instructors from getting to know their farmers well and from establishing the close personal contacts which are so desirable for successful extension work.

In India a "total approach" to community development has been adopted, all aspects being dealt with at the village level by a village level worker (or *Gram Sevak*), who receives 18 months' training in a variety of subjects, including agriculture, animal husbandry, forestry, cooperatives, public health, village industries, rural engineering, and extension methods and principles. A similar approach was recommended by the East Africa Royal Commission. However, it seems that the type of man available in Tanganyika would be incapable of dealing with such a variety of subjects, and that a service so widely based would be too difficult to administer.

The following organization is suggested as being suitable to conditions in Tanganyika. An extension department should be established within the Ministry of Natural Resources. This department would cover the subjects of crop husbandry, irrigation agronomy, animal husbandry, elementary animal hygiene and health, and forestry insofar as it concerns the establishment of tree plantations on farms. It is envisaged that junior staff for this department would receive elementary training at a "natural resources school." This training would cover all the subjects just mentioned, and also extension methods and principles, community development and cooperative organization. The sole object of training in principles of cooperation would be to help the workers to understand the principles and practice of cooperative societies, with and through which they would often have to work: the establishment and supervision of such societies would remain the function of the Department of Co-operative Development. Similarly, the extension service would only concern itself with routine matters of animal hygiene and health and would refer all other matters connected with animal diseases to the Veterinary Department.

It is envisaged that this extension department would have staff of the following categories:

a. Junior staff, equivalent to existing Field Assistants. These would receive elementary training in natural resources subjects (as indicated above) at a "natural resources school" in Tanganyika.

b. Intermediate level staff, equivalent to the present Field Officers in the Department of Agriculture. These would normally hold diplomas in agriculture.

c. Senior staff equivalent to present Agricultural Officers. These would normally be graduates in agriculture or men of experience and ability promoted from the second category.

d. Administrative staff, equivalent to present Provincial Agricultural Officers and Assistant Directors.

Promotion should be possible from category (b) through (c) to (d) and, for men of exceptional ability capable of successfully undergoing further training, from (a) to (b). Category (c) should include men fully qualified in crop husbandry, animal husbandry, agricultural engineering, etc., to whom non-routine problems could be routed from the lower categories. Similar problems in more specialized fields, such as those of entomology and plant pathology, would be referred to officers of the research and specialist division.

Training of Staff

At present, Field Assistants are trained, after a probationary year of field work, in the natural resources school at Tengeru. As funds allow, and as the number of candidates of suitable educational level increases, it will be desirable to establish perhaps two more similar schools, in different types of ecological environment.

In the past, staff of category (b) could be trained in the agricultural diploma course at Makerere College in Uganda. However, in 1957 the diploma course at Makerere was replaced by a degree course, and no further diploma students were accepted. At present, the limited number of local candidates does not justify the establishment of a diploma course in Tanganyika. It may, however, become desirable to establish one at some later date.

Present government policy places emphasis on the training of Africans for agricultural extension work. This is clearly of the greatest importance. In the first place, it would be difficult to find sufficient expatriates to man a further-expanded agricultural extension staff. Perhaps a more important reason for increase of the number of African extension workers is that Africans are more likely than Europeans to be able to secure the confidence of the farmers, especially if their efforts were to be supported by the political leaders.

Role of the Cooperatives in Agricultural Improvement

In an increasing number of areas, the marketing cooperatives form a natural rallying point for the cultivators and are institutions commanding confidence and respect. In such areas, it is natural that agricultural extension work should be channeled through the cooperatives if they are willing to give their support.

To some extent this is done already. Some cooperatives distribute seed and cuttings, and organize or help to organize spraying against pests and diseases. These activities have had their value, but they also have some severe limitations. Cooperative societies find it necessary to treat all members alike and this may lead to waste, particularly in such matters as free distribution of seedlings. On the other hand, free provision of services may be highly justified, for example to ensure comprehensive coverage in spraying to protect against pests and diseases. In practice, the cooperatives have not yet fully replaced all the valuable work of this kind which used to be done by the marketing boards before their executive powers were withdrawn. Because of limitations of staff and funds, cooperatives can only undertake operations which are relatively simple and inexpensive.

The cooperatives could and should in an increasing measure be used as a channel of communication and information between individual growers and extension officers. The grouping of social development and cooperatives in a single department should facilitate the integration of cooperatives into community development programs. But there is also an urgent need for very close cooperation with the agricultural and veterinary officers.

C. REORGANIZATION OF AGRICULTURAL CREDIT FACILITIES

Improvement of methods in African agriculture will increase both the demand for equipment for the cultivators and also the assurance that it will be productively used. The farmer who can secure a good return on increased and improved equipment should be given every help in acquiring it, not only in order to assist increase of production, but also because a farmer who makes a success of improved methods and equipment is a valuable example to his neighbors.

The African farmer cannot borrow from a bank, since he has no security to offer. He may be able to borrow from a trader, although under the Credit to Natives (Restriction) Ordinance of 1923 no debt is enforceable by legal process against an African (other than one holding a trading license), unless the original loan agreement received the assent of an administrative officer. In these circumstances, African farmers obtain credit largely from public bodies or from cooperatives.

Several Native Authorities operate revolving loan funds. Some cooperatives are prepared to make loans to their members. Finally, there exist two government institutions designed to extend credit to Africans: the Local Development Loan Fund, established in 1947, makes loans for agricultural and livestock purposes; and the African Productivity Loan Fund, set up in 1955, lends for purchase of agricultural equipment, for agricultural and livestock improvement schemes, for processing machinery and also for equipment for cottage industries.

This present credit situation is by no means satisfactory. The

Native Authorities can lend only on a small scale, and the lending activities of cooperatives have been very limited up to the present. As for the two government Loan Funds, it is hardly too much to say that they are partly paralyzed at present by a feeling of crisis induced by many difficulties and failures experienced in their operations to date. The Mission therefore considered the nature of the need for rural loans and how the administration of the loans might be improved.

The Need for Equipment

The productivity of African agriculture is limited by the great lack of capital and productive equipment. Many cultivators have little or no equipment beyond a hoe, an axe and a knife. In only a few places have ox-drawn implements or carts been introduced to any extent. The peasant, his wife and children carry loads on their heads or backs, thereby diverting time and effort from cultivation. The women spend many hours daily laboriously pounding grain.

Despite the extreme shortage of equipment, the additional amount that Africans could use economically appears at present to be somewhat limited. As is usual in underdeveloped areas, ability to make effective use of capital is limited by lack of technical knowledge.

By contrast, there is often demand for implements which cannot be economically used given present levels of skill and the present organization of African agriculture. This point is illustrated by the experience of the African Productivity Loan Fund in making loans for the purchase of tractors. Although some African farmers have managed to operate tractors profitably, many others have failed. A number of factors make the economic use of tractors by African farmers somewhat difficult. Operating costs are high because of the relatively high cost of fuel and on account of the small size and irregular shape of fields, increasing operator-hours per acre. Numerous failures and breakages occur because the drivers lack skill in using tractors and because of inadequate clearing and stumping of the land, resulting in breakage of implements and damage to tires. Breakdowns commonly result in tractors being out of service for considerable periods, often at the busiest time of the year, because spare parts have to be obtained from a distance and depots frequently carry inadequate stocks. A tractor must be used to good effect in order to pay, but most tractor owners are not very competent in organizing and man-

aging tractor work. Furthermore, only a limited number of operations can be done economically by tractor. Tractors pay in plowing
and land preparation, but their further use in weeding, cultivating,
harvesting and transport frequently costs too much in proportion to
the increased yield produced or the value of the labor saved. Consequently, a major difficulty is that, whereas there is more than enough
work which can profitably be done by tractors during a short period
of the year, it is difficult to employ them economically for much of
the remainder of the year. The conclusion is therefore widely accepted in Tanganyika that there are rather few farmers who can at
present benefit from loans to buy tractors. In many areas it is thought
possible to promote the adoption of ox-drawn equipment. Even the
successful introduction of ox-drawn plows depends on extension
work. Attempts in some areas have failed through lack of sustained
follow-up.

Nevertheless, some types of modern equipment have been adopted
in various areas and have proved their value. The use of sprays for
cotton and coffee has become popular. Here the cooperatives have
played an important part. Agricultural credit needs to be linked to
extension work to assist producers to select suitable types of equipment and to put it to good use. There should be the closest possible
collaboration between extension workers and the credit-providing
agencies.

The requirement appears to be for a rather large number of small
loans, of tens of pounds rather than of hundreds, for fairly simple
articles of equipment or improvements such as ox-plows, ox-carts,
wheelbarrows, groundnut shellers, improved livestock, fertilizers or
spraying and dusting equipment. The smallness of many of the loans
required creates the difficulty that the administrative costs of lending
will inevitably be high in relation to the sums lent, the more so
because in many areas potential borrowers are widely scattered and
often rather inaccessible.

The Experience of the African Loan Funds

At the end of 1959, the Local Development Loan Fund had 252
loans outstanding, to a total value of £ 56,831. These loans were all
for agriculture and agrarian activities such as fishing, poultry keeping,
livestock and milling. The African Productivity Loan Fund had 308
loans outstanding, to the total amount of £ 92,456. Of these loans,

just over £ 71,000 were for agriculture, fishing, etc., and the remainder for small-scale industry. Over half of its agricultural loans were for small maize mills, and over one third for agricultural machinery, largely tractors. For each institution, the number of loans outstanding and their total amount were somewhat smaller than at the end of 1958. There was, however, an increase in the first half of 1960 in the number of new loans made.

TABLE 17   Outstanding Loans of the African Loan Funds Compared with Arrears of Interest and Repayment, Position at End of 1959

		(Figures to nearest £)
	Local Development Loan Fund	African Productivity Loan Fund
*Total sums outstanding*ᵃ	29,032	43,562
of which:		
on loans on which only interest due..	17,879	24,644
on loans on which repayments due ..	11,153	18,918
Interest and repayments six months or more overdue		
Interest	161	378
Repayments	4,921	10,021
Total	5,082	10,398

ᵃ These figures represent disbursements less repayments made, whereas the larger figures mentioned in the text above are on the basis of commitments.

SOURCES: Local Development and African Productivity Loan Funds Report and Accounts for 1959; Government of Tanganyika.

Each of the Loan Funds has at its disposal £ 100,000, so that the funds remaining uncommitted at the end of 1959 amounted to just under £ 51,000 in total.

The difficulties encountered by the two Loan Funds are shown by the figures for defaults and arrears of service payments. Service payments are applied first to interest, and the remainder over and above the interest liability to repayment. Table 17 shows that repayments six months or more overdue amounted to as much as 44 percent of the total outstanding amount of all loans on which repayment had become due for the Local Development Loan Fund and 53 percent for the African Productivity Loan Fund. Interest and repayments

three months or more overdue to the two institutions increased from
£ 16,155 at the end of 1958 to £ 20,561 at the end of 1959. It is
apparent that the problem of loan service by African borrowers is an
extremely serious one.

Some defaults have come from loans for purchases or projects
which were technically or economically unsound. Others reflect failure of borrowers to accept their responsibilities.

In addition to loans for equipment, the Loan Funds have made
loans for the planting of permanent crops. The original practice was
to grant periods of grace (referred to as "moratoriums") on these
loans, so as to delay repayment until the crop began to come in. The
African Loan Funds Committee (see below) now feels that these
periods of grace reduced the sense of connection between the loan
and repayment, and so augmented rather than reduced defaults. In
June 1959, the African Loan Funds Committee decided to cancel the
period of grace, and make the first repayment due not later than the
harvest following payment of the first instalment of the loan. The
Committee considers that expansion loans should only be given to
cultivators who have demonstrated their worth and ability by having
mature permanent crops or annual crops which already yield sufficient income to take care of the early service instalments on the loan
before the expanded acreage comes into production. This is, perhaps,
a sound precaution. There are, however, limits to the extent to which
the risk of defaults can be met by progressive tightening up of repayment terms. Beyond a certain limit, loans would cease to be worthwhile and potential borrowers would be forced back on financing
improvements from their own funds.

A similar consideration applies to the requirement, made on loans
for the purchase of equipment, other than mills in towns, that the
borrower should himself make a deposit of at least 25 percent of the
cost of the equipment: i.e., that the loan should be limited to 75
percent of the cost.

It is clear that the administration of loans to the African farmers
must encounter many serious problems. The borrowers have no
security to offer. The taking out of a chattel mortgage over equipment financed by a loan has not been found particularly satisfactory.
Many borrowers fail to appreciate the distinction between a loan
from the government and a windfall gain, and take rather lightly
their obligation to service the loan. Many think that lack of commercial success or unexpected financial embarrassment ought to excuse
them from the obligation to repay. Thus, the success of loans requires

close supervision which is apt to be costly, since the borrowers are scattered and the amounts of individual loans small.

Administration

At present, the African Loan Funds are virtually run by one man in Dar es Salaam, under the general direction of the African Loan Funds Committee, an interdepartmental body augmented by several unofficial members. Preliminary vetting of loan applications—in fact, often, their preparation—and the supervision of loans is left to local administrative, agricultural, veterinary and other officers. To these officers, often hard-pressed with other work, the applications, said to "flood into District Offices," are frequently a nuisance, taking valuable time needed for other work.

Some decentralization of administration and responsibility is clearly desirable. In Uganda, the African Loan Fund has secured a certain decentralization of responsibility by requiring that local governments guarantee 50 percent of loans made to persons in their areas. By this procedure, defaults have been reduced to 15 percent. In Tanganyika it has been found that defaults are relatively low on loans from the Native Authority revolving funds, because of pressure of public opinion. In Tanganyika, however, no acceptable way of associating Local Government Authorities with loans from a central body appears to have been found. Originally, all the loans of the Local Development Loan Fund were channeled through the Native Authorities. In 1952, as a result of representations by the Provincial Commissioners, it was agreed that all loans should be direct to the borrowers, Native Authorities being asked to give a 50 percent guarantee. In 1953, the guarantee was made to apply only to loans of over £500. Native Authorities have in fact become increasingly reluctant to guarantee loans. In November 1959 the African Loan Funds Committee agreed that Native Authorities should be enabled to take bulk loans from the Local Development Loan Fund for specific purposes at a low rate of interest: the Native Authorities would relend to individuals at higher rates of interest. By mid-1960, no such loans had been taken up.

Another possibility of decentralization would be to have cooperative societies act as the agents for the Loan Funds. Those cooperatives which have a monopoly of purchase of a crop are in a particularly good position to ensure that loan service obligations are met. This possibility should be further investigated. However, the cooperatives clearly cannot provide a full solution to the problem of the organization of agricultural credit.

The Mission concludes that, for the administration and supervision of the Funds' agricultural loans, there is a need to establish a trained specialist Loan Funds Officer in each major agricultural area. There is at present one Loan Funds Officer working in the field, stationed at Bukoba and covering West Lake Province and the southeast Lake area. The presence of this officer is said greatly to have improved the administration of loans in these areas. The additional loan officers should be seconded agricultural field officers.

The cost of, say, six loan officers distributed around the territory would admittedly be high in relation to the value of loans to be expected. Each officer might cost a total of, say, £4,000 per year, including salary, paid leave, accommodation, traveling costs and all other expenses. Even if the rate of interest on loans were to be raised from the present 5 percent to, say, 7 percent, it would require full payment of the interest on loans totaling some £ 345,000 to cover the costs of the loan officers alone, leaving out of account central administrative costs.

It therefore seems likely that the cost of administering agricultural and other local loans will have to be subsidized for several years to come, as indeed is done at present, when loans are administered by administrative and agricultural officers. Such a subsidy can be justified by a number of arguments: successful loans increase revenue-yielding activity, and so bring in an indirect return to public authorities; successful operations may provide valuable demonstrations to others, and so lead to further acceleration of development; and, finally, the Loan Funds can perform an educational function in instructing Africans in the value and responsibilities of credit.

Administrative and financial arrangements for agricultural loans will be further discussed in Chapter 11, pp. 220-23.

Cooperatives' Lending Activities

There are at present no cooperative credit societies for African farmers, and the extension of credit for productive purposes by marketing societies is very little developed. A considerable amount of credit has in fact been given by marketing societies, some of which have lent excessive sums in relation to their financial resources; but this credit, which is often unlawful as being outside the authority of the bylaws of the societies, has generally not been for productive purposes. Recently, however, there have been signs of new and more healthy developments.

In the Lake Province, the Victoria Federation of Co-operative Unions is experimenting with the provision of chemical fertilizers against payment from the proceeds of the ensuing crop. In 1959, 100 tons of fertilizer were made available as a pilot project. In fact, only 20 of these 100 tons were taken up by cultivators, so that the initial reaction to what appeared a promising experiment was disappointing. Nevertheless, the Mission recommends that the experiment should be repeated. The reasons for the poor response in the first year should be carefully examined, and any indicated adjustments made. In the pilot scheme, no interest was charged; but if the use of fertilizers increases, the operation should become a regular credit transaction.

In the West Lake Province, the Bukoba Native Co-operative Union has recently embarked upon a very interesting general credit scheme for its members, after first making the requisite changes in its by-laws. The Union distinguishes between agricultural productivity loans and emergency loans. The latter category in particular (covering such purposes as funerals, reconstruction of a house after a fire, payment of school and medical fees and maintenance of orphans and twins) is rightly tied to stringent limitations as regards justification, amount and terms.

For both types of loan, payment is to be made from the next final payment for the coffee delivered, within 12 months. However, security is required through a commitment on crops including those of following financial years, together with the applicant's coffee garden and house. The Mission notes with interest and approval that a pledge on individually held land under African customary rights is being turned into an instrument of credit policy. Interest, at 6 percent a year, is charged only on loans totaling more than Shs. 250/-. The existence of this lower limit may simplify administration, but it introduces an element of charity. If the system expands, a flat rate of, say, Shs. 5/- may be introduced for administrative expenses, over and above the interest charged for larger loans. Agricultural Productivity Loans are primarily tied to the ability and prospects of the applicant —in the words of an official of the Union: "A person who wants to employ labor and himself sit idle is unsuitable." The purpose of the loan must be well established. In general the loan sum is paid in instalments. For this class of loan the period of repayment can be extended to more than one year.

Such schemes encounter inevitable initial difficulties and have to be put to the test of practice. They may, however, constitute a major breakthrough in the provision of productive credit to African peasants, and are strongly recommended for careful follow-up and for study by other cooperatives.

In due course, cooperative credit administered by marketing societies could become of major importance in Tanganyika. The possibility is already under consideration of a central cooperative bank, which could undertake a fairly large volume of lending through the individual cooperative societies. This bank would attract deposits from the cooperatives as collective bodies and from their individual members. The possible organization and functions of such a bank are discussed in Chapter 11. A bank of this kind would confer on cooperative lending the advantages of a large-scale operation, and would bring the collective credit of the cooperative movement into support of the lending operations of any single cooperative.

D. MARKETING AND INCENTIVES

In many British territories, administrators have felt the need to intervene in the free workings of the market in order to ease the growing pains of the money economy. Such intervention has been less extensive in Tanganyika than in many other British territories, including Uganda. Only for cotton is there a statutory price-stabilization fund and prescription of a fixed price to the producer for each season. The present policy in Tanganyika places emphasis on the development of marketing cooperatives as a means of strengthening the bargaining position of African producers. The strength of the cooperatives in certain areas is enhanced by legal regulations making them the sole outlet for certain types of produce.

The marketing of the major African export crops seems to be rather satisfactorily organized in Tanganyika at present, though certain specific problems remain. Greater problems, and problems which have not yet been fully investigated, affect some of the lesser export crops and African crops for consumption within the territory.

It should be one of the tasks for the proposed economic section of the Treasury to keep a watch on the development of marketing problems and to suggest such measures as they may appear to require. Policy should be kept flexible. Circumstances may change so rapidly that particular measures or institutions become outdated after only a few years.

Further development of the money economy depends not only on the presence of markets where producers can secure a satisfactory cash price for their produce, but also on the existence of incentives to earn the cash. This raises the controversial question, briefly discussed at the end of this chapter, of the adequacy of the supply of "incentive goods" in rural areas of Tanganyika.

Marketing Cooperatives

The cooperative societies fall into two categories: those grouped into three giant associations, and the rest (see Table 24). The three giants are: the Victoria Federation of Co-operative Unions, Ltd., handling all the cotton of the Lake Province; and the Kilimanjaro Native Co-operative Union, Ltd. (KNCU) and the Bukoba Native Co-operative Union, Ltd. (BNCU), which have the sole right to trade in African-grown coffee in their respective areas. Mention should also be made of the Tanganyika Co-operative Trading Agency, Ltd., to which all African coffee cooperatives belong and which handles sales for all its member cooperatives except the KNCU and the BNCU.

The total value of products marketed through cooperatives was over £ 10 million in 1958. Over 60 percent of this was coffee and nearly 35 percent seed cotton. Only for cotton and coffee do cooperatives handle the bulk of the crop. The total number of African producers selling through cooperatives is larger than the number of members, and is estimated at some 400,000.

Over vast areas, the establishment of cooperatives is hampered by the sparse distribution of cash crop production and the economic weakness of producers.

The three giants are now operating rather smoothly. The main problem at present affecting the marketing and processing of *cotton* has concerned the remuneration of the ginners. In the years to 1959, this remuneration was fixed according to a formula accepted by the Government. Starting in 1960, the fixed price for the season to be paid by the Lint and Seed Marketing Board is the price ex-ginnery, and in the Lake Province the remuneration to the ginners thus becomes a matter for negotiation between the Victoria Federation and the Lake Province Ginners Association. By either procedure, the ginning charge affects the price which the cooperatives receive for seed cotton, and is thus a matter of great interest to the cooperatives. In August 1957 the Minister for Natural Resources requested Messrs. Cooper Brothers and Co. of London to review the organization and economics of the cotton industry in Tanganyika, with specific reference to the cost of the services rendered by and the basis of remuneration of those engaged in the buying and ginning of cotton. The resulting report confirmed the view that the remuneration to ginners in the Lake Province had been too high. Recently an old ginnery changed hands for £ 200,000, whereas a new and more efficient plant could be erected for £ 150,000. The cooperatives have reacted to this situation by themselves going into the ginning business in order to secure a share of the profits obtainable from it. This policy must have the incidental effect of giving them practical knowledge of the costs of ginning, knowledge which must be valuable under the new bargaining procedure. The Victoria Federation now owns six ginneries, constructed largely with money borrowed from the Marketing Board. This method of transferring the profits of ginning from private operators to the members of the cooperatives has been made economically justifiable, in the face of the general scarcity of capital in Tanganyika, by the considerable expansion of the Lake Province cotton crop in recent years, an expansion which has in itself justified the construction of new ginneries.

The question of ginners' remuneration is still not finally settled. The 1960 negotiations between the Victoria Federation and the Ginners Association reached a deadlock, which had to be broken by the intervention of the Minister for Natural Resources. The general agreement between the Federation and the Association will come up to be reconsidered in 1965. It will then be important to make further arrangements which protect the interests of the cooperative members while at the same time reassuring the Asian community that it can expect satisfactory returns on its enterprise and capital, elements which have a valuable part to play in the future development of the Lake Province and Tanganyika as a whole.

The main question at present concerning the marketing of *coffee* is whether Tanganyika should join in an international coffee agreement and, if so, on what terms. The coffee producers of Tanganyika,

European as well as the African cooperatives, are able to concert their policy through the Coffee Board, a consultative body on which the various producers' associations are represented. Tanganyika was represented at the international coffee talks in September 1959 by the Chairman of the Coffee Board and by the Minister for Social and Co-operative Development, who was formerly an official of the Bukoba Native Co-operative Union. The United Kingdom declined to commit the East African territories to the Coffee Agreement signed in Washington, but put forward a "declaration of intent" under which Tanganyika has agreed to a voluntary cut of 2.3 percent in exports from its current crop.

The most urgent need at present is for measures to improve the quality, and so enhance the marketability, of Tanganyikan coffee. The Meru Co-operative Union, Ltd. has recently led the way in erecting a central pulpery. The Mission recommends that other coffee societies should pay close attention to the results of this venture, since central pulperies may well be an effective way of improving quality and securing a higher return (see Annex II, p. 366).

Compulsion and the Voluntary Principle

Although the Mission would maintain that compulsion in marketing should be avoided so far as possible, it would hold as a general proposition that compulsory grading and marking of exports may be highly desirable in order to preserve the reputation of Tanganyika's products by preventing the export of low quality, adulterated or dirty lots.

One general issue affecting cooperative marketing concerns "single-channel marketing," i.e., compulsion to sell through a cooperative or other prescribed body. The Co-operative Societies (Amendment) Ordinance of 1960 has established new procedures whereby the Governor in Council may order that a certain class of producer of a specified product ". . . shall sell such commodity produced by him in accordance with any directions given by [a] registered society (including any directions to sell to or through such registered society), whether such producer be a member or not." While there are strong practical reasons for the establishment of one-channel marketing for certain agricultural products in certain areas, and while the powers given by the ordinance are hedged around by a number of provisos, the Mission urges that every effort should be made to avoid serious infringement of the voluntary and democractic character of the cooperatives.

Matters relating to the promotion, registration and management of cooperatives will be discussed in Chapter 11.

Local Authority Markets and Produce Cesses

As has been pointed out, the creation of cooperatives for the marketing of many products, whether for export or for local consumption, is often difficult. Producers will often be widely scattered, and thus difficult to organize. Further difficulties are created by the fluctuations of the market. The well-known phenomenon of isolated local markets with gluts and dearths of the products following each other in rapid sequence makes marketing very risky. Cooperative organizations cannot shield producers from these uncertainties, whereas these uncertainties can prevent the formation of viable cooperatives.

The task of providing markets for African products which are not produced on a large scale in particular areas is laid upon Native Authorities. On the whole, the Native Authorities have done a commendable job in constructing simple market places where the farmer and the merchant can come together in controlled conditions designed to ensure fair weights and measures.

However, in many areas both producers and merchants have an incentive to trade outside the Native Authority market. The Native Authority market is commonly used for the collection of a produce cess, based on the value of all sales made there, so that there is an incentive to trade outside the market in order to evade the cess. Moreover, some traders prefer to trade outside the markets in order to conceal the size of their turnover from the income tax authorities. In order to enforce the collection of the produce cess, trading in the Native Authority market is commonly made compulsory. Nevertheless the Mission was informed that up to 75 percent of produce sales in some districts are made illegally outside the Native Authority markets.

The Mission received from various sources strong representations that Native Authority produce cesses should be abolished. With these representations the Mission is in agreement. It will be suggested in Chapter 16 that produce cesses should be abolished and the Native Authorities compensated by being given access to other sources of revenue.

Supply of Incentive Goods

The argument is widely advanced in Tanganyika that the spread of the money economy is hampered by the fact that consumption goods which would give to cultivators an incentive to increase their money incomes are not sufficiently widely available in rural areas. On the other hand, shopkeepers argue that goods outside the range of those which they already stock would simply remain on their shelves unsold. There is no doubt a certain truth on both sides. It is often difficult to predict what articles will appeal to people who are gradually emerging from a subsistence economy and from the conformism of tribal life.

Certain firms appear to have created markets for themselves among Africans throughout the territory by energetic selling campaigns. Others seem to have been too easily discouraged. The Mission gained the impression that for a number of products, including sugar, markets could be expanded, especially in the more remote areas.

Public policy enters the question, particularly through the system of licensing of non-African traders. A licensing system inevitably brings the danger that administrators will think of reasons for using it restrictively. In fact, the interests of the African consumer are best served by the maximum of competition between traders, and the growth of the economy is benefited by the greatest possible availability of consumer goods and small implements.

At present, in accordance with the general land tenure system of the territory, non-African traders are confined to prescribed trading centers, and can only trade outside these centers if they can obtain itinerant traders' licenses. In most of the more populated and more prosperous parts of the country, trading centers are only a few miles apart, and thus the agrarian population has fairly good access to consumer goods. Nevertheless, any restriction which prevents maximum exposure to consumer goods seems, at the present stage of development of the money economy, to be undesirable.

The Mission advocates a more positive attitude towards non-African traders, who perform a most valuable function as catalytic agents in economic activity. The desire to facilitate entry of Africans into trade should be met not by restricting others, but by such measures as training and provision of appropriate credit facilities.

CHAPTER 6 *AGRICULTURAL TRANSFORMATION AND RESEARCH*

Continuation of present agricultural programs in Tanganyika, coupled with the adoption of some at least of the modifications suggested in the last chapter, should be sufficient to ensure a considerable increase of agricultural production over the next few years, and even some small improvement here and there in land use.

To a major degree, the hope for better land use lies in African leaders becoming convinced of the urgency of the need and in their convincing the farmers. There are already African ministers who are well aware of the need for measures to safeguard the land, and leaders in the cooperative unions who see the benefits of suggested changes of methods and who are prepared to encourage farmers to adopt them. It may be hoped that the new Government, with an elected majority, will be able to carry the people with it in action to improve land use, and even to back that action, where necessary, by legislation to ensure soil conservation measures.

The importance which the Mission attaches to the institution of more productive farming methods, making more intensive use of the land on a sustainable basis, has been explained in earlier chapters (see pp. 6 and 91). The Mission considers that the promotion of this aim cannot be left wholly to "improvement" activities of the kind described in the last chapter. To achieve more rapid progress, something more is required, whether through intensive campaigns in settled areas, involving a variety of coordinated measures, or through planned and supervised settlement of areas which are at present uninhabited or thinly inhabited. In fact, the Mission judges that the second of these approaches is in general the more promising in the present conditions of Tanganyika.

Attempts to impose new agricultural patterns on the land of Africa have all too often failed. Past failures show that the task is difficult, not, however, that it is impossible. The chief lesson of the past is the need for careful investigation, trials and planning. The main emphasis in this chapter is therefore on the necessity for further research and experiment. While we indicate the general nature of the schemes we have in mind, we can do so only in rather general terms, since the details must depend on the results of further investigation.

TYPES OF TRANSFORMATION

Reorganization of Farming in Settled Areas

It is natural to consider first how far the desired ends—considerably greater production coupled with preservation of the fertility of the soil—can be achieved in settled areas.

Experience in Kenya under the Swynnerton Plan shows one approach to this type of change. In certain parts of Kenya, a government program aims at bringing about a rapid reorganization of farming.

The first step was to do away with customary land tenure and inheritance, and the considerable degree of fragmentation of holdings which resulted therefrom, and to replace them by a system under which everyone so entitled obtained a consolidated holding of economic size. Secondly, each owner of such a holding was provided with a farm plan, which indicated the soil conservation layout to be adopted and showed how the holding could be efficiently operated on an improved and intensive farming system. This has been followed up by close supervision and advice, which will have to be continued over a prolonged period, to enable the farmer to understand the farm plan, gradually to implement it and eventually to develop his holding to a high standard. This close supervision appears to be necessary for success, because of lack of managerial ability on the part of the farmers. One further essential for the ultimate success of the reorganization is the provision of loans to farmers in order to enable them to develop their holdings by putting up buildings for stock, erecting fencing, providing water supplies, buying fertilizers, etc. Such loans will obviously have to be provided on a very large scale, and the problem of where the finance is to come from has proved difficult to solve.

It is quite unlikely that any such reorganization of farming could be achieved on a large scale in the settled areas of Tanganyika in the near future. In parts of Kenya, the degree of overcrowding and fragmentation of holdings had reached a stage involving such hardships for the majority of farmers that they were able to see the advantages of reorganization. In Tanganyika this is not the case. Severe over-crowding and fragmentation are still confined to quite limited areas; and this, coupled with the present resistance to any measures which attempt radically to change land tenure or land use, makes it im-probable that wholesale reorganization of farming in settled areas could be achieved.

It remains the case that agricultural extension work and the other parts of the improvement program should aim at increasing produc-tion on planned holdings; at improving yields per acre rather than at expanding acreage under methods which deplete the fertility of the soil; and at promoting methods which safeguard soil fertility and guard against erosion. An important possibility, demanding further investigations and trials, is the integration of livestock with arable farming in mixed farming systems.

The ultimate ends to be aimed at by "improvement" and "trans-formation" programs are the same. However, the Mission concludes that quicker progress towards these ends is likely to be made, within the limitations of the resources available for government action, by planned settlement of empty areas than through exclusive concentra-tion on improvement of methods in settled areas. When people move to new areas, they are likely to be more prepared for and receptive of change than when they remain in their familiar surroundings. And where people are under pressure to move or see the advantage of doing so, they can be required to abide by rules and to adopt new practices as a condition of receiving new land.

It will in any case be necessary to open up new areas for cultivation in order to relieve local overcrowding in some parts of the territory. And it is important that, when new areas are settled, they should be brought under cultivation by methods which give returns adequate to justify the expense of opening them up for settlement and which protect the soil from deterioration and erosion. All these considera-tions focus attention on the importance of systematic programs of planned settlement of empty or thinly populated areas suitable for agricultural development. To allow such areas to be brought under cultivation by the old, low productivity methods which threaten the fertility of the soil is an opportunity wasted.

Planned Settlement of New Areas

When the Government spends money on opening up of new areas for settlement, by tsetse clearing, provision of water supplies, flood control or building of access roads, it should whenever possible take the opportunity of introducing methods and organization designed to secure reasonably high yields on a permanent basis.

The first step must be to secure agreement from those who have rights over the land to be settled that settlement should be made conditional on the observance of certain rules. This may present certain difficulties when the land is part of the tribal area of the people who are to settle it. However, the need for government investments to make the land productive or accessible gives to the Government a not inconsiderable bargaining point.

As to methods of securing the adoption of new methods and new forms or organization, the Mission envisages two approaches:

a. supervision by extension workers;

b. partnership schemes, in which the Government or some other agency would provide certain services to the tenants and possibly also a certain element of management.

Supervised Settlement. Supervised settlement schemes involve:

 i. laying out holdings of economic size;
 ii. working out the farming system to be adopted, and laying down the necessary rules of soil conservation and good husbandry;
 iii. helping and inducing the settlers to farm efficiently and to follow the rules.

Ways in which people can be induced to accept the rules of supervised settlement schemes need to be explored. At present, even if settlers could be induced to accept rules as a condition of settlement, there would probably be difficulty in ensuring that they continue to observe the rules. Preliminary vocational training of a rather elementary nature for potential settlers should be experimented with, only the most responsive trainees being accepted for settlement in the early stages of each settlement scheme. Such training might well give good returns by increasing and accelerating improvement of yields.

The financial implications of supervised settlement schemes also need to be carefully investigated. These schemes will often involve relatively high costs in preparing the land for settlement, putting in roads, laying out holdings, and providing close supervision. It may well prove difficult for the Government to recover these costs, even taking into account the return by way of increased tax revenues. Attempts to charge rents sufficient to ensure an adequate rate of return to the Government might run into difficulties, not only by discouraging Africans from participating, but also by making it difficult for the farmers to make their holdings sufficiently productive to yield them a good standard of living as well as to pay the rent.

The immediate need is for further pilot projects to explore the inducements and financial arrangements required to make a success of planned settlement schemes.

Partnership Schemes. In planned settlement schemes, the role of public authorities is limited to initial planning, advice and supervision. An alternative form of organization is the partnership scheme, in which an effort is made to increase the productivity of the holdings by provision by government, or some other agency, of management, supervision and capital for the acquisition of stock and equipment, or installation of irrigation or other facilities. Experience in running partnership schemes is being built up by the Tanganyika Agricultural Corporation (TAC) in its farming settlement schemes (see Annex IV).

In designing partnership schemes, it is particularly important to ensure that the yields to be expected will justify the cost of the centrally provided services. These costs are likely to be high, especially if mechanization is involved. Very few of the mechanized schemes so far attempted in Africa have succeeded both in covering overheads and in yielding a return to the farmer appreciably greater than he could obtain by farming his own land by traditional methods. This is true of the TAC farming settlement schemes at Nachingwea and Kongwa. Moreover, there is likely to be a delay of several years before there is much return on the capital invested, since it takes time to train the tenants to adopt efficient methods.

For the immediate future, further experience of agricultural partnership operations can be secured at Nachingwea and Urambo (see Annex IV). The Mbarali Irrigation Scheme will give further experience in a different set of conditions (see Chapter 8, p. 187). Further partnership operations should be planned only after the necessary preliminary investigations have been completed (see below).

The Mission considers that partnership schemes should as a general rule be run by the Tanganyika Agricultural Corporation, which has already built up staff and a valuable body of experience. This proposal presupposes a financial reorganization of the Corporation (see Chapter 11, pp. 224-25).

Irrigation and Flood Control. Irrigation and flood control projects are, or should be, analogous in many ways to planned settlement schemes. They give the opportunity to introduce improved methods while at the same time making such methods necessary in order to secure adequate returns on the investment involved. While the program of irrigation and flood control proposed by the Mission may be considered a part—and an important part—of the transformation program, it raises a special set of technical issues, and is therefore considered in another chapter, Chapter 8.

THE PREPARATORY STAGE

The immediate need, in relation to the transformation approach, is for an expanded and accelerated program of research and trials. These should be undertaken immediately, so far as available resources allow. What is required is a continuous production line leading from the initial collection of basic data to the institution of improved farming systems, and involving, broadly, the following stages:

a. Collection of basic data, mainly by soil and hydrological surveys.

b. Land use classification and broad land use planning.

c. Planned experiments on various factors of land utilization, to yield the bricks from which improved farming systems may be built: e.g., experiments to determine the response of various soils to fertilizers, to find out appropriate pasture grasses for different areas and work out methods of pasture establishment and management.

d. Planned experiments of a longer-term nature in which a number of factors are combined into a farming system and its effect on yields and fertility maintenance is determined.

e. Study of the economic and managerial aspects of farming systems, either on unit farms under departmental control or on the holdings of progressive farmers.

f. Promulgation of the improved systems within partnership or planned settlement schemes, or by persuading progressive farmers in settled areas to try them out on their own land.

Certain aspects of these stages are considered below in some detail.

The Need for Expanded Research

The research services of the Department of Agriculture have recently been expanded and reorganized. Present arrangements are a great advance on the former inadequate provision for research, but the research staff is still small in relation to the size of the territory and the diversity of conditions and problems encountered within it.

In the past, the bulk of the agricultural research effort in Tanganyika has been directed towards investigating the problems of the three crops of greatest economic importance, cotton, sisal and coffee. There has been no consistent and sustained research on any scale on other crops and their pests and diseases, nor on the general agronomic problems of African farming and land use. Work on soils and their utilization has also lagged behind. In the past, this has been the responsibility of the Government Chemist's Department, an unsatisfactory arrangement because the chemists concerned were not necessarily trained in soil science, had a lot of other work to do in quite unrelated fields, and were not in close touch with agronomists and others as they would have been if they had been working in the Department of Agriculture.

Under the new arrangements, there are four regional research centers, at Tengeru, Ilonga, Ukiriguru and Nachingwea, each of which has an establishment of one entomologist, one plant pathologist, at least one plant breeder, at least one agronomist and one soil scientist or land utilization officer, plus ancillary and subordinate staff. The work of these centers, and also that of the coffee research station, is directed and coordinated by a Chief Research Officer in Dar es Salaam. The sisal research station continues as before to be managed by the industry. The expanded research division of the Department of Agriculture is still not fully staffed, and, indeed, experienced staff for this type of work is not easy to find. The services of several able and experienced officers have recently been lost through retirement or transfer.

The research division should draw all possible advantage from cooperation with the East African Agricultural and Forestry Research Organization, the regional organization concerned primarily with longer-term research, and by collaboration and exchange of visits with staff of the research divisions of the agricultural departments in Kenya, Uganda and the Central African Federation. The Mission recommends that more adequate provision of funds be made to cover traveling costs of Tanganyika research officers visiting these other territories.

Suggestions are made below for certain specific additions to the present research staff.

Surveys of Rainfall and Land

The first question relating to planned settlement schemes or partnership schemes is where they should be located. The choice of sites should be influenced by accessibility to markets and transport facilities, in order to keep down the capital costs of access roads and the transport costs bearing on the prices received for the produce of the areas. But an overriding consideration is the need to find areas where water supply and soils are favorable.

A major problem in the development of new areas will be to decide what crops can be economically grown under a rather low and unreliable rainfall, or, if irrigation is possible, how much irrigation water is needed as a supplement to rainfall to ensure optimum growth and yields of a crop. Much knowledge concerning the water requirements of tropical crops has been accumulated in various parts of the world; but further research and experiment are needed to apply this knowledge in the conditions of Tanganyika. Variations in water need due to different climatic conditions, and at different periods during the growth of the crop from planting to maturity, require further study. In so far as non-irrigated agriculture in Tanganyika is concerned, even if the water requirement of a crop were known, it would need to be supplemented by good information on rainfall reliability, so that a decision could be made as to whether the rainfall would be adequate in the majority of seasons to meet that requirement.

The Mission therefore recommends work on two projects which are largely complementary, namely:

a. to make a close study of rainfall reliability in different parts of the territory; and
b. to obtain data on the water requirements of important crops.

These projects might qualify for external grant assistance.

The statistical analysis of rainfall data should be continued, and studies of seasonal rainfall should investigate the reliability of amounts both of 25 inches and of 30 inches. The expanded analysis of rainfall data should be related to more comprehensive studies of water requirements of various crops. These studies should include the observation and interpretation of data on available moisture during the growing period in its relation to rainfall, runoff, subsoil losses and crop use. This type of investigation will result in more accurate recommendations as to the types and varieties of crops which can be grown in the different parts of the roughly half of Tanganyika's area which at present appears marginal for crop production. It may also give further indications for the breeding of varieties of crops adapted to the specific rainfall and soil-water patterns found in various parts of Tanganyika. This work will of course benefit the "improvement" aspect of agricultural development as well as preparing the way for "transformation" schemes.

While the work on water requirements and on crop breeding would be of great value to Tanganyika, it must be borne in mind that it would be of equal value to the other two East African territories, and that some work on both projects is already being done by the East African Agricultural and Forestry Research Organization (EAAFRO), and, with particular reference to cotton, by the Cotton Research Station in Uganda. If such a technical assistance project could be brought into being, it might appropriately be placed on an interterritorial basis and administered by EAAFRO.

Settlement schemes will frequently depend on the provision of irrigation; and it is in general desirable that where irrigation facilities are provided, these should be in a context of planned settlement or partnership arrangements. The research required for the proper planning of irrigation schemes is discussed in Chapter 8.

Soil survey or reconnaissance has so far only been carried out over limited areas in Tanganyika, and for much of the country there is very little information on the nature and fertility of the soils. Such information is basic to agricultural development. As an example, in many places where water is available and irrigation practicable it is impossible to say whether it would be worth while because the nature of the soil which could be commanded is unknown. The Mission encountered instances where irrigation works have already been constructed and only subsequently has it been appreciated that the soils commanded are somewhat unsuitable for irrigation or at least require some amendment.

The land utilization and planning division of the Department of Agriculture is, of course, working in this field. It is, however, too small (four soil scientists only) and is a new and largely inexperienced section. The Mission therefore suggests that efforts should be made to obtain from some outside organization the services of four experienced soil classifiers and an experienced soil chemist for a period of three years. Such assistance has been given by ICA to the Kenya agricultural department with very beneficial results. The soil classifiers, one of whom at least should be knowledgeable in land use classification for irrigation purposes, would carry out detailed surveys in selected areas believed to be of good potential, in conjunction with the local land utilization officers. They might also endeavor to obtain something of an over-all picture of the soils of Tanganyika by carrying out in certain areas reconnaissance or transient surveys which would serve as a basis for more detailed surveys later. The soil chemist, working in conjunction wth the surveyors, would carry out laboratory examination of soil samples, and, in particular, would develop the laboratory organization and training of junior staff necessary for the routine examination of large numbers of soil samples by modern methods.

Trials of Cultivation Systems

An aim of transformation operations is to institute systems of farming which give relatively high yields while maintaining or increasing soil fertility. In the present state of technical knowledge, it would not be possible to recommend for all parts of the country more intensive and productive farming systems which could maintain fertility and at the same time be practical and economic. For considerable areas possessing reasonably good soil and rainfall it would be possible to recommend with some confidence a mixed farming system, in which crops would be rotated with grass utilized by productive stock. This system would include, wherever possible, an area under a relatively high-priced, and preferably perennial, cash crop. The best pattern in different areas needs to be determined by field trials.

The information available on the requirements of various soils for fertilizers or on the economics of the use of fertilizers for different crops is still inadequate. As a follow-up of the soil surveys recommended above, there should be an expansion of fertilizer trials. The Mission believes that in some areas the use of fertilizers will prove to be economic and a valuable aid in increasing yields and maintaining fertility. Here again, results will benefit improvement operations as well as the transformation program.

Trace element deficiencies affecting crops, particularly in volcanic soils, and mineral imbalance or deficiencies in livestock are known or suspected in a number of areas. In various places there appear to be deficiencies of boron in coffee, wattle and pines, of zinc in coffee, of sulphur in tea, and probably of iron or manganese in various crops. Such deficiencies should receive increased investigation. Many of them should be susceptible to ready and economic correction once their existence is understood and mapped.

Farm Economic Studies

Farm economic studies are likely to be needed for several purposes, amongst which are the following:

a. When an improved system of farming has reached an advanced stage of technical development as a result of research, it will be necessary to put it into operation on a holding, as nearly under normal conditions as possible, and to make a close study of its economic and management aspects. Some trial holdings on improved systems have already been established in some parts of the country.

b. In some areas a few progressive farmers have already abandoned shifting cultivation, have enclosed holdings of varying size which are virtually on individual tenure, and have begun to farm them on improved lines, sometimes using tractors on the larger holdings. If the Agricultural Department is to be in a position to advise and help such farmers it must clearly obtain data on the economics of various sizes of holdings and on various methods.

At present there is no one in the Department of Agriculture with experience of such work, and a number of difficulties and problems are likely to be involved in the design of such enquiries, the sampling techniques involved, and their general organization. It is, therefore, recommended that outside assistance should be sought for the provision of an agricultural economist experienced in the work. With the aid of one or two local agricultural officers (preferably Africans) this agricultural economist should initiate economic studies.

Pilot Projects

Beyond the stage of research, investigation and field trials, the problems of transformation operations will be analagous to those of all extension work. The effort and money devoted to devising improved agricultural techniques adapted to particular parts of the country with reasonably high potential will be wasted if cultivators cannot be attracted to the schemes and induced to conform to the patterns of activity which they require.

In this matter of persuasion, again, it will be desirable to start with pilot projects, designed to perfect the techniques required. Such pilot projects should be used also to instruct supervisory staff for further schemes.

Planned settlement schemes and partnership schemes will have to include provision for overcoming the lack of managerial ability on the part of African farmers. Costs for supervision and assistance will inevitably be high.

CHAPTER 7 *LIVESTOCK DEVELOPMENT*

Much of Tanganyika is potentially fit for stock keeping, but for little else. Over roughly one third of the territory, there is a 15 percent or greater probability of receiving less than 20 inches of rain during the rainy season (October to May). In this huge area, largely in the north and center of the territory (see Map 2), conditions are in varying degrees unfavorable for the production of arable crops, except in those limited areas where irrigation is economically feasible; but a very considerable part of this area is suitable for livestock, provided that tsetse fly is controlled and water supplies are provided. These areas of small and uncertain rainfall are already occupied, though sparsely in parts, by nomadic pastoralists, and in them stock outnumber humans. Livestock are also kept by the majority of farmers, both European and African, in many of the higher rainfall areas where arable farming is practiced. In 1958 there were in total 7.4 million head of cattle, 2.8 million sheep and 4.1 million goats (see Table 18). At present Africans keep about 98.5 percent of the cattle and sheep and over 99.5 percent of the goats in the territory, and a little more than half of the pigs.

While the number of animals is great, the contribution which they make to the material product of the territory is small. Further, livestock are running down the land in many areas. If a fair valuation were put on deterioration and erosion of soil due to overgrazing, the contribution of animals to the economy might well be found to be negative in many places. In the words of the Royal Commission, the way of life of the pastoral tribes ". . . portends both a danger and a deficiency. The danger is that they may turn their lands into desert; the deficiency that, without management of their herds, and in some cases better usage of their lands than mere pastoralism, they will contribute far less than their lands' potential to the growing needs of the community" (Royal Commission, p. 281). A similar judgment applies in general to stock keeping by African tribes primarily engaged in crop production. The deficiencies of African animal husbandry have been considered in more detail in Chapter 4, pp. 79-81.

The product of the livestock sector was estimated by the Statistical

TABLE 18   Tanganyika Livestock Census and Primary African Sales of Stock, 1957 and 1958

('000 head)

Province	Year	Livestock Census			Primary Sales				
					Cattle				
		Cattle	Sheep	Goats	Mature	Immature	Heifers	Sheep	Goats
African Owned									
Lake and West Lake	1957	2,785	1,178	1,277	91	23	8	11	18
	1958	2,785	1,062	1,175	81	13	4	9	16
Western	1957	861	207	442	30	14	2	5	15
	1958	878	214	450	33	10	2	3	16
Northern	1957	1,240	589	952	49	4	—	8	30
	1958	1,357	656	873	48	4	4	14	26
Central	1957	962	608	900	42	22	4	24	53
	1958	1,156	562	988	40	18	2	11	32
Southern Highlands	1957	796	120	179	11	2	0.5	0.4	0.8
	1958	771	117	178	11	3	0.6	0.4	0.8
Tanga	1957	222	116	260	6	0.3	—	0.7	4
	1958	268	120	257	6	2	—	1	4
Eastern	1957	68	30	87	4	0.2	—	0.1	0.8
	1958	67	29	87	4	0.4	—	—	0.8
Southern	1957	17	13	120	—	—	—	—	—
	1958	18	13	100	—	—	—	—	—
Total	1957	6,951	2,861	4,217	232	66	14	49	121
	1958	7,300	2,773	4,107	224	50	8	39	95
Non-African Owned									
Total	1957	107	24	16					
	1958	115	33	17					
African and Non-African Owned									
Total	1957	7,058	2,885	4,233					
	1958	7,415	2,806	4,124					

SOURCE: Annual Reports of the Department of Veterinary Services.

Unit at a peak figure of £ 17.4 million in 1959, of which about a quarter was estimated to have been marketed. On this basis livestock contribute to the monetary and subsistence sectors combined only about one-fifth as much as does crop production. Meat consumption by Africans is roughly estimated at 8½ oz. per head per week, not including consumption of game meat, poultry and fish, which is estimated at a further 4½ oz. per head per week. It must be emphasized that all these figures are extremely rough. As will be stressed below, the statistical evidence on the production of the livestock sector is still very unsatisfactory (see p. 164).

Exports of meat and meat products reached a peak value in 1959 of £ 1.7 million, including a considerable element of processing, while exports of hides and skins reached a value of £ 1.9 million. Thus in this year the livestock sector contributed 8 percent of total exports as compared with slightly under 5 percent in the preceding years. These exports have been partly offset by imports of slaughter stock, meat and meat products from Kenya, which appear to have been running at about £ 0.5 million a year.

For animal husbandry as for agriculture, the Mission's recommendations fall into two categories, an "improvement" approach and a "transformation" approach.

Step-by-step improvement of African methods remains extremely important. There are in fact certain encouraging signs of progress towards increased productivity within African cattle keeping: in some areas, stock owners are showing an increased tendency to regard their animals as a cash crop, and to take a more active interest in disease control, pasture management, improved animal husbandry and better quality stock. It must be emphasized, however, that so far there are only the beginnings of progress, in spite of many years of work by the Veterinary Department. It is likely to be many years before the traditional African cattle industry can be raised to anything approaching a reasonable level of efficiency and productivity. The Mission therefore considers that expenditures designed to improve animal husbandry within the framework of present African practice should be scrutinized very critically, in order to avoid outlays the returns on which are smaller than the economy can afford.

Side by side with efforts to improve African cattle keeping by modifications of the traditional pattern, the Mission recommends an increase of partnership cattle ranching, in which Africans would run cattle under skilled management provided by the Tanganyika Agricultural Corporation or some other public body.

The final section of this chapter deals with dairying.

THE MARKET FOR BEEF

The Mission considers that demand, within the territory and for export, justifies the aim of increasing annual production of beef animals by 100,000 head. It would be time enough to reappraise the situation when such a figure had been attained.

The Domestic Market

The consumption of meat by the African population is low and, in view of the deficiency of their diet in animal protein, increased consumption is desirable from the point of view of health and nutrition. A rough calculation suggests that it would be desirable on nutritional grounds for the African population to increase its present consumption of meat by at least 40 percent: that is to say, to consume over 100 million pounds more than at present, thus necessitating the slaughter of at least 700,000 cattle of 150 pounds dead weight.[1]

It seems probable that Africans will in fact be prepared to purchase more meat as money incomes continue to increase. Of the 33,000 head of slaughter cattle imported from Kenya, it is known that about half are consumed in the Northern Province, mainly by the coffee growers around Kilimanjaro and Meru, and about half in Tanga Province, mainly by laborers on sisal estates. It may be noted that if the labor employed by the sisal industry received a meat ration at the rate prescribed by the Employment (Care and Welfare) Regulations, the meat requirements for this alone would amount to approximately 10 million pounds per annum, equivalent to some 67,000 head of native cattle of 150 pounds dead weight.

Even the present meat consumption is not being fully met from

---

[1] The estimates quoted above put African per capita consumption of meat, excluding meat from game, at 8.6 oz. per week, though this figure is subject to a very wide margin of error. If it be assumed that a desirable consumption is 18 oz. per week per head of population over 16 years old, and 6 oz. per head per week for those under 16, then the additional annual meat requirement for the present population would exceed 100 million pounds per annum. These per capita amounts are in fact less than those recommended in the Tanganyika Employment (Care and Welfare) Regulations, 1957.

production in Tanganyika. In 1957 just over 1½ million pounds' weight of fresh meat, bacon, ham and sausages, valued at £ 161,000, was imported; and, in addition to the recorded imports of slaughter stock on the hoof from Kenya, i.e., 32,984 cattle and 17,642 sheep and goats, valued at about £ 300,000, it is also known that there were appreciable unrecorded imports on the hoof from Kenya. Thus it is safe to assume that Tanganyika is importing at least £ 500,000 worth of meat per annum.

Exports

There seem to be fair prospects for at least a moderate expansion in the export trade in canned meat and meat extracts. In 1959 the value of these exports was £ 1.7 million. The main plant of Tanganyika Packers Ltd. at Dar es Salaam, which in preceding years had been running well below its maximum capacity, handled 80,000 head. The smaller plant at Arusha, capable of processing 20,000 head per annum, had a through-put in 1959 of 13,000 head plus 4,000 carcasses of chilled beef imported from Kenya. At present there is a good market for Tanganyika canned beef, and no difficulty is being experienced in disposing at good prices of all that is produced though the market for beef extracts was rather less favorable in 1959. It is true that the present generally favorable market is to a considerable extent due to the fact that over the past few years supplies from Argentina have been much less than formerly; but while it is expected that the latter will increase over the next four years, it seems unlikely that they will reach their previous volume. While it is not easy to assess the future market, it seems reasonable to suggest that if the Dar es Salaam cannery were enlarged to take 100,000-150,000 head per annum, there would not be much difficulty in disposing of the resulting canned meat and extract. As the factory is at present capable of dealing with the slaughter of 100,000 head per annum, the delivery of that number would only necessitate an increase in canning machinery; but to deal with more than 100,000 would mean a major extension and reorganization. It should be added that, except for 1953 and 1959, the through-put of the plant in Dar es Salaam has been well below capacity each year, and obviously the profitability of the enterprise would be appreciably raised if arrangements could be made to ensure that its present capacity is fully utilized.

Beef Production Target

To increase the through-put of Tanganyika Packers from the 1959 figure of 97,000 to 120,000 per annum (both plants), and to replace imports of slaughter cattle from Kenya would require some 60,000 head of cattle; then only a small allowance has to be made for increased domestic consumption in order to justify the interim target of increasing production of beef animals by 100,000 per annum.

IMPROVEMENT OF AFRICAN ANIMAL HUSBANDRY

Policy towards African cattle keepers has to aim as much at prevention of overstocking as at increase of production. As was emphasized in Chapter 4, the combination of communal ownership and grazing of pastures with unrestricted individual or family ownership of herds leads to failure to adjust stocking rates to carrying capacity and to complete disregard of pasture management. Where there is added to these human factors the restrictions imposed on pasture utilization by the presence of tsetse over large areas and the inadequacy and maldistribution of water supplies, the result is gross overstocking, deterioration of the pastures and severe erosion. Since, in addition, the people are reluctant to sell stock and their standards of animal husbandry and disease control are poor, the productivity of the cattle industry is extremely low. In drought years many animals die, or are sold as immatures, there being a great waste of a potential asset in either case.

The take-off from the African cattle stock is at present comparatively small. On the one hand, the rate of natural replacement in the herds is low: under the average conditions of African animal husbandry the calving rate is only about 50 percent, about 20 percent of the calves fail to survive the first six months and a further 20 percent do not reach maturity. On the other hand, except in years when widespread drought induces exceptional take-off and a high rate of deaths from natural causes, the cattle population increases at a fairly high rate. From 1954 to 1958, the average annual increase appears to have been over 3 percent. There is obviously considerable scope for increasing the take-off by improving calving rates and reducing mortality. On European-run ranches, where the essentials of pasture management are practiced, where water supplies are reasonably adequate and where there is adequate disease control, a calving rate of 85 percent is readily achieved, and this allows an annual take-off equivalent to 20 percent of total numbers.

It would be technically possible to secure a considerable increase of livestock products from smaller numbers of animals—that is to say, to increase production while at the same time reducing the danger to the land. The object of policy must be to persuade African cattle keepers of the great advantages of systematic management of stock and pasture and to induce them to adopt the requisite methods. While production can be somewhat increased and the danger to the land somewhat reduced by limited changes, measures to increase calving rates, decrease calf mortality, improve the quality and condition of the animals and increase the carrying capacity of pasture land are best presented as a coherent whole, capable of converting cattle into a valuable cash crop.

Measures to Increase Sales of African Cattle

In African stock keeping, given the present conditions of lack of management and of overgrazing in many areas, a higher rate of take-off is needed, even with the low rate of natural replacement, in order to adjust stocking rates to the carrying capacity of the land. Efforts to increase sales serve the two purposes of increasing production and reducing overgrazing.

The present problem is not so much overstocking in relation to the real potential of the land as overstocking in relation to the present lack of pasture management. Consequently, except in some locations where the land has already been irretrievably ruined (as, for example, in Kondoa-Irangi), an initial reduction of stock numbers, if followed by better pasture management, would in due course allow the land to carry more stock than it does at present.

Efforts to increase the number of animals sold have been made for many years. In addition to propaganda and persuasion, compulsory de-stocking rules were latterly enforced in some areas, whereby stock owners were compelled to sell a proportion of their animals. These rules were always very unpopular, could never be fully implemented, and were not very effective in reducing the pressure on the land.

In the face of increasing opposition, attempts at compulsory de-stocking have now been discontinued. Despite this, the stock sales from the areas concerned have not fallen. This fact, together with certain other evidence, suggests that Africans are, in fact, beginning to sell more cattle, probably because of an increased desire for consumer goods. It is, however, likely that this tendency to sell more stock will only increase slowly and that efforts to develop a commercial attitude amongst the pastoralists will have to continue for some time.

Three cattle cooperatives have recently been registered in the Lake Province. It is to be hoped that these will increase appreciation of cattle as a cash crop in their areas, and will show the way for useful development of similar institutions in other areas.

Markets and Stock Routes. Various means of facilitating the movement and marketing of cattle have received attention but require further development. In some areas, particularly in the huge Masai pastoral area of the Northern Province, the provision of more primary cattle markets and of access roads to them, is desirable. The existing main stock routes seem fairly adequate in number and coverage, but there is a need to provide them with more water supplies and with fenced holding grounds. A program to increase and improve markets and stock routes has been worked out by the Veterinary Department. Its cost has been roughly estimated at £ 28,000 a year over the next five years. The Mission recommends that this program be carried through.

Mobile Meat Processing Plants. The purchase and operation of two mobile meat-processing plants for the production of meat and bone meal has also been considered by the Veterinary Department. The case for these arises from the fact that in certain areas of dense cattle population and in certain droughty seasons it is necessary to take off a proportion of very poor-quality animals which are only suitable for canning. These animals are often not brought into markets because the owners are unwilling to trek them long distances when the chances are that they will be rejected. The use of mobile processing plants, which can go out into the affected areas, has proved successful in Kenya in preventing these low-quality animals from continuing to clutter up the land or from dying in bad seasons, and a ready market has been found for the meat and bone meal produced. It is now considered that such plants would not cover their costs in Tanganyikan conditions and that they would have to be subsidized. However, taking into account the value of checking overgrazing, the Mission considers that it would be worthwhile to put at least one such plant into operation and to check the results to see whether more may not be justified.

Provision of Holding Grounds for Immatures

Partly as a result of the African's tendency to keep too many cattle, there is inadequate pasture and water to feed them in dry years, with the result that in such seasons large numbers of animals either die of starvation or are offered for sale as immatures. The purchase and slaughter of these immatures before they have grown out and fattened represents a great waste, and while a number are now bought by Tanganyika Packers and others for growing and fattening on their holding grounds, this procedure is not yet adopted on a large enough scale to avoid considerable waste in bad years. Furthermore, the availability and prices of immature cattle fluctuate considerably; in drought years they are available in large numbers at low prices, while at other times the supply is limited and the price is high. At present no adequate arrangements exist to even out these fluctuations as much as possible and to ensure a fairly steady supply to the cannery and to the urban butchers. Consequently, if this waste of immatures and fluctuation in their supply were dealt with by providing additional holding grounds or ranches on which they could be fattened, there would be an immediate increase in the supply to the market. More concrete proposals are made below (pp. 161-63).

Pasture Management and Improvement

It has already been pointed out that African pastoralism is characterized by a virtual absence of pasture management, and that in consequence the herbage, and the land itself, suffers from overgrazing, destruction and deterioration of the grass cover due to uncontrolled burning, and reduction in carrying capacity owing to bush regeneration. Various authorities (see, for example, report of an FAO team, *Milk Development Possibilities in East Africa,* 1958) have indicated that the disadvantages of communal land tenure and grazing are at the root of the trouble, and have suggested the development of individual livestock holdings. In most areas however, the establishment of individual holdings would be impracticable, not only because such a major change in land tenure would be resisted by the people, but also because of difficulty in providing access to the limited water supplies and because some grazing areas can only be utilized at certain seasons of the year. Consequently, it will generally be necessary to try to effect improvements while accepting a continuation of communal land tenure and communal grazing.

The primary needs are usually for an initial reduction in stock numbers by sales, for the introduction of simple systems of rotational grazing and/or the provision of grazing reserves, and for doing away with indiscriminate burning and its replacement with a controlled use of fire in those areas where this is needed to deal with bush regeneration.

All these are matters on which the Veterinary and Agricultural Departments have been working for years, but progress has been and is likely to continue to be slow, although in certain areas rotational grazing and grazing reserves have been successfully introduced. In some places a further desirable step would be the rehabilitation of denuded areas by sowing or planting suitable grasses after a minimum of preparatory cultivation. This has been done successfully on a considerable scale in Kenya.

Bush Clearing and Elimination of Tsetse Fly

In many areas where the cattle population is dense, the pastures heavily overgrazed and the land deteriorating, the provision of expansion areas by clearing bush to eliminate tsetse fly is a prerequisite to the rehabilitation of worn-out occupied areas. However, bush clearing is costly. The normal method of eliminating tsetse fly is first to survey the tsetse position over the whole area, then to clear the 5-10 percent of the bush which forms the breeding places of the fly and finally to clear fly barriers around the area in order to prevent the reentry of the fly from adjacent infested bush. Formerly the clearing was done by voluntary local effort; now, however, it is often necessary to employ hired labor, in which case the average cost of the whole operation is from Shs. 8/- to Shs. 25/- per acre depending on the type of bush. In thicket country (though not in miombo), further clearing is necessary to permit the development of a reasonable grass cover. Consequently, clearing of thicket country for cattle would be quite uneconomic if it had to be done by paid labor. Much tsetse-infested country is of inherently low potential, and can at best be expected to yield only a low return on capital invested. Moreover, past provision of additional land by bush clearing has all too frequently relieved matters only temporarily, since it has not been accompanied by any permanent reduction in stock density or improvement in land use.

The Mission does not consider that any large-scale central government investment in tsetse clearing to open up land for cattle is justified, but rather that clearing by the Central Government should be limited to areas of high potential for ranching or mixed farming and to localities where only limited further clearing is needed to safeguard existing fly-free areas, or to extend them considerably. Central government operations should be concentrated on areas of strategic importance in the struggle against tsetse, and the task of opening up areas for use should be left to a considerable degree to local effort. Consultations with the Veterinary Department suggest that a reasonable central government program would cost £ 10,000 a year, enough to clear about 25,000 acres annually. This is rather less than double the present allocation.

Water Supplies

Additional water supplies are needed in pastoral areas both for the general welfare of the population and better growth of the cattle, and also as a concomitant to pasture improvement. Lack of water is one of the main factors restricting livestock to about one third of the territory (cf. Map 3). It also shapes the pattern of cattle keeping. For example, members of the Mission visited many areas where large herds of cattle are walked down from the villages to streams, lakes or pools over distances exceeding five miles and sometimes even exceeding 15 miles. The permanent cattle "bomas" are often located at some distance from streams to avoid flooding and insect pests. In the dry season, cattle are often concentrated around the limited remaining water sources, with an attendant risk of erosion caused by overgrazing and trampling. In some years the streams and pools may dry out completely and a great loss of animals will be suffered. It is in part as a reaction to this hazard that the cattle-holding Africans tend to build up their herds to the greatest extent possible in the good years in the hope that a larger number may survive in dry years.

Problems of water supply are particularly acute over much of the two thirds of the territory to the northwest of a line Mbeya-Tanga. Over much of this area, streams are dry during the dry season. Consequently in many areas it is necessary to look to ground water or to storage in reservoirs if year-round water supplies for men and beasts are to be provided. In most parts of the territory, there are in fact technical possibilities of providing rural water supplies, from reservoirs created by digging tanks or constructing dams in small catchments, from boreholes or by piping water from springs or small brooklets. In all these cases, relatively high expenditures are involved.

Recent Development. Of the capital funds made available in recent years for the improvement of land and water resources, some 20 percent, or roughly £125,000 a year, have been allocated to the provision of water supplies mainly for the supply of livestock. The postwar increase of government effort has in part merely replaced construction of tanks, hafirs and small dams which used to be carried out by tribal turnout, but it has also made possible increased provision of water supplies and the undertaking of water supply projects of a more complicated nature. Larger dams have been constructed, storing large amounts of water and capable of providing for a perennial flow in the river downstream of the reservoir. Pipelines have been built, bringing water from perennial streams or springs to dry parts of the country nearby. For example, the pipeline system near Leguruki transports 250,000 gallons of water daily from springs on the slopes of Mount Meru to a dry land area 14 miles away. In Kondoa District, where heavy overgrazing has occurred on the slopes of escarpments, water is now brought down through pipeline systems to the plains, in an effort to bring about movement of cattle from the overgrazed slopes to the flatter land below. A third type of water supply consists of boreholes equipped with hand pumps, engine-driven pumps or windmills to bring underground water to the surface. Some eight drilling teams with equipment operate in Tanganyika and provide some 50 boreholes a year.

In recent years, there have been constructed in each year something like 20-30 major surface schemes, 15-20 pipeline schemes and 25-30 boreholes (not including boreholes to provide water for industrial and similar purposes, but including some village water supplies which did not provide water for cattle, and some works which have also provided water for irrigation). These works have been mainly in the cattle areas in the Northern, Lake, Central and Western Provinces, and also in parts of the Southern Highlands and in the extreme southeast of the Southern Province.

The program for establishment of water supplies for livestock is progressing satisfactorily in terms of numbers of watering points installed. The Government envisages a gradual speeding up over the coming years to meet the great demand for new water supplies. However, there are still technical problems to be overcome. Even more important, the economics of the return to this form of expenditure is open to a certain amount of doubt. The Mission therefore urges that there be no great acceleration of the program until further investigations and planning have been undertaken to assure that this form of investment shall indeed make an adequate contribution to the economy of the territory.

Risk of Local Overgrazing. A particularly serious technical problem, to be borne in mind in future planning, is that of overgrazing in the immediate surroundings of the water supply points. Large numbers of cattle concentrate there, with the result that the vegetation is destroyed, the soil becomes denuded and erosion may result. The first parts to be eroded are the tracks by which the cattle find access to the reservoirs and other watering points. The inflow of water to the reservoirs is often loaded with silt. During its travels through the country the Mission found some striking examples of this type of damage. In some cases the surrounding area of the reservoirs becomes swampy because of the great number of cattle approaching over this area.

One possible solution might be to erect fences to prevent the approach of cattle near to the reservoir. Water should then be provided for the cattle in cattle troughs at the end of pipes bringing water from the reservoir. Thus the number of cattle at any one watering point could be restricted. However, fencing of reservoirs, by scrub or sisal plants or by artificial means, is impracticable unless the collaboration of the people can be obtained. This is especially so in very dry years, when it can be expected that people will break down the fences to let their cattle reach the water. Another solution may be to construct fairly large dams from which water can be released steadily over the dry period of the year to provide a steady flow of water in the river bed downstream for a considerable distance. This solution however is applicable only under conditions where the water does not seep into the soil and where the river traverses an area which is not susceptible to erosion.

Where water is made available by boreholes or by pipeline systems, it may be possible to restrict the amount of water made available at a particular place. However, efforts to circumvent such a restriction are to be expected. For example, in Masailand an effort was made to limit the number of cattle round a borehole by providing only a limited amount of oil to drive the engine of the pump. The local people soon bought oil themselves to operate the engine over the whole day, with the result that overgrazing did in fact occur.

Economics of Water Supply for Livestock. In order to avoid erosion in the neighborhood of watering points, it will be desirable to aim at not more than 1,250 head of cattle to each watering point, or 1,500 at the utmost. If the water supply takes the form of a running river or of a pipeline with a number of cattle troughs, then calculations should be made on the basis of the carrying capacity within a range of two or three miles. The average cost of water supply points as constructed in recent years can be put at £ 2,000-3,000, but the cost could be somewhat reduced in cases where a number of supply points are constructed in a limited area. The fairly small dams, the tanks and hafirs may be less expensive. Pipeline systems, however, are in general rather more expensive. The figures are based in part on an analysis of a large number of reservoir projects, an allocation of construction costs being made as between rural water supplies (especially for livestock) and irrigation. On this basis, a representative figure for the capital cost of providing water may be put at about £ 2 per beast.

The question arises in what circumstances an investment of this size is justified. Given the low rate of take-off in African cattle keeping and the poor quality of many of the beasts, the returns to the investment in terms of increase both of incomes and of public revenues may be low. A major goal of the water development program has been to open up new land for grazing, and thus to spread population and cattle from overpopulated and overgrazed areas towards new areas, and to allow an improved ratio of land to cattle. Such improvement has indeed been temporarily achieved in some areas. Examples were mentioned to the Mission, for example in the Lake Province, where overcrowding in certain regions gave way to a more normal occupation of the land, after opening up of new areas by a combined policy of tsetse clearing and provision of water supplies. In general, however, overgrazing has not been alleviated to any considerable extent by the installation of new watering points. Indeed, provision of new watering points may well lead to such an increase of total cattle numbers as to extend significantly the area exposed to overgrazing.

There exist no systematic factual data on the effects of new water installations in Tanganyika. Given the general uncertainty about the economics of African cattle keeping, it is virtually impossible at present to make useful calculations concerning the rate of return to the economy as a whole and the rate of financial return to the public sector resulting from investment in provision of watering points for livestock in particular conditions. The situation is further complicated since in some areas the opening up of new grazing land will depend not on provision of water alone, but on a combination of water development and bush clearing; and in some it may be possible to use provision of water as an inducement to secure the acceptance of other desirable changes, thus bringing about an increase of production greater than would be achieved by any of the changes in isolation.

In order to establish criteria for future projects, factual data should be accumulated on the economics of watering points. Developments at new watering points of various kinds in various parts of the territory should be studied over a period of several years. Such studies should be planned with the assistance of an economist to be seconded to the Ministry of Natural Resources from the economic section of the Treasury (see p. 210).

Water Charges and Local Rates. As will be seen in connection with irrigation, the effect of investment on the public finances is considerably influenced by the amount of any direct charges which can be levied on the beneficiaries of the investment (see Annex VII, p. 428). In Tanganyikan conditions it is not practicable to establish water charges to be assessed per head of cattle coming to the supply point. On the other hand, it may be possible to obtain a direct return through increase of cattle tax. Many Native Authorities impose cattle taxes at rates from Shs. 1/- to Shs. 3/- per beast. In Singida District, some £ 12,500 was collected over one or two years by the Native Authority from a special cattle tax to be set aside for water development. In 1957 the basis of sharing the costs of installing cattle water supplies was changed from 50/50 to 75 central/25 local, with the proviso that a higher proportion might be met from local funds where finances permit and where there is a strong popular demand for a large water development program. In order to promote direct contributions to the cost by the beneficiaries, the Mission recommends return to a 50/50 sharing of costs of cattle water development between the central government and local government authorities. However, local authorities should not necessarily be allowed to "buy" water development unless there is a reasonable assurance that this development meets the criteria suggested below.

Where local government authorities are unable to pay in advance their half of the capital cost of desirable water development, the central government might well lend them the amount of their contribution, on terms not less hard than those of "hard" loans from external sources.

Policy for Cattle Water Development. The provision of additional water supplies should form part of a planned program in which watering points are sited with regard to the pasturage available and arrangements are made for the control of stock numbers and for pasture management. Careful attention should be given to the possibilities of using provision of improved water supplies as an inducement to improved cattle and pasture management. In certain circumstances, the control of water supplies could be directly used to bring about improved pasture management: for example, if water is provided by a borehole or by piping from some distance, then, if it is desired to rest the grass in the area for a given year or season, this can be assured by cutting off the water supply.

If for any reason it appears essential to install watering points in areas where there is no great assurance that reasonable grazing control will be realized, then only water supply points of a type with a restricted and controlled supply should be installed. This points to borehole supplies and pipeline supplies from springs or streams. Reservoir schemes should only be installed if there is reasonable assurance of adequate grazing control. Only in a very small number of severe hardship cases should exceptions be made to this rule.

Future Capital Expenditures. The Mission considers that capital expenditures on the various types of schemes for provision of water for livestock might well develop as shown in Table 19. Actual rates of investment should depend on the extent to which the conditions stated in the last two paragraphs can be attained.

Other Measures to Improve Animal Husbandry

Disease Control. Much has been done in the past to reduce the losses from disease among African stock by the establishment of numerous Veterinary Centers, the provision of free medicines and vaccines, and the initiation of dipping schemes for the control of tick-borne diseases. The response to these efforts has been variable. In many places there has been opposition to dipping schemes for which the people had to pay a small fee, and as recently as in 1958 the Iringa dipping scheme had to be finally closed down because of the mass noncooperation of the people. On the other hand there has been increased interest in anti-tick measures in the Lake and Western Provinces, and in many districts a former indifference is being replaced by an awakening interest in the provision of free vaccines.

TABLE 19   Suggested Scale of Provision of Watering Points for Cattle

Type of Installation and Year	Number of Installations	Capital Cost	Number of Animals Watered
		(£)	
Reservoirs and Tanks [a]			
1958/59	10	30,000	12,500
1963/64	15	45,000	18,750
1968/69	50	150,000	62,500
Boreholes			
1958/59	20	40,000	20,000
1963/64	30	60,000	30,000
1968/69	40	80,000	40,000
Piped and Other Supplies			
1958/59	20	50,000	25,000
1963/64	30	75,000	37,500
1968/69	40	100,000	50,000
All Types			
1958/59		120,000	57,500
1963/64		180,000	86,250
1968/69		330,000	152,500

[a] Some of the reservoirs would also provide water for irrigation. Capital costs shown are the part of the total allocated to livestock supply.
SOURCE: Mission figures.

While it is desirable to increase facilities for disease control, the prime task is to promote increased use and appreciation of these facilities.

The following operations, envisaged by the Veterinary Department, appear to the Mission to deserve early attention:

a. Expansion of the existing scheme whereby financial assistance to cover the cost of dipping or spraying facilities to control tick-borne diseases is given to the Native Authorities in districts where stock owners apply for such assistance. Under a Colonial Development and Welfare Scheme which comes to an end in 1960, £ 12,500 a year has been provided for this purpose. The Veterinary Department estimates that provision in the capital budget of £ 15,000 a year will be required over the next ten years, to finance in part 100 dipping centers.

b. The construction of permanent crushes for the accommodation of cattle receiving inoculations against such diseases as rinderpest, anthrax and blackquarter, or antrycide treatment against trypanoso-miasis. The construction of a further 100 crushes a year over the next ten years is desirable; it would cost £ 20,000 a year. If present trials of a portable type of crush prove it to be satisfactory, this cost will be somewhat reduced.

c. The provision of quarantine stations at strategic points on the stock trade routes. There are no quarantine stations on these routes at present. About ten stations would ultimately be desirable. The most urgent requirement is for three stations on the routes by which cattle enter the Northern and Tanga Provinces from Kenya, primarily for the control of foot-and-mouth disease. The capital cost would be of the order of £ 10,000-20,000 per station. Allowance for this item has been made in the program to improve stock routes (see p. 148). Annual operating costs would be about £ 1,200 for each station.

Improved Care of Cattle. There is a general need for improvement in the present low standards of animal husbandry, particularly in the matter of provision of dry season feed, the correction of mineral imbalance or deficiencies by the provision of licks, the better housing of stock and the provision of bedding for calves. Obviously most of these points have reference to stock kept in the arable areas rather than in the drier ranching zones. The need here is for continuation of existing extension efforts, but with the changes of methods and organization suggested in Chapter 5 (pp. 112-13).

Selection and Improvement of Stock. At present the average growth rate, mature weight and quality of African cattle are all poor. This, of course, is partly due to the relatively severe conditions in many areas, to poor management and husbandry and to lack of disease control; but it is also partly due to the inherent poor average quality of the stock.

In the past, virtually no attempt at selection and improvement has been made by African cattle owners. There was no culling of poor heifers or castration of scrub bulls, and breeding was therefore indiscriminate. Of late, however, efforts of the Veterinary Department to get poor bulls castrated have begun to meet with some response. For some years, also, the Veterinary Department has bred and made available for sale a limited number of improved heifers and has placed improved bulls at stud at veterinary centers. At present, however, neither the numbers of improved cattle available for distribution nor the interest shown by the Africans are adequate to effect any major improvement in the average quality of the stock.

The production and distribution of earlier-maturing and more productive stock will only be effective if it is accompanied by parallel improvements in pasture management, animal husbandry and disease control. At present, these latter improvements are of more urgent importance than the breeding of better stock; but in the long run the availability of more productive types of cattle will be an important factor in the successful development of improved beef production or of dairying in both the pastoral and the arable areas. The Veterinary Department should continue its work of selection and breeding. In addition, the partnership breeding ranches proposed later in this chapter should be of great value as cattle improvement centers.

Comprehensive Improvement Schemes

Government provision of water or tsetse clearing should be used to the greatest possible degree as an inducement to secure improved management of cattle and pasture. Effort should be concentrated in particular places in the main cattle areas, where there is the best chance of securing adoption of a range of improvements allowing higher calving rates, lower calf mortality, better quality of stock, better condition of the animals and improved pasture. If a few communities in different parts of the territory can be thoroughly convinced of the benefit of the necessary combinations of measures and practices, then these communities can be used as demonstrations to others.

Introduction of Cattle into Certain Arable Areas

There are certain arable areas in Tanganyika which would benefit by the introduction of more cattle, provided that they were integrated with crop husbandry in the farming system. This is particularly so in the Southern Province, where few stock are kept at present. The possibility of promoting mixed farming in such areas is worthy of exploration.

PARTNERSHIP CATTLE RANCHING

So important is African cattle keeping on the traditional pattern, in terms of numbers of persons and areas of land involved, that its improvement clearly justifies some considerable government effort. However, large and rapid results are not to be expected. In many areas, the adoption of methods based on the view of livestock as a cash crop would amount to no less than a social revolution. With the spread of the monetary economy this revolution is inevitable; it can no doubt be accelerated by measures of persuasion and inducement; but experience shows that the pace remains slow at best.

To take early advantage of the possibilities of increased beef production in Tanganyika, the Mission recommends further establishment of organized, large-scale ranches under expert management. Such ranches, established in selected localities on land cleared from tsetse and provided with water supplies, would have several advantages:

a. By expert management and supervision of the tenant cattle keepers, efficient land use and a good level of productivity should be achieved. This would enable a reasonable return to be obtained on the capital invested, and yield a fair living to the tenants.

b. A proportion of the land could be used for the growing out and fattening of immature cattle purchased from the African areas, thus reducing the great waste which at present occurs from the slaughter of large numbers of young cattle in drought years.

c. A part of the land could also accommodate a breeding herd entirely under expert control. This would have three advantages. First, it should provide the enterprise with a profitable nucleus in the establishment of a really well-run herd of improved quality cattle from which production would be maximal. Secondly, from this herd it would be possible to provide the African tenants with improved heifers and with the service of selected bulls. Thirdly, the supply of marketable steers from the breeding herd could help to even out the supply of stock to the butchers and canners, by off-setting the fluctuations resulting from the fact that the off-take of immatures from the African areas is abundant in drought years but more limited in good years.

Development of Three Existing Ranches

It is suggested that the first step should be to provide the Tanganyika Agricultural Corporation (TAC) with the additional capital needed for the full development of the already partly developed and partly stocked Kongwa, Ruvu and Mkata ranches. The first two are already under the management of the Corporation, while the last is being run, so far as it is possible to do so with the very limited funds available, by the Veterinary Department. These three areas, totaling approximately 388,000 acres, are all suitable for ranching, and are conveniently situated not too far from the fresh meat market and the cannery at Dar es Salaam, with which they have good road and rail communications.

In these three ranches there is the possibility of carrying out a useful experiment, and at the same time making a profit. The present position is that none of these ranches is fully developed or fully stocked, so that the overhead charges per head of stock reared are higher than they should be. At Kongwa a considerable proportion of the land cleared is not at present being used, and as it is steadily reverting to bush, much of the initial investment in clearing will be lost unless the ranch is fully developed. Similarly, if the Veterinary Department, for lack of funds, were to close down at Mkata, or reduce the scale of its operations, then at least a part of the investment already made would be lost. The further investment suggested would increase efficiency and profits, check loss of existing investments and at the same time be of considerable benefit to African tenants and to Africans elsewhere, from whom immatures would be purchased.

Present operations at *Kongwa* and *Ruvu* are described in Annex IV. The Mission recommends: that operations at Kongwa should be progressively concentrated on the breeding and rearing of stock from the herds on the ranch, and that buying in and fattening of immatures should be tapered off as breeding activities are developed to full capacity; and that Ruvu should for the time being continue to concentrate on purchase and fattening of immatures, but that a partial switch to breeding activities should be considered when the ranch is fully developed. *Mkata* is a ranching area totaling 220,000 acres, which has been run by the Veterinary Department for the primary purpose of breeding improved Zebu stock for the benefit of the African cattle industry; but immatures have also been purchased and fattened on the ranch, the revenue derived from them being used to finance the breeding activities. Funds available for Mkata have been limited, and it is far from fully developed or stocked. The Mission considers that it would be appropriate to transfer the Mkata ranch from the Veterinary Department to the TAC, which would become responsible for building it up to full capacity. Initially, at any rate, it might be considered advisable to continue to run Mkata partly with improved cattle bred on the ranch and partly with immatures for fattening. When fully developed its total carrying capacity would not be less than 20,000 head, so that 10,000 immatures might be carried, giving an off-take of 3,000 per annum, together with a breeding herd of 2,500 yielding about 2,125 calves per annum; these would take three and a half years to reach slaughter weight.

It appears that these ranching operations should be sufficiently profitable to justify borrowing as necessary to cover the costs of expansion. It is considered that a further investment of £ 75,000 in small sums over a fairly long period of time would be required for the full development of ranching at Kongwa, and that £ 25,000 may be required to develop the Ruvu ranch to full capacity. No similar estimate is available for Mkata.

Establishment of Additional Ranches

It would be wise to await some results from this experiment before attempting the further development of partnership ranches. The building up of further suitable breeding herds could in any case only be done gradually and could probably be most satisfactorily and economically achieved by drawing breeding stock from the Kongwa and Mkata ranches after they had become fully stocked. Thus for the next five years at least, effort would be concentrated on building up the ranches at Kongwa, Mkata and Ruvu.

A preliminary calculation suggests the possibility of setting up additional breeding ranches as self-liquidating ventures under the TAC or some other public corporation, even if they have to be financed by borrowing on "hard" terms (see Annex VII, pp. 438-41). Thus, provided that demand for beef appears adequate, it will be advantageous to set up further breeding ranches as adequate supplies of breeding stock become available.

There is rather more doubt concerning the prospective finances of additional ranches for the fattening of immatures. It seems that such ranches, regarded as self-contained business operations, would be unlikely to earn surpluses sufficient to service debt equal to their capital cost. However, the Mission considers that their real value to the livestock sector of Tanganyika as a whole justifies the establishment of a certain number of partnership operations for fattening of immatures. It is possible that the total return to public finances, including all forms of return by way of increased tax receipts, would cover the cost of borrowing to establish these (see Annex VII, pp. 435-38).

The economics of ranches for fattening immatures should be further investigated, with due attention to the additional income put into the pockets of African cattle keepers from whom immatures are bought, and the effects of these purchases on the development of African cattle keeping. If further investigation confirms the Mission's preliminary judgment that these ranches are a good investment, then a number should be set up on suitable sites as near as possible to major areas of African cattle keeping.

If new fattening ranches were to be established and operated by the TAC or some other public corporation, then the corporation would probably have to be subsidized in some form, possibly by way of a loan on easy terms to finance establishment of the ranch. As an alternative, such ranches might be operated by the Veterinary Department.

It is contemplated that both types of ranch, breeding and fattening, should be run on a partnership basis, the whole or part of the herds being managed by African tenants or partners, but with central provision of capital, services and skilled supervision. Eighty thousand acres appear to be the minimum economic unit which, allowing for a carrying capacity of one beast to ten acres, would support the overheads entailed in expert supervision and management.

RESEARCH

The Veterinary Department has a research program covering a number of aspects of animal husbandry. The chief inadequacy in the present program of research related to livestock appears to be in questions of pasture improvement and management. Under the recent reorganization of the research activities of the Ministry of Natural Resources, responsibility for pasture research was transferred to the Department of Agriculture. In view of the fact that problems of pasture improvement and management are likely to be important in relation to ranching development, it is desirable that more attention be given to this subject.

In addition to the pasture research of the Ministry of Natural Resources, further work has been done at a pasture research station maintained by the TAC at Kongwa. This station has now largely solved the immediate problems relating to bush regeneration and the establishment of perennial pasture species on the ranch. The results and experience obtained appear to have wide application over the central areas of the territory. The maintenance of a research station of this kind is hardly an appropriate activity for the TAC, and the

Mission proposes that the station should be taken over by the Government.

Another aspect of livestock research which merits further attention is the collection of information on the characteristics of the African cattle population. Present figures of sex and age composition of the cattle population, calving rates and mortality rates are little more than general impressions, and, when compared with the rate of increase of the total population as shown by livestock census counts, involve some rather obvious mutual inconsistencies. In attempting to assess the contribution to the economy made by livestock, it has consistently been found that exports of hides and skins are surprisingly small by comparison with the numbers of deaths and slaughters, as estimated by comparing the number of calves which may be supposed to be born with the apparent increase of the total cattle population. More accurate knowledge of calving rates, mortality rates, composition of the cattle population and rates of take-off would help to define the problem of improvement of African cattle keeping. Comparison of the figures for African herds with those for breeding herds under skilled management might in time prove of some persuasive power in demonstrating the shortcomings of present African methods. It is therefore desirable that the estimates of the relevant magnitudes made by veterinary officers should be checked for internal consistency and plausibility, and that veterinary officers should be encouraged to improve upon their present estimates.

DAIRYING

The per capita consumption of fresh milk by the African population is very low. Milk supplies to towns are expensive, of poor quality and subject to seasonal fluctuations. There thus appears to be scope for efforts to improve the milk supplies to the towns. It is with this object that a program of dairying development should obviously begin. In many rural areas, fair quantities of milk must already be available for home consumption; and in any case, the problems of distribution to the widely scattered consumers in such areas are formidable. One exception is the Kilimanjaro-Meru area, where the dense population of rural coffee growers presents a considerable potential market.

Little is at present known about the economics of milk production by African farmers, and further investigation is clearly desirable. It is nevertheless possible to make certain suggestions of methods whereby African as well as European milk production might be advantageously increased.

The Market

The figures presented in Table 20 show that the per capita consumption of fresh milk by the total population of four out of a group of five major towns is only about one tenth of a pint per day. Iringa stands out as an exception, but with a consumption of only about one sixth of a pint per day. These figures cannot be regarded as indicating with any precision the average milk consumption of African town-dwellers. On the one hand, the figures are averages of African consumption and the certainly very much higher per capita consumption of non-African town-dwellers. On the other hand there is an appreciable unrecorded direct producer-to-consumer African milk trade in some of the towns. Nevertheless, the figures may be taken as a firm indication that the average consumption of milk by Africans in the towns is very low. No figures are available for rural consumption; but although it might reach as much as one pint per person per day in a very few districts, such as Kwimba, such areas are very limited; and in those provinces and districts where there are very few stock, milk consumption must be negligible.

Although it is generally considered that the nutritional status of the adult African population is fair, it is known that the diet is commonly deficient in protein, calcium and certain vitamins. It would appear therefore that an increase in milk consumption would be

TABLE 20   Milk Consumption in Five Towns

Town	Population	Milk Supplies	Price		Consumption
			Bulk	Bottled	
		(gals. per day)	(cents per pint)		(pints per head per day)
Dar es Salaam	129,000	1,650		80	0.10
Tanga	38,000	500		65	0.10
Mwanza	20,000	200		75	0.08
Dodoma	13,000	150			0.09
Iringa	10,000	200	50	60	0.16

beneficial. This applies particularly to children. Children are usually breast fed for as long as possible, but between four to eight months after birth the supply of breast milk does not meet the child's requirements and is usually supplemented by pap made from the protein-deficient staple food, which may be maize, sorghum, millet, bananas, cassava or sweet potatoes. It is also known that deficiency diseases caused by lack of proteins, vitamins and calcium are common among school-age children.

The main reasons for the low consumption of fresh milk, at any rate as far as the urban population is concerned, are as follows:

a. The high price of milk in relation to the income of the average African. In the towns milk prices range from 50 to 80 cents per pint while the income of the majority of Africans is only Shs. 2/- to Shs. 3/- per day.

b. The poor quality of much of the milk. Fresh milk has to be boiled, making it somewhat unpalatable, and will not keep. It is consequently less popular than tinned milk.

c. Irregularity in the supply of milk due to the big seasonal fluctuation in its production and to the poor distribution services.

Non-African Dairying

Non-African milk production is mainly in the two parts of Tanganyika which are best suited to dairying, namely the Arusha-Moshi area of the Northern Province and parts of the Southern Highlands Province, particularly the Iringa district. There are also small-scale non-African dairying activities elsewhere, particularly in the neighborhood of Dar es Salaam.

Arusha and Moshi Districts. On the alienated lands of the highland parts of Arusha and Moshi Districts, conditions are very suitable for keeping of grade European breeds of dairy cattle, or of European breeds crossed with Zebu; and since 1955 farmers have been tending to switch from the production of cereals, the prices of which have fallen, to milk production.

The farmers of this area are not at present receiving an economic return for the bulk of their milk; but it is considered that if steps were taken to organize the collection, processing and distribution of milk, the farmers could again receive an economic return and production could be doubled. Proposals to this effect have been put forward by a recent FAO-UNICEF Mission.[2]

The expansion of European milk production in Arusha-Moshi, although hampered by shortage of capital and lack of adequate marketing facilities, was encouraged by payment of a guaranteed minimum price of Shs. 2/- per gallon for approximately twelve months by the Tanganyika Farmers Association. Herds have been increased by the purchase of dairy animals from Kenya, and production from about eighty European farms has now reached about 5,000 gallons per day. Unfortunately, however, the Tanganyika Farmers Association has been forced to drop the guarantee, since the price of Shs. 2/- per gallon involved it in a certain loss, and the farmers are at present receiving an uneconomic return for the bulk of their milk. One of the difficulties is the seasonal fluctuation in milk production. In the dry season the limited production can readily be disposed of as fresh milk in the towns of Arusha and Moshi and to the African coffee growers on Kilimanjaro and Meru, but in the rainy season there is a surplus which realizes a lower price because it has to be processed into butter, ghee or cheese. This difficulty is accentuated by the fact that there is no central processing plant. Part of the wet season milk surplus, or skim milk derived from it, might be utilized if the pig industry were developed.

The scheme aims at developing milk production on both European and African farms by improving facilities for collection, processing and marketing; and at providing a stable market by improving distribution and by making available good quality, low price milk to the African population. In addition it proposes that free or subsidized milk should be supplied to school children as a counterpart of any UNICEF assistance.

The main proposals are:

a. A dairy farmers' cooperative should be formed which should:
   i. Coordinate the collection and transportation of milk from the farms. This would necessitate the erection of a collection and cooling station at Dutch Corners.
   ii. Erect a pasteurizing and processing plant at Arusha (where only a small cooling and pasteurizing plant at present exists) for bottling of milk, for sale of pasteurized milk in bulk con-

[2] FAO, *Report to the Government of Tanganyika on a Dairy Survey of the Arusha/Moshi Area*, 1959.

tainers and for processing surplus milk or surplus butter fat into butter, cheese, etc.

iii. Make arrangements for the Express Dairy to be utilized on an agency basis for pasteurization of milk at its plant in Moshi and for the distribution of milk and dairy produce in that area.

iv. Erect and operate five distribution depots on the slopes of Kilimanjaro.

It should be noted that about 60 percent of the milk is produced in the Arusha district whereas about 75 percent of the consumers are the somewhat scattered coffee growers living on Kilimanjaro in the Moshi district. The intention is that all fluid milk sold in both areas would be standardized to not more than 3 percent butter fat. Milk would be separated daily at Arusha and a portion of the resulting skim milk sent in bulk to Moshi, where it would be mixed with whole milk from the Moshi area to produce standardized milk for distribution in Moshi and on Kilimanjaro. The butter fat would be manufactured into butter or ghee at the Arusha plant, which would also process all daily and seasonal surplus of milk into butter or ghee, and would distribute standardized fluid milk in the Arusha and Meru areas.

b. A Milk Board should be established to maintain over-all coordination of production and marketing, to register producers and other handlers of milk, to establish quality standards, to develop a pricing system, and to consider ways and means of expanding consumption and of increasing milk production by African farmers.

c. Government should undertake:

i. To secure technical assistance to help in market development, administration, and dairy plant management.

ii. To develop training facilities for dairy production, extension workers and dairy plant technicians.

iii. To support the development of the industry by upgrading of roads in both the producing and consuming areas.

iv. Possibly, to purchase or subsidize dairy products for free distribution.

The estimated capital required to be obtained locally is £65,000, made up of £40,000 for buildings and plant and £25,000 for working capital. It is likely that the Tanganyika Farmers Association would be prepared to find the working capital and to borrow the remainder, the latter possibility requiring a government guarantee to a bank.

It is likely that UNICEF would be prepared to provide the capital for equipment, the cost being repaid with interest over a period of ten or fifteen years by the issue of free or subsidized milk.

Although details of how to finance and implement this scheme have not yet been fully settled, there is a good prospect of its being put into operation. The scheme appears to be workable. However, the following points should be borne in mind:

a. There is no doubt that present milk production could readily be doubled from the European farms alone; but, although there is excess capacity at present, this would require some further capital investment in buildings, fencing, stock, etc. It is unlikely that many of the farmers would have the capital required. However, it should be possible for them to obtain it by loans from the Land Bank (or its successor agency).

b. The UNICEF report estimates that the retail price of the standardized 3 percent butter fat content milk would be 45 cents per pint. It does not seem certain that this price would be low enough to increase consumption amongst the Chagga coffee growers to the extent required to absorb a large proportion of a doubled production. In 1957-58 the proceeds of coffee sales distributed by the KNCU to approximately 40,000 members totaled £ 1,865,451 or rather under £ 47 per member, equivalent to an income of Shs. 2/56 per day. This is not very much from which to purchase one-and-a-half pints of milk per day at 45 cents per pint. On the other hand, should milk production exceed the requirements of the Arusha-Moshi area, it is very probable that a further market could be found in Tanga Province.

c. If the Government should be involved in the purchase or subsidization of milk for free issue to school children, some difficulty might arise from the fact that this service was being provided for only two districts in the whole of Tanganyika, and two of the highest income districts at that.

Iringa District. In the Iringa District of the Southern Highlands Province, the number of dairy cattle kept has also recently increased; present production of fresh milk is about 350 gallons per day of which about 200 gallons is sold in Iringa Township and 150 gallons sent to Dodoma and Dar es Salaam. Farmers have been endeavoring to cooperate in the organization of milk collection and marketing and in the operation of a small pasteurizing plant, but so far with only limited success. There is certainly a dairy potential in this area, but conditions are not as good as they are in the Northern Province.

The severe dry season of six months makes seasonal fluctuations in supply a major problem, the pastures are rather poor and there is an indication of a mineral deficiency.

African Milk Production

Milk is produced to some extent from African-owned cows in all cattle keeping districts, but it is impossible to estimate how much is produced. It can be taken for granted that production is low, since the cows only calve about once in two years and many of them are not milked at all, while the yield per cow is small: The FAO Mission on milk development possibilities in East Africa (1958) suggested that in all probability it does not exceed 75 gallons per lactation, but the Mission believes that it is more likely to be from 80-100 gallons. An unknown quantity of this milk is used for home consumption. A further unknown quantity is sold in local village and township markets by producer-retailers or by middlemen who collect it from the farms. Estimates of the amount of this milk are only available for a few towns. A further quantity, approximately 3,100,000 gallons in 1958, is processed into ghee, producers receiving 10 cents per pint and the skim milk being returned to them. Ghee production has been well established for many years, particularly in the Lake, Western, Central and Southern Highlands Provinces, where a large number of cooperative or Native Authority creameries are in existence. Production has, however, been declining—to, say, 44,472 tins of 36 lb. in 1958, compared with 76,034 tins in 1952, presumably because the financial return to the producer is small and he often has to carry his milk daily anything up to seven miles to a creamery.

Over the dryer areas, constituting something like half of the territory, conditions are more suitable for beef production than for dairying, and in many of the wetter arable areas it may well be that a greater return is obtainable from crop production than from milk. Consequently, and despite the fact that there are certainly areas where a combination of dairy cattle and crop production in a mixed farming system would appear to be a highly desirable objective, we agree with the FAO Mission that a study of the economics of African milk production is needed before it can be decided whether, and where, an expansion of this activity is desirable. We also agree that in the meantime efforts should be made to make the most economic use of available milk supplies from African farmers, particularly those in the neighborhood of some of the towns, where some encouragement of increased production might also be given. The main requirements for this purpose are as follows:

a. The development of the fresh milk market, which would give a greater return to the farmer than ghee production and would result in his having a greater interest in dairying.

b. The improvement of milk collection and marketing facilities. At present these are almost totally unorganized, the milk either being brought in and sold by producer-retailers or collected with varying degrees of inefficiency by retailers. What is required is the provision of milk collecting and pasteurizing centers to which the milk is delivered by the producer or to which it is brought by vehicles which pick it up from the producers at collection points on the roads. An example is the milk collection and pasteurizing plant established at Mariakani in Kenya; this was financed by two African District Councils, is run by the Veterinary Department under their general supervision, and supplies about half a million gallons a year to Mombasa.

c. Improvements in simple dairy hygiene are necessary in order to avoid wastage of milk which goes bad before reaching the collecting center, or the delivery of poor quality milk to the consumers. This is mainly a matter of avoiding contamination of the milk during milking, and of ensuring the provision of suitable containers, their cleanliness and their protection against dirt and flies until they reach the collecting center. It would require an increase in simple extension activities among the producers. Subsidiary and longer-term requirements for the improvement of African dairying would be the provision of more water supplies, better disease control, and breeding stock of improved milk-producing capacity.

Supply of Milk to the Towns

It would be impracticable greatly to increase the supply of whole milk in many areas, not only because of the distances over which milk would have to be transported and the bad condition of the roads, but also because of the problem presented by the large seasonal variations in milk production. At the same time there is available a large quantity of skim milk, a by-product of production of butter and ghee. Much of this skim milk, which is of high nutritive value, is at present wasted.

A means of making cheaper milk available to Africans in the towns would be the preparation of a toned, or standardized milk of, say, not more than 3 percent butter fat but with its original content of non-fat solids, or possibly an enhanced content. A 3 percent butter fat content is adequate to provide a product of high nutritive value; and, of course, the protein and calcium content would be equal to, or greater than, that of whole milk. Such a standardized milk would be produced by:

a. Separating from whole milk a part of the cream for manufacture into butter or ghee;

or

b. Adding to whole milk a preparation of fluid skim milk derived from the manufacture of butter or ghee at another center;

or

c. Reconstituting dried skim milk and adding to whole milk.

Method (c) would be the most effective means of using the present surplus of skim milk. Dried skim milk resulting from processing surplus milk during the rainy season at, say, Iringa, could be stored and transported to Dar es Salaam for toning purposes. This would augment the inadequate supplies available during the dry season. This method, however, would necessitate the installation of suitable drying plants.

Supply of Milk to Dar es Salaam. The milk supplied to Dar es Salaam at present averages about 1,650 gallons per day, equivalent to the very low consumption of about 0.1 pints per day per head of the population. Moreover, the supply is subject to considerable seasonal variations. Milk is sold at 80 cents per pint, an extremely high price, particularly in relation to the low average income of the Africans.

The FAO Mission (1958) emphasized the difficulties of milk production around Dar es Salaam and stated that they must inevitably result in high costs of production. It considered that the possibility for increasing production in the area is limited. This is generally true. But it should be noted that a large part of the present supply comes from 47 companies and individuals keeping the dairy cattle in or near the Municipality. Only four of these producers rely solely on dairying for a livelihood, and the majority are thoroughly inefficient.

Although the conditions in the Dar es Salaam area are far from ideal, they by no means rule out profitable dairying. This has been demonstrated by the Veterinary Department, which for some years ran a government dairy farm at Temeke. This farm produced about 50,000 gallons of milk per annum for Dar es Salaam, at a production cost of rather less than 50 cents per pint, and showed a small profit. The farm was closed down in 1958, since the Government did not wish to compete with local enterprise; but in view of the present inefficiency and high-cost production, it seems a pity that it was not maintained. There seems little doubt that dairying could be profitably carried on in the area if undertaken with skill and good management. It could most probably be advantageously combined with other enterprises such as coconut production, pig keeping and fruit and vegetable growing.

On the other hand, available land near Dar es Salaam is probably rather limited and the possibility of alienating such land at the present time is likely to be small. There is suitable land at Ruvu, about 50 miles from Dar es Salaam. This land was alienated with the object of increasing milk production for Dar es Salaam; but the farmers there are said to have found beef production more profitable, mainly because of the transport costs on milk.

There would be no point in increasing the supply of milk to Dar es Salaam unless the price could be reduced to a level which would considerably increase African consumption and at which fresh milk could compete with canned milk. Although the present price of canned milk is from 76 to 83 cents per pint, it has advantages in that it is sweetened, does not require boiling and keeps for three days. The most promising possibility of increasing the supply of milk to Dar es Salaam seems, as suggested above, to be to expand production at Iringa or elsewhere and to market a low-priced toned or reconstituted spray-dried skim milk, which could be distributed from bulk containers. This would necessitate the erection of a milk processing plant and of facilities for drying skim milk at Iringa or elsewhere, and the provision of reconstituting equipment, milk cans, etc. at Dar es Salaam. Before such an investment could be contemplated, it would be necessary for the whole matter to be investigated by dairy experts.

Such an investigation appears to be well worth while. Dar es Salaam is easily the largest urban African market for milk. If economic means of increasing supply and consumption in Dar es Salaam could be found, they could then be applied to other townships. It is suggested that FAO-UNICEF might be asked to send a Mission similar to the one which recently visited the Arusha-Moshi area.

CHAPTER **8** *A PROGRAM FOR IRRIGATION AND FLOOD CONTROL*

A considerably enlarged program of irrigation development and flood control works occupies a prominent place among the Mission's recommendations. Such a program not only would open up new areas for cultivation or increase the productive potential of certain areas already cultivated, but also may provide the means whereby cultivators may be persuaded to adopt improved farming systems.

The first part of this chapter outlines the program which the Mission recommends should form the basis for immediate preparatory work. The second part of the chapter is concerned with the nature of the preparatory work required and with the administration of schemes.

OUTLINE OF A PROGRAM

Present Extent of Irrigation

Irrigation is practiced only on a limited scale in Tanganyika at present. Much of such irrigation as exists is on non-African estates, but there is also a fair number of small irrigated areas farmed by Africans.

On certain estates, techniques of irrigation are highly developed. The largest irrigation scheme, on the Arusha-Chini estate of the Tanganyika Planting Company south of Moshi, grows 7,500 acres of irrigated sugar cane, and employs some 3,000 laborers, a striking example of the contribution which can be made by irrigation to the economic life of Tanganyika and its population.

The extent of African irrigation is not accurately known, but a number of small irrigated areas are found on the slopes of Mount Kilimanjaro and Mount Meru, and throughout the country near perennial streams and in valleys. In the Weru Weru catchment area near Moshi over 400 furrows divert water from the river and its tributaries. Also in the Usambara Mountains, a large number of furrows conveying water from streams to irrigate land are found. It is estimated that about 25,000 acres are irrigated by Africans in Tanga Province. Irrigation is also carried on from a number of small dams in the Western Province. Crops grown include coffee, paddy, maize and onions. African irrigation methods are generally primitive and result in considerable waste of water.

The eventual possibilities of irrigation development are somewhat limited by the restricted amounts of water available over much of the territory. It appears that irrigation and flood control together can make available for cultivation rather less than a further 2 percent of the total area of the country, or about 4 million acres. Much of the irrigable land is found in large flat valleys in the eastern part of the territory. Here, flood control will usually be a necessary prelude to irrigation development. Perhaps 4 percent of the area to the southeast of a line Mbeya-Tanga could be brought into use by a combination of flood control and irrigation. To the northwest of the line, numerous opportunities exist for irrigation development in small schemes, in many places in combination with the provision of rural water supplies. Perhaps 1 percent of this part of the territory could be irrigated. It must be emphasized that the figures given are very rough. The way in which they have been calculated is shown in Annex III (pp. 399-401).

Scale of Program

The Mission proposes that preparations should be put in hand forthwith for a program of irrigation and flood control works to reach an annual development of 25,000 acres a year from about 1969/70. It considers that a program of this size is needed to make a sufficiently appreciable contribution to Tanganyika's development, while at the same time it should be feasible to build up the staff and knowledge required for such a program.

To undertake irrigation and flood control works on this scale, it will be necessary to build up a considerably increased specialist staff and to make extensive preparations. While this is being done, the extent of properly designed capital works which can be executed will necessarily be somewhat limited. Thus the Mission recommends a cautious program in the first years, reaching not more than 7,500 acres per year in 1965/66. In the period from 1965/66 to 1969/70, the acreage under construction should be increased from 7,500 to the full 25,000 acres per year.

Location of Projects

Although there are big areas suitable for development as unified projects, for instance the Rufiji Valley or the middle flat plain of the Ruvu Basin, the Mission recommends the spread of development over different parts of Tanganyika. The overriding factor in planning a program of irrigation and flood control must be the financial considerations discussed below and in Annex VII. However, subject to these overriding considerations, attention should also be given to such aims as:

a. improvement or diversification of food supply in areas where the present supply is inadequate in quantity or variety;

b. relief of overcrowding, with its attendant risks of destruction of fertility and erosion;

c. demonstration at points distributed throughout the territory of irrigation methods and the advantages to be secured by their adoption.

Within this framework, development should be directed towards areas of high potential. Projects in areas of low potential, for instance alkaline and saline soils, tend to be costly and to give a lower return. The scope of the proposed program, 100,000 acres between 1965/66 and 1970/71 or $2\frac{1}{2}$ percent of the whole area for which irrigation or flood control development are technically feasible, makes it possible to concentrate first on the very best lands. On a longer-term view, also, the scarcity of water in many parts of Tanganyika leads to the conclusion that the best lands should be selected for development of water resources.

In Table 21 the Mission gives in very rough outline a possible program for irrigation and flood control. All these areas will provide opportunities for increased agricultural output. Many of the developments, especially those in the various river basins and valleys, are intended to be on a partnership basis. They will result in training of African farmers in better systems of farming. The proposed development in the Central, Western, Lake and Southern Provinces is especially directed towards production of a better food supply for the population. For all areas a gradual development is foreseen. The selection has also been influenced by specific factors which are related to population pressure and possibilities of future development. Drought hazards were also taken into consideration.

TABLE 21   Possible Areas of Irrigation and Flood Control
Development, 1965/66-1970/71

Upper Pangani Basin, near Moshi	20,000 acres	Irrigation
Upper Ruvu Basin, near Uluguru Mts.	20,000 acres	Irrigation
Kilombero Valley	5,000 acres	Flood Control (empoldering)
Rufiji Valley	5,000 acres	Flood Control (empoldering)
Bohoro and Pawaga Flats	10,000 acres	Irrigation
Central Province	15,000 acres	Irrigation
Western Province	10,000 acres	Irrigation
Lake and West Lake Provinces	10,000 acres	Irrigation
Southern Province	5,000 acres	Irrigation

SOURCE: In selecting areas of possible development, the Mission has made use of a
number of reports from earlier surveys and from recent investigations including
those in which FAO teams have participated (cf. Annex III). This information
was supplemented by discussions and field trips in the territory.

The role of irrigation in the Upper Pangani Basin and in the
Upper Ruvu Basin in relieving population pressure on the slopes of
neighboring highland areas has been stressed in Chapter 4. The
development in the Upper Ruvu Basin will also offer an opportunity
of exploring the possibilities of future development of the large areas
which are available for development in this basin.

Development of the Kilombero Valley and of the Rufiji Valley is
recommended, though in the first stage only on a restricted scale.
Over-all development of these very fertile and promising areas can
only be undertaken in very large projects. These projects would
involve the expenditure of over £ 10 million, and it is recommended
that this work be postponed until sufficient information has been
obtained on the desirable type of development. For 1965/66 to
1970/71, two flood control projects are foreseen as a start to investigating possibilities of future development.

Although the Bohoro and Pawaga Flats are not very favorably
located from the point of view of marketing conditions, the proposed
development aims at releasing population pressure on the highlands
between Iringa and Mbeya.

The distribution of acreages over the different areas is, of course,
very tentative. The possible distribution of such a program by

cropping patterns and degree of supervision is shown in Annex VII, pp. 433-34. It appears that the average annual gross product of such a program might be some £ 37 per acre, or 30 percent of average construction costs estimated at about £ 120 per acre (Annex VII, p. 434).

Special attention will have to be given to the need for the construction of new feeder roads or the improvement of existing roads in the various areas of potential development. The following examples may be given. For the development of the Upper Ruvu Basin the improvement of the road between Morogoro and Kisaki is highly desirable. The development of the Kilombero Valley will be greatly influenced by improvement of the road between Mikumi and Ifakara. Construction of feeder roads will also be necessary in areas of development in the Bohoro and Pawaga Flats.

Possible Investment Program

According to the programs for irrigation and flood control outlined in this chapter and that for rural water supplies considered in Chapter 7, capital expenditures for all forms of non-urban water development (other than for any major industrial projects) might develop as illustrated in Table 22. It must be stressed that these figures merely illustrate a reasonable future development of the scale of the program, financial circumstances allowing, and that they are not intended as a "plan" to be rigidly implemented.

TABLE 22　Possible Development of Capital Expenditure for Water Development

(£ '000)

Category	Budget Estimates 1960/61	1965/66	1969/70
Irrigation, etc.	176	900	3,000
Empoldering		90	150
Flood control, etc.		80	250
Rural water supplies	358	240	415
Other small water supplies		200	300
Total	534	1,510	4,115

SOURCE: *Estimates of Expenditure, 1960/61;* Mission estimates.

Staffing

In 1959 the staff of the Water Development and Irrigation Department numbered roughly 550 engineers, assistants and subordinates. Thirty staff members had higher degrees in engineering and there are 15 others in senior posts.

Total recurrent expenditure per senior official was in the neighborhood of £ 6,000 per year. This staff has been responsible for a program of capital works of some £ 300,000-400,000 and for part of the program of surveys and investigations. Its output, calculated in this way, is rather low. This is due to three factors. First of all, a great deal of the capital works consists of small projects involving much traveling and a high staff expenditure per project. Secondly, much time is taken up by training and supervision of subordinate staff. Thirdly, the department is still in the stage of collecting data and establishing its offices and administration.

Because present staff is large in relation to the present level of capital expenditures, it will not be necessary for current expenditures to increase by anything like so large a proportion as the increase envisaged for capital works. It is estimated that the capital program of £ 4 million in 1969/70 could be managed by a staff of some three times the present size (leaving out of account, for the moment, staff requirements for special investigations and surveys).

It will be necessary to increase staff well in advance of any considerable enlargement of capital expenditures, in order to be able to undertake the extensive preparatory work required before each phase of construction. In accordance with its proposal for the enlargement of the program of capital works, therefore, the Mission recommends that the indicated increase of water development staff should be largely undertaken, so far as practicable, over the next five years.

The present accounting procedure of the Government of Tanganyika is to charge the cost of water development staff and associated expenditures to the current budget, and then to make an allocation of part of these costs, according to formula, to capital works, the net total appearing in the current budget being adjusted accordingly. Assuming a continuance of something like present accounting procedures, the Mission assesses current expenditures (net) as building up from £ 359,000 provided in the budget estimates for 1960/61 to a peak of perhaps £ 1 million in 1965/66 and 1966/67. At this time, staff expenditures would be approaching their maximum, while the sums to be charged to capital works would still be on the increase. (The figure of £1 million is perhaps rather too high, since it may prove unnecessary to complete the full tripling of the staff by 1966/67.) With capital works at the target level of £4 million in 1969/70 and subsequent years, the charge on the current budget, similarly computed, would be of the order of £650,000 (see Annex VIII, p. 446).

In addition to the current and capital expenditures already outlined, a sum of the order of £150,000 a year will be required for special investigations and surveys. In accordance with present practice, this provision is put in the capital budget. It would allow for consultants to be assigned to preparatory surveys and design, and for acceleration of topographical surveys in areas where early development is envisaged.

Provision has also to be made for agricultural officers to carry on extension work on the development schemes. If the staff requirement is put at one senior staff member to 3,000 acres, and it is considered that rather over 100,000 acres will have been developed by 1970/71, then 30-35 senior staff members will be required by that year. Including assistants, travel costs and offices, the total expenditure might rise from £95,000 in 1965/66 to £125,000 in 1970/71. It has not been possible to make an estimate for staffing requirements and management costs in partnership schemes.

ECONOMICS OF IRRIGATION AND FLOOD CONTROL

Irrigation and flood control schemes involve rather high initial capital costs. A program on the scale suggested would necessitate a considerable increase of external borrowing, and would thus involve the Government in the obligation to service increased foreign debt. Unless the schemes lead to a total increase of government revenues sufficient to cover the increase of debt service, they cause a net deterioration of government finances.

These considerations lead to the conclusion that, as a general rule, irrigation and flood control projects should only be undertaken provided that the expected annual gross output on the projects is of the order of 30 percent of the original total capital cost. The actual ratio of gross output to construction costs which would be required in order to assure that total returns to public authorities cover service on additional debt needed to finance the projects will differ considerably according to the circumstances of particular projects (see Annex VII). Calculations of the type shown in Annex VII should be carried out in more refined form for various types of project in Tanganyika. Until this has been done, it is only possible to suggest a general rule of thumb of the kind just indicated. To be more specific, it may be suggested that only for exceptional reasons, such as relief of acute local hardship, should irrigation or flood control projects be carried out in which the expected value of the annual gross product is less than 20 percent of the original construction cost. In a territorial program of irrigation and flood control development, it will be necessary to look for average gross product of the order of 30 percent of construction costs. (These figures are subject to correction when more refined calculations have been carried out.)

Construction costs for irrigation schemes may be estimated at about £ 100-150 per acre, including cost of leveling the land (see Annex VII, pp. 425-26). Thus the minimum product which should normally be considered acceptable may be tentatively put at £ 20-30 per acre, according to the level of construction cost, and the desirable average product at something like £ 30-45 per acre. For the program of development suggested later in this chapter, average construction costs are estimated at about £ 120 per acre, thus indicating the need of an average product of the order of £ 36 per acre.

Estimates of the gross output which might be obtained on irrigated areas in Tanganyikan conditions are set out in Annex VII, pp. 432-34. They are based on certain assumptions concerning future development of suitable crop varieties and cultivation techniques. They suggest that paddy schemes will give gross output of £ 35-50 per acre. Other schemes with mainly cotton, oilseeds and maize should give a gross output of £ 20-40 per acre. A third type of scheme with mainly cotton, paddy and oilseeds should give gross output of £ 25-45 per acre.

In estimating the economics of irrigation schemes, the multipurpose character of many of them should be borne in mind. The smaller schemes will supply livestock with water and also provide water for domestic use. In many reservoirs, fisheries will be developed. Experience shows that in most areas fish are readily welcomed as an addition to diet. However, the contribution of fish to the financial result is rather small. Available data indicate the gross output of fish to be of the order of £ 3 per acre of reservoir (amounting, perhaps, to £ 1 per acre of irrigated land).

Direct Charges on Cultivators

The effect of a scheme on the public finances depends to a considerable degree on the size of the charge which can be made for water, land rent and any services provided to the cultivators. It is desirable that these charges should be at the highest levels consistent with attracting a sufficient number of cultivators: for the more the Government can secure in direct charges, the more the schemes for which it is feasible to borrow, and the faster irrigation development can progress.

However, the farmer has to develop his land in the scheme and to accustom himself to irrigation agriculture. Yields in the first years are not likely to reach the level eventually attainable. For this reason, a period of, say, three years should elapse before charges are assessed at the full rate. In schemes which are operated on a partnership basis, the collection of water charges will become a part of the general administration of the farms by the management of the scheme.

Size of Plots

At present it is envisaged that each farmer will cultivate 3 to 6 acres in the new irrigation schemes. The Mission considers that a slightly larger area per farmer is desirable. If a representative figure for annual gross output is taken at £ 35 an acre, water charges are reckoned at 20 percent and other money costs to the farmer at £ 8 an acre, then a five-acre holding would yield a money income of £ 100 a year, and a 10-acre holding of £ 200 a year.

Studies should be made of the economic size of holdings in new schemes. The possibility of a gradually increased degree of mechanized cultivation should be taken into account, and also the level of income which has to be envisaged for the future.

Economics of Small-Scale Flood Control (Empoldering) Schemes

On small flood control projects in areas of good rainfall, likely crops are oilseeds, cotton, maize, etc. It is considered that gross annual output would be some £ 15-20 per acre. This indicates a gross return of 25-35 percent on the estimated construction cost of £ 60 per acre. For such schemes it will be necessary to consider whether a direct charge on the cultivators is necessary to secure that public authorities are adequately compensated for the cost of borrowing to finance the projects, and, if so, how these charges could be administered.

PLANNING, PREPARATION AND SUPERVISION

Government experience to date in irrigation development in Tanganyika points to the need for careful and thorough preliminary investigation and preparation. The difficulties which have been encountered will be set out here, not in a spirit of criticism, but in order to emphasize the need for a planning stage before any large program of irrigation development is attempted.

In 1955 the Government started the construction of a number of irrigation schemes, in an attempt to increase the application of irrigation in Tanganyika. The Water Development Department became the Water Development and Irrigation Department, and funds up to roughly £ 100,000 per annum were made available.

Contrary to expectations, development has been slow, and the returns on the investment in terms of increased production appear often to have been smaller than they should have been. A number of problems of organization and technique have been encountered.

It struck the Mission that construction of many irrigation projects was undertaken before it had been fully ascertained that sufficient land of good quality and topography was under command. It is clear that irrigation development should be preceded by soil and topographical surveys to determine suitable sites. Departmental policy now rightly requires a land planning survey before a decision to execute a project is made.

In some projects, land tenure problems have arisen. The local land authorities have sometimes refused to allot available irrigated land to farmers from elsewhere. In some irrigation schemes much land was taken up by only a few farmers, resulting in holdings larger than could be properly tended and consequent neglect of the accurate cultivation practices which are needed under irrigated conditions.

Leveling of the land has normally been left to the farmers in the schemes. With their lack of equipment and their lack of knowledge of irrigation, these farmers have generally neglected this important aspect of the layout of the land. Even preliminary surveys to indicate the necessary leveling have frequently been neglected. In one scheme, however, the government department decided to do the leveling on behalf of the farmers. The results in themselves were very encouraging: crop yields improved and the number of farmers applying for land in the scheme rose above the number for which irrigated land was available. The cost of leveling was however very high.

Further difficulties have arisen from lack of knowledge of the crops to be grown under irrigated conditions in Tanganyika. The green irrigated areas in an otherwise dry country attract many insects and thus promote the spread of pests and diseases on a considerable scale. Water applications are not always well timed as there is no knowledge available of irrigation techniques.

In many schemes, however, trial fields have been laid out by the Department of Agriculture. From these fields the first indications can be obtained of crops to be grown and information will be obtained on cultivation and irrigation practices to be applied.

African Participation

In the matter of African participation, experience has varied from scheme to scheme. In schemes with a good layout of land and land of good quality, Africans have usually shown a keen interest in participating. In several of these schemes there are waiting lists of African farmers who have applied for land to be made available in future expansions. In some schemes the farmers are willing to do a lot of work to make the ridges round their land. Crop yields are often very satisfactory. However, it is noteworthy that in nearly every scheme the farmers maintain a foothold on agricultural land elsewhere, and continue to grow their traditional food crops outside the scheme. There have also been cases where African farmers have been slow to respond to the possibilities of the schemes. This lack of response arises from lack of traditional knowledge of irrigation farming and resistance to the idea of paying water charges. In some projects, crop yields have been low due to inadequate leveling of the land, and in some, African farmers were discouraged from taking up land because it had still to be cleared.

Surveys and Investigations

No further major irrigation schemes are at present envisaged by the Government. It is clear that the next few years should be spent largely in assimilating the experience already available, in careful planning of future development and in building up the staff for future programs.

The estimate that only about 2 percent of the total land area of Tanganyika can be brought under cultivation by irrigation and flood control projects indicates the need for careful over-all planning. Except in certain valleys in the eastern part of the territory, where water is abundant and land restricted, the situation generally prevails that water is definitely scarce. Careful planning and design are needed to ensure the best eventual use of scarce water.

Such planning necessitates the collection of many additional data.

Mapping. An acceleration of topographical and contour mapping is needed in connection with irrigation and flood control development as also for geological surveys, mineral prospecting, planning of lines of transport and communications, routing of power lines and for a number of other developmental purposes.

By the middle of 1959 about 40 percent of the total area of Tanganyika had been covered by topographical mapping, but not all of the maps are as yet complete in all details. The completed maps cover an appreciable part of the principal productive regions, but important areas, notably round Lake Victoria and in the Southern Province, remain to be surveyed and mapped. At present, only 4 percent of the territory is mapped each year: at this rate it will be 1975 at the earliest before adequate maps exist for the whole territory.

In the past, part of the cost of mapping has been met from CD&W funds, and free services have been provided from the United Kingdom by H.M. Survey.

The Mission urges that means should be found of accelerating progress in topographical mapping. The total capital cost of completing the coverage to the present standard of 1 in 50,000 with contours at vertical intervals of 50 feet is estimated at £ 2 million.

Hydrological Surveys. The next most basic need in planning water development is to continue the general appraisal of Tanganyika's water resources. Hydrological survey work was interrupted by the war, but has been somewhat accelerated in the last few years. Effort has been directed both to the collection and study of general information on hydrological conditions over major areas of the territory and also to the collection and analysis of data relevant to specific projects.

The two aims are of equal importance. Without general insight into the hydrology of the territory as a whole, it is impossible to plan soundly or to make efficient allocation to different areas of funds, staff and equipment. Without sufficient and detailed investigation of project areas, construction becomes a hazardous affair.

During the last five years the number of river-gauging stations has been increased from a bare 10 to over 275. Plans are in hand gradually to enlarge the study of silt loads in rivers and streams and of the quality of available water for domestic and irrigation purposes. The number of groundwater surveys is steadily increasing. An important contribution to general hydrological information can be made by analysis of the water balances of the increasing number of reservoirs, especially in the central and northwestern regions. Such analysis will result in valuable information on annual yield of catchment areas of different rainfall, topography, soils, vegetation and size. Thus it will contribute to general planning and to specific project planning. The Mission stresses the importance of these studies and hopes that the plans to undertake them will be put into effect.

Hydrological survey work is restricted by lack of funds and by shortage of trained observers, and also by the size of the territory, the inaccessibility of many places and also by the lack of topographical and contour maps of much of the territory.

The training of hydrometrists has been taken in hand. The Mission considers that this training deserves the full attention which is given to it by the responsible authorities.

Surveys of Three Major River Basins. The collection and processing of hydrological data in three major river basins in the eastern part of the territory has been greatly aided by the Food and Agriculture Organization of the United Nations (FAO). Under an agreement between the FAO and the Government of Tanganyika, a number of experts have studied, in collaboration with experts selected by the Government, the water resources and their possible development in the important basins of the Rufiji River, the Ruvu River and the Pangani River. Roughly half of the cost has been met by FAO, the remainder being largely covered from CD&W funds.

The Mission stresses that such hydrological surveys should be maintained even after the foreign experts leave the territory on termination of their assignments. Provision is made for the continuation of these surveys in the estimate of financial requirements set out earlier in this chapter.

Soil Surveys. The importance of soil surveys and further research into the water requirements of crops is stressed in Chapter 6. Such investigations are particularly important in relation to irrigation projects, where the returns to be secured by considerable investments are at stake. Although much knowledge has been made available in recent years about the irrigation potential of the Rufiji, Ruvu and Pangani basins, data on the suitability of the land for irrigation agriculture have still to be collected for a number of areas. Hydrological surveys appear to be ahead of soil surveys at present.

Trial Farms and Pilot Projects. If irrigation and flood control works are to be usefully stepped up to the scale of 25,000 acres a year by the end of the decade, then it will be necessary in the meantime to build up a body of knowledge and experience of the agricultural and organizational problems involved. This focuses attention on the major importance of irrigated trial farms and pilot projects. The history of irrigation trial farms in Tanganyika up to the present has been rather melancholy. It is now desirable to start up several more such farms in the various areas of potential irrigation development, avoiding so far as possible the difficulties encountered in the past.

The trial farms have all been in the Rufiji Basin. So far only one of them has contributed considerably to the increase of knowledge in the field of irrigation: this is the trial farm in the Bohoro Flats near Rujewa. The other trial farms, one in the Kilombero Valley and two in the Rufiji Valley, have encountered a number of difficulties. Two had to be closed down because of flooding. For the third, the design of a proper layout had taken several years, and at the time of the Mission's visit the future of this farm was insecure.

The largest trial scheme is located in the Bohoro Flats near the Mbarali River and bordering on the Rujewa trial farm. Its main purpose is to determine the organizational implications of irrigation on a large scale. It is intended eventually to establish supervised irrigation farming of 5,000 acres by African farmers.

Various organizational difficulties have been encountered in the design and construction of this project. It may, however, be expected that these difficulties will be overcome in the near future. A number of considerations have applied particularly in selecting the site of the scheme. Preference was given to a location near a main road and near a rather densely populated area, but there are still some doubts whether the scheme is well situated with regard to marketing of the crops. Nevertheless, the Mission is very definitely of the opinion that the completion of the scheme should get the full attention of the Government. The disadvantages of the scheme are of a minor nature compared with the advantages to be expected from a major scheme under which organized and supervised irrigation agriculture with African farmers can be tried out. It is estimated that the construction cost of the scheme will be about £ 300,000 to £ 400,000 for 5,000 acres, work being spread over three to four years.

A particularly important function of trial farms and pilot projects is the training of skilled irrigation men of all classes from laborer to manager.

Planning, Design and Preparation

Problems of Coordination. There has at times been a lack of coordination, in water development, between agricultural and civil engineering staff. Even while it remained in the Ministry of Natural Resources, the Water Development and Irrigation Department tended to form a rather isolated civil engineering enclave within its mainly agricultural surroundings. The danger of inadequate collaboration between agronomists and engineers appears to have been aggravated by the recent transfer of water development and irrigation from the former Ministry of Natural Resources (now Ministry of Agriculture and Co-operative Development) to the new Ministry of Lands, Surveys and Water.

The organizational problem involved in the distribution of departments between ministries will be discussed in Chapter 11. The point to be stressed here is the importance of adequate integration of engineering and agricultural functions. This applies not only in the definition of the objectives of the schemes, but also in the project design stage. Agronomists, specialized in irrigation, should be involved in the design of the projects, in order to secure a proper layout of the fields, a proper determination of water requirements, etc. The necessity of matching land classification surveys with hydrological and topographical surveys has already been sufficiently stressed. Integrated planning design should be promoted by establishing planning groups consisting of members of the design staff of the Water Development and Irrigation Department together with agronomists specially assigned by the Department of Agriculture.

General Appraisal of Projects. On the basis of preliminary investigations of projects, master plans should be designed and presented to the Land Use Committee. This Committee should ascertain that preliminary investigations have been sufficient to warrant a decision. The ultimate decision on the priority of the project should depend on firm criteria concerning the relationship of prospective benefits to costs. The nature of these criteria has been discussed on pp. 176 and 180-81. The objectives of schemes should be clearly defined. The appraisal of the objectives should include, within reasonable limits, the expectation that the population in the development area will react favorably to the execution of the project and be willing to cooperate.

In considering the feasibility of a project, it may often be desirable to investigate the costs and potential effects of alternative projects of different sizes or types.

Preparatory Steps. The first stage in execution of any project would be to secure the agreement of the local land authority or Area Land Board to the use of the land on the basis proposed.

Another important preparatory step, as already mentioned, is to ascertain whether enough farmers are interested in taking irrigated plots subject to the various conditions which have to be imposed. Every precaution should be taken to avoid expensive, large-scale schemes which fail because of lack of response.

Even if the initial reaction is favorable, some preliminary extension work will usually be desirable. An irrigation scheme will revolutionize farming in the area concerned. The population should be prepared for this revolution. Groups of farmers should be taken to visit other irrigation areas. Future participants should be prepared for the fact that they will be starting on a completely new type of land use. The economic consequences, including the necessity of paying water charges, should be made clear. It may also be appropriate to direct preliminary extension work to the preparation of cooperative ridging and plowing schemes, cooperative marketing, etc.

Supervision.

In existing irrigation schemes where cultivation is carried on by Africans, the Department of Agriculture has usually given much attention to the development of good agricultural practices. In many areas, field officers of the Department of Agriculture have been assigned the task of concentrating on the development of irrigation farming techniques. Such extension work is of great importance to the success of a scheme, through inducing the farmer to plant at the right time, to apply water correctly, to control weeds, etc.

In the Mbarali Scheme on the Bohoro Flats, irrigation development is in charge of the Tanganyika Agricultural Corporation. The Corporation will probably itself cultivate the land at first, and subsequently bring in African cultivators on a partnership basis or as tenants, in each case under strict supervision. Development of irrigation farming on a partnership basis may well be feasible in large projects, whereas a more limited type of supervision of independent cultivators will probably be appropriate in smaller schemes.

In the smaller schemes, it may well be desirable to implicate Native Authorities, as at present, or Area Land Boards in the necessary regulatory measures, the Central Government providing technical help. In particular, the control of use of water would probably best be left to a local body.

There is reason for concern whether the water will be used efficiently. There are a few examples of firm regulations with regard to land and water use applied by Native Authorities or irrigation committees, but at the same time there are many examples of wasteful use of water. The Mission recommends the establishment of firm water rights under the new Water Ordinance. The purpose should be to make as much water as possible available for irrigation and to discourage waste of water. In the future, water laws will be necessary, providing the framework for regulation of water distribution, construction and maintenance of works, and assessment of water rates.

Up to now, insufficient attention has been given even to the establishment of rules for the regulation and release of water from reservoirs. Regulation is of particular importance since the reservoirs have to carry water through the dry season to the beginning of the next growing season.

Where irrigation is developed on a large scale, special attention will have to be given to the catchment areas above the reservoirs. It may be desirable to control grazing in these areas. In places the eventual aim should be to establish forest reserves to prevent the deterioration of the soil cover and resulting erosion.

FLOOD CONTROL

In many areas in Tanganyika, flood hazards and arid conditions alternate with the seasons. In some of these areas, there are possibilities of land development by flood control. In particular, there are a number of flood plains, notably in the river basins of the east of the territory, where flood control would be an essential prerequisite for agricultural development.

However, there are probably rather few places where flood control alone would be sufficient. Further investigation is required, but on present knowledge it appears that flood control alone is sufficient for development only in areas with mean annual rainfall of at least 45 inches; and for such crops as paddy and sugar cane, more than 45 inches of rain are needed if they are to be grown without irrigation. In areas where average rainfall is less than 45 inches, flood control alone can only provide conditions for pastoral use of the land and for very limited cultivation. Flood control on a large scale will nearly always involve conservation of water by storage dams and reservoirs. Small-scale flood control could however be achieved on certain favorable sites by the construction of embankments, thus empoldering parts of the area. In schemes of this kind, drainage facilities would have to be provided.

Where flood control has to be combined with irrigation, total capital costs will be rather high. It will nevertheless be desirable to carry out some pilot projects of flood control, both coupled with irrigation and also in high rainfall areas where irrigation is unnecessary, to gain experience of the technical problems and economics of such schemes.

FORESTRY

Economic Value of Forests

Forest and woodland cover a large part of the territory: 2 percent of the total land area is classified as forest and forest woodland intermediate, 16 percent as woodland bushland intermediate and 35 percent as miombo-type open woodland. (The distribution by province is shown in Table 59). Over 43,000 sq. miles, or nearly 13 percent of the territory, have been declared forest reserve.

The wooded areas provide timber of all sorts, charcoal, bark, honey and beeswax and a variety of other forest products. The Statistical Unit estimates the total annual value of forest products at some £ 5.5 million, about 60 percent in the monetary economy and 40 percent in the subsistence sphere. These estimates are very rough, due to incomplete recording of timber production.

The commercial part of these operations is regulated by the Government under various forms, mainly through sawmill concessions. There are 66 sawmills operating both in the governmental forest reserves and in forests or woodland under Native Authority control.

Hardwood and mangrove poles are export articles of some importance. The value of exported wood and poles has ranged between £ 600,000 and £ 750,000 a year in recent years.

For the African rural people, forests are important as a source of raw material for their huts and other domestic uses, as an additional source of labor income through collecting wild products or through wages. Some glades bordering montane forest and a few tsetse-free areas of miombo and acacia woodland are important grazing grounds.

At least part of the forests is hydrologically and ecologically an important asset of Tanganyika as a whole and of the mountainous populated areas in particular. Although it is possible that they have little effect on total rainfall and that they increase evaporation on the spot and thereby decrease total runoff, at the same time they regulate and regularize runoff to a large degree, a function of vital importance for settled areas downstream. It is hard to evaluate in detail this important function, but its economic value must be far greater than the value of forestry products.

Protection of Forests

The Government's policy, over the last decade, of consolidating and expanding its natural function as a protector of the forests to the benefit of the whole economy and future generations, is to be applauded.

The Government has adopted the policy of engaging the interest of local people in forest reservation by inducing Local Government Authorities to undertake the management of forests of local importance. Native Authority forest reserves now amount in total to 4,400 sq. miles, or 10 percent of the total forest estate. Plantations belonging to Local Authorities total 10,000 acres, or one third of total forest plantations. Local Authorities spend about £ 40,000 per annum on plantations; revenue is about £ 15,000. These activities should be continued and, if possible within the financial limitations, be expanded.

The Government has, together with the demarcation and management of forest reserves, built up a competent staff, distributed over the territory and entrusted with regulatory and protective duties. Effort must now be directed to increasing income to the territory from forests, so as to cover part of the expenditures made to promote responsible forest exploitation.

Assessment of Future Demand for Wood and Timber

Because forests are a productive asset with a very long gestation period and productive lifetime, forest policy must to a large extent depend upon forecasts—rough as they may be—of future demand. It is expected that towards the end of 1960 forestry economists from the FAO will make a detailed study of the probable development of demand. This study may be expected greatly to improve knowledge of potential—and, indeed, of present—demand, and so provide a firmer basis than exists at present for future forestry policy.

Development Program

In 1959 the Forestry Department prepared an investment program, aiming at the production of the quantities of timber which it estimated would be demanded in the territory in the year 2,000. Although the FAO study may point to some revision of the demand estimates on which the program was based, it is nevertheless clear that the growth of demand which may be expected gives scope for a considerable afforestation program. Over a long period (and with forests it is necessary to plan 40 and more years ahead) consumption of sawn timber may be expected to rise very substantially. One factor among others is the replacement of poles and grass by timber and corrugated iron or tiles in house construction.

The area which the Department proposed to plant with trees in the first five and ten years amounts to:

	1960-65	1965-70
	(acres)	
Softwoods	18,500	31,700
Hardwoods	5,900	8,000
Total	24,400	39,700

In comparison with the areas under forest reserve (27 million acres), the proposal to plant or replant, in 10 years time, 64,000 acres or one quarter of one percent, is very modest. Yet it poses important policy and financing problems.

The capital costs of the full program proposed were estimated to average about £ 180,000 a year for the first five years and £ 160,000 for the second five years. The estimated cost, reckoned per acre, falls as the program proceeds, because many preparatory investments in access roads and buildings have to be made in the first years. For the whole 64,000 acres program, capital investment would amount to £ 1.7 million, or about £ 26 per acre.

An advantage of the proposed program is that it would make full use of existing staff, who have to be maintained in any case for regulatory and protective duties. The Department estimates that it could carry out the proposed program with a less than 10 percent expansion in staff—ranging from a few specialists down to forest guards and patrolmen. With half of this capital budget, only one third of the program could be carried out, and the cost per acre would rise to about £ 40.

In view of the territory's budgetary difficulties, the Mission proposes (in Chapter 3) capital expenditures for afforestation somewhat smaller than those proposed by the Forestry Department, amounting to £ 180,000 in 1961/62 and 1962/63, and falling off to £ 140,000 in 1965/66. Expenditures of this size seem sufficiently large to keep costs per acre down to a reasonable level. The proposal is in any case only tentative. It will have to be reviewed in the light of the findings of the FAO team.

On the basis of capital cost of about £ 26 per acre, the department estimated that, on reasonable assumptions on yield in cubic feet and fees to be paid by sawmillers, the Government would, over a period of 40 years, retrieve its initial outlay three times in sawmillers' fees alone. Such a calculation does not take into account the considerable value at the end of the century of the standing hardwood forests. The difficulty, in view of present financial stringency, is the delayed nature of the return.

Mechanization. Up to the present, the Forestry Department has largely relied on manual labor. It attracts laborers by allowing them, for a limited number of years, to grow food crops and even some cash crops on land to be planted in trees. In its plans for an expanded afforestation program, the department reckons on mechanizing operations to a large extent. The investment program is based upon this assumption.

A certain degree of mechanization is no doubt a technical necessity. However, the Mission's advice, based on social as well as economic considerations, is to mechanize only to the degree absolutely necessary, and to experiment carefully with various mixtures of mechanization and hand labor. This advice need not have an appreciable effect on the scale of the program and may, if anything, reduce cost per acre.

Location. Forestry policy in a territory so large as Tanganyika must pay careful attention to questions of location—accessibility of markets and local needs to supplement the supply of wood from natural forests. These considerations point to an emphasis on the

Northern and Lake Provinces. If the railroad were to be extended into the Kilombero Valley, production forests might also be established around Sao Hill.

In some places, clashes may arise between technical considerations of forestry and the economic interests of the territory. One case in point is the competition for land of forestry and pyrethrum growing on Mount Kilimanjaro (see Annex II, pp. 374-75). Similar competition might arise between forestry and cocoa growing in the Usambara foothills and between forestry and tea in some places. It has been laid down that, "Until a Reserve is placed under planned management, its boundaries may be adjusted to the extent necessary to accord with major decisions of planned land utilization."[1] The Land Use Committee should ensure that forestry policy pays proper regard to the value of land in alternative uses.

Beeswax and Honey

Beeswax is a minor, but by no means negligible, product coming under the Forest Department. Exports of beeswax reached nearly £ 250,000 in both 1957 and 1958.

There is a real danger that production of beeswax and honey will disappear in Tanganyika as has happened in Uganda, collection of honey being looked upon as an inferior occupation. Beeswax, however, is demanded for a wide variety of pharmaceutical, cosmetic and other uses, and the market prospects are favorable.

The need is to stimulate interest in beekeeping, and to promote the creation of facilities for collection and for proper separation of the honey. An informal cooperative in the Western Province has been hindered by the lack of funds with which to purchase honeycombs offered for sale. This case gives a striking example of the possible value of financial arrangements ensuring adequate credit to small-scale cooperative marketing and processing organizations.

The 1960/61 budget makes increased provision for Beeswax Officers, raising the total number to five. The prospect of increasing marketed production of besswax and honey by as little as 5 percent per annum would appear to justify some further increase of expenditure on extension work in this field.

[1] *Forestry Policy,* Sessional Paper No. 1 of 1953.

FISHERIES

It is difficult to assess at all accurately the product of fishing in Tanganyika, since the marketing of fish is not canalized to the same extent as that of agricultural produce. Available evidence suggests that the total catch of fish has been increasing rapidly in recent years, but that there remains great scope for increased exploitation of this valuable asset.

Tanganyika fisheries can be broadly divided into three categories: marine; the two great lakes; and other inland fisheries. Lake Victoria and Lake Tanganyika still appear to contribute the greater part of the total catch. However, other inland fisheries have been growing very rapidly, due in considerable measure to deliberate stocking of lakes and dams with quick-maturing tilapia. Marine fishing is still little developed.

Marine Fisheries

Government effort in marine fisheries has been mainly directed to improving the techniques used by African and Arab fishermen in coastal, inshore fishing. Activities have been largely concentrated on the coast of the Tanga and Southern Provinces, where some success has been attained in introducing new or improved types of gear. Some purchases of improved equipment have been assisted by the African Productivity Loan Fund. Attention has also been given to the introduction of mechanized fishing craft, but this program is still in the experimental stage. On the advice of an expert provided by the Food and Agriculture Organization, a project is now being carried out to demonstrate a small mechanized native sailing craft (30-foot *mashua*) which it is hoped could be produced at a cost of £ 350-400. Should this experiment prove successful, it will presumably result in a substantial amount of applications for loan assistance.

Fishing in waters further from the coast is not considered susceptible of early development by the established fishermen, and has not attracted large-scale operations.

Lake Victoria

Lake Victoria continues to be the main area of fishing activity in the territory. The further development of this area requires a combined approach through improved marketing arrangements and better methods of fishing in the more remote areas offshore.

Lake Tanganyika

The main catch from Lake Tanganyika is of *dagaa,* a small fish which is dried and eaten whole. The recorded marketed catch has been of the order of 2,000 tons a year, dry weight, and it is thought that the total catch may be some 3,000 tons dry, or about 10,000 tons wet. Fisheries experts have estimated the maximum safe catch at three times this figure.

The fishermen have taken advantage of loan facilities to buy outboard motors and pressure lamps (used to attract the fish, which are caught at night). An officer from the Agricultural Department spent some time in Kigoma experimenting in improved drying techniques designed to allow activity to continue through the long rainy season, and having the additional effect of improving the quality and market price of the dried product. Although the technical and economic possibilities appeared distinctly promising, this officer has now been withdrawn on grounds of absence of local support. The Mission sympathizes with the argument that scarce personnel should be posted to the places and tasks which may be expected to give the largest returns on their efforts. However, there is an obvious danger of impatience in cases where results are slow to materialize. Without feeling able to judge the merits of this particular case, the Mission would point out that the possibility of large returns may in certain cases justify some uncertainty and delay.

A major problem in further expansion of dagaa fishing is to open up new markets. Sales in the main existing markets, along the Central railway line and in the sisal estates, could not be greatly increased without depressing price. Efforts are already being made to develop markets in the Rhodesias. While there would appear to be scope for greatly increased sales of dagaa in Tanganyika, it seems that the Asians who handle the trade are not very interested in opening up new channels of distribution. This problem appears to deserve further attention.

Some fish other than dagaa are taken from Lake Tanganyika, but lack of refrigeration facilities confines these to the local market. On two occasions European entrepreneurs have offered to start up highly capitalized operations for the catching and distribution of fish from the deep lake, but they have been refused licenses in the face of opposition from the local Africans. Thus a valuable resource remains unexploited. If any further opportunity of this kind arises in the future, means should be explored of working out an arrangement which will win local assent.

Other Inland Fisheries

In the remainder of the territory the chief potential development appears to be through stocking dams and small lakes with various species of tilapia. During the past several years such activity has been expanding with considerable success under the aegis of the Department of Agriculture. For example, in the Central Province, Lake Kitangiri in Iramba District is now yielding 16 tons of tilapia a month. In Dodoma District, the newly-opened Hombolo Dam is supporting a population of 70 fishermen whose catch is 12 tons a month. At Lake Babati in the Northern Province, some 60 fishermen are engaged in producing about 15 tons of tilapia a month.

As additional dams are constructed in the territory for agricultural and livestock development, it is obviously desirable that their potential for fisheries development also be exploited. As noted in Chapter 8, the annual yield of fish obtainable from such sources may be roughly estimated at £ 3 per acre of reservoir. Agricultural extension workers, particularly those working in areas of irrigation development, should have at least a minimum training in matters of fishery development.

Future Development

In shaping policy for development of fishing, it has to be remembered that, in addition to its direct value in increasing activity and incomes, increased production of fish gives indirect benefits by increasing the supply of protein in the diets of the people. Thus the Mission considers that there is little doubt that a fair degree of priority should be given to expanding government effort to promote development of fishing.

As a preliminary to any substantial expansion of the staff and resources devoted to fisheries development, however, the Mission considers that it would be desirable to undertake a general survey of the fishing industry, covering potential production and potential markets in the various parts of the territory. On the basis of such a survey, it should be possible to make recommendations for the development of production and marketing and to provide a guide to the allocation of increased efforts by the Fisheries Division of the Department of Agriculture.

CHAPTER 10 *ESTATE AGRICULTURE*

Estate agriculture under non-African management presents very much less extensive problems for public policy than does African agriculture. Nevertheless there are certain issues which need to be discussed.

It is the view of the Mission that estate agriculture on alienated land makes a valuable contribution to the economy of the territory, and that policies hostile to the continuance of estate agriculture would be shortsighted. Indeed, public authorities should be prepared to provide help for established estates according to the same criteria on which assistance is given to African agriculture.

One percent of the land area of Tanganyika, 2.14 million acres, has been alienated for agriculture under non-African control. The alienated area is thus relatively small, though it contains some of the more fertile and better-watered land of the territory.

Although the estates are relatively small in total, the value of their product per acre is several times that of African farming. Thus the estates account for around 45 percent of the value of Tanganyika's agricultural exports and some 35 percent of the value of the total marketed agricultural product. The activity of the estates makes an important contribution to the government revenue of Tanganyika, the sisal estates in particular being among the main income tax payers of the territory.

The estates also have a certain value in demonstrating to Africans relatively advanced methods of production. It is said that several of the more successful Chagga coffee growers have learned their methods while working as laborers on European coffee estates. Elsewhere, the impact of the example given by estates is said to be extremely small, but the effect may well increase with the passage of time.

In what follows, it is convenient to discuss separately the strong and well-established sisal industry on the one hand, and on the other hand the other estates, many of which are less able to meet their problems unaided.

SISAL ESTATES

Sisal is the premier industry of Tanganyika, contributing almost a quarter of total exports in recent years, and accounting for a little under 10 percent of the total product of the monetary economy, and nearly a quarter of the value of marketed agricultural produce.

Exports of sisal have been growing in recent years at a rate of around 5 percent per annum, production increasing from 121,000 tons in 1948 to 197,000 tons in 1958. During the same period world output and consumption has about doubled, from 256,000 tons in 1948 to about 500,000 tons in 1958.

The market depends on the general business level, and its expansion depends in particular on the demand for baler twine for hay. World demand seems likely to continue to grow steadily at a rate of about 5 percent a year, provided that the present price relationships between the major hard fibers do not greatly change. However, it would not be safe to assume more than a modest rate of increase in the Tanganyika sisal output during the next few years. While production has greatly increased elsewhere, notably in Brazil, increase of production in Tanganyika is held back by certain local factors.

The main problems connected with production which require solution if the industry is to continue satisfactorily are:

a. to find practicable and economic means of increasing yields per acre and, at the same time, maintaining or improving soil fertility;

b. to find means of economizing labor.

As the industry is well organized and strong financially, there seems every reason to expect that it can solve its own problems, and that in the future profitable production will be maintained and probably somewhat increased. No special public action appears to be needed. Nevertheless, in view of the importance of the industry to the economy, it seems worthwhile to review briefly the changes in methods which appear to be required.

Intensive Production and Maintenance of Soil Fertility

In the past, it has been customary to grow sisal continuously on the same land for several cycles without application of fertilizers or other means of maintaining soil fertility and, in consequence, with some degree of soil exhaustion and decline in yields. The diminishing returns from such land have been partly offset by opening new land which, initially at any rate, has given high yields; but this is no longer possible, as no considerable areas of suitable alienated land are now available for sisal growing. Hence, for the future of the industry, it appears necessary to find means, which are practicable both technically and economically, of growing sisal intensively and continuously, either as a monoculture as at present or in a rotation, while maintaining both yield and soil fertility.

If intensive production and high yields prove to be practicable, then an appreciable reduction in acreage, basic cultivation costs and handling charges should be possible and land would be released which might be used for other purposes. The land released would be the poorest and most worn out, and would require considerable expenditures to restore its fertility. Nevertheless, it might prove suitable for some purposes, such as pasture or cashew nuts. On the other hand, if economic means of maintaining fertility are not found, then the industry will be faced with steadily declining yields and rising costs of production.

Means of intensifying production and increasing yields per acre and per annum and of maintaining fertility are, to a considerable extent, already known as a result of research, but the economy of applying these methods on estates is largely unproven.

Certain measures, such as improved nursery techniques, spacing and cutting methods, have already been shown to be economic and are being adopted fairly widely on the estates.

As regards the use of fertilizers, there is no doubt that potash pays handsomely on potash-deficient soils; and it has been shown that, except in a few limited areas, the application of phosphate is unnecessary. On soils of pH less than 5.8, lime gives marked increase in yields; on most soils nitrogen also increases yields; and on all soils application of sisal waste increases yields; but, the economy of the use of all these materials is uncertain. Similarly, there is some evidence that growing leguminous cover crops between sisal rows increases yields, but there is no information on the economics of the practice.

A major difficulty in endeavoring to assess the profitability of the use of fertilizers, waste or cover crops is that it is essential to obtain figures for at least one complete cycle of sisal, lasting 6-8 years, and during such a period the price of sisal and costs of production may alter considerably. Rough calculations based on a price of £70 per ton c.i.f. London for No. 1 suggest that the application of lime, nitrogen and waste, if combined with other means of increasing yield per acre, such as good nursery and planting techniques and optimum spacing and cutting, will show a small profit. It should be remembered that without the application of these materials, and possibly the use of cover crops, yields seem certain to decline steadily.

There is little doubt that better equipment and better organization for the application of sisal waste to the fields would reduce costs of application, but this would involve large capital expenditures on equipment: for example, the cost for one large group of estates is estimated at £12,000. Smaller estates might not be able to afford such equipment, but it is possible that estates could combine in its purchase and use, or that it might be owned and operated by contractors.

The industry is well aware of the need to assess the economics of methods for maintaining fertility and intensifying production, and a number of estates have already planted fields of 10-15 hectares in which they are applying new methods and keeping records of costs. It has also been virtually decided that an additional area of land shall be added to the Sisal Research Station on which large-scale, costed trials of new methods can be carried out.

One other factor of importance is the possibility that yields per hectare and per annum might be appreciably increased by the introduction of a new hybrid variety of sisal. Several promising hybrids are at present under observation at the Research Station. However, types giving increased yields would demand higher standards of culture and fertilization for the maintenance of fertility, and cost of production per ton of fibre might be rather little reduced.

Economizing Labor

Present methods of sisal production involve a great deal of hand labor. Wages have recently increased, and the industry has had a fair amount of labor troubles. Hence it is important, in view of the competition from other producing countries, that efforts should be made to economize in labor. Economies seem possible in three fields:

a. In land preparation and cultivation. Much has already been done to mechanize land preparation, but there is scope for further labor saving, especially in weeding. The indications are that at the present price of effective herbicides, weed control by chemicals in the field is more expensive than hand weeding, but trials should continue with new techniques and new herbicides, as they might well result in the discovery of economic methods. One estate is already using flame guns extensively for weed control, and claims that this is cheaper than hand weeding.

b. In the handling of the leaf from the time it is cut until it enters the decorticator. At present this involves a very great amount of hand work. An appreciable economy would probably be immediately effected by switching from a system of paying for a task based on the number of leaves to piece rates based on weight; but there are possibilities of much greater improvement in finding means of mechanizing, or partially mechanizing, the collection and transport of leaf from the field to the rail trucks or lorries, of mechanizing the loading and unloading of the trucks, and in the evolution of a satisfactory automatic leaf-feed through the decorticator.

c. In the handling of the fiber after it leaves the decorticator. Here again much hand labor is involved in carrying fiber to and from the drying lines and in sorting, grading and brushing. Much more labor-saving methods have been used in sisal factories in Indonesia and it seems certain that investigations could provide means for considerable improvement in the Tanganyika factories.

The industry is proposing to erect an experimental factory in conjunction with a new plantation at the Sisal Research Station and to employ an engineer to work on means of labor saving and increasing efficiency in the handling of both leaf and fiber.

OTHER ESTATES

Certain other types of estates are less able than the sisal industry to handle the problems confronting them, and there is a case for public assistance, particularly in marketing and provision of credit.

Size and Nature of Non-Sisal Estates

Of the 2.1 million acres in Tanganyika alienated for non-African agricultural or pastoral use, 25 percent is under sisal, 9 percent under other crops and 4-5 percent fallow, 32 percent is used for grazing and 29 percent is not in use. Food crops occupy 96,000 acres, tree crops 55,000 acres and other crops (excluding sisal) 34,000 acres. Although tree crops thus occupy only 2½ percent of the alienated land, several of them are of considerable economic importance, notably coffee (19,000 acres), tea (15,000) and coconuts (9,000).

Many of the non-sisal estates are comparatively small. Out of 900 farms responding to a recent census inquiry, about 15 percent had less than 100 acres. One sixth of the estates have a labor force of less than five.

Among the non-sisal estates there are several, mostly producing tree crops, which are held by companies and run by paid managers. These estates have less serious financial, technical and social problems than the second type. These are run by European or Asian yeomen farmers, very often pioneers on new land, many of them having settled after the first World War. Some of these latter farms grow coffee, but more are occupied with animal husbandry and annual crops.

The Problem of Succession

Many non-African farmers are concerned for their future security. It is said that many British and Western European owners and leaseholders would sell their estates if they could obtain a satisfactory price, and many estates are in fact being sold to Greeks and Indians, who appear to have more confidence in their future in the territory. In the circumstances, many owner-operated estates are being allowed to run down. Successful farmers send their children to schools and universities in the United Kingdom and elsewhere, and the chances are great that the heirs will not choose to return to Tanganyika. Retirement, even if keenly desired, then becomes difficult for the owner, and the farm may become undercapitalized because profits are withdrawn and new investments avoided.

With a view to preventing the running down of valuable assets, the Mission suggests that the Tanganyika Agricultural Corporation (TAC) should be prepared as a temporary measure to bid for estates which are offered for sale, thus giving assurance to the present owners that estates and their equipment, if maintained in good condition, will always command a reasonably good price. Estates bought by the Government or by a public body might be run as partnership operations or as demonstration farms. Alternatively, the TAC might act as an agency house, taking over estates and installing competent paid managers to run them, the present owners being compensated by the device of issuing shares to them.

Investment

Many of the smaller estates find it difficult to raise finance for desirable improvements or modernization.

To some extent the Land Bank of Tanganyika, an official body established in 1947, has been able to meet this need. The Land Bank lends on first mortgage terms, and will lend up to 70 percent of its valuation of land and permanent improvements. In 1957 the maximum amount which might be lent to a single borrower was raised from £ 10,000 to £ 15,000.

The recent financial situation of the Land Bank has been somewhat precarious, due to the large weight of its short-term liabilities (cf. Chapter 11, pp. 222-23). Too much of the Bank's limited funds is tied up in marginal investments. Farmers have tended to turn to the Land Bank for short-term as well as for medium-term accommodation, and in mid-1959 the Land Bank was driven to raise its short-term lending rate above the longer-term rate in an effort to induce short-term borrowers to turn to the commercial banks.

In the reorganization of lending institutions, proposed in Chapter 11, attention should be given to the capital needs of estates.

Management

Many farmers are retired men from the civil service and other professions and lack technical knowledge and managerial ability. The following measures to improve methods and management in areas where there are concentrations of non-African farming are endorsed by the Mission:

a. The continued provision of specialist coffee advisory officers.

b. The provision of a tobacco advisory officer for the main tobacco area near Iringa. This is already in hand.

c. The continued provision of a farm planning and advisory service for the mixed farming area in the highlands of the Northern Province.

d. If further land is alienated, or Crown land leased, the policy should be strictly observed of ensuring that the occupant has sufficient knowledge and experience to enable him to farm the land efficiently.

Marketing Problems

Marketing arrangements for a number of products, including tobacco, vegetables, dairy products, poultry products, pig meat and beef are unsatisfactory. Domestic markets are narrow, and success on the part of a few producers may rapidly attract considerable competition. European producers have often found their costs of production relatively high in the face of competition from Indians and Africans, and the result has often been an understandable, but not always workable, desire for semi-monopolistic organization of marketing.

Marketing arrangements should as a rule be financed by the producers themselves, with the aid of borrowing from commercial banks. The role of government should be to assist in the solution of organizational problems. Government policy should aim at the organization of marketing in the interests of the economy as a whole.

CHAPTER 11 *INSTITUTIONS FOR AGRICULTURAL DEVELOPMENT*

Preceding chapters have discussed the future functions of a number of different institutions: the Ministry of Natural Resources and its various Departments; Local Government Authorities; Area Land Boards; cooperative societies; marketing boards; a cooperative bank; the African Loan Funds or a possible successor agency; the Land Bank; the Tanganyika Agricultural Corporation. Certain possible relations between various of these bodies have been suggested, but it remains to give a coherent picture of the part which each institution would play in promoting and guiding development.

This chapter also discusses organization and finance. Some of the proposed bodies do not yet exist: e.g., Area Land Boards, the cooperative bank and a successor agency to the African Loan Funds. Other bodies are in need of financial reconstruction, notably the Land Bank and the Tanganyika Agricultural Corporation.

THE MINISTRY OF NATURAL RESOURCES

The task of the Ministry of Natural Resources will continue to be to promote, assist and guide development of agriculture, animal husbandry, forestry and fisheries. It is desirable that all the departments concerned with these subjects shall remain within a single ministry, but some reorganization is required to secure adequate coordination between the several departments of so large a ministry.

The Land Use Committee

The Land Use Committee should continue as the final arbiter of the feasibility and priority of natural resources development projects. It should remain, as at present, a committee of heads of departments within the Ministry of Natural Resources, unless the Water Develop-

209

ment and Irrigation Department is in fact transferred to another ministry, in which case the Land Use Committee will have to become an inter-ministerial body. It should direct the common effort of the various departments concerned with a development project.

The Mission suggests that the Permanent Secretary of the Ministry of Natural Resources should be the formal chairman of the Committee, but that it might be presided over at ordinary working meetings by a Chief Technical Officer, who would also be the director of the Committee's specialist staff.

Planning Staff

A small specialist staff should be built up to assist the Land Use Committee, in particular by preparing appraisals of projects.

One member of this staff should be an officer seconded from the Economic Section in the Treasury. This officer should be made a member of the Land Use Committee. His task should be not only to ensure that economic reasoning and information receive sufficient attention at headquarters level, but also to teach officers in the field to give proper attention to the economics of programs and projects and to collect the data required for proper economic evaluation.

Reorganization of the Ministry

There are at present certain defects in coordination between the various departments of the Ministry of Natural Resources: various examples have appeared in the preceding pages. The Mission recommends that a study be undertaken with a view to effecting some reorganization.

The following list of departments or divisions is given as an example of the type of reorganization we have in mind. The list is not necessarily exhaustive, nor is the composition of the various departments necessarily that which would prove the most convenient.

Extension (see Chapter 5, p. 113), farm planning and mechanical services to producers;
Research—covering all aspects of crop and animal husbandry, including irrigation agronomy;
Water development and irrigation;

Animal health (including research);
Forestry;
Fisheries;
Planning staff;
Administration and finance.

Division of Responsibility Between Ministries

The foregoing suggestions for the organization of the Ministry of Natural Resources presuppose that the Ministry will continue to have the same major responsibilities as it had when the Mission was in Tanganyika. It is in fact proposed to make some reallocation of departments as between ministries, following the elections in August 1960 (see below). This reallocation would transfer water development and irrigation from the Ministry of Natural Resources into a

Distribution between Ministries of Responsibilities
Related to Agricultural Development

	To July 1959	From July 1959	Proposed Reorganization 1960
Agriculture	Ministry of Natural Resources	Ministry of Natural Resources	Ministry of Agriculture and Co-operative Development
Veterinary Services (including Tsetse Control)	"	"	"
Water Development	"	"	Ministry of Lands, Surveys and Water
Land Tenure	Ministry of Lands and Mineral Resources	Ministry of Lands and Surveys	"
Co-operative Development	Ministry of Natural Resources	Ministry of Social and Co-operative Development	Ministry of Agriculture and Co-operative Development
Rural Social Development	Ministry of Local Government and Administration	"	"

Ministry of Lands, Surveys and Water, would bring cooperative development back into the same ministry as agriculture and veterinary services (as was the arrangement before July 1959), and would also bring rural social development into the Ministry of Agriculture and Co-operative Development.

On balance, the Mission prefers the division of responsibilities as established in July 1959 to that contemplated in the proposed new reorganization. The underlying problem is, of course, that the collection into a single ministry of all the central government functions having a direct bearing on agricultural and livestock development would result in a very large ministry, and in an excessive burden of work for a single minister. It will be seen from the last page that in the past few years these functions have always been divided between three ministries. However, for reasons set out on p. 188, the Mission considers that it is highly desirable that water development and irrigation should remain in the ministry responsible for agricultural development. There are certain advantages in having cooperative development and rural social development (or community development) also in this same ministry; but, if it is considered necessary to limit the range of responsibilities given to a single ministry, then the Mission would prefer that cooperative development and community development should be placed under another ministry, rather than that water development and irrigation should be separated from agriculture.

COMMUNITY DEVELOPMENT DEPARTMENT

The Mission envisages that the present Social Development Department will be converted into a Department of Community Development.

In accordance with the proposals for the shape of a community development effort set out in pp. 110-11, the Mission considers that the main activity of the Department of Community Development should be the organization of intensive community development schemes, at first on a pilot basis and in one or two limited areas. However, the Department should also provide a certain amount of technical guidance and specialized services to the wider, less intensive community development effort to be carried out through local authorities and other existing bodies.

An effort should be made to recruit a nucleus of skilled senior officials with experience in the practical execution of community development schemes.

The question arises of the organizational arrangements to be made for agricultural and veterinary staff working in the intensive community development projects. The Mission considers that these officers should continue to be members of the appropriate division of the Ministry of Natural Resources, rather than that the Department of Community Development should have its own agricultural and veterinary staff. Especially if community development is the responsibility of a different ministry than deals with agricultural and livestock development, it will be necessary to give careful attention to devising administrative arrangements which ensure close collaboration between the Department of Community Development and the agricultural and veterinary departments. The Department of Community Development will also have to establish close working links with certain other ministries, for example the Ministry of Education and the Ministry of Health.

LOCAL GOVERNMENT AUTHORITIES

In the past, the Local Government (Native) Authorities have taken part in the public programs of agricultural development mainly as regulatory bodies. They have been the instruments for the attempts to induce improvements in agricultural and animal husbandry methods by way of large numbers of ordinances and regulations. Such ordinances are very useful in enforcing pest or disease control and similar measures; but they have little educational value. As has been seen in Chapter 5, the attempt to enforce better methods by legal sanctions was unpopular, became unworkable, and has been largely abandoned.

The Mission considers that in present circumstances the Local Government Authorities are well suited to take an extremely important part in the organization and execution of local development programs and projects. The attempt to promote a type of community development approach to development on a Tanganyika-wide scale should call on Local Government Authorities to play a key role. Many construction projects and useful activities, which would be out of the question if they had to be financed from the central budget, could be undertaken with great benefit on the basis of locally organized contributions of labor, materials or money.

LOCAL LAND BOARDS

The suggested composition and role of the proposed Area Land Boards have been considered at some length in Chapter 4. These Boards would be principally concerned with the administration of types of land tenure appropriate in particular areas. In this, it would be essential that their activities should conform with systematic planning of land use. The Land Boards might also in some instances regulate the way in which land is used by the occupants.

THE COOPERATIVES

In a remarkably short period, African producers of coffee, cotton and some other products in Tanganyika have organized themselves into powerful marketing cooperatives. Although most of the cooperative societies of Tanganyika are concerned first and foremost with produce marketing, many of them now form a natural focus for efforts to improve the productivity of African agriculture, whether by advice or by material assistance. The role of cooperatives in marketing, processing and other aspects of agricultural development has been discussed in Chapter 5, pp. 114-15, 120-21 and 121-27. The following paragraphs, after outlining the development of cooperatives up to the present, discuss various issues of policy in matters concerning the regulation, organization and staffing of cooperative bodies.

TABLE 23   Development of Cooperatives, 1948 to 1959

	1948	1953	1957	1958	1959
	(end-year figures)				
Number of registered societies	62	188	474	546	617
Total membership ('000)	52	153	305	319	325
Share capital (£ '000)	78	87	207	228	249
Reserves and surpluses (£ '000)	276	1,059	1,961	2,265	2,618

SOURCE: Annual Reports on Co-operative Development.

TABLE 24   Classification of Registered Cooperative Societies, End 1959

	Federations	Unions	Affiliated Primary Societies	Unaffiliated Primary Societies	Membership	Gross Proceeds in Preceding Season (£'000)
African Marketing Societies						
Victoria Federation of Co-operative Unions Ltd.	1	15	318	—	128,500	4,439
Bukoba Native Co-operative Union Ltd.	—	1	71	—	57,000	2,312
Kilimanjaro Native Co-operative Union Ltd.	—	1	42	—	[40,000]	1,852
Other affiliated societies	—	7	64	—	[50,138]	1,086
Unaffiliated societies	—	—	—	78	27,034	534
Total	1	24	495	78	302,672	10,223
Multi-Racial Marketing Societies	1[a]	—	—	5	1,664	1,302
African Consumers' Societies	—	—	—	9	17,521	—
Asian Loan Societies	—	—	—	5	3,137	—
Total, all societies	2	24	495	97	324,994	11,525

[a] Tanganyika Co-operative Trading Agency Ltd.
SOURCE: Annual Report on Co-operative Development, 1959.

Development of Cooperatives to Date

Table 23 shows the increase over the last decade in the number and importance of cooperatives. New societies continue to be formed at a rapid rate. In 1958, 82 new marketing societies and three others were registered, while registrations of 13 cooperatives were canceled. In 1959, there were registered 70 primary marketing societies, one secondary marketing society and three consumers' societies. These registrations included the conversion of a single coffee marketing society into a union and three affiliates. Two probationary societies became registered societies, and two new societies were given probationary status. There were two genuine cancellations.

The 13 cancellations in 1958 included eight maize marketing societies in a single area and were exceptionally high; five or six cancellations in a year is considered more normal—i.e., a mortality rate of a little over one percent.

The distribution of cooperatives by type at the end of 1959 is shown in Table 24. It can be seen that marketing societies predominate. In comparison, other types of cooperative have made little progress. The virtual absence of credit cooperatives is a striking feature of the cooperative movement in Tanganyika.

As is to be expected, marketing cooperatives have developed most rapidly in areas where there are major cash crops and a fair density

TABLE 25 Geographical Distribution of Registered Primary Cooperative Societies, End 1959

Province	African Marketing	Multiracial Marketing	Other Types	Total Membership
Lake	324	—	1	130,382
West Lake	76	—	1	80,402
Southern Highlands	55	—	2	31,945
Northern	54	2	2	47,575
Southern	31	—	—	15,440
Eastern	27	3	4	9,522
Tanga	6	—	2	9,412
Central	—	—	1	116
Western	—	—	1	200
Total	573	5	14	324,994

SOURCE: Annual Report on Co-operative Development, 1959.

of population, and not at all in thinly populated areas with no major cash crops. This is illustrated by Table 25. A coffee cooperative recently formed in Kasulu District is the first marketing cooperative to be registered in either the Western or the Central Province.

Regulation and Promotion of Cooperatives

The Department of Co-operative Development has a staff in the provinces of about 100 Co-operative Officers and Inspectors, answerable to a Commissioner for Co-operative Development who is also the Registrar of Co-operative Societies. The main function of this staff is regulatory, though it also performs useful work in encouragement and guidance.

The conditions for registration of cooperative societies are laid down in the Co-operative Societies Ordinance (Cap. 211, Supp. 55):

"If the registrar is satisfied that a society has complied with the provisions of this Ordinance and the rules and that its proposed by-laws are not contrary to the Ordinance or to the rules, he shall register the society and its by-laws unless he is of the opinion that—

"a. proper provision has not been made for the financing of the society; or

"b. there is already a society in the same locality which is substantially performing similar activities for persons of the same race, tribe, class or occupation or that the registration of another society would serve no useful purpose; or

"c. the by-laws do not contain sufficient safeguards for the proper administration of the society."

The judgment whether proper provision has been made for the financing of the society is based, in the case of marketing societies, on the amount and value of the crop which they can be expected to handle. For crops which are already handled on a considerable scale by cooperatives, this judgment has been largely reduced to rule-of-thumb.

In cases where the conditions for registration are not judged to have been fully met, a cooperative society may be given probationary status. The principal difference between a probationary and a registered society is that the former does not enjoy limited liability and may be terminated at the absolute discretion of the Registrar. The lack of limited liability does not appear to be a serious obstacle to the establishment of a society, since it is not as a rule necessary that a new society should incur liabilities substantially in excess of its realizable assets.

Without having been able to investigate in detail how the procedure for registration of societies works in practice, the Mission approves the principle that reasonably high standards must be maintained in requirements for registration, and also in auditing and in the general conduct of the societies' business. It is essential that requirements and standards should be stringent enough to ensure the reputation of cooperatives in commercial circles, for on this their value as economic institutions depends. Insistence on high standards inevitably places a heavy burden on the staff of the Co-operative Department in helping the new and smaller cooperative societies, in particular, to meet these standards.

The Co-operative Department rightly takes the view that cooperatives must come into existence by the demand of the potential members, and that societies which are artificially fostered are not likely to be successful. Nevertheless, the role of cooperative officers (and of their colleagues in other departments) in stimulating interest in the cooperative form of organization, and of the cooperative officers in nursing societies through their difficult early years, is extremely important. A delicate balance has to be struck in assisting the formation and successful operation of cooperatives without endangering their vitality and self-reliance.

As has been suggested in Chapter 5, the cooperatives can play a most important part in the improvement of agricultural methods and increase of production. To this end, there is a need for close collaboration between cooperative officers and, for example, officers of the Department of Agriculture. The lines of such collaboration have to be decided in Dar es Salaam, but it is at provincial and district level that collaboration must be made effective.

A Central Cooperative Body

In January 1960 a meeting was held for the first time of representatives of all the cooperative unions and unaffiliated societies, and the establishment was approved in principle of a central body to perform common services for the cooperatives. The Mission believes that such a body would be useful, though there may be difficulties in staffing it adequately.

Staffing of Cooperatives and of the Cooperative Department

So rapid has been the growth of cooperatives in Tanganyika that it has been difficult to find permanent staff for them of an adequate level of education.

In 1959, eight students from cooperative societies in Tanganyika and 22 from the Department of Co-operative Development attended the East African School of Co-operation. Although a high proportion of students from the societies fails to secure a passing grade, the course is said to be of benefit to them. A further 65 students from societies annually attend the School of Co-operation at Mzumbe. This school aims to bring students up to the standard of bookkeeping required to strike a trial balance. About 80 percent of students are given passing grades. In addition, various courses are conducted throughout the territory by Departmental and Union Staff to train cooperative employees and committee members, and an increasing number of employees of cooperatives are going overseas for specialist training in a variety of subjects.

The capacity of these facilities nevertheless remains inadequate, and creation of the proposed central cooperative body would create further need for staff. On the other hand, the new central body might well be successful in organizing, and attracting funds for, additional training facilities. Some thought might be given to using the facilities of the KNCU College of Commerce in Moshi, at present under-utilized, more specifically for training staff for the cooperative societies and unions, for the proposed new central body and also for the Department of Co-operative Development.

A Cooperative Bank

The possibilities are already being explored in Tanganyika of establishing a cooperative bank. This idea has a number of merits, and warrants careful consideration.

To some extent different cooperatives have different seasonal requirements for money, so that a pooling of liquid resources through a central institution would economize the amount of liquid resources needed by the cooperatives as a whole.

However, in general the cooperatives have little money beyond their immediate requirements, and thus it cannot be expected that a cooperative bank could raise any very considerable sums from cooperatives as collective bodies. How much a central cooperative bank could attract in deposits from individual members of cooperatives remains uncertain, but the experiment is worth trying.

The main function of a cooperative bank would be to act as an intermediary between individual societies on the one hand and commercial banks and other potential lenders on the other hand. A central institution with the backing of the whole cooperative movement might be able to borrow on more favorable terms than would be available to any but the largest cooperatives or cooperative unions. A cooperative bank should not only make medium- and long-term loans to cooperative societies to finance buildings and equipment, but should also help cooperatives to obtain the necessary working capital. New cooperatives often have great difficulty in securing adequate working capital, and their success may be prejudiced because they are unable to pay cash immediately for crops brought in by members. Of course, if the cooperative bank were to lend to young and financially insecure cooperatives, it would have to exercise a certain supervision over their finances. It might be psychologically advantageous for this function to be transferred progressively from a government department to a central cooperative body, provided that the cooperative bank could find staff of the necessary caliber. Government would, of course, still need to retain the ultimate regulatory function.

To the extent that a cooperative bank was successful in attracting savings from individual cooperative members, it would need to hold a considerable part of its assets in a secure and liquid form, such as Treasury Bills.

The cooperative bank would require management of high caliber, which is inevitably expensive. The Mission therefore suggests that the cooperative bank might be under the same management as a government small loans institution (see the following section). By this device, the overheads of both institutions could be reduced. The cooperative bank would of course publish its own separate accounts, and it would be important that it should be felt by the cooperatives to be a separate institution belonging to the cooperative movement.

REORGANIZATION OF LENDING INSTITUTIONS

There is a clear need for reorganization of the various public lending institutions. The Mission recommends that an expert consultant should be called in to study the future organization of the Local Development Loan Fund, the African Productivity Loan Fund,[1] the Urban Housing Loan Scheme, the Land Bank,[2] and, in general, institutional arrangements for the provision of credit for small-scale agricultural, industrial or commercial ventures, African or non-African.

The lending functions to be covered go wider than the agricultural sphere, but are conveniently grouped here, since agricultural and related lending will certainly predominate in the immediate future.

The functions are:

a. agricultural lending against security (the present function of the Land Bank) ;

b. agricultural lending without security;

c. credit for small-scale industrial and commercial ventures;

d. housing loans;

e. possibly public works loans to local authorities (see Chapter 16, p. 330).

Without wishing to prejudge the findings of an expert investigation, the Mission sees certain advantages in the combination of most or all of the public small-scale lending activities under a single small loans institution. This single body would handle such a volume of business as to be able to afford headquarters staff of high caliber. In addition, amalgamation of the African Loan Funds with the Land Bank would do away with the present psychologically undesirable division of lending operations along racial lines.[3]

Combination of some or all of the existing lending agencies would raise certain institutional difficulties. For example, the African Productivity Loan Fund was financed by a grant from the United States, carrying certain conditions as to the purposes and terms of loans. It might be possible, in the context of a general reorganization, to renegotiate the terms attached to the grant. Failing this, it would be necessary to continue to distinguish the operations of the African Productivity Loan Fund, as is done at present even though this fund is under the same management as the Local Development Loan Fund.

[1] These two bodies and their operations have been described in Chapter 5.

[2] The operations of the Land Bank have been described in Chapter 10.

[3] The Land Bank will lend only on mortgage terms, and few Africans have adequate security to offer.

Existing Problems of Organization and Finance

Apart from the possible economies of combination, there are various outstanding problems of administration and finance which require early attention.

The present difficulties of the Local Development Loan Fund and the African Productivity Loan Fund have been examined in Chapter 5. It is there suggested that local loan officers should be posted in the main agricultural areas of the territory in an effort to combine a positive lending policy with a reduction of the number of defaults on loans. The lending agency or agencies should not necessarily be expected to meet the full cost of these officers. Similarly, the Mission sees much merit in the proposal of the Ministry of Mines and Commerce to establish field units to assist Africans to operate commercial projects and small-scale industrial enterprises, to give courses to African traders and to administer loans for commercial and small industrial projects. However, under this scheme it would be necessary to guard against the growth of favoritism, by which loans might become merely a reward for those making a good showing in the training courses, to the exclusion of other, equally worthy borrowers.

At the end of 1959 the Local Development Loan Fund and the African Productivity Loan Fund together had uncommitted resources amounting to some £ 51,000. The Urban Housing Loan Scheme, by contrast, finds its operations limited by shortage of funds, and the financial structure of the Land Bank has been distinctly precarious.

At mid-1960, the Land Bank had loans outstanding of nearly £ 1.2 million. Part of these loans was financed from the Land Bank's permanent capital of £ 300,000. However, the greater part had been financed from short-term deposits made by the public. The Land Bank is authorized to accept deposits up to £ 700,000, and such deposits were in fact at this level at the end of 1959. Subsequently there was a considerable net withdrawal of deposits, which amounted to £ 583,000 on March 31, 1960. The first buffer against financial difficulties due to withdrawal of deposits by the public is a government guarantee of overdrafts up to £ 200,000. At March 31, 1960, overdrafts amounted to £ 166,114, and the Land Bank was in receipt of a temporary government loan of £ 100,000. By the middle of the year, this temporary government loan had been increased to £ 200,000, short-term deposits were up to £ 604,500 and the overdraft had been reduced to £ 88,577. The financial vicissitudes of the Land Bank in the first half of 1960 were only such as were to be expected, given the Bank's financial structure. The Government of Tanganyika has now made provision to increase the Land Bank's permanent capital to £ 1 million.

Capital Requirements

As a rough indication of order of magnitude, the Mission considers that the public lending institution(s) under consideration should have an extra £ 2 million-£ 2½ million over the next five years. This sum has been estimated on the assumption that the public body or bodies would avoid lending in cases where money could be obtained from the commercial banks or other sources. A large part of the sum indicated would be for development of agricultural processing facilities.

FUTURE STATUS OF THE TANGANYIKA AGRICULTURAL CORPORATION

The Tanganyika Agricultural Corporation (TAC) was set up in 1954 with the original purpose of taking over the assets in Tanganyika of the U.K. Overseas Food Corporation (Groundnut Scheme). The Corporation maintains and operates large farming and ranching areas at Kongwa, Nachingwea and Urambo. In addition, the Corporation also carries out certain projects as managing agent for the Government of Tanganyika. These include the Rufiji Basin Survey, carried out with assistance from the Food and Agriculture Organization of the United Nations, the Ruvu Ranching Scheme and an experimental tobacco growing scheme at Lupa Tingatinga. The present operations of the TAC are described in Annex IV.

The Corporation has built up a considerable body of experience, and is the logical body to take responsibility for the proposed additional partnership schemes and cattle ranches. The Mission recommends that TAC should be established on a permanent basis. This necessitates immediate consideration of the future finances of the Corporation and careful definition of its relationship with the Government.

The Finances of the TAC

The financial future of the TAC is at present uncertain. The present arrangement, whereby the operating deficits of the Corporation are covered by direct annual grants from the United Kingdom Colonial Services Vote, runs only to September 30, 1962. The provisions are such that the Corporation is unable to build up financial reserves.

The question of the Corporation's financial future is divisible into two parts: on what terms should the Corporation be cut loose from existing financial arrangements in September 1962; and how should new operations of the Corporation be financed after that date?

The terms on which the present financial arrangements will be terminated will have to be discussed between the Governments of Tanganyika and the United Kingdom.

At present the buildings and installations of the "Transferred Undertaking" (Kongwa, Nachingwea and Urambo) are carried on the books at values which are high in relation to their earning capacity. Under existing arrangements, this high valuation is in practice of benefit to Tanganyika. The Corporation includes in its income and expenditure account an expenditure item for depreciation of fixed assets related to the book value of these assets. This item contributes to the operating deficits covered by grants from the United Kingdom. By this means it has been possible for the Corporation in effect to convert old assets of little or no earning capacity into new ones appropriate to the Corporation's present activities.

The question to be settled by September 1962 is what liability the TAC or the Government of Tanganyika is to assume to the United Kingdom in respect of the Corporation's fixed assets which have, by one means or another, been financed by the United Kingdom.

Whatever the agreement reached on this point, the Mission recommends that the ownership of these assets should be transferred to the Government of Tanganyika, and not to the TAC itself. The TAC should then have an obligation to pay service to the Government, whether on fixed or some variety of equity terms. By this means the Government will be enabled to ensure that the Corporation is paying proper attention to commercial considerations, while at the same time being able to adjust service terms as may seem desirable for reasons of public policy.

In relation to the financing of new investments, the most immediate problems are those connected with the operations at Nachingwea. Provided that a suitable valuation is put on the existing assets of the cattle ranches at Kongwa, Ruvu and Mkata, it appears that the TAC should be able to earn a fairly good rate of return on the additional funds needed to bring the ranches up to full capacity, as recommended in Chapter 7. The expansion of operations at Nachingwea, as recommended in Annex IV, raises greater financial problems, by reason, in part, of the experimental aspects of the farming settlement scheme.

The Mission recommends that an effort should be made to distinguish between the experimental and commercial aspects of the Corporation's operations, even when these are combined, as at Nachingwea. Experimental operations should be carried out against direct remuneration by the Government, while commercial operations should be expected to yield reasonable rates of return on the capital employed.

For commercial-type operations, it should be the general rule that the Corporation should borrow to finance new investments at the full commercial rate. Nevertheless, there might be a case for some degree of continued subsidization by the Government for certain projects of importance to the development of the territory. To limit the TAC to operations which promise to the Corporation itself returns sufficient to cover debt service charges may in some cases be unduly restrictive (cf. the discussion of the finances of cattle ranching schemes in Annex VII). Any requirement that the TAC should meet in full from its earnings all costs, including debt service charges, should be applied with a certain discretion, although at the same time the financial arrangements should be such as to discourage waste and inefficiency. While it is in general desirable that subsidies should be clearly recognizable in nature and amount, it may be appropriate in some cases for the Government to lend to the TAC at service terms "softer" than those which the Government has to pay on its own marginal borrowing. In deciding how far it should authorize and enable the TAC to engage in commercial-type operations which will not be self-liquidating if financed on normal commercial terms, the Government should take into account, as one factor in the calculation, the indirect returns which it may expect to receive by way of increased revenue as a result of the operations in question.

Relations between the TAC and the Government

Given the potential scale of the TAC's operations and their importance in relation to total public agricultural and livestock development activities, it is essential that the working relationships between the

TAC and the Government should be clearly defined. The chief points concern the power to decide what operations the TAC should undertake and what general policies it should follow, and the stage of planning of operations at which the TAC should assume responsibility for them.

The TAC ought to be given considerable independence in its day-to-day operations. However, the Mission suggests that the Minister for Natural Resources should have power to decide what operations the TAC should undertake and to issue directives on broad matters of policy, and that the Minister should be answerable for the Corporation's broad policies, but not for the details of its operations. This arrangement would be similar to that applied to the public corporations in the United Kingdom. It should be further considered whether the Directors of Agriculture and of Veterinary Services should be on the Board of the Corporation, or whether this would tend to confuse the constitutional relationship.

It is essential that the respective responsibilities of the Government and of the Corporation in the design of projects should be clearly laid down. The Mission considers that initial surveys and the investigation of projects up to the stage of drawing up the master design should be in the hands of the specialist staff of the Ministry of Natural Resources. The Corporation should become involved at the stage of detailed design, and should be able to express an opinion on the technical and commercial feasibility of proposed projects. One advantage of the proposed arrangement is that the TAC would not be obliged to keep a large specialist staff duplicating the survey and planning staff of the Ministry of Natural Resources. For its participation in detailed design of projects, the TAC could call in consultants as needed to supplement its own resources of operational knowledge.

The Government should be given full facilities to investigate costs and returns on TAC projects, not merely in order to be able to keep a check on the Corporation's commercial efficiency in cases where government subsidy is involved, but also in order to obtain data of relevance to the selection and planning of future development projects, whether to be executed by the TAC or by the Government itself.

MANUFACTURE, MINING AND TRANSPORT

CHAPTER 12 *INDUSTRIAL DEVELOPMENT— MANUFACTURING AND POWER*

In the last fifteen years, there has been a substantial growth of industry in Tanganyika. Starting from small beginnings, the net value of manufacturing appears to have at least doubled between 1948 and 1958, while mining production increased about fourfold and generation of power fivefold (see Table 26). However, these activities are still small in relation to the economy as a whole. Manufacturing and mining each contribute only about 4 percent of domestic product, including subsistence. The number of persons employed in manufacturing, mining and power generation—roughly 35,000— is considerably less than one tenth of the number of persons in paid employment. About as many persons again are employed in the first processing of the main agricultural exports, an activity excluded from the conventional definition of manufacturing.

MANUFACTURING

Existing Manufacturing Enterprises

Over half of the output of manufacturing, as shown in Table 27, is accounted for by certain types of secondary agricultural processing, such as grain and oil milling, and by food products and beverages. Other important manufacturing activities are carpentry, furniture production and sawmilling, and motor vehicle repair and general engineering (including the repair shops of the East African Railways and Harbours Administration, the largest industrial employer in the territory).

On a broad count, but excluding the initial processing of agricultural export commodities, there are some 2,600 establishments engaged in manufacturing and related service industries in the territory. A listing by detailed categories, together with employment figures, is

229

TABLE 26   Industrial Production in Tanganyika, 1948-58

Year	Gross Output of Mining	Net Output of Manufacturing	Electricity Generated
	(£ '000)	(£ '000)	(millions of kWh.)
1948	1,827	n.a.	24.3
1952	5,875	(3,800)	64.5
1953	3,743	(3,300)	73.2
1954	5,068	3,745	85.2
1955	5,494	4,085	95.7
1956	5,481	4,016	106.8
1957	5,434	5,727	113.9
1958	6,766	6,826	123.2

NOTE: Manufacturing refers to net output, and excludes subsistence production. The figures in parentheses are based on Peacock and Dosser, *The National Income of Tanganyika, 1952-1954*, with an adjustment to conform to the official estimates for the following years.

Mining refers to gross output, including internal transport costs. The value of net output in 1958 is estimated at £ 6,186,000. Comparable data are not available for the years before 1954.

Electricity production excludes power generated by industrial enterprises for their own use.

SOURCE: Tanganyika *Statistical Abstract, 1959.*

TABLE 27   Net Output of Manufacturing Industries, 1958[a]

Industry	Number of Employees[b]	Net Output	
		(£ '000)	(percent of total)
Food, drink, tobacco, milling, etc.	6,396	4,485	59
Carpentry, furniture, and sawmilling	8,079	1,599	21
Clothing and footwear	448	200	3
Motor vehicle repair and general engineering	2,691	872	11
Brick, block and tile making ...	893	150	2
Other	1,194	310	4
Total	19,701	7,616[c]	100

[a] Preliminary estimate.

[b] African employees only.

[c] Includes indirect taxes, estimated at £ 790,000.

SOURCE: East African Statistical Department, Tanganyika Unit.

given in Table 75. Most of the establishments are extremely small, and the official survey of industrial production, which excludes concerns with fewer than five employees, covers only about 300 enterprises with a total of about 20,000 employees, as shown in Table 27. Most of these 300 establishments are private companies or partnerships with fewer than 50 employees, owned and managed by residents, mainly of Asian or European origin. A second group consists of a relatively small number of larger firms engaged in the production of such items as cans, canned meat for export, vegetable oil products, wheat flour, beer and paint. About three fourths of the value of manufacturing output is accounted for by this category. Using fairly advanced techniques and employing a relatively high ratio of capital to labor, a number of these firms are owned and managed by overseas enterprises, mostly of British origin. Several enterprises in this category are now in process of establishment, the two most important being engaged in the production of cigarettes and footwear; in both cases the investment in Tanganyika represents the branching out of an enterprise already established in Kenya. During the past several years the bulk of the new investment in manufacturing, which has been on the average just under £1.75 million a year, has gone into these relatively large firms.

Except for the brewing of beer (*pombe*) by Africans, there is little "cottage" industry engaged in the production of traditional handicrafts for the African market. In the towns and villages, however, in numerous small establishments, the production of footwear, clothing, simple furniture and other household items is carried on, mainly by Asians. Many establishments of this type are included in Table 75.

The recent growth of Tanganyika's manufacturing industry, both small scale and large scale, has depended predominantly on non-African enterprise and capital, both resident and foreign. It cannot be expected that this situation will change materially during the next five or ten years. The emergence of an African business community will necessarily be a gradual process, though it may be aided by a training scheme at present under consideration. As the participation of Africans in commerce and the service trades develops, this should provide the nucleus of a business class which can shift to small- and medium-sized industrial activity as opportunities arise. The same may apply to Africans who achieve success as settled farmers. Also, the growth of a class of African artisans and technicians in industry should form a base from which small businessmen may be recruited in time.

Asians form the largest element of the resident non-African community, and their role in commerce is particularly important. Many of the technical and managerial skills acquired in commerce and the service trades should be applicable to manufacturing enterprises, and this community, which is rapidly expanding in numbers, should be able to provide recruits for the industrial sector, not only as businessmen and managers but also as technicians. This would also facilitate the reinvestment in industry of profits earned in commerce, a pattern that has been followed in many underdeveloped countries.

For the rest, the expansion of industry, particularly of the capital-intensive type, must rely heavily on enterprise, technicians and, to a substantial degree, capital coming from outside the territory. Even if some of these elements are provided through governmental or quasi-governmental channels, such as a development corporation, in the final analysis they must be drawn to a large extent from the private sector of industrial countries overseas. For this reason, it is desirable that the Government should encourage to the maximum possible extent the entry of technicians, professional persons and businessmen.

The Path of Industrial Development

At this stage of Tanganyika's development it is desirable that the Government and the public should form some idea of the path which further development of industry might reasonably take. A realistic appraisal of the outlook for industrial development would help in the formulation of general policies and in the resolution of specific issues as they arise.

While some expansion of manufacturing for export can be foreseen —mainly in the form of processing of domestic agricultural products —the scope for further development of manufacturing is determined principally by the size and nature of the domestic market. This may be said to set an outside limit to the expansion of manufacturing. Within this limit there remains the basic question of the degree to which it pays to give special encouragement, through protection or other forms of special assistance, to the development of secondary industries.

Protection. The Government of Tanganyika, in considering its attitude toward the East African tariff, has taken the position that the circumstances of Tanganyika are such as to call for no more than a moderate application of protection as a measure for encouraging secondary industry.[1] The Mission considers that this position is well founded. The scope of the domestic market is limited, and its expansion must depend primarily on the growth of agricultural incomes. There is neither the need for, nor the possibility of, rapid absorption of a large volume of unemployed or underemployed labor through industrial expansion. In these circumstances, a policy of "forced draft" industrialization would not accord with economic realities in Tanganyika. Nevertheless, there may be arguments for protection of certain particular types of enterprise; and certain measures to promote and assist the establishment of manufacturing enterprises will certainly be appropriate.

Thus far, import duties have been levied in East Africa mainly for revenue; in Tanganyika they are, in fact, the largest single source of governmental income. As production for the domestic market has expanded, however, these duties have afforded a measure of fortuitous protection to domestic industries, and recently certain import duties have been adjusted with the object of fostering industrial development. Among the commodities locally produced in Tanganyika and which are now dependent on a measure of protection are paint, nails, rayon knitwear, insecticides, and footwear. A cotton textile industry, if established, would make an important addition to this list. A local cement industry might also require some degree of protection, possibly supplemented by quantitative restrictions in view of unsettled conditions in the international market for cement.

Because of the *de facto* customs union between Tanganyika, Kenya and Uganda, the domestic market for Tanganyika's manufacturing industries might in principle be taken to include the other two East African territories, and the existence of this wider market might be thought to help industrial development in Tanganyika. In practice, however, Tanganyika's exports of manufactures to Kenya and Uganda are now negligible, though a plant fabricating metal containers exports an appreciable part of its output to the other two East African territories; and it is difficult to think of many manufactures that might be developed in Tanganyika in the near future for sale in the East African market as a whole. Indeed, the existence of the customs union raises the question of the extent to which the growth of the domestic market in Tanganyika will be satisfied by imports from Kenya, where

[1] The Government's position is stated in a paper submitted to the Legislative Council, *Protection of Secondary Industries Through the Customs Tariff*, Sessional Paper No. 7, 1956.

industrial development is considerably more advanced. The question of interterritorial relationships in connection with development of manufacturing in Tanganyika will have to be further discussed below.

Manufacturing Development and the Domestic Market. The scope for a further expansion of manufacturing in Tanganyika for the domestic market can be said to depend (a) on the possibility of displacing existing imports of manufactures and (b) on the extent to which the growth of demand for manufactures consequent upon rise of incomes in the monetary sector can be effectively met by local production rather than imports. At the present stage of Tanganyika's development, increased demand for manufactures remains largely dependent on expansion of agricultural output. Thus the most important single condition for further industrial expansion is the development of agriculture. Within the limits set by total demand, consideration must be given to the possibilities of import substitution.

The main categories of imports into Tanganyika are shown in Table 69. There are obviously many manufactured items which it would be difficult or impossible to displace by domestic production, either because the technical conditions for their production do not exist or because the local market is still too small to permit production on a profitable scale, even with substantial protection against imports. There are, however, certain imported commodities for which a "mass market" already exists and which appear capable of being produced at costs which, if not fully competitive with imports in all cases, are at least in the range requiring a relatively low degree of protection.

An examination of the list of imports contained in Table 69 suggests that the most promising possibilities for import substitution include the following:

Commodity	Imports, 1958[2]
	(£ '000)
Beer	592
Cigarettes	3,105
Cement	1,145
Sugar	848
Textiles	5,791
Footwear	583
Rubber tires and tubes	794
Total	12,858

[2] Including imports from Kenya and Uganda.

For all these commodities consumption has increased substantially since the end of the war, and they now amount together to over one fourth of the territory's total imports (including trade with Kenya and Uganda). Some possibilities of import substitution no doubt exist also in the group of manufactured foodstuffs and other miscellaneous manufactures, but not to any great extent in the categories involving the processing of metals (although a razor blade plant has recently been opened in Dar es Salaam, in addition to the metal containers plant already mentioned). Machinery and transport equipment, which comprise one fifth of total imports, must clearly be excluded.

Perhaps the most significant feature of the above list is that the large-scale production in the territory of all the commodities included either exists or is under serious consideration. Another interesting feature of the list is the extent to which certain of the commodities are now imported from the other two East African territories. This is the case particularly for beer, cigarettes, sugar, cement and footwear.

European-type *beer* and refined *sugar* are already produced in Tanganyika in substantial amounts, and recently initiated projects, when operating at full capacity, should satisfy most or all of the local demand for these products. The per capita consumption of these products has risen sharply, but is still much lower in Tanganyika than in the other two East African territories. As incomes rise further, a considerable increase in production, over and above the present level of imports, should be stimulated.

A large *cigarette factory*, a branch of an enterprise established for some years in Kenya and Uganda, is being built in Dar es Salaam, and it is reasonable to assume that in due course local production will fully meet domestic requirements, except possibly for some specialized types. A *shoe factory*, also a branch of an existing Kenya enterprise, is in the course of construction. Its output initially will consist mainly of rubber-soled canvas shoes, but it seems reasonable to assume that it should in time satisfy the territory's requirements for low-cost footwear of all kinds. The conditions for establishing a plant to fabricate *truck tires* have been under discussion.

Establishment of *cotton textile* plants in Tanganyika has been delayed, in part, by a dispute under the licensing procedure (see pp. 240-41) as to the appropriateness, given the structure of import duties, of allowing a concern to begin operations on the basis of weaving imported yarn. Recently, in response to difficulties experienced by a large vertical textile mill in Uganda as a result of competition of imports from India and Japan, specific duties on cotton cloth have been introduced in East Africa, resulting in effective rates of from 50 to 75 percent of the landed cost of various grades of imported cotton and rayon textiles respectively. These rates of duty appear to make the manufacture of cotton piece goods in Tanganyika an attractive proposition even on a fully integrated basis.

Tanganyika's imports of *cement* in 1958 amounted to about 125,000 tons, with a value of over £ 1 million. Deposits of limestone suitable for cement production are available in several locations, but some of the best deposits are unfavorably placed in relation to markets or to accessibility of suitable clays. There have been several proposals from commercial interests for the development of cement production in Tanganyika. The position is complicated, however, by the fact that cement is already being produced on a large scale in Kenya, from which Tanganyika now imports roughly half its supply. Further, the plant from which Kenya supplies Tanganyika has a large amount of unused capacity. In addition, the international market in cement is unstable, with a tendency toward price wars and dumping. The minimum feasible size for a plant is estimated to be 60,000 tons. The issue that arises is whether it is desirable to go ahead with a cement industry now—a development which would presumably depend on a quota on imports, including, possibly, imports from Kenya—or wait until demand expands further in East Africa, thus preserving the unity of the East African market.

If the projects described in the preceding paragraphs should all materialize, it may be estimated that the gross value (including ocean freight) of the imports displaced within, say, five years might be in the neighborhood of £ 6 million. The net contribution to aggregate territorial output would, however, be somewhat less, owing to the import content of some of the products in question. The bulk of these items—textiles, cigarettes, cement, sugar and beer—would utilize largely locally produced raw materials. At least in the cases of cotton and tobacco, local fabrication would probably be to some extent at the expense of exports of the raw product. If the net contribution to aggregate output of these potential industries is taken at roughly £ 5 million, this would represent an increase of only about 3 percent of present gross domestic product (including subsistence), even though it would be a substantial growth in the value of manufacturing production. This estimate, though, is based merely on the displacement of existing imports, and does not take into account the fact that the market for the items under consideration may be expected to expand more than proportionately to any increase in per capita incomes.

Possibilities of Expanding Manufactures for Export. There is also the possibility of growth of exports of manufactures based largely on locally produced raw materials. At present *canned meat* is the chief item in this category. As indicated in Chapter 7, the outlook for an increase of exports of this product is favorable. The production of *wattle extract* has recently begun on a moderate scale, though here the outlook for expansion is clouded by market uncertainties. The development of a higher degree of processing of existing agricultural exports in the near future is not very promising, but certain possibilities can be foreseen. The most promising, provided technical and organizational difficulties can be overcome, is the local processing of *cashew nuts,* which are now largely exported in the raw state for processing in India. No significant processing of sisal occurs in Tanganyika, whereas in Kenya there is a large factory which is engaged in the production both for the domestic market and in some instances for export of a variety of *sisal products,* including mattings, rugs, and bags incorporating a blend of sisal and imported jute. Other exports based on local agricultural production may develop in time. Among those which have been surveyed recently are *lime juice, soluble coffee, desiccated coconut,* and *starch products based on cassava.*

Smaller-scale Activities. The foregoing discussion has focused attention on a limited number of manufacturing possibilities giving scope for operations classifiable as large-scale, at least by East African standards; their development in many cases will no doubt require expatriate management and substantial amounts of capital from external sources. Further possibilities, by no means unimportant in total, exist for increasing production of a range of commodities which can be produced locally by simpler techniques and sometimes on a smaller scale at reasonably competitive costs, or which, by their nature, must be produced locally if at all. Some of the recent growth in manufacturing, as indicated in Tables 26 and 75, has consisted of production of this type. Included in this category are commodities which enjoy a degree of natural protection against imports because of their bulk and hence of high transport costs. Examples are *furniture, building materials* such as bricks, tile and pre-cast concrete products, *soap* and *soft drinks.* Other products are perishable, such as *dairy and bakery products.* Mention should be made also of the growing importance of trades sometimes classified as service industries such as *printing and publishing, repair and servicing* of machinery and vehicles, including agricultural machinery, and *retreading of automobile tires.*

Effects of the East African Customs Union

It has been suggested above that the existence of a *de facto* customs union between Tanganyika, Kenya and Uganda is not in practice a significant aid to industrial development in Tanganyika. Indeed, the Mission could not fail to observe the extent to which opinion in Tanganyika, both official and private, tends to emphasize the disadvantages for Tanganyika of present arrangements. The Mission strongly believes that economic cooperation, and the prevention of the growth of barriers, between the three East African territories is in the best interests of the long-run development of the area as a whole. It would, however, be unrealistic—and in the end self-defeating—to ignore the possibility of certain conflicts of interest, actual or potential, among the territories.

The administrative advantage to all the parties from a common customs and excise system is clear, particularly in view of the problem of smuggling that would be posed if the common market were abolished. An economic advantage from the point of view of the region as a whole lies in the inducement to investment and development generally offered by a market composed of all three territories. Potentially, at least, the industrial and agricultural perspectives of each territory are broadened by access to the larger common market; promising "infant industries" are thus in a position to enjoy economies of scale and reach a position of maturity—presumably at lower costs—more rapidly than if each territory were sheltered not only from the outside world but also from its neighbors. Finally, the expansion of production induced by the common market in any one of the territories may indirectly benefit its partners through growth of interterritorial trade and investment.

Concern in Tanganyika arises from the tendency of industry to gravitate to Kenya. The reasons for this tendency are complex and rooted in the historical development of the region, but a basic factor is the concentration in the Lake Victoria Basin and Kenya Highlands of over half the population of East Africa and much more than half of East African purchasing power. Once established, the industrial center in Kenya tends for various reasons to expand with the growth of the common market area which it serves.

From Tanganyika's point of view, this development appears to threaten two undesirable consequences. In the first place, to the extent that Tanganyika's actual or potential imports from overseas are displaced by imports from Kenya, Tanganyika loses the revenue which it would otherwise obtain from import duties. In Kenya, on the other hand, the loss of revenue from import displacement will tend to be offset by increased revenue from income tax on companies and their employees. Since there is at present no integration between the fiscal systems of the two territories, there is no mechanism for adjustment of the fiscal incidence of the possibly unbalanced growth of industry within the common market.

Even if the balance of fiscal advantage could be adjusted to the satisfaction of the territories, there would remain a second problem arising from the possible imbalance in industrial development within the common market. From the point of view of Tanganyika, an argument may be made for some measure of "infant industry" protection not only against imports from overseas but against imports from the other members of the customs union, and in particular from Kenya. The case for regional integration—particularly in the absence of an integrated fiscal system—assumes a high degree of mutuality in the development of sheltered industries. In this sense the problem, from Tanganyika's point of view, is how the advantage of the common market can be preserved without unduly prejudicing such industrial development as would be feasible and desirable if Tanganyika were to be considered in isolation.

Important as these issues of interterritorial trade relations may be in principle, their practical significance in East Africa up to the present should not be exaggerated. It has been noted above that as the Tanganyika market grows, certain industries originally located in Kenya and Uganda are beginning to decentralize and to establish branches in Tanganyika: examples are sugar, beer, cigarettes, footwear and, in the not-too-distant future, possibly cement. Also, so far as the Mission can judge, there is little evidence that any considerable number of the recent industrial investments that have been made in Kenya have been at the expense of investment in Tanganyika, in the sense that similar investments would have been made in Tanganyika had the common market not existed. Except possibly for cement, the Tanganyika market alone is yet too limited to have led to this type of industrial development.

The importance of the East African common market for all parties concerned appears to lie more in its potential development than in actual results thus far, either favorable or harmful. It is in this light that an effort should be made to harmonize the interests involved. Recommendations to this end will presumably be made by the Raisman Commission (see pp. 34-35).

Industrial Licensing

In general, the legal and administrative framework affecting private investment in industry in Tanganyika appears to the Mission to be satisfactory and to leave little room for suggestions for change. The Government's policy toward foreign private capital and enterprise is receptive and non-discriminatory. In conformity with the policies of the sterling area, once approval has been given to an application for the investment of foreign capital, there is no restriction on the repatriation to the country of origin of profits and dividends. The Mission wishes to stress the desirability of continuing these policies and of making them known to potential investors throughout the world.

The Mission's examination of the "investment climate" in Tanganyika did disclose, however, two aspects of some importance in which we consider a modification of policy to be desirable. One, which is discussed in the following chapter on mining, concerns the awarding of licenses for mineral exploration. A second is the Industrial Licensing Ordinance.

The Industrial Licensing Ordinance of 1952 is administered jointly with the other two East African territories with the object of effecting the "orderly promotion and development" of manufacturing industries in East Africa as a whole. An East African Industrial Council, on which each of the territories is represented, has the responsibility of determining a list of "scheduled" industries, and any proposal for investment in a scheduled industry must be approved by the Council.

Thus far, eleven industries have been scheduled, of which the production of cotton yarn and piece goods is the most important. The full list is: cotton yarn; cotton piece goods other than knitwear; cotton blankets; woolen piece goods other than knitwear; fabrics spun or woven from soft fibers other than fibers of animal origin; steel drums; glassware; sheet or window glass; metal window frames; doors and door frames; and enamel hollow-ware.

Licenses have been issued to firms in ten of the eleven scheduled industries.

A judgment on the incentive effect of industrial licensing can never be conclusive, since the alternative outcome is unknown. The substantial postwar development of enterprises in non-scheduled industries in East Africa demonstrates, however, that when the scope of the market is sufficient, business enterprises are prepared to risk their capital without official assurance of protection against competition. The development of the cement, cigarette and footwear industries, for example, seems to support this conclusion.

While the incentive effect of licensing is questionable, the danger of granting a monopolistic position to any enterprise is apparent. This is particularly true when, as for certain of the scheduled industries, competition is further limited by substantial protection against imports. The administrative difficulties inherent in any system of licensing new investments reinforce the Mission's doubts as to the usefulness of such a system. It is possible that the necessity to seek a license may in fact prove a deterrent to potential investors.

The Mission considers that, on balance, the policy of industrial licensing has contributed little, if anything, to the industrial development of East Africa in general or Tanganyika in particular, and that its probable contribution to future development is equally limited. It is recommended that consideration be given to abolishing the system. At the least, the Mission recommends that no additions should be made to the list of scheduled industries.

Objects and Functions of a Development Company

The industrial development which has occurred in Tanganyika thus far has been largely the result of private initiative. The Government itself does not operate any industrial enterprises, and, although it has participated jointly with private capital in several industrial ventures, such participation has been on a limited and *ad hoc* basis. The only substantial governmental investments for developmental purposes have been in a meat-packing plant and in a mine producing base metals.[3] The Government recently acquired a large interest in Wil-

---

[3] The business enterprises in which the Tanganyika Government has an interest, either as a principal or as a lender or guarantor of loans are the following:

Williamson Diamonds Limited

Tanganyika Packers Limited   *(footnote 3 continued)*

liamson Diamonds Limited, a going concern, but this transaction clearly reflected considerations other than the promotion of industrial development. The United Kingdom Colonial Development Corporation, on the other hand, has been fairly active in the field of mineral development, and has also undertaken the development of wattle extract. As a generalization, it can be said that governmental financial participation thus far has been directed mainly to mining rather than to manufacturing projects.

Recently, however, there has been discussion of the establishment of an industrial development company. To this end, a sum of £ 200,000 was put aside in the 1960/61 capital budget, the intention being to provide a further £ 300,000 over the following two years. At the same time, discussions have been conducted with the Colonial Development Corporation (CDC) to explore the possibility of setting up an investigatory company to be financed in part by the CDC and in part by the Government of Tanganyika, a nucleus of staff to be provided by the CDC. The functions of this company would be to investigate and publicize opportunities for the establishment of new enterprises. An advantage of such an arrangement would be that the investigatory company would have access to the expertise and experience built up by the Colonial Development Corporation, and that the connection would give the company a certain recognizable commercial standing. It is to be noted that, while the CDC is precluded

---

(footnote 3 continued)
    Uruwira Minerals Limited
    Nyanza Salt Mines (Tanganyika) Limited
    Liganga Iron Limited
    Tanganyika Coal Fields
    Rungwe Coal Company Limited
    Mbeya Exploration Company
    East African Airways Corporation
    Tanganyika Electric Supply Co., Limited

In Williamson Diamonds the Government owns 600 shares representing 50 percent of the share capital. Of this amount, 320 shares were acquired in payment of death duties and 280 shares were secured by a special purchase arrangement (see p. 256). The other sizable government interest is in Tanganyika Packers, in which the Government acquired 51 percent of the equity for £ 350,184. It also for a time guaranteed a loan to Tanganyika Packers of £ 200,000. The Government's stake in Uruwira Minerals has been £ 470,000 in the form of guarantees of loans. The Government has an 81 percent interest in the Nyanza Salt Mines, the main producer in the territory. The Government's interest in the other enterprises listed is minor; in the case of the iron and coal ventures, it consists of a 12½ percent share of the equity, taken in consideration of the Government's expenditure in preliminary exploration.

by its present charter from undertaking new investment operations in territories after they become independent, it is authorized to provide managerial and advisory services on the request of any Commonwealth government though it must obtain sufficient remuneration to cover the cost of such services.

A danger to be guarded against in establishing an investigatory company and, as a possible second step, an investment company is that overheads may be too large in relation to the amount of additional development which the institutions would promote. Another danger in the case of an investment company is that it may be inclined to make a show of its worth by rapidly committing the funds provided to it, without due regard to the soundness of the enterprises financed. This risk would be reduced by the participation of an experienced outside body.

In relation to the proposed development company (or companies), as to other aspects of policy affecting industrial development, it is important to maintain a realistic appraisal of the results which can be expected. The Mission did not find any major potentialities in the field of manufacturing or mining which appeared to be blocked for lack of financing or entrepreneurial initiative. However, an investigatory company might discover and make known some promising opportunities; and it is possible that in certain cases the willingness of an investment corporation to participate in the financing of projects with foreign enterprises might be of some importance in persuading expatriate investors to commit themselves to new ventures.

The greatest potential value of a development company or companies appears to be in promoting small-scale enterprise in manufacturing (e.g., production of furniture and building materials), in service trades such as vehicle repairs, road transport, hotels, in agricultural processing and in industries such as dairying and fisheries.

As indicated earlier in this chapter, the main element of the local business community to be considered in this connection consists of Asians and small numbers of other non-African businessmen. It is the Mission's impression that the Asian business community is held back from expanding its activities into the industrial field more by lack of technical knowledge and entrepreneurial initiative than by financial considerations. The relatively high rate of expansion of Asian participation in private construction and commercial activity in the postwar period seems to support this conclusion. In certain cases, a development company might find it desirable to act as a financial partner with members of the local business community, but its main role is conceived to be promotional and advisory. One useful function would be to promote industrial research likely to lead to business development—for example in the processing of agricultural products. The actual research, however, should continue to be done as far as possible on a joint East African basis or by outside agencies working on contract.

The Mission concludes that an investigatory company would be useful provided that it could draw on the assistance of the CDC or some other suitably qualified outside body, and provided that the net cost to the Government of Tanganyika could be kept rather small. The possibility has been canvassed that such a company would receive a return by way of fees from, or free equity participation in, enterprises established as a result of its advice. However, it seems impossible to count on any very considerable returns of this kind. A final decision on the establishment of an investment company, and on the organization and functions of such a company, could well be left until the work of the exploratory company has thrown more light on the nature of the opportunities.

Enterprises below a certain prescribed size should continue to receive assistance from the loan fund(s) discussed in Chapter 11 rather than from the development company.

Income Taxation and Tax Incentives

For a country as dependent as is Tanganyika on the inflow of capital and skills from abroad, the influence of the tax system on this inflow is obviously of the greatest importance. The Mission did not study this complex question in detail, but had the benefit of the recent *Report of the East African Commission of Inquiry on Income Tax, 1956-57* and of other studies.

The present basic rate of income taxation on public companies is Shs. 5.50 on the pound, or 27.5 percent. This is low by comparison with most industrial countries and is in fact lower than the rate charged in many areas, in Africa and elsewhere, with which Tanganyika may be considered to be in competition for foreign capital.[4] As the rates and related allowances are practically uniform among the

---

[4] A foreign investor is usually liable to taxation in the country of his residence, at rates which may be higher than in the country of investment. An important

three East African territories, there is no problem of competition within the area.

The opinion is heard that, in view of the need for increased government revenues, the basic rate of company tax should be raised, this rise being accompanied by increased allowances of various kinds. The policy followed in East Africa appears to be based on two major considerations: first, that it is desirable to have a tax structure favorable to capital inflow, since at present East Africa cannot to any great degree offer the attractions of large, proved mineral deposits in favorable locations or of large purchasing power for manufactured goods; second, that to tax the net earnings of enterprises at a relatively low rate helps to assure the viability of enterprises once established. The Mission has considerable sympathy with these latter arguments in their relation to conditions in Tanganyika. However, assuming the continuance of the East African Customs Union, the rates of company taxation have, in practice, to be kept roughly uniform in the three territories; and, as between low basic tax rates and rather higher basic rates accompanied by increased allowances, possibly including "tax holidays" for new enterprises, the balance of advantage may well be somewhat different in each of the three East African territories. In this matter as in others, differences in interest and approach will have to be settled by negotiation.

It remains to consider the appropriateness of the various tax allowances granted to companies, notably initial allowances in respect of capital expenditure and depreciation allowances.

The allowances permitted under the East African Income Tax Act compare favorably with those of most African countries and with many of the countries from which overseas capital might be expected to come. In general they offer certain incentives to investors, by recognizing the principle of accelerated depreciation, thus reducing the burden of taxation until all or most of the original investment has been recovered. For industrial buildings, an initial deduction of 10

---

exception, however, is the company organized as a subsidiary of a foreign enterprise, which may, in so far as it reinvests in the country of investment, escape liability to the possibly higher tax rates in its "home" country. As regards United Kingdom companies, recent legislation creating a special category of Overseas Trade Corporation has increased the scope for effective tax concessions in capital-importing countries. This, and similar arrangements, provide a strong incentive to a company to earn and reinvest profits in a capital-importing country having a tax rate lower than the capital-exporting country.

percent of the cost, and annual deductions of 2 percent, are allowed. A more generous allowance is granted to hotel buildings. For industrial plant and machinery, the initial deduction allowed is 20 percent, and annual rates, varying with particular items of equipment, seem to afford considerable incentive.

The Mission concurs with the East African Commission of Inquiry on Income Tax that there is no need to depart from the existing East African system in favor of a system of full tax exemption over a period of years for "pioneer industries," such as is practiced by a number of underdeveloped countries. This view is based not only on the belief that the existing system in East Africa offers reasonably adequate incentives to investors, but also on considerations of the problem of administration likely to be associated with a system of concessions to individual enterprises or industries. Only in the case of mining enterprises does the Mission consider that some additional tax concessions would be advisable (see pp. 270-71).

The preceding paragraphs have described the tax rates applied to public companies. The taxation of "private" or closely held companies is also of importance in Tanganyika, since this form of organization is found convenient by many small and medium-sized industrial enterprises and is common in estate agriculture. The same low basic rate of tax applies to private as to public companies. Much thought has been given in East Africa to the problem of taxation of undistributed profits of "controlled" companies (that is, roughly speaking, companies in which five or fewer persons have a more than 75 percent interest). The present law, dating from 1958, appears reasonable, but is the subject of a certain amount of controversy, in part because its provisions have not been thoroughly understood by some interested parties. The object of the law is to give reasonable encouragement to private as well as public companies to increase their productive capacity in part at least by plowing back profits, while at the same time preventing the abuse of the "controlled" company as a device for surtax evasion.

The law applies an "undistributed income tax" to the part of income of "controlled" companies which is not distributed though considered to be distributable. This tax is at a high basic rate, being the difference between the regular company rate of Shs. 5.50 on the pound and the maximum surtax rate of Shs. 15/-. However, a private company is allowed certain deductions in determining the income subject to undistributed income tax. The regulations allow a minimum percentage deduction which may be supplemented by a deduction for amounts spent on fixed assets of the type normally subject to depreciation allowance. The deduction for such expenditure may be carried forward over a period of years, and the liability to tax readjusted accordingly. The provisions do not apply, however, to the acquisition of assets in the form of stocks in the hands of trading companies, and this apparently accounts for some of the criticisms expressed by the local business community. The present law does not put private companies on precisely the same footing as public companies so far as the incentive to plow back earnings is concerned, but the Mission feels that it goes a long way in this direction, and represents a reasonable balance of the conflicting objects of policy in this field.

Industrial Sites and Estates

Most industrial activity is concentrated in Dar es Salaam and its environs, and the remainder largely in a few other towns. Land for industrial purposes may be acquired in these areas under long-term lease and at reasonable rates: with rare exceptions, the acquisition of sites and related facilities for business purposes does not seem likely to present serious difficulty in the foreseeable future. Planning provision has been made for industrial areas in all the major commercial centers of the territory. A scheme is in hand to make available for immediate occupation a certain number of industrial sites in Dar es Salaam, Moshi, Tanga, Morogoro and Mwanza. These sites, which are in government ownership, are being cleared of non-industrial interests and supplied with water, electricity, roads, and in some cases rail access. In Dar es Salaam and Moshi this work is completed, and in the other towns mentioned it is well in hand. There is no evidence that industrial development has been hampered by the existing scope of measures to make available land for industrial development.

Some countries have had success in attracting industry by providing not only planned industrial sites and facilities but also factory buildings for lease to enterprises which may be hesitant to commit capital for this purpose. Often the low rental on such buildings is, in effect, a form of subsidy. The larger industrial establishments which have recently been established in Tanganyika or are in prospect require buildings suited to their special needs and would not normally be influenced by this type of arrangement. In the future, consideration might be given to providing such facilities to small and medium-sized enterprises, but at present there is no evidence of a demand for such facilities that would warrant expenditure by the Government.

One favorable factor in the Dar es Salaam area is the existence of adequate sites for construction of housing for African labor. Firms establishing plants in the area do not as a rule have to face the additional cost of providing housing for their labor force.

Industrial Research and Surveys

The East African Industrial Research Organization, a department of the East Africa High Commission, is at the disposal of the three East African territories to study the technical possibility of establishing new industries and to assist existing industries in increasing their efficiency. It maintains headquarters and a technical laboratory in Nairobi and, with a current operating budget of about £ 50,000, employs a small staff including specialists in such fields as chemistry, chemical engineering, fuel technology, ceramics, crop drying and processing, and metallurgy. In view of Tanganyika's limited industrial development, the Mission is impressed with the advantage of continuing work of this type on a joint East African basis.

While there seems to be no need for establishment of separate industrial research facilities in Tanganyika, the Mission is concerned that the East African Industrial Research Organization—as well as other sources of technical and industrial advice—be used as effectively as possible. One advantage in the proposal to establish an investigatory company would be that it could press for the carrying out of industrial research closely related to projects that it had under consideration. Of particular importance would be research leading to new uses for agricultural materials now produced or capable of being produced in Tanganyika, and particularly for their further processing in the country. A substantial part of the research program should be directed to projects which show promise of being successfully exploited by small or medium-sized enterprises.

ELECTRIC POWER

As shown in Table 26 at the beginning of this chapter, the expansion of electricity generation during the past ten years or so has been rapid. There has been not only a relatively high rate of growth in industrial and commercial consumption but also a sharp increase in household use. The large proportionate increases were, of course, related to a very low initial level of per capita consumption. During the past several years the rate of expansion has slackened, but it has nevertheless averaged about 9 percent a year. At this rate, consumption by 1964 would be in the neighborhood of 200 million units, as compared with 123 million units in 1958.

Between 1948 and 1958, generating capacity grew about three-fold. Generating capacity is now about equally divided between hydroelectric and thermal facilities, but since 1953 the growth of capacity has been almost entirely in the form of thermal plants, mainly powered by imported diesel oil. Beside the capacity shown in the official statistics, a considerable number of private thermal power plants have been installed.

The cost of thermal power, based as it is on imported fuel, is relatively high. Some growth of thermal capacity must be regarded as inevitable in the territory's present stage of development, given the great distances over which hydroelectric power would have to be transmitted to reach certain users. However, the main part of the territory's growing power requirements, which are still concentrated in the Eastern, Tanga and Northern Provinces, can be most economically met by hydroelectric development. The recent increase of thermal capacity to meet the steadily expanding requirements of Dar es Salaam and the adjacent area along the Central Line can be considered a makeshift.

Tanganyika is fortunate in having in its system of rivers a hydroelectric potential far exceeding its requirements in the foreseeable future. The full development of the lower reaches of the Pangani River alone—the logical source of power for the settled areas in the Tanga, Eastern and Northern Provinces—would afford a potential capacity of 68.5 megawatts capable of supplying 321 million units (kilowatt hours) of electricity per year, more than twice the output of power now generated by all sources in the territory. Development of the territory's hydroelectric potential is favored by the fact that the configuration of the Pangani River, one of the main power sources, permits the expansion of generating capacity by relatively small stages, thus avoiding the cost of maintaining a large investment in idle capacity while consumption grows. On the other hand, the main areas of actual and potential demand for power are at substantial distances from the possible generating sites and are rather scattered.

The Hale Hydroelectric Project

Since 1954, when a careful survey was made of the territory's electricity needs and potentialities, both the Government and the private power company which holds a franchise to supply power in the territory, the Tanganyika Electric Supply Company, Limited (TANESCO) have supported the view that the logical way to meet the growing needs of the Dar es Salaam area is to expand hydroelectric facilities on the Pangani River. This would entail the construction of a transmission line 140 miles in length. The plans were based on the assumption that the increased generating facilities would also help to meet the growing demand of the Tanga area and of Mombasa, to which electricity is already exported from the existing Pangani Falls Station. Also, potential expansion of demand along the Central Line in the direction of Morogoro and Kilosa was considered to be capable of being economically met by linking up with the Dar es Salaam–Pangani transmission network.

The existing hydroelectric station at Pangani Falls is now being utilized to its full capacity. Electricity demand in Dar es Salaam is expected to absorb the full capacity of the local thermal installations by 1964. The construction of the Hale station has therefore become a matter of some urgency.

Construction has been held up by two problems: first, of obtaining finance on suitable terms; and, second, of determining the appropriate capacity of the installation in relation to the flow of the river.

The financial problem has been to raise money on terms which allow for the fact that such an installation cannot meet the full service charge on debt for three years or so, until demand has built up to a certain level. In mid-1960 it was felt that the problem of raising finance on suitable terms was within reach of solution.

The estimated capital costs, for the design contemplated at mid-1960, are:

	£ million
Hale Power Station	1.9
Transmission lines to Dar es Salaam and Morogoro—first system	2.3
Miscellaneous finance costs, etc.	0.4
Total	4.6
Second transmission line (by 1969)	0.7

The problem of capacity relates to the consideration that the installation at Hale involves a series of underground tunnels, which have to be designed according to the flow specification envisaged. It is thus not possible to recommend that the project be started on a limited scale, with the possibility of future expansion. The scale has to be decided once and for all.

A minimum flow of 450 cusecs is already guaranteed to the neighboring Pangani Falls power station. For Hale, TANESCO is asking that the flow duration curve below 700 cusecs should become not less favorable than at present, so that it will be possible to count on the availability of 700 cusecs for 70 percent of the time and of 650 cusecs for 75 percent of the time.

In order to maintain this flow while the demand for water for irrigation grows in upstream areas, it will be necessary to construct a storage dam. A suitable site has been surveyed at Nyumba ya Mungu. Indeed, such a dam will in due course be required in order to safeguard the minimum flow of 450 cusecs guaranteed for the Pangani Falls station. A single-purpose storage dam at Nyumba ya Mungu would cost about £ 600,000, a dam with provision for future hydroelectric development about £ 700,000.

The company argues that design on the basis of a flow of 700 cusecs is required to make it possible to deliver power to Dar es Salaam at a sufficiently lower cost than thermally generated power to be worth while, and also to provide a large enough installation at Hale to meet increasing demands over a period of eight years, from 1964 to 1972. The criterion as applied, however, appears to be somewhat arbitrary. The flow of 700 cusecs would allow installed capacity at Hale of 21 MW, giving a cost at Dar es Salaam, according to the company's calculations, of 7.3 cents per kWh. This figure compares with the present cost of thermal generation of over 10.5 cents per kWh generated for fuel and water alone. It is to be noted that the company estimates that a flow of 550 cusecs would allow a cost at Dar es Salaam of 10.3 cents per kWh, and would enable the expected increase of demand for electricity to be met up to 1970. Also, when the capacity installed at Hale is fully absorbed, there will remain several other sites in the lower reaches of the Pangani River allowing ready exploitation for hydroelectric development of heads of water in excess of 100 ft.

The company's cost calculations make no allowance for the cost of constructing a storage dam at Nyumba ya Mungu, it being assumed that this dam will be constructed at government expense as and when it is required to maintain the present pattern of flow below 700 cusecs. This dam has to be regarded as a cost of power rather than of irrigation. Irrigation alone would not necessitate the construction of a large storage dam at Nyumba ya Mungu, were it not for the necessity of maintaining the flow available for power generation. Whether the Government is justified in assuming the whole cost of providing the dam at Nyumba ya Mungu depends on estimates of the benefits to be obtained, in terms of both increased production and increased government revenues, by making possible the generation of electricity cheaper than can be obtained by expansion of thermal capacity. In any case, the cost of the Nyumba ya Mungu dam is not such as to make any very appreciable difference to the true total cost of electricity to be generated at Hale, particularly when suitable allowance is made for the facts that regulation of the river flow will benefit subsequent stages of hydroelectric development in the lower Pangani, and that it may prove economic to generate at Nyumba ya Mungu electricity for the Moshi-Arusha area.

A recent decision in principle by the Government to assure TANESCO of the flow required to build Hale to the 700-cusec specification entails an obligation to build the Nyumba ya Mungu dam, and also involves a decision on the allocation of water as between power development and irrigation in the middle Pangani Basin. This latter decision must have been somewhat difficult to make, by reason of imperfect knowledge of the potential under irrigation of the soils in the middle basin. While a survey of a limited part of the area has shown the soils there to be largely unsuitable for development under irrigation, it is not clear to what extent this finding can be extrapolated to the rest of the area. At the same time, population pressure in the neighboring Usambara Mountains gives rise to an increasing demand for water for irrigation.

A decision which remains to be taken is whether Nyumba ya Mungu should be built solely as a storage dam, eventual hydroelectric installations being put in nearer to Moshi and Arusha, or whether the extra cost should be incurred of building Nyumba ya Mungu with a view to subsequent power development on this site.

The case of the Pangani Basin illustrates the need for advance planning of the long-term development of a river basin as a whole. Though there may be possibilities in certain cases of sharing costs between power and irrigation, in other situations there is bound to be a conflict between the use of water for power generation and for irrigation. For the long-term development of the territory, it is important that the relevant data should be collected, and the appropriate analysis carried out, in advance of the planning decisions which have to be made.

CHAPTER 13 *MINING*

Until recently, minerals played a minor role in the economy of Tanganyika. Before the first World War, the recovery of gold and mica in small, scattered operations was the principal mining activity. There were subsequent discoveries of various other minerals, but their exploitation was held back by the world economic depression in the 1930's and by the dislocations of the second World War.

Several minerals have contributed to the growth of the importance of mining since the war, but the preponderant factor has been the development of diamond production, principally by the Williamson diamond mine. Diamonds now account for roughly two thirds of the total value of all mineral production (see Table 28). A fairly considerable increase of gold production up to 1953 has also been of some importance in the general increase of mining activity. Gold still contributes one sixth of the total value of mineral production. Minerals as a group now provide about 15 percent of Tanganyika's export earnings, nearly as much as either coffee or cotton. Furthermore, the mining industry makes an important contribution to public revenue, through taxes and also by way of government equity participation in certain mining operations.

The variety of known mineral occurrences in widely scattered locations in the territory, and the geological setting in mineralized areas, give promise that further exploration may result in long-range development. Large sections of the territory have not been prospected to a degree which excludes the possibility that economically significant mineral deposits may exist. While the outcome of geological mapping and exploration is naturally uncertain, the Mission believes that the potentialities are sufficiently promising to justify the Government on the one hand in taking a calculated risk by allocating its own resources to facilitate mineral exploration and, on the other, in framing its policies with a view to attracting the greatest possible interest of private enterprise in mineral exploration and development.

TABLE 28   Gross Value of Mineral Production, 1938, 1948, 1958

(£'000)

Commodity	1938	1948	1958
Diamonds	4	1,070	4,415
Gold	587	496	854
Lead	—	—	314
Building minerals	2	40	252
Salt	54	86	243
Copper	—	—	337
Silver	1	4	235
Mica sheet	12	61	51
Lime	—	16	19
Gypsum	—	—	22
Tin concentrates	50	52	13
Tungsten concentrates	1	—	—
Other minerals	1	2	11
Total	710	1,827	6,766

SOURCE: Tanganyika *Statistical Abstract, 1959.*

THE PHYSICAL SETTING

Although it is a land of plains and plateaus, Tanganyika contains two extremes of topographical relief: Mount Kilimanjaro, rising over 19,000 feet above sea level near the northern boundary, and Lake Tanganyika, the world's second deepest lake, occupying a trough on the western border. Topographical divisions are broad. To the east are the wide flat reaches of the coastal plains. These are generally bounded on the west by an irregular series of mountain ranges, reaching elevations of 7,000 feet. West of these ranges, the great central plateau and rolling plains form the greater part of the area. Deeply eroded escarpments then drop abruptly into the troughs of the Western Rift system along the western boundary, as exemplified by Lake Tanganyika.

More than two thirds of the surface area is composed of very ancient rocks of both igneous and metamorphic derivation, and less than one third of unaltered sediments. Broadly, a large central core is formed by an extensive altered shield of igneous rock occupying the west central area. Flanking this are very old gneisses and schists, variously divided into banded ironstones to the northwest followed by altered sediments in the extreme northwest area; metamorphic series crumpled into mountain ranges on the eastern side, and ancient metamorphosed sediments and volcanics gradational to the west. After deposition of these ancient rocks, a long period of geologic time elapsed followed by deposition of sediments, including the coal-bearing formations in the south, and possible oil formations along the seacoast. Igneous formations cover a wide range. The extensive granite areas forming much of the central part of the country are the oldest; late volcanic activity in the southwest and northeast forms the most recent.

Tanganyika's mineral deposits cover a wide range of diverse types. The principal gold deposits in the northwestern section are usually found in the banded ironstones which border the granite. In the extreme northwest, tin and tungsten deposits occur in metamorphic rocks. At Mpanda in the central western portion, a large lead-copper deposit has been mined. In the north central section is the Williamson diamond mine in the form of a large diamondiferous "Kimberlite pipe," which breaks through the granite. Many other known pipes are barren, however. In the southwest a large deposit carrying columbium (niobium) is being developed and other similar types of deposits are known. Extensive deposits of titaniferous magnetites have been found in this region.

Deposits of secondary origin are also important. A large phosphate deposit, formed from leaching of guano deposited in an ancient lake is under development southwest of Arusha. There are very large coal deposits in southern Tanganyika, not far from the magnetites. Extensive gypsum deposits are known. Salt deposits are abundant. Most commercial production of salt is derived from springs near Lake Tanganyika in the west. A great deposit of rock salt has been found in a drill hole during exploration for oil on the east coast. Finally, there are a host of minerals of minor economic importance: mica, of which there is a steady but limited production; graphite; garnet; kaolin; meerschaum; vermiculite; bentonite; and others. Building materials, mainly stone and gravel, are produced quite extensively. Limestone for cement manufacture is available in several locations; however, as mentioned in Chapter 12, some of the best deposits are not well located in relation to markets or to suitable clays.

THE RECORD OF MINERAL DEVELOPMENT

Diamonds

Diamond-bearing gravels were discovered before the first World War in the Shinyanga area of the Lake Province. Commercial production on a small scale began in 1925 but declined during the 1930's. It was not until 1940 that a major discovery was made at Mwadui by the late Dr. J. T. Williamson operating as an individual prospector. The subsequent history of diamond mining is essentially that of the Mwadui deposit, most of which has been developed by a single enterprise, Williamson Diamonds Limited. A small adjoining deposit is worked by a neighboring company, Alamasi Limited.

The diamonds in the Williamson mine are found in a kimberlite pipe and in the gravels forming the surface of the pipe which has an area of about 250 acres. Thus far, mining has been limited to the richest sections in the near-surface gravels, which contain an exceptionally high concentration of diamonds with a high proportion of gem quality.

In 1958 the Government acquired a half interest in Williamson Diamonds Limited. The Government's holdings consist of 600 shares, of which 320 shares were acquired in satisfaction of estate tax due from the estate of the late Dr. J. T. Williamson, who died in 1958. The remaining 280 shares were purchased with the proceeds of a 20-year loan of £ 1,317,272 made to the Government of Tanganyika by the De Beers Corporation. The Government's income from this venture, which in 1959 earned a net working profit of nearly £ 3 million before income taxes, now consists of royalties, income taxes and dividends. Part of these dividends is applied to pay the service on the loan with which the Government purchased the 280-share portion of its holding, but the general importance of the enterprise in the territory's budget can be seen from the fact that in 1958/59 total mining royalties, of which Williamson Diamonds was the main source, were £ 600,000, while total dividends paid by the Williamson enterprise in 1959 were £ 1 million and reserves set aside for taxation in that year over £ 0.5 million.

The output of Williamson Diamonds rose from 100,000 carats in 1945 to 624,291 carats in 1959 with a value of over £ 4 million. The mine's reserves are not fully known, but indications are that they will easily support the current scale of operations for many years. Exploration of the unaltered kimberlite below the weathered formation and enriched surface gravels is now in progress, and a shaft is being sunk to permit development to a depth of 1,000 feet. The grade of ore may decrease at the lower depths, but it is considered that a considerable expansion of present operations should be profitable.

The agreement concluded between the Government of Tanganyika and De Beers Consolidated Mines, Limited, at the time of the Government's acquisition of its shares, provides that so far as is commercially practicable the operations of the Williamson mine will be carried on at full plant capacity. If a general curtailment of diamond production becomes necessary, De Beers undertakes that the Williamson mine will not be required to reduce its output any more than the lowest curtailment applied to any mine in the De Beers group. As regards marketing arrangements, the volume of diamond sales is subject to an arrangement between Williamson Diamonds and the Diamond Corporation, a marketing subsidiary of De Beers. Tanganyika is entitled to a specified quota of the sales made by the Corporation, which accounts for the preponderant share of the world diamond trade. As Tanganyika's quota is considerably larger than the current output of Williamson Diamonds, no obstacle stands in the way of marketing an increased volume of Tanganyika diamond production.

	1957	1958	1959
Diamond revenue[1]	(£) 2,308,998	3,506,860	4,221,277
Mining expenditure[2]	(£) 1,055,447	1,181,057	1,551,955
Operating profit[3]	(£) 776,366	2,030,625	2,872,326
Reserve for taxation	(£) 154,155	248,553	545,000
Dividends paid	(£) 48,000	597,801	1,000,000
Tons treated	1,314,779	2,163,417	2,236,192
Carats produced	371,871	502,780	624,291
Grade (carats per 100 tons)	28.28	23.24	27.92
Cost per carat recovered (shillings)	63.59	54.22	
Cost per ton treated (shillings)	17.98	12.60	

[1] This figure differs from the value of diamond exports for the year in question, presumably owing to changes in stocks held.

[2] Including royalties paid but excluding depreciation on fixed assets.

[3] This figure differs slightly from the balance between revenue and expenditure owing to the inclusion of other items in the profit and loss account.

As production has grown, the capacity of the installations of Williamson Diamonds has been increased; at present the fixed assets of the enterprise are carried at a book value of over £ 8 million. A major part of the installation is a modern treatment plant, capable of handling 7,000 tons of diamondiferous gravel a day. The financial results have become increasingly satisfactory, as indicated in the figures from the company's financial statement, cited at the foot of page 257.

Gold

Gold has consistently occupied second place in Tanganyika's mineral production in recent years. Production from reef and alluvial sources declined from about £ 900,000 in 1954 to £ 700,000 in 1958, but a substantial increase was expected in 1959 in consequence of increased output of the Kiabakari Mine, the largest producer.

Gold mining is principally confined to four areas: (i) east of Lake Victoria, the site of the Kiabakari mine; (ii) south of the lake, where the Geita mine maintains a substantial output; (iii) the Lupa district in southwestern Tanganyika, which was an important source in former years but has declined; (iv) the Singida District in the Central Province, scene of the earliest gold mining operations during the period of German administration.

In the early phase of development, the gold mining industry was based on the exploitation of fairly rich alluvial ores, particularly in the Lupa field. This was succeeded by a phase of operations that has continued to the present, based on the working of low-grade ore bodies. With rising costs of production, some mines have been forced to shut down. Recent improvements in mining efficiency and metallurgical practice have reduced operating costs and permitted more profitable operation by larger companies. Geological information indicates that in many districts further systematic exploration efforts would result in new ore discoveries comparable to those now being mined. Unless the price of gold is increased, however, no substantial change in the outlook for increased production is likely.

At present 80 percent of gold output is accounted for by the Kiabakari and Geita mines. The Kiabakari mine, with a potential output estimated at 4,500 ounces of gold monthly at full-scale operations, is now the largest producer in the territory. After intermittent operations since the early 1930's, the mine was reorganized during the 1950's with increased underground development and a new refining plant, which reached full-scale operation in 1959. The mine is operated by the Tangold Mining Company in which the United Kingdom Colonial Development Corporation has a 51 percent interest, a private mining concern holding the remainder.

The Geita mine, until recently the territory's leading gold producer, has an output of about 3,500 ounces a month. Gold mining in the area being mined has passed through several phases following a large-scale development in the 1930's. An extension of part of the area now being mined was explored in 1959 by the Geological Survey. The financial results of operations during the postwar period have not been very satisfactory, owing to rising costs of operation. In 1958 the company operated at a substantial loss. In 1959, operations were based on treatment of a lower tonnage of better grade ore at an increased recovery rate, following new capital installations. A small working profit was earned during the year and the outlook is considered to be improving.

The Lupa district was one of the most important areas in the early phase of gold mining in the territory. The biggest producer in the area, the New Saza Mine, operated profitably from 1939 to 1956 but closed after exhausting its reserves. Alluvial production, once an important feature, has now sunk to insignificant amounts, mainly from individual African diggers. Despite geological formations which make prospecting difficult in the Lupa area, it is believed that a number of worthwhile occurrences remain to be found.

Production in the Singida district is now small, and several mines formerly worked are now idle. However, the grade of indicated ore remaining in the idle mines and the geological setting of the district encourage the belief that the area still contains promising exploration and development possibilities. In both the Singida and Lupa districts, any further development would probably have to be based on the exploitation of low-grade ore by relatively large enterprises.

Lead

In the course of prospecting for alluvial gold in the Mpanda area, a significant lead deposit was discovered in 1942. Underground exploration and diamond drilling indicated the presence of large ore reserves which were believed in 1945 to be about 2 million tons containing $6\frac{1}{2}$ percent lead. Associated with the lead were copper, silver and gold deposits.

In 1954 a large plant was installed by Uruwira Minerals, Ltd., for the recovery of ores, primarily lead. The cost of the installation exceeded £ 2 million, of which over half was financed by the Tanganyika and United States Governments through loans and guarantees. To move the output to market, a spur railway was built to join the Central Line.

The production of lead, copper and associated gold and silver at Mpanda was slightly over £ 1 million in 1958. However, the estimates of reserves on which the large plant installation was based have proved to be overoptimistic. Indicated sulphide ore reserves in mid-1959 were estimated to be adequate for less than one year's operation. Mine exploration and deep level drilling by the Geological Survey have yielded disappointing results. In mid-1960 the mine was accordingly being closed down.

Tin

Karagwe District in the northwestern corner of Tanganyika forms an extensive area carrying widely distributed tin ores and some minor tungsten occurrences. It was hoped that large alluvial deposits would be found, but by 1930 it became clear that most of the material was to be found in reefs or in small alluvial deposits which are a much less promising source. Mining operations have been on a small scale, the maximum production of tin ore (cassiterite) being only about 400 tons in 1938.

In 1950 the Colonial Development Corporation took over a series of claims from individuals and carried on an extensive exploration with the hope of being able to work the Karagwe deposits cheaply on a large scale. The fall in the price of tin metal was partly responsible for the withdrawal of the Colonial Development Corporation from this project.

The only operating tin mine at present is the Kaborishoke open pit mine. The mill is now handling 1,000 tons of low-grade alluvial gravels a day and producing 5 to 7 tons of tin concentrate per month; tonnage treated may increase when more water is available. A survey in the vicinity of the Kaborishoke Mine, made by New Consolidated Gold Fields Ltd., in the hope of finding deposits of a grade suitable for large-scale working, has been abandoned. In general, Karagwe District is best suited to small-scale operations, and the outlook is for a continuation of a small volume of production over an extended period.

Mica

Mica-bearing formations are found in many parts of the territory and have been mined on a small scale for many years, particularly in the Uluguru Mountains near Morogoro in the Eastern Province. During the past several years, however, production has declined, and the value of exports has dropped from about £75,000 in 1954 and 1955 to £51,000 in 1958. This is due partly to a weakening of demand for the poorer grades of mica, but also to an exhaustion of visible reserves and an unwillingness of producers to invest in the exploratory work involved in searching for underground deposits.

A recent development has been the taking over of a lease of one of the more important producers by two African cooperative societies, the original members of which were former employees of the company. The lease covers an area producing "ruby" Muscovite mica, which is of high quality and in relatively great demand. Marketing is carried out through licensed European dealers.

Because of the scattered occurrence of deposits, mica mining is best carried on by individuals or cooperatives. The Government already offers geological advice to potential producers. It should be investigated whether any further government assistance in exploration and development work is appropriate.

Other Minerals

The production of *salt* amounted in 1958 to about 36,000 tons with a value of £250,000. The principal source, which has been worked for many years, is a brine spring at Uvinza, near Lake Tanganyika in the Western Province. Production has been increasing gradually and approached 18,000 tons in 1958 with a value of £165,000. Half of the output is exported to the Republic of the Congo and the Federation of Rhodesia and Nyasaland. Production is carried out by one enterprise, the Nyanza Salt Mines, Limited, which is controlled by the Tanganyika Government. Along the coast a substantial but fluctuating volume of salt is produced by solar methods; in recent years output has been in the neighborhood of 10,000 tons.

Garnet occurrences are widespread in the territory, but the only commercial production of abrasive garnet of marketable quality is from a small mine in the Southern Province, the annual output of which has a value of about £ 4,000. A moderate increase of production from other sources is possible.

A *meerschaum* deposit, discovered in 1953 on the border of Kenya and Tanganyika near Mount Kilimanjaro, is being exploited commercially. The material is used principally in the manufacture of tobacco pipes, carried on in Kenya by the same company.

PROSPECTIVE MINERAL DEVELOPMENT

Phosphate

A major deposit of phosphate, at Minjingu Hill east of Lake Manyara in the Northern Province, was discovered accidentally in 1956 during the course of an aerial geophysical survey for the purpose of testing radioactivity. The origin of the deposit is unusual; it is believed to have been formed originally from bird guano accumulated around an island at a time when the level of the lake was much higher than at present. Development of phosphate production at Minjingu Hill has been entrusted to New Consolidated Gold Fields, Ltd., which holds a special exclusive prospecting license over the area and also over an adjacent area where a similar deposit has been discovered and is now being investigated.

The size and quality of the deposit indicate that a basis exists for substantial development of phosphate production. Thus far, proved reserves of phosphate-bearing rock amount to 10 million tons with a relatively high content of phosphorous.

The ore consists of two main types. Roughly half consists of powdery material with clay as the principal impurity. This type can be upgraded cheaply by dry separation from clay. The other half of the reserves is classed as hard and semi-hard ore with silica as the principal impurity. Some of this material can also be upgraded mechanically by breaking and screening. For other types, refinement by a flotation process may be necessary.

Tests have indicated that all types of ore are suitable for direct application in agriculture after grinding where necessary. The upgraded products may be used in several ways, including (i) direct application as fertilizer, (ii) admixture with superphosphates, (iii) manufacture of superphosphates, and (iv) manufacture of phosphorous and its chemical compounds.

The key question is whether the product would bear the cost of transport to Tanga or Mombasa for export, given obtainable f.o.b. prices. The deposit is located 70 miles from the present railhead at Arusha, and, although operating costs at the site are estimated to be comparatively low, road transport to railhead would make the cost at seaport prohibitive. Similarly, rail transport at the lowest rate charged on other export goods in the territory would subtract too much from the f.o.b. price to allow production costs to be covered. At mid-1960 the plan was, therefore, to limit production to 30,000 tons a year for internal consumption.

Development for export, if feasible, would make a considerably larger contribution to the economy of the territory. It is believed that the deposit is large enough to support profitable production of 300,000 tons of upgraded products per year. The Mission recommends renewed investigations to determine whether it might not in fact be justifiable to charge a specially low railway freight rate on phosphates for export, after construction of the necessary rail-spur. It may be noted as a factor in the calculation that the prospective dam at Nyumba ya Mungu (see pp. 251-52) could provide electricity for operations at Minjingu Hill. Here again is a case of a particular operation which has to be considered in the wider context of a number of interrelated developments.

Columbium (Niobium)

Columbium (known in British usage as niobium) is a metal whose properties make it of increasing interest as an alloy in the production of steel used under high temperatures, particularly in jet engines. The mineral pyrochlore has become a large potential source of columbium with the discovery of a large number of deposits in several African countries, Canada and Brazil.

A large deposit of pyrochlore was discovered at Panda Hill near Mbeya in the Southern Highlands Province by the Geological Survey Department. In 1955 the Government granted a prospecting license in the area to the Mbeya Exploration Company, Ltd., of which 70 percent is owned by a Netherlands concern, N. V. Billiton Maatschappij, and the remainder by the United Kingdom Colonial Development Corporation.

The development of the deposit is proceeding in stages. The first stage, to determine the size of ore reserves, was completed in November 1955. This has disclosed large reserves which can be exploited by low-cost mining. The second stage has been the installation of a pilot plant with a daily capacity of 100 tons, to indicate possible methods of treating the ore. Some success appears to have been achieved in solving the technical difficulties in the production of a satisfactory concentrate, but the profitability of a full-scale treatment plant capable of handling several thousand tons of ore a day has still to be established.

The future development of colombium production in Tanganyika is somewhat difficult to foresee. Assuming that the mineral dressing problem can in fact be overcome, it remains the case that development of world consumption is somewhat uncertain, owing to the existence of substitutes; also numerous sources of supply exist throughout the world.

Following the discovery of pyrochlore in Mbeya, further search for similar formations was undertaken in the territory. This disclosed a deposit in the Northern Province in the Lake Manyara area, with definite possibilities of providing ore of a payable grade. Preliminary investigations were undertaken by New Consolidated Gold Fields Ltd., but have now been abandoned.

Coal

Surveys have revealed the existence of large deposits of coal of good quality in the southwestern part of Tanganyika. The development of coal production on a commercial basis at this stage of Tanganyika's development is, however, blocked by the remoteness of the region from the sea coast and from rail transport facilities.

The main coal fields lie in the basin of the Ruhuhu River, a short distance east of Lake Nyasa. An option for the development of these deposits has been granted to Tanganyika Coalfields, Limited, an enterprise in which the Colonial Development Corporation has a major share; smaller shares are held by two private overseas concerns, and the Tanganyika Government holds a 12½ percent interest, by virtue of the lease assigned to Tanganyika Coalfields, Limited.

From 1949 to 1953 a large-scale program of prospecting was carried out in the Ruhuhu basin, involving an expenditure of over £ 500,000. Some 284 million tons of good quality, non-coking steam coal were proved by drilling; including lower grades, total reserves are estimated at over 400 million tons. The formation of the deposits is such that only a small portion can be extracted by cheap open-cast methods. Most of the deposits would require mining by more expensive underground methods.

Another coal deposit of smaller dimensions has been surveyed in the same vicinity. This is the Songwe-Kiwira field, near the northern end of Lake Nyasa. Drilling operations here proved reserves of over 20 million tons, of a quality that is good but somewhat inferior to the deposits in the Ruhuhu basin.

These coals appear to be assets for the future rather than for the present. The coal fields are remote from major centers of economic activity, and are 500 miles from the coast. It has been seen that the power needs of some of the major centers of potential industrial development in Tanganyika can be well met by hydroelectric development. Present world prices of coal are low, and the prospects are that they will remain low. Large stocks of coal have accumulated in Europe, and Japan's import needs, which are in any case for coking coals, are readily met from nearby sources. No prospective development of the southwestern part of Tanganyika is in view such as would permit the cost of coal shipment by rail to be shared with other traffic. The high cost of the underground mining operations required also dims the outlook for commercial development in the near future.

Iron

The existence of large iron ore deposits in southwestern Tanganyika has been known for many years. The deposits occur at Liganga in a rather inaccessible area north of the Ruhuhu. In 1957 and 1958 a comprehensive examination by drilling was undertaken by the Geological Survey. This indicated a minimum of 45 million tons of ore with an average iron content of 49 percent. Evidence of substantial additional deposits was also found. The ore is in the form of magnetite, which is associated with a high percentage of titanium-bearing minerals. The presence of titanium means that the ore cannot be treated economically by standard smelting methods. Alternative methods of reduction exist, however, and tests have shown that iron of an acceptable composition can be produced from the ore. If the metallurgical problem can be overcome at a suitable level of cost, the future development of the Liganga iron ore deposits on a large scale will depend, as in the case of coal, on finding export markets and hence on the solution of the transport problem. No immediate prospect of such development can be foreseen. However, the possibility exists of producing pig iron on a small scale by direct reduction utilizing the nearby Ruhuhu coal deposit.

Petroleum

During the past several years exploration for petroleum has been carried out by the B.P. Shell Petroleum Development Company in the coastal belt, adjacent islands and territorial waters. Substantial sums have been spent on surface mapping, geophysical surveys and the drilling of three deep test wells. All three wells were dry and the results of exploration thus far are inconclusive; however, the search is continuing. A by-product of this activity has been the discovery of large deposits of gypsum and rock salt, which may be commercially valuable.

MINING POLICIES

Surveys, Exploration and Prospecting

The effective development of mining involves a number of interrelated steps leading from topographical and geological surveying to exploration and prospecting and finally to the commercial exploitation of mineral discoveries. For each stage, consideration must be given to the action which the Government may take and the policies and measures best calculated to maximize the territory's return from mineral development.

While the known geological structure of Tanganyika tends to support the view that new, economically significant mineral occurrences may be found, their discovery is complicated by a number of natural obstacles. A mantle of soil capping as well as weathering and oxidation hide or obscure the surface appearance of ore deposits in most areas. The ancient nature of most geological formations renders them obscure, and capable of being defined only after prolonged study. Highly advanced techniques of prospecting may be needed at certain stages of exploration—including photogeological, geochemical and geophysical procedures—and these are costly. Interesting unprospected areas are typically remote from transportation. In brief, the surveying and discovery of commercially attractive mineral deposits can well be a slow and expensive process, even though the ultimate rewards may be great.

The Government's Program. The Government maintains a well-organized and well-equipped Geological Survey Department, whose main function is the preparation of geological maps to serve as a guide to more intensive exploration efforts. The laboratory facilities and staff of the Department also perform a variety of other functions, such as analytical assay, and the provision of mineralogy, petrology and mineral-dressing services which are of assistance in developing the mineral potential of the territory.

Since 1954 the main long-term program of the Geological Survey has been the preparation of geologic maps on a scale of 1:125,000, a scale which is considered of sufficient detail for all practical needs. With the personnel available, supported by an annual budget of £ 140,000, it has been possible thus far to map on this scale only about one tenth of the territory. At this rate, it would take a staff of the present size 30 years to map the entire territory.

More rapid progress in geologic mapping would be helpful in attracting further interest in exploration by venture capital. While some areas may be of little geological interest, the goal of mapping the greater part of the territory should be maintained. Proposals are now being considered to speed up the program of basic geological mapping with the object of achieving territory-wide coverage in seven years. The Mission believes that this aim is a sound one, provided that it can be achieved without unduly cutting into the budgetary funds available for other necessary purposes. This rate of geological mapping has implications for the program of topographical mapping, which should be planned to fit in with it (cf. p. 185). The present intention is to abandon the interim program of geological mapping to reconnaissance standard, so far carried out for just over one quarter of the territory, and to concentrate effort on the more rapid production of maps of lasting value.

As a general rule, large-scale exploration should be carried out to the greatest possible extent by private companies. There seems, however, to be a gap between the purely theoretical work of the Geological Survey and the private exploration now going on. This need is partly met by a small Economic Geology Section of the Geological Survey Department, which has successfully undertaken limited prospecting activity, notably in the case of the columbium-bearing pyrochlore deposits which are now undergoing development. Previously this section had undertaken important surveys of deposits of coal, iron, lead and gold, among others. Following the initial discovery of phosphates in 1956, the section began a systematic search for similar deposits.

The Mission considers that this work should be expanded. It recommends, therefore, that a mineral reconnaissance survey should be undertaken by the Geological Survey Department on a more systematic and sustained basis. The object of this survey would be to make a careful and detailed search for mineral indications in areas considered to be geologically interesting as shown by previous mapping. The project would require extensive field work by geologists and should employ advanced techniques and equipment. Following the Mission's visit to the territory, the Geological Survey Department has prepared a project for a reconnaissance mineral survey involving expenditure of £ 225,000 over a six years' period.

In the Mission's view, the acceleration of the mapping program and the organization of a systematic mineral reconnaissance survey both represent programs for which external assistance in the form of grants is highly desirable for a country in Tanganyika's economic position. The possibility of lifting Tanganyika's mineral development to a new level seems to the Mission to warrant external support of this nature.

A course for African prospectors has recently been conducted by the Department of Mines, assisted by the Geological Survey Department. The Geological Survey Department also organizes an annual field training course for departmental field assistants at which suitable staff from mining and prospecting companies can be catered for and are welcome. Simple geological mapping and mineral exploration techniques make up the bulk of the training. The Mission considers that activities of these kinds should be continued or even increased, according to the response encountered.

Private Exploration and Prospecting. In recent years a considerable amount of large-scale exploration for minerals has been undertaken by private interests or by private firms in association with the Colonial Development Corporation or the Tanganyika Government. Projects on which large sums have been spent include the coal and iron deposits in the southwest, the pyrochlore and phosphate deposits, and tin and gold occurrences in several areas.

A recent and extensive program has been that of the Western Rift

Exploration Company which holds a special exclusive prospecting license covering 34,000 square miles in the southwest, bordering on Lake Tanganyika. A large staff was employed and the most modern techniques used. However, only indications of minor interest were found, and this project has consequently been discontinued. As mentioned above, a search for oil has been carried out along the coast by the B. P. Shell Development Company. Williamson Diamonds has been carrying on a prospecting program for diamonds which was to be expanded in late 1959. No prospecting rights for diamonds except those held by Williamson Diamonds have been granted for a number of years.

In Tanganyika prospecting is lawful only under a license which is granted at the discretion of the Government to qualified adults for a nominal fee. The law provides for several types of prospecting license. An "Exclusive Prospecting License" may be granted for an area of eight square miles. By negotiated arrangement a "Special Exclusive Prospecting License" over larger areas may be granted. The Government can also control prospecting activities by formally closing any district or the whole territory to prospecting for any specified mineral or by a policy of withholding prospecting licenses. At present prospecting is not permitted throughout the territory for diamonds (with the exception of the arrangement with Williamson Diamonds), coal, iron, helium and salt. For various reasons prospecting is not permitted in specified areas for gold, gypsum, meerschaum, kaolin, radioactive minerals and raw materials for cement production.

In general, exploration for minerals under the conditions prevailing in Tanganyika requires the resources and technical background of large mining concerns. To encourage venture capital to undertake exploration, mineral legislation must be attractive and flexible. The present regulations which provide for granting special or exclusive prospecting licenses are usually necessary to attract concerns willing to make substantial exploration expenditures. However, such rights should be granted only for short periods and should be renewed on the basis of performance rather than of stated intentions. Closing the territory or various districts to prospecting for certain minerals may be advisable at times to prevent speculative pegging of claims or generally to ensure the orderly development of a deposit by financially responsible and technically competent groups. But over-application of this policy—which now covers a good part of the present mineral potential of Tanganyika—may defeat the very purpose it is designed to serve.

The Mission recommends as a first step in attracting fresh mining capital to Tanganyika that the territory be opened to diamond prospecting by any reputable mining group. It is also suggested that all Exclusive Prospecting Licenses and Special Licenses be periodically reviewed, and renewed after present termination dates only if satisfactory developmental efforts by the holder have been shown.

Taxation

It is the Mission's view that venture capital is the single element most vitally needed to explore and develop Tanganyika's mining potential. One measure to attract such capital is the provision of tax incentives. Specially favorable tax treatment of mining enterprises in the early stages of development is widespread in both developed and undeveloped countries. This policy is based on a recognition of the unusually risky nature of mineral exploration expenditures as well as of the advantages accruing to a country from successful mineral development. After the cost of finding, developing and equipping a mining property has been repaid from profits, however, an established mine should be able to bear an appropriate share of taxation on a basis similar to the rest of commerce and industry.

Tanganyika's income tax law incorporates a moderate tax incentive for mineral enterprises by allowing an initial deduction from net income of 40 percent of capital expenditure, including exploration and other pre-production costs. Under special conditions applicable to short-lived mines, the remainder may be written off in the following six years. Mining enterprises are also subject to the payment of moderate royalties. The highest rate, 15 percent of net value as determined by an official valuer, applies to diamonds. Lower charges are assessed on other minerals at fixed rates or according to a sliding scale based on the ratio of net profit to net value. As mentioned in the preceding chapter, the basic rate of company taxation—27.5 percent—is low in comparison with most industrial countries and not unfavorable compared with countries with which Tanganyika is in competition for venture capital.

The Mission feels that additional tax incentives would help to attract new capital into mineral development. While the details of such incentives should be the subject of expert study, it is suggested that certain provisions patterned after those successfully used elsewhere, for example in Canada, should be adopted. In particular, a brief tax-free period is recommended—perhaps of three years' duration as in Canada. This should be supplemented by an allowance for full deduction of exploration and other pre-production expenses which would, in effect, extend the initial tax-free period for several more years. In addition, Canada permits an annual "depletion" allowance for all mines of one third of taxable profits and extends special tax benefits to marginal gold mines. It also allows a more rapid write-off of investment in mining machinery and equipment than Tanganyika. The Mission recommends that these measures be given careful consideration.

Mining Consultant

The administration of the mining laws and regulations, including the issuance of prospecting licenses, the registration of claims and leases and supervision of safety regulations is in the hands of the Mines Department. In addition, a special post of Mining Consultant was established some years ago for the purpose of maintaining relations between the Government and the mining industry. This post has been, to all practical purposes, vacant for some time. The Mission believes that a full-time resident Mining Consultant, responsible directly to the Minister of Mines and Commerce, could make a valuable contribution to the territory's mineral development.

The primary function of the consultant would be to attract mining capital to the territory by maintaining contact with foreign enterprises and development groups. He would draw their attention to the possibilities for mineral exploration and development as revealed by various surveys. His responsibilities should include advising the Government on general policies relating to mineral exploration and development and also on specific projects as they arise. To perform these tasks effectively calls for a highly qualified person, preferably with engineering experience, and the remuneration should be fixed accordingly.

CHAPTER 14 *TRANSPORT, COMMUNICATIONS AND THE TOURIST TRADE*

There is a widespread belief in Tanganyika that lack of transport facilities is holding back the economic development of the territory. The Mission's investigations suggest this view to be commonly exaggerated. The main routes by land, water and air reach every corner of the territory, and their capacity is now underemployed. The present deficiencies are largely local in character, affecting inland access routes to the main transport arteries.

The problem of providing an adequate transport and communications system in Tanganyika is intrinsically of great difficulty. The area to be served is vast; the population and many centers of economic activity are scattered around the periphery of the territory (see Map 4); the density of traffic is therefore very low. In these conditions, future development of transport and communications will have to be planned with care so as to avoid duplication which the territory cannot afford.

The inland transport system is based on three ocean ports, each serving its own hinterland: Tanga in the north, Dar es Salaam in the center and Mtwara-Lindi in the south. Dar es Salaam serves by far the largest area, the Central railway line running across the entire width of the country from east to west and northwest, to Lakes Tanganyika and Victoria; and a main trunk road leads to the extreme southwest in the Southern Highlands. The port of Dar es Salaam and the Central railway line also serve the transit traffic of the Republic of the Congo.

Tanga serves a compact but densely populated and prosperous hinterland along the northeast border with Kenya, but shares this with the much larger port of Mombasa, which is the only port serving Kenya and Uganda. In the south, the modern port of Mtwara and its sister port Lindi together serve a much less developed and sparsely populated hinterland, stretching along the Mozambique border as far as Lake Nyasa. Both Tanga and Mtwara are linked with their hinterland by rail, and the same is true of Mombasa, which has a rail connection with the Moshi-Arusha area.

272

A road system, its main density in the coastal and Lake Victoria areas but with its principal long-distance routes running north to south, forms the link between the separate hinterlands of the three ports. Coastal and lake shipping complete these links in the east and west.

Thus, the lines of communication by road, rail and water largely complement each other. It is of the highest importance to maintain this pattern as new links are added to the transport system.

ROADS AND ROAD TRANSPORT

The road system has been by far the most affected by the difficulties posed by the territory's geography and the location of its economic activity. These conditions have required an extensive road network far out of proportion to the volume of traffic it is called upon to carry. There are at present 19,143 miles of roads maintained from central government funds, of which 8,114 miles are classified as main roads and 11,029 as district roads. Another 8,000 miles of rural and village roads, often in very poor condition, are the responsibility of local authorities. In contrast, the total number of registered vehicles is only 35,000—of which some 13,000 are private passenger vehicles— and a large majority of these circulate in urban areas and on short sections of inter-urban routes. In these circumstances the Government applies the only defensible policy of providing a country-wide "Low Cost Road" system, defined as follows at the Tenth International Road Congress, Istanbul, 1955:

> "A low cost road is one which, having regard to considerations of climate and traffic, has been located and built to geometrical standards commensurate with future requirements, but has been constructed with bases and surface to meet the present traffic requirements. It is, however, one which should be so designed, constructed and maintained that it allows for stage construction when traffic requires it and improvement in economic conditions permits."

The Ministry of Works' road department is carrying out this policy with commendable efficiency, skill and frugality.

Within the broad framework laid down by this policy, there remains a number of important issues: the plan of the system of main roads and the priority of the development of its various sections; the balance between the development of main roads and feeder roads; and the standard of construction to be applied on the different sections of the road network.

Main Roads

Map 8 shows the present road network, together with the more immediate plans for additions and improvements, plans with which the Mission is in general agreement.

The basis for the Government's long-term program for the construction of main roads has been described as a grid of three routes running north and south and three running east and west. The grid is conceived of as comprising the following routes:

North-South:

a. Mombasa, Tanga, Segera, Mkata, Chalinze, Dar es Salaam, Kilwa, Lindi-Mtwara.

b. Kenya border, Arusha, Babati, Dodoma, Iringa, Mbeya, Rhodesia border.

c. Uganda border, Bukoba, Biharamulo, Kasulu, Mpanda, Sumbawanga, Rhodesia border.

East-West:

d. Tanga, Korogwe, Moshi, Arusha.

e. Dar es Salaam, Morogoro, Dodoma, Manyoni, Singida, Sekenke, Nzega, Biharamulo.

f. Mtwara (Lindi), Songea, Mbeya.

With the exception of the Sekenke-Nzega section of route (e), and of a planned link in route (a) further east than the present route from Segera to Chalinze, roads already exist over all the routes indicated. However, to bring the grid up to true main road standards would involve not only the completion of the missing sections, but also upgrading and even realignment in parts of many of the roads.

In general this grid forms an acceptable basis for a fairly long-term plan of development of the main road system. However, construction or improvement should have very much higher priority for some parts of the grid than for others; and a number of roads which are not included in the grid are of economic importance equal to or greater than that of parts of the grid itself.

At present, the highest priority is being given to upgrading and improvement of the link Segera-Mkata-Chalinze, in order to facilitate communications between Dar es Salaam and the important centers of economic activity in the north of the territory—Tanga and also Moshi and Arusha (by way of routes (a) and (d)). In this case, we consider that the new railway link between the Tanga and Central lines does not wholly meet the need for improved communications between these important parts of the country, and that the combination of parallel routes—coastal shipping, railway and two roads—is spread out so as to serve a suitably wide area. The intention is to allow the more westerly road, passing through Kwadihombo, to drop down to the status of a local main road.

The next highest priority is to be given to completing the link from Singida to Nzega. This link may be regarded not only as completing route (e), from Dar es Salaam, via Nzega to Biharamulo, but also as extending route (d) by providing a link from Moshi and Arusha to the Lake Province. Some increase of internal trade based upon increase of specialization appears to be growing up between the Northern and Lake Provinces, cultivators in the Lake Province specializing in cotton and relying to some extent on supplies of food grains from the Arusha area. This growth of specialization and internal trade would be helped by the provision of a road link of a satisfactory standard between Babati and Nzega. In due course there will be a case for a more direct link between Arusha and Malya, further to the north. But this link would be expensive, and must be given considerably lower priority than the link by way of Sekenke.

The third priority is for improvement of the road leading from Dar es Salaam into Morogoro and Iringa and thence into the Southern Highlands where it connects with Mbeya in the southwest, a combination of part of routes (b) and (e) according to the above presentation of the grid. This route forms the main line of communications between the Southern Highlands and the rest of the country. Although most of this road is already developed to an all-weather standard, parts of it have still to be brought up to all-weather standard.

The Mission agrees with this allocation of priorities. In the next five years further development should also be undertaken of a number of link and branch roads such as Mpwapwa to the Dodoma-Dar es Salaam road, Tabora-Nzega, Songea-Lake Nyasa and Mbeya-Lake Nyasa.

The grid as developed and supplemented in this way will have a main emphasis on east-west routes, reflecting the fact that the natural flow of traffic carrying the territory's main export crops and the bulk of the trade in imported and locally produced goods is along lateral routes.

An important consideration in the planning of main road development must be the avoidance of the superfluous expenditures involved in duplication of railway and water routes. It is for this reason that the grid quite rightly does not include a central route east-west from the coast to Lake Tanganyika. Such a route would cross for a distance of 400 miles—more than half its total length—an area of unproductive land, already traversed by a well-equipped railway. Similarly, the improvement of the coastal road from Dar es Salaam down to Mtwara and Lindi, the southern part of route (a), must for the most part be given a low priority, since it duplicates a shipping route. The cost, which would run into several million pounds, would not be justified in relation to other pressing needs. Certain sections of the route, however, especially that from Kilwa for a distance southward, are feeder roads to ports and as such require early attention.

The north to south route in the west (c) does not run through areas of high potential production except over its extreme northerly section from the Uganda border to Biharamulo. This route serves a number of towns of no great importance, but it forms their only connection with the country's main lines of communication. For this reason it must receive some attention, although economic considerations would permit of only lower standards of construction at this time.

The remaining north to south artery is the middle route (b), known as the Great North Road. For most of its length it does not serve highly developed production areas. The only usefulness of a road over the whole stretch is as a territorial link between north and south and as a transit road for international traffic between Kenya and the Rhodesias and beyond. Thus on a purely internal basis, this road would have lesser priority than other Tanganyika main routes, particularly the three east to west arteries. The only portion of the north-south artery of primary internal importance is the stretch leading from Iringa into the Southern Highlands and Mbeya. As an international link, however, it may be suitable to develop its entire length to a uniform stabilized all-weather standard, provided the bulk of the funds so required is forthcoming from the other interested territories to the north and south of Tanganyika. Tanganyika's share of the cost of development should be no more than is justified by the potential growth of internal traffic.

Feeder Roads

Up to the present, the Government's policy has been to build up the main road system to an all-weather standard, passable at all seasons, and to attend to feeder road improvement on a strictly limited scale. This was the right policy to start with; a feeder road could serve little purpose until the main road could take its traffic. The alternative of providing a complete system of main and feeder roads, area by area, would have prejudiced the economic development of important areas of the territory and would have severely hampered administration. With the growth and improvement of the main road network, the Government considers that the time has arrived at which the rate of main road improvements should be gradually reduced and expenditure on the improvement and expansion of feeder roads proportionately increased. The Mission is in full agreement with this change of policy.

The expansion of feeder roads should, of course, reflect plans and prospects for the further development of agricultural output. For example, the Mission's recommendation of certain irrigation projects (see Chapter 8, pp. 177-78) in the Upper Ruvu Basin, the Kilombero Valley and the Bohoro and Pawaga flats carries with it the corollary of the development of feeder roads in these areas. In many areas, it should be investigated whether improvement of feeder roads or provision of storage facilities is the more economic solution of local problems. This applies in areas where the main problem is that crops cannot be evacuated and consequently deteriorate if early rains make the tracks impassable, or where food supplies cannot be brought in to meet occasional emergencies during rainy seasons.

TABLE 29   Proposed Expenditure on Road Development, 1960/61-1965/66

(£ '000)

Category	1960/61 Budget Estimates	1961/62	1962/63	1963/64	1964/65	1965/66
Main roads	1,082	1,000	1,000	900	800	675
Feeder roads	304	340	380	475	575	700
Total	1,386	1,340	1,380	1,375	1,375	1,375

SOURCE: *Estimates of Expenditure, 1960/61;* Mission proposal.

During the past several years the Central Government has spent around £ 900,000 a year on road construction (not including the sums provided for maintenance). This is substantially below the outlay during the early 1950's; the budget estimate of £ 663,000 for 1959/60, which was abnormally low in part for technical reasons, was by far the smallest of the past decade. About one eighth of recent expenditure has been for feeder roads. Allowing for total expenditure on roads at some £ 1.4 million a year over the next few years, the Mission suggests allocations up to 1965/66 as listed in Table 29.

Road Standards

The standards of road construction affect not only the initial cost but also the maintenance charges. An all-weather standard requires the bridging of streams and flood openings, culverts and side drainage, a certain amount of re-alignment and regrading, and an all-weather surface which may be earth, stabilized earth, gravel or similar material, macadam, tar or bitumen. After experience of some over-expensive sections, reasonably cheap yet adequate standards have been designed and adopted. For feeder roads a lower standard has been accepted, but one which allows passage for at least eight months of the year, and more often up to ten months.

With the growth of the road network, maintenance has become an increasingly important element in the Government's recurrent expenditures, having risen from under £ 300,000 in 1951 to over £ 1,000,000 (budget estimate) in 1960/61. Even at this level, maintenance expenditures appear to have been insufficient to keep many roads up to the intended standards, and the Mission's current budget projections in Chapter 3 allow for some raising of standards of maintenance. The growth of maintenance expenditures has been due in part to the improvement in the quality of the roads to meet the requirements of increasing numbers and weights of vehicles; in such circumstances, maintenance costs increase sharply.

In view of the high maintenance cost as well as the initial cost of bitumenized roads, it is essential that the density of traffic and other conditions should be carefully considered in every case where the provision of a bitumen surface is proposed. The present policy is to provide a bitumen surface where very steep gradients make maintenance of other surfaces costly, and in conditions of high traffic density. The first condition is appropriate for a bitumen surface. As to traffic density, however, this is extremely low on all roads, except those within the largest towns. Only short stretches leading out of Dar es Salaam and half a dozen of the provincial towns have a traffic density up to 300 vehicles in 24 hours; a few short sections in the Tanga province and around Arusha and Moshi have a density between 200 and 300. A density of 170 vehicles in 24 hours is now considered to qualify for bitumen surface. The Mission feels that this qualifying limit may be too low, and should be carefully examined.

Maintenance needs are unduly increased by vehicles which are too heavy traveling along roads at excessive speeds. The road department has correctly set maximum limits to the weights of vehicles allowed to use the different roads, but these limits are frequently exceeded. Far more serious is the effect of excessive speed. The damage a heavy vehicle running at excessive speed does to an unpaved road is quite out of proportion to that caused by an average vehicle running at a normal speed; the former may do as much damage as eight or ten of the latter vehicles. These evils can only be controlled by more effective administration of licensing and by enforcing a speed limit on certain roads for buses and lorries of not higher than 30 miles per hour.

Regulation of Road Transport

Tanganyika's road transport system is still in its infancy. Until 1957 it was uncontrolled. In 1957 a licensing system was introduced, primarily to deal with what was considered to be an unhealthy situation arising from excessive competition among different types of road transport. The licensing system distinguishes between public carriers of goods and passengers on the one hand, and private traders carrying their own goods on the other. The Transport Licensing Authority is empowered to limit the number of licensed public carriers and to determine the route and conditions of operation of the carrier. While competition within the road transport system was the main problem aimed at, the system of transport licensing also affects road-rail competition which, while yet a minor problem in Tanganyika, is a growing one. Reference to this aspect is made in a separate section below.

The object of the licensing system, as in other countries, is twofold: (i) to enforce minimum standards of safety and efficiency, and (ii) to prevent disruptive competition which, in the long run, might lead to higher average costs of transport or to serious dislocation,

waste or even discontinuance of normal transport facilities. The
Mission considers that some degree of regulation is desirable but it
feels equally that there is a danger of attempting too much in the field
of transport regulation in the relatively primitive conditions prevailing in the territory. What is needed is effective regulation over the
main long-distance routes; in the rural areas not only is regulation
impractical but it is important not to discourage African enterprise
which, while not necessarily maintaining the standards of regular
long-distance public carriers, provides a service which would otherwise
be unavailable.

On the main long-distance routes the road transport industry still
shows abundantly the disorderly features of a growing but, as yet,
uncoordinated system: passengers carried on lorries, goods traffic on
buses, running on unauthorized routes, and various deviations from
minimum standards of safety and efficiency, such as unroadworthiness
of vehicles, unsafe accommodation of passengers, overworking of drivers, nonobservance of published timetables, excessive speeds and over-
loading. There is a nucleus of competent operators and haulers,
large and small, but its position is being undermined by wasteful and
in some instances illegal competition by large as well as small operators, particularly private carriers. A country in Tanganyika's position
should not expect to have a road transport system of the same standards as prevail in more developed countries; but it should be possible,
by effective regulation, to establish a firmer basis for the industry.

Two reasons are primarily responsible for the present state of
affairs. One is a widespread misconception of the true cost of furnish-
ing road transport services of a minimum acceptable standard. Entry
into the transport business is deceptively easy: there is abundant
evidence of the misguided notion that it is only necessary to buy a
bus or lorry to be ready to embark on road transport. Costs of maintenance and administration are underestimated. The result is that
there are far too many vehicles on a number of road sections for the
traffic offered for carriage. Many transport enterprises fail, defaults
on hire purchase of vehicles are widespread and there is considerable
evasion of income taxation.

A second factor is the illegal competition by traders operating
under private carriers' licenses who offer long-distance service. This
competition tends to undermine the position of the full-time public
carriers by depriving them of a profitable portion of their potential
business. The long-distance private carrier, conveying his own goods
to his customers, cannot possibly compete against public carriers

unless he also carries other people's goods against payment. The possible exception may be the private trader who carries his raw materials on the return journey, a rare case. But attempts by the private carrier to stabilize his own position by engaging in partial competition with the public common carrier inevitably means that the private carrier skims the cream off the public carrier's business. This threatens the position not only of the important road haulers operating fleets of vehicles on the main roads but also of the individual African owner-driver who should be the mainstay of the road transport system in rural areas.

The basic remedies for the situation are a revised licensing policy and better enforcement of the regulations. During the initial period of its existence, the Transport Licensing Authority has been hampered by the fact that a transition from a free-for-all to a regulated system had of necessity to be gradual. A large number of public carriers' licenses had to be issued "as of right." The time has arrived, however, when the number of licenses issued to public carriers and the conditions of issue of such licenses can be effectively regulated. The Mission supports the position taken by the Licensing Authority that the full-time long-distance haulers should be protected by limiting the number of licenses issued to public carriers along a determined route. The issue of public carriers' licenses should be conditional on the demonstration of some proof of understanding of the cost, obligations, and requirements of the intended operations, as well as compliance with safety regulations governing vehicle, passengers, load and crew and the observance of approved published timetables and tariffs and of insurance requirements.

It is important, however, that the protection of the regular long-distance hauler should not be allowed to stifle the growth of local transport services off the main scheduled routes, particularly in areas where it would not pay the regular haulers to operate. For this reason, the Mission considers that the licensing conditions should be administered with a considerable measure of flexibility to allow a higher degree of competition in limited areas (including exceptions to the rule limiting private carriers to their own goods), particularly where transport requirements are seasonal. Further, where large numbers of small operators are now licensed to cover the same route, they should be encouraged to pool their resources and also to shift their business off the main routes to the feeder road systems as they are developed. Standards of service in these areas need not necessarily conform to those applied on the main routes.

The administration of the licensing system also requires improvement. The Transport Licensing Authority lacks means of effectively enforcing the existing regulations. Steps should be taken to strengthen the Authority, including the appointment of officers with power to charge and prosecute offenders. This should be accompanied by a campaign to inform the public of the reasons for the licensing policy and its specific regulations.

RAILWAYS

The railway system has made a major contribution to Tanganyika's economic development and is destined to continue to do so. The bulk of the main cash crops rely on rail facilities to reach the ports, and the flow of imports to the richer areas in the north and northwest of the territory is heavily dependent on rail traffic. Interterritorial trade with Kenya and Uganda is also dependent largely on rail links, supplemented by lake shipping. Part of the agricultural and mining areas that are developed in the future will probably be most economically served by an expansion of the rail network.

TABLE 30   Statistics of the East African Railway System, 1948 and 1958

	1948	1958
Route mileage[a]	2,930	3,398
Tanganyika	1,278	1,589
	(millions)	
Goods traffic (tons)	2.6	3.9
Goods traffic (ton-miles)	769	1,517
Capital assets[b] ($£$)	37.5	100.5
Operating revenues ($£$)	7.3	18.9
Operating expenses[c] ($£$)	5.6	15.9
	(units)	
Locomotive stock	234	459
Tanganyika	74	115
Wagon stock	5,764	9,545
Tanganyika	2,006	3,592

[a] Including branch lines.
[b] Including harbor installations.
[c] Including renewals.

SOURCE: Tanganyika *Statistical Abstract, 1958;* East African Railways and Harbours Administration, *Annual Report, 1958.*

Throughout East Africa the railways' business has grown steadily since the war, as indicated in Table 30. Goods traffic (ton-miles) roughly doubled between 1948 and 1958; the number of passenger journeys, however, remained practically unchanged as more and more short-distance travelers took to the roads. During the early part of the period traffic demand rose out of proportion to capacity, which suffered from under-maintenance during the war and from difficulty in procuring equipment during the early postwar years. By 1955, however, the rehabilitation problem had been overcome, and since then there has been a substantial growth of rolling stock and a moderate increase in route mileage, financed mainly by foreign loans. The increase in route mileage was mainly outside of Tanganyika, but the three East African territories have shared more or less equally in the expansion of rolling stock. The railway system is now the largest single employer in the territory and its central workshops in Dar es Salaam are the largest industrial establishment; it also provides hotels for travelers and tourists, certain road transport services, and housing and training facilities for its staff.

Administration

Since 1948 Tanganyika's railways have been operated with those of Kenya and Uganda as one system by the East African Railways and Harbours Administration (EARH) with headquarters at Nairobi in Kenya. The amalgamation has been of benefit to each of the three territories. The unified system is financially stronger, the utilization of its rolling stock and equipment is better, the administration, staff establishment, offices and other services are cheaper and tariffs lower than would have been the case if the systems had continued as separate entities.

The EARH Administration, operating as an agency of the East Africa High Commission, is essentially independent in both its administrative and financial arrangements. Its annual budget and major policies are, however, subject to review or approval by various bodies including an interterritorial Transport Advisory Council, on which the three Governments composing the High Commission are represented. Under the provisions of the Merger Act of 1948 the railways have been efficiently and economically operated. Future political changes may require some organizational adjustment, but since the Administration is already practically autonomous and a well established economic and technical entity, these adjustments should be kept to a minimum.

The idea is sometimes voiced of separating the Tanganyika railways, ports and inland waterways from the present system. This would be a retrograde step. The size of the system as it is today—comprising 3,400 route miles, serving a population of over 25 million, carrying a traffic of just over 2,000 million combined passenger miles and goods ton-miles, with a staff establishment of 50,000—is within the range of the most successful of the world's railway systems, neither too small nor too large, as shown by extensive research and experience. The trend in railway reorganization everywhere is towards even closer integration. Certain measures of decentralization are no doubt feasible without harm to efficiency or operating results, and might help to increase the responsiveness of the system to local requirements. But, for the reasons mentioned, no major reorganization should be contemplated.

Finances

The financial position of the Administration is sound. Capital assets are properly maintained, adequate reserves are provided for renewals and maintenance, and no financial difficulties have been encountered during the postwar period. By law the railway is required to operate according to business principles, but on a "nonprofit" basis. This means that any surplus, after provision for interest charges, renewals, reserves and betterment funds, must be applied to reduce rates and fares. The Mission recommends that this requirement be dropped, in order to enable the Administration to apply any surplus to improvement and expansion.

Revenue from goods traffic is about eight times that from passenger traffic and the proportion is increasing. Goods traffic therefore requires most of the attention in the search for a proper balance between rates and costs. Under the present schedule of freight rates—which provides differential rates for ten classes of commodities—the over-all revenue amounts to a little over 20 cents per ton-mile and the average total cost per ton-mile to just under 19 cents. The Mission considers that the tariff structure is sound, reflecting the variations in the relationship between value and bulk of the goods carried in accordance with general practice.

The advent of road competition has recently forced the Administration to revise the rate structure in an attempt to halt the diversion of high-rated traffic to road transport. From January 1, 1959, the five highest classes of rates have been drastically reduced and in compensation the five lowest classes, which apply to East Africa's major export crops, have been increased by 5 percent. The modified structure of rates represents a reduction in average charges, the first during the postwar period. The effect of these revisions will be known only after a year's application, but so far the financial results are not particularly encouraging.

As indicated in the preceding discussion of road transport, part of the competitive pressure exerted by road haulers reflects the disorganized state of the road transport industry. The impact of such pressure on the railways reinforces the case for effective regulation of road transport. The policy of shifting the burden of "irregular" competition by road transport onto the commodities now being carried by the railways at the lowest rate may have prejudicial effects on the trade in these commodities as well as inequitable effects on the consuming public. Continued attention to the problems of road-rail and intra-road competition is needed in the interest of securing the maximum return from the territory's investment in its transport system considered as a whole.

One way of dealing with the problems of undesirable road-rail competition is to give the Railway Administration more freedom to adapt certain rates to the needs of the moment. The Mission supports a policy allowing the Administration to exercise the necessary freedom and flexibility in this regard. A measure which has already proved of considerable help in meeting road competition is the application of through rates for the combined use of the Railway Administration's road and railway services. Other measures that should be explored in this connection are the introduction of special containers for road-rail-water, through-carriage and of refrigerated and insulated wagons for long-distance rail transport.

While operations of the EARH Administration as a whole are financially satisfactory, it should be pointed out that certain portions of the Tanganyika rail network are in a weak position. The short branch from the Central Line to Mpanda is threatened with losses, at any rate over a period, as a result of the closing down of the mine at Mpanda. Efforts are being made to promote increased agricultural production in this area to provide enough traffic to justify keeping the railway open. The Southern Province railway, connecting Mtwara with Masasi and Nachingwea and isolated from the rest of the system, still falls far short of covering its purely operating costs in spite of drastic operating economies. As was seen in Chapter 3, the losses on this railway and the associated port of Mtwara give rise to a considerable burden on the budget of Tanganyika. The decision on whether the railway should be kept open must depend on the assessment made of possible future agricultural development of the Southern Province. It has been pointed out elsewhere that the future of the Tanganyika Agricultural Corporation's activities at Nachingwea is closely bound up with the future of the railway.

Railway Development

The only substantial additions to the rail network of Tanganyika since the end of the war have been the two lines just mentioned: one of 154 miles from Mtwara to Nachingwea in the Southern Province, built in connection with the Groundnut Scheme, and having a link to Masasi; and the other a branch line of 131 miles which was built to provide access from the Central line to the lead-zinc mine at Mpanda in the Western Province.

Work is now in progress on two further lines. One is a 44-mile branch line due for completion in 1960, from Kilosa on the Central Line to Mikumi, a provisional terminus on the main road serving the Southern Highlands. Among other things, this would provide transport for the projected sugar scheme referred to in Chapter 4. The second is a connecting link, 117 miles long, between the Central line and the Northern (Tanga) line.

This connection is long overdue. It will close the gap between the two main parts of the railway system and make possible substantial savings in operations, particularly by permitting an interchange of rolling stock. The advantage of this interchange is heightened by the fact that the seasonal peaks of traffic on the Central Line and on the Northern Line and the Kenya-Uganda lines with which it is connected occur at different periods without any overlap.

The value of rolling stock that will be released by economies made possible by completion of the link is conservatively estimated at £ 550,000. On the other hand, to make the rolling stock interchangeable will require unification of the different types of braking systems on the two lines at an estimated cost of £ 400,000. The cost of construction of the line itself will be approximately £ 2 million. Preliminary traffic estimates, necessarily rough, indicate a first year's operating deficit of £ 36,000, an acceptable figure in view of the ensuing benefits to be expected from the line.

The Mission envisages that further extension of the main transport network should be largely by way of road building, as suggested above. However, two further railway building projects come up for consideration:

a. The extension of the Mikumi branch, referred to above, to the site of the Kilombero Sugar Company plant in the Kilombero Valley. This link, which may be made feasible by the traffic to be provided by the sugar company (20,000 tons of refined sugar per year initially, with the intention of increasing to 30,000 tons per year) would assist in the opening up of the Kilombero Valley for agricultural development. However, careful attention will have to be given to the relative merits of road and rail communications in the area to the southwest of Mikumi, it being borne in mind that an eventual extension of the railway out of the Kilombero valley in the direction of Lake Nyasa would be very expensive to construct.

b. A 70-mile extension of the Northern Line from Arusha to reach the projected phosphate mine at Minjingu on Lake Manyara. It has been seen in Chapter 13 (p. 263) that the future of this project depends on whether it is feasible to transport phosphate from mine to port at a charge not greater than the difference between the cost of production and the f.o.b. export price.

As has been seen in Chapter 2, it is the task of the Railway Administration to find finance for construction of new lines, loans raised by the Administration being covered by the joint and several guarantee of the Governments of the three East African territories.

OCEAN PORTS AND SHIPPING

Tanganyika has four ports on the Indian Ocean: Tanga in the north, Dar es Salaam in the center, Lindi and Mtwara in the south. As shown in Table 31, Dar es Salaam is by far the most important, followed by Tanga, which is the main outlet for sisal exports. The importance of Tanga is diminished by the fact that its hinterland is also served by the port of Mombasa in Kenya. Mtwara and Lindi serve an area of the country whose development lags behind that of the areas served by the other ports. These ports are operated by the East African Railways and Harbours Administration.

TABLE 31   Operations of Tanganyika's Ports, 1958

Item		Tanga	Dar es Salaam	Lindi	Mtwara
Revenue	(£'000)	279	972	48	69
Working expenditures[a]	(£'000)	273	846	45	72
Traffic	('000 tons)	264	692	51	75
Petroleum imports	('000 tons)	10	227	—	7
Ships calling	(number)	721	1,203	156	162

[a] Excluding interest, renewals and betterment provisions.

The capacity of all ports is adequate; their equipment is capable of handling an appreciably larger volume of traffic than the present. Access to all is free from hazards, except for Lindi which is obstructed by a bar restricting the use of the port at low tide to vessels of not more than 12 feet draft. The entrance channel to Dar es Salaam allows no vessel of greater length than 625 feet, but such vessels do not normally sail these coasts.

Deep-water berths are available at all ports, alongside wharves at Dar es Salaam and Mtwara and at buoys or anchorages in all four ports. Transit and storage sheds, stacking ground areas, cranes and other handling appliances, lighters and port craft, lights and navigational aids, fire and health services, and dockworkers' amenities are modern and in good shape.

During the ten years ending 1958, traffic through the Tanganyika ports has practically doubled, but the increase has not been regular. After a fairly steep rise during the first four years, held back only by the limited port capacity in the years immediately after the war, two or three years of little or no increase followed until the railway and port congestion problems had been mastered. A sudden increase in traffic volume occurred in 1955, since when the volume has remained roughly the same.

With three new deep-water wharves at Dar es Salaam completed in 1957, the deep-water port at Mtwara built mainly for the Groundnut Scheme still underemployed, and the port of Tanga now well equipped for a considerably larger traffic volume, there is no need for further development for several years to come. However, the margin at Dar es Salaam is such that a more than normal increase in traffic may well require additional berthing facilities in the not too distant future. It is therefore recommended that a project for one or two additional deep water wharves be worked out in sufficient detail to be ready for construction at short notice should the need arise.

Shipping

The country's ports are in general well served by the world's shipping lines and tramp steamers, though problems are liable to arise concerning the adequacy of coastal services. The flow of imports and exports is regular and at reasonable charges.

Coastwise shipping is operated by the regular lines, international as well as local, all subject to international rules and regulations, and by small local craft, subject only to the territorial Government's "Regulations Governing Native Craft."

The regular ocean cargo liner has been the backbone of coastwise shipping. But the operation of these vessels is now seriously threatened by competition from two sides: from seasonal road transport on land and from mechanized dhow traffic on the sea. Several services have been withdrawn or have given notice of withdrawal during the past year or so, as a result of losses incurred.

It should be realized that road transport and mechanized dhows together could not replace the normal coastwise shipping: road transport, however flexible and speedy, cannot compete in cost on a year-round basis, and the mechanized dhow or schooner cannot carry all traffic at all seasons. Thus the full-time coastal shipper faces a problem similar to that of the railways and the regular long-distance road hauler. If appropriate conditions are not established to allow regular, scheduled shipping services along the coast at reasonable levels of profitability, the community will pay the price in irregular and probably dearer alternative transport. Immediate steps are required to assure orderly development of coastal shipping.

Recommendations to regularize the competition on shore have been set out above. On water a distinction will have to be made between the long established native dhow traffic and motor schooner traffic of modern days. The native dhow has its special place in coastal transport; its operations are adequately controlled by the existing regulations governing native craft. The motor schooner has developed from a small native dhow fitted with a motor to a vessel of the size of small coasters, and her size is still increasing. She carries passengers and valuable cargoes owned by others, but she escapes the laws and rules covering the safety of craft, passengers, cargo and crew. She is allowed to use native dhow port facilities without paying a reasonable and adequate proportion of the cost. The operation of dhow wharves in fact results in a yearly deficit.

The Mission recommends that motor schooners of all sizes, and sailing schooners of 125 tons and over, be subject to regulations governing seaworthiness of vessel, safety and comfort of passengers and cargo, qualifications and conditions of service of crew, and also that the use of dhow wharves at standard charges be restricted to genuine dhows and that motor vessels be surcharged appropriate rates.

When these steps have been taken, it will be necessary to consider whether any further measures are necessary to maintain or secure adequate services.

Most of the coastal shipping calls at the port of Zanzibar, which is outside the jurisdiction of the East African customs and excise authorities. Hence customs formalities are necessary in all coastal ports. This in turn requires additional documents for all consignments, even those passing from one Tanganyika port to another. Traders have been complaining of the excessive formalities required and of the delays in forwarding documents and consequently in taking delivery of the goods covered by them. It is suggested that the customs and excise authorities invite the shipping companies to consider together with them the simplification of these formalities for all purely internal transport, formalities which are entirely absent when the same goods are carried between ports by inland routes.

INLAND WATER TRANSPORT

Tanganyika's rivers are unsuitable for navigation, and with a growing road transport system, inland water transport on rivers could not possibly be developed economically to compete with the roads. Nature has, however, provided the country with excellent waterways on lakes which are among the largest in the world. Inland water transport thrives on Lake Victoria, which serves two of the most prosperous provinces. On Lake Tanganyika, whose coastal area is less fertile and only thinly populated, its activities are proportionately less.

The principal services are provided by the Inland Water Transport division of East African Railways and Harbours. They are supplemented by native craft. The floating equipment is of good standards, well maintained, and new craft have been added recently to the lighter and tanker fleets. A new passenger and cargo ship is under construction and is expected to be in service on Lake Victoria about the middle of 1961.

Mwanza, in Tanganyika, is the main port on Lake Victoria. Through it a steadily increasing traffic is handled, exceeding 100,000 tons per annum. A new port area with ample wharf lengths, sheds and storage space, cranes and appliances is nearing completion. Further developments will not be required for a number of years to come. There is, however, a need for considerable improvement in access roads from the ports and jetties into the hinterland, and these roads deserve priority over extensions to the coastal roads.

Mechanized native craft on the lakes are increasing in numbers, and there is a tendency to divert their operations from their most appropriate function of feeder transport to inter-port traffic. As a parallel to similar coastwise traffic along the ocean coast, these craft escape safety regulations for vessel, cargo, passengers and crew. The need arises for proper regulation before their operations become damaging to regular public transport. It is recommended that regulations governing these craft, similar to those for coastwise schooners, be adopted, so allowing them to compete under orderly conditions. As in the case of road transport, the object of regulation should be to prevent the undermining of a service which is only partially duplicated by the unregulated small-scale operator. But such regulation should be administered flexibly to avoid suppression of desirable initiative and excessive protection of the "regular" shippers.

AIR TRANSPORT

Dar es Salaam is Tanganyika's main airport, built to international standards. Internal airports are well distributed over the territory and served by scheduled services. A number of landing strips, government and private, provide air access to otherwise inaccessible and remote small centers of activity. Thus the present needs of the country are adequately served. The airports and landing grounds are in adequate shape, with the exception of Tanga, where the runway will soon require attention.

The Dar es Salaam airport is modern, well planned, though on a small scale, and well equipped, calculated to handle comfortably one aircraft arrival and one departure at a time. Plans have been prepared to extend the main building at both ends. It is right to have these plans in readiness, though there is at present no urgent need to carry them out.

At the smaller of the internal airports, where only one or two aircraft, or none at all, call during a day, there appears to be a surplus of attending administrative and ground staff. Considerable economies may well be found in the combination of one or more departments' and airlines' posts in one person, and it is recommended that this possibility be jointly examined by the organs concerned.

The air services inside Tanganyika and with neighboring territories are operated by the East African Airways Corporation (EAAC) with its own aircraft. Since 1957 the Corporation also operates international services to the United Kingdom and Continental Europe and to the Indian continent, using aircraft chartered from the British Overseas Airways Corporation or wholly owned. The combination of internal and international services has been efficient and has contributed towards satisfactory operating results.

The Corporation, like the railways and ports, is operated under the High Commission's control, as a business concern. Since 1955 the Corporation's operating results have shown a surplus after paying interest and provision for depreciation and reserves. Tanganyika's own internal services contribute under 10 percent of the total revenues; the international services accounted in 1958 for nearly half of the total revenues and the proportion is still rising. Most of Tanganyika's internal services are operated below capacity, and their earnings do not fully cover their actual operating costs. However, they provide an essential passenger and freight service to remote places, and must be maintained.

The Corporation has ordered two Comet-4 jet aircraft for delivery in 1960 for international services, confident that their part in the expected increase in world air traffic will cover the cost, capital and recurrent. This is a reversal of the policy hitherto followed, under which the EAAC international operations, which are in effect complementary to those of the larger airlines, were handled by used aircraft, displaced from service in the major lines, with their severe competition, while still having a long remaining serviceable life. These second-hand aircraft, in excellent shape, have in fact been procured at very low cost. There need be little fear that the Corporation's confidence in the future is overoptimistic. Nevertheless, the cost involved is considerable, and the results of this departure from the existing policy will have to be analyzed with care, to make sure that the balance between attractive and remunerative international traffic, and weak but essential internal traffic, is not disturbed at the expense of the latter.

Meteorological Service

The meteorological service is an East Africa department, directly responsible to the High Commission. It is much concerned with air transport, internal and international; in the latter field it will find increasing duties with the expansion of high-speed aircraft routes. In the field of weather observations, statistics and forecasts generally, the department is naturally handicapped in Tanganyika by the extensive area and low density of population. Up to the present the department has been able, by efficient operations and stringent economies, to keep abreast with developments generally.

The future will certainly require some expansion, particularly for aviation requirements. In the immediate future it is desirable to establish a modern long-range Sferics network for the detection of thunderstorms; this is all-important because a closer network of ground stations is not only very costly but difficult to operate in the sparsely populated areas, most of them in Tanganyika. This Sferics network requires four centers in East Africa, at Entebbe, Nairobi, Dar es Salaam and Tabora. Tanganyika's share would thus be two out of the four stations.

A second project, also essential in the immediate future, is the extension of storm-detecting radar, already in operation at Dar es Salaam, to Tabora and Mwanza, to cover the large inland land mass and the expansive water area of Lake Victoria. Wind-finding equipment exists at Tabora, but it is not being worked, since adequate funds are not available for its operation and maintenance. The extension of the storm-detecting radar system to the two stations mentioned and provision for their regular operation are recommended.

POSTS AND TELECOMMUNICATIONS

The East African Posts and Telecommunications Administration is another agency of the East Africa High Commission. A regional director for Tanganyika, to whom wide authority is delegated for day-to-day management, administration and operations, has his head office at Dar es Salaam.

The department meets with considerable difficulties, financial and technical, in providing services over vast distances not only to outlying small centers but also between the larger towns and cities. In spite of these handicaps, the postal and telecommunications network covers the country well, the rates are not high, and the financial operating results are satisfactory. There are now 172 post and telegraph or telephone offices in the country, and since 1950 £ 2,500,000 has been spent on new works and extensions to buildings, plant and equipment.

A recommended development program for the Tanganyika Directorate over the five years 1959-63 is summarized in Table 32.

TABLE 32   Posts and Telecommunications: Recommended Program of Capital Expenditures in Tanganyika, 1959-63

(£ '000)

	1959	1960	1961	1962	1963
Construction (postal service) ..	82	94	32	32	32
Telegraph	2.7	1.5	1	1	1
Telephone					
Lines	85.2	11.1	19.1	18.7	9.8
Exchanges	5.6	7.5	15.8	7.8	2.7
Installation costs	125.8	99.3	87.3	92.0	86.7
Total	290	213	155	152	132

Two major projects for telephone lines, for which public pressure is strong, are not included in the program above because of prohibitive costs. One is the link from the coast with the Lake Province via Singida, waiting for an all-season road beyond Singida to be available. It would appear that this link could well wait for the road to be built, after which the cost of construction and maintenance of lines will be reasonable. For the present the telephone link along the central railway line is regularly available.

The other project is the improvement of the coastal link south from Dar es Salaam. Elephants and giraffes, in addition to climatic upheavals, cause too frequent interruptions of this line, and its maintenance and repair are extremely difficult because of inaccessibility. These interruptions are a definite hindrance to trade and the public in the Southern Province. The Mission is satisfied, however, that any alternative telecommunications link would be too costly in construction and future maintenance. Yet the Mission would suggest that further study of the problem be made, particularly the solution of a VHF radio link with substations at the requisite distance along the coast, using such points as may become accessible as new feeder road sections along the coastal route are constructed.

Requests have been made for public call boxes along main roads. The Mission finds that the cost of such a service would far outweigh the expectation of resulting revenues. This is a case where the long routes and the low density of population cannot justify heavy expenditures.

THE TOURIST TRADE

The almost unique game reserves and the varied natural scenery of Tanganyika offer a strong attraction for tourists. With the growth of international air travel, the territory's accessibility to tourists from Europe and even from North America has greatly increased. Additional tourist trade comes from in-transit sea passengers through Dar es Salaam and from travelers coming from the Rhodesias and other parts of Central and South Africa.

During the past several years Tanganyika has received close to 10,000 visitors a year, of whom about 2,500 were classified as "intransit." The number of visitors increased sharply from 1954 to 1957; there was a sharp drop in 1958, possibly as a result of the unsettled economic conditions abroad, but the level remained well above that of the earlier 1950's. It is estimated that gross tourist expenditure in 1957, the peak year thus far, exceeded £ 1 million. Further promotion of tourism offers promise of substantial benefit to the territory's economy.

A fair amount of public and private effort has gone into this endeavor, but there is scope for more. In general, tourism in Tanganyika is organized as part of tourism in East Africa as a whole, particularly on the part of visitors from overseas, and it seems that this circumstance should be accepted as the basis of certain joint efforts regarding international publicity and the organization of tours by groups. Thus far both Kenya and Uganda, especially the former, have secured a substantially larger share of the East African tourist trade than Tanganyika. This is due to a number of factors, including better links with international air transport, better road conditions and superior hotel facilities. There is no reason, however, why Tanganyika should not share in the potential general expansion of the East African tourist trade, by developing facilities that would increase the attraction of its special natural assets such as the Serengeti National Park, the Selous game sanctuary, the Ngorongoro Crater, the area around Mounts Kilimanjaro and Meru, the dramatic scenery south of Lake Victoria, the fine, shark-free beaches and reefs on the Indian Ocean and many others. With future developments in mind, it may be noted that Kilimanjaro, Meru, the Ngorongoro Crater, the Serengeti and the south shore of Lake Victoria up to Mwanza are all in a stretch of just over 300 miles.

Numerous projects for developing and improving hotel facilities and other services catering to the tourist trade are under consideration by various private interests, and the Government has been attempting to promote the construction of a large hotel in Dar es Salaam. Should a development corporation be established, it could play a valuable role in promoting, and possibly assisting financially, development of hotels and other facilities, such as road transport for tourists. In the 1960/61 capital budget, allowance is properly made for construction and improvement of access roads to areas of interest to tourists.

Game Protection and Management

In its Serengeti National Park alone, Tanganyika claims to have the largest concentration of plains game animals left in the world. Their number, variety and seasonal migrations afford a spectacle which it is becoming increasingly difficult to parallel anywhere else in the world. This should be recognized as one of the territory's greatest assets for the future, and should be unswervingly protected.

It seems clear, however, that sentimentality over game cannot be expected to influence Africans in the areas concerned in favor of the protection of animals from hunting and the reservation of large areas of land—even dry, tsetse-infested land. So far, revenue from tourists is not enough to provide any very persuasive argument.

In these conditions, thought is being given to the possibilities of game cropping, with the object not only of increasing the economic value of the game reserves but also of giving them value, as sources of meat, obvious to those who live on their borders. There is a growing body of evidence to show that, in areas such as the Serengeti, the ungulate fauna are better adapted for survival than are domestic stock. Thus there is reason to believe that, under a proper system of game management and cropping, certain areas protected for game can be made to yield a higher return of protein per acre from game animals than could be achieved by the introduction of stock, with the attendant risk of overgrazing and erosion. The Mission considers further investigation of the methods and the economics of systematic game cropping to be highly desirable. This is an activity for which technical assistance from outside agencies might well be sought.

The Price of Access

Policy in promoting tourism should probably aim at increasing the volume of middle-income tourists rather than of the luxury trade or big-game hunting safaris. The role of the East African Railways and Harbours Administration in promoting low-cost package tours in East Africa is already important and should be further developed. A major contribution to an expansion of the tourist trade in East Africa as a whole, and hence in Tanganyika, would be a substantial reduction in air fares from Europe; this has recently been under consideration.

EDUCATION

CHAPTER **15** *EDUCATION*

The provision of school places for Africans in Tanganyika has greatly increased over the past dozen years. There are now primary school places for over 50 percent of children reaching school age. However, only about one in eight of those entering school receives more than four years of education, and the number completing 12 years of education and sitting for the School Certificate examination passed 300 only in 1959, but has been brought up to some 480 in 1960.

The number of African children receiving more than the beginnings of formal education is clearly inadequate, especially in view of Tanganyika's progress to political independence. The declared aim of a civil service recruited wholly from the inhabitants of the territory is still frustrated by the absence of candidates of the required level of education.

The need to expand African educational facilities is fully recognized in Tanganyika. However, due to financial difficulties, a Five-Year Plan for African Education, 1957-61, was lengthened to a seven-year plan, and even as such has not been fully implemented. There is a clear need to increase the numbers of potential university graduates, of school certificate students, and of those with a moderate level of technical training. Even though the effect of additional education expenditures on the growth of the economy, and hence of the revenues needed to meet the bill, is delayed and somewhat uncertain, nevertheless the claim of education to increased government funds is beyond dispute. However, it is necessary to keep in mind that expenditures on education are in competition with expenditures on programs likely to have a more immediate effect on production and the growth of revenue. It is therefore necessary to select educational priorities with great care.

The educational situation of non-Africans creates less acute problems at present. It appears that very few Asian children do not receive at least primary education, and the Asian-Arab group, out of their comparatively small population, secured in 1959 280 School Certificate passes and 112 passes in the General Certificate of Education examina-

TABLE 33   Structure of the African Educational System

	Standard											
	I	II	III	IV	V^a	VI^a	VII^b	VIII^b	IX	X	XI	XII
a. Numbers enrolled in 1959	107,273	96,003	88,397	83,835	13,850	10,479	8,334	7,208	1,686	1,562	474	318
b. Numbers enrolled in previous standard in previous year	—	107,261	96,650	86,305	76,474	11,882	10,480	7,795	6,454	1,619	1,378	328
c. Numbers enrolled in corresponding Standard I ....(year)	107,273 (1959)	107,261 (1958)	110,493 (1957)	110,034 (1956)	103,312 (1955)	93,297 (1954)	85,173 (1953)	76,661 (1952)	67,158 (1951)	58,180 (1950)	53,563 (1949)	56,205 (1948)
d. Percentage surviving from previous standard in previous year.	—	89.5	91.5	96.6	18.1	88.2	79.5	92.5	26.1	96.5	34.4	97.0
e. Percentage surviving from corresponding Standard I enrolment	100.0	89.5	80.0	75.7	13.4	11.2	9.8	9.4	2.5	2.7	0.9	0.6

a Including District School enrolment.
b Including Pre-Secondary enrolment.
NOTE: These figures cover all registered schools: government schools; local authority schools; government-aided private schools; and unaided private schools.
SOURCE: Annual Reports and Summaries of the Department of Education.

tion. Most of the Europeans in Tanganyika were educated outside the territory and a high proportion of their children are sent for education outside the territory.

AFRICAN EDUCATION

Structure of the System

From 1951 to the present, African education has been organized in terms of three stages comprising four standards (forms, grades) each. Each standard is normally the work of a year. Some pupils may be made to repeat standards, but there is no provision for faster progress. The first stage, covering Standards I to IV, is provided in primary schools, the second (Standards V to VIII) in middle schools, and the third (Standards IX to XII) in secondary schools.

The main function of primary schools is training in the basic skills and tools of learning.

Middle schools are selective institutions and entrance into them depends on a competitive examination. They provide four years of "English and general education" aiming at: (a) further education or training, e.g., secondary education, teacher training Grade II, trade schools; and (b) practical orientation towards useful citizenship and immediate employment.

Secondary schools provide diverse streams which lead to different goals. For example, a student completing Standard X may (a) begin the Teacher Training course for Grade I teachers, (b) enter a Technical Institute or a Natural Resources School, or Departmental Training Courses, (c) continue secondary education, or (d) seek "general employment." Specifically in the case of girls, completion of Standard X would qualify them for further training courses for "medical assistants, policewomen, clerks and social development workers." After Standard XII a student takes the Cambridge Oversea School Certificate examination and may proceed to higher studies, take Departmental Training Courses or seek "general employment."

Until recently, the further two years of education required for the Higher School Certificate and university entry have been available only at Makerere College in Uganda. The present policy is to make this additional schooling available in Tanganyika, and four schools at this level have been opened.

The majority of middle schools and all secondary schools are board-

DIAGRAM OF EDUCATIONAL
SYSTEM FOR AFRICANS, 1959

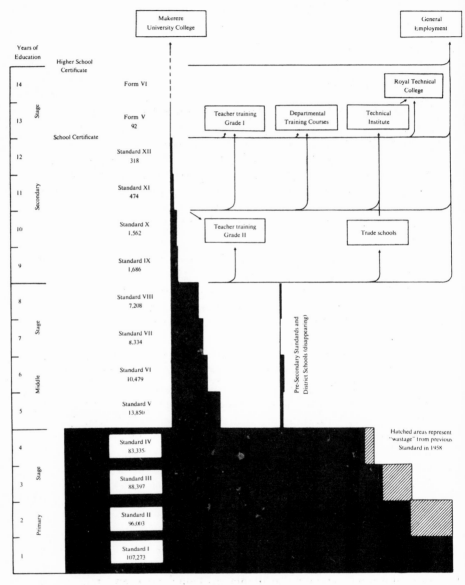

Diagram 3

ing schools. This arrangement is clearly inevitable outside the larger towns, given the present selectiveness of post-primary education and the wide dispersion of the population; and it has certain educational advantages. Its obvious disadvantage is that it makes middle and secondary education rather costly.

The organization of education, the enrolments at each level and the occupational goals after various standards, have been presented by the Department of Education for the year 1958 as shown in Diagram 3. The diagram highlights one of the most important facts about Tanganyikan education—the limited educational opportunity, especially at the middle and secondary levels.

The number of children entering Standard I appears to amount to about 45 percent of the population reaching school-going age. Many fall out, particularly after the first and second grades, and in recent years only around 75 percent of those enrolled in Standard I have reached Standard IV. But it is after Standard IV that there comes the first great curtailment of the number of places available: less than 20 percent of Standard IV pupils pass on to Standard V (see row (d) of Table 33). Similarly, little over a quarter of those reaching Standard VIII pass on to Standard IX, so that in 1959 the Standard IX enrolment was less than 3 percent of those who had entered Standard I in 1951 (see row (e) of Table 33). In 1957, only 178 African pupils reached Standard XI, but by 1958 the number increased to 328.

The African educational system has been greatly expanded over the postwar period at every level. Standard I enrolments increased from less than 50,000 in 1947 to over 110,000 by 1956. The number of African school certificate candidates increased from 28 in 1948 to 101 in 1953, 175 in 1958 and some 480 in 1960. This last figure nevertheless remains extremely low.

A Program for Further Expansion

In the Mission's opinion, the aims for further development of the African school system should be, in order of importance:

a. Expansion and diversification of post-primary education (secondary and technical in particular). An important aim should be to bring the school certificate class as soon as possible up to, say, 2,000-2,500. Special attention should be paid to expansion of facilities for, and improvement of girls' education on the middle and secondary levels.

b. Re-examination of the existing pattern of African education. Establishment of an Institute of Education, which should carry out research into the theory and practice of education in Tanganyika.

c. Full utilization of space in the existing primary schools and reduction of wastage (drop-out), particularly in the case of girls.

These aims have implications, of course, for expansion of teacher training.

Expansion of Secondary Education

An immediate and urgent aim of policy in Tanganyika is to secure a sharp increase of the number of secondary places available for Africans. This is to be done in two ways: by provision of new schools and classrooms; and by racial integration of the educational system which, while desired on other grounds, will have the effect of opening up secondary places for Africans in schools which have been reserved up to the present for the other races.

Present plans aim at increasing the Standard IX places available in "African" schools to 2,835 by 1964, an increase of 1,150 over 1959 enrolments, and at increasing Standard XII places to 2,275 in 1964, an increase of nearly 2,000 over 1959 enrolments. The additional places would be provided to a considerable degree in grant-aided, voluntary agency schools (largely mission schools), and it is believed that sufficient teachers of adequate standards can be found.

The Mission is in sympathy with these plans, subject to the financial provisos considered at the end of this chapter. From the data available to us, it is not clear what assumptions are being made as to the number of extra secondary places for Africans which will become available as a result of integration. The pupils to reach Standard XII in 1964 will come from the total of 8,334 who were in Standard VII in 1959. In estimating the feasible increase of school certificate candidates, it is necessary to make allowance for the requirements for teacher training and for various departmental training courses including training of agricultural Field Assistants, for entrants to trade schools and to the Technical Institute and for those who will wish to leave the educational system for other destinations. Expansion of the higher levels of the educational system obviously has its costs in terms of keeping pupils in school longer and away from productive employment, and is possibly siphoning off some of the best pupils from vocational training courses of high importance to the territory. It is clearly desirable that the Development Committee of the Council of Ministers should plan the development of education on the basis of a view of the balance of requirements for those emerging from the educational pipeline. While it is hardly possible in a free society directly to allocate the products of the educational system to particular professions and trades, it has to be borne in mind that while educational opportunities inescapably remain limited, the differential expansion of various parts of the educational system can be in itself an indirect type of vocational allocation.

The Mission further urges that every effort should be made to avoid dilution of teaching standards.

4-4-4, 6-6 or 8-4

A major issue of African education below the secondary level has been whether to maintain the present primary-middle-secondary, 4-4-4 pattern, or whether to split up the educational structure up to school certificate in some other way. The influential Binns Report[1] came out strongly in favor of the present 4-4-4 organization and supported it on the following grounds:

a. "Basic skills and tools of learning, as well as general adaptability can be communicated to the average African pupil under present conditions in four years."

b. The holding power of the former 6-year primary course was not strong. It was found to be difficult if not impossible to get the majority of the African children to stay at school for even four years, let alone six.

c. Concentration on the strengthening of a 4-year course as a limited objective would reduce wastage and hence increase literacy.

d. A limited objective of a primary education for all would be accomplished more easily if such an education extended over four years.

[1] This is the name habitually given to the Report of the East and Central African Study Group in *African Education, A Study of Educational Policy and Practice in British Tropical Africa*, a report produced on behalf of the Nuffield Foundation and the Colonial Office, 1953.

e. A break after completion of Standard IV, followed by another 4-year intermediate course, would strengthen the educational value and the holding power of the latter.

f. A stronger and more integrated intermediate course would in turn facilitate the work of the secondary schools.

The Binns Report noted that this type of organization was strongly opposed by African opinion; and, judging by what was said in the 1959 Legislative Council debate on the Budget, this opposition has not died out. It is argued that four years of primary education is inadequate, while eight years up to the end of the middle school course is either not enough or too much: that is to say, that it leaves the pupil dissatisfied to return to agriculture or to unskilled work, while not equipping him adequately for other careers. The 4-4-4 system is also resented since it sharply distinguishes the educational system for Africans from those for Asians and Europeans, which still have two stages, primary and secondary.

Plans are now being made to reorganize African primary education in rural areas to bring about the extension of the present four-year primary course to one of six years. It is envisaged that this process will take ten years to complete. This is regarded as an intermediate step towards the eventual aim of a fully integrated system consisting of an eight-year primary course followed by a four-year secondary course to school certificate and two further years to higher certificate and university entrance. As primary schools take over Standards V and VI, classrooms in middle schools would become available. It is planned to use such classrooms to double over the next three years the number of pupils who complete Standard VIII in rural middle schools.

The Mission is in sympathy with the more immediate aim of lengthening African primary education to a six-year course, though at such a pace as financial considerations may permit. The further aim of an eight-year primary course for a considerable proportion of the territory's children seems rather more questionable. We are concerned not merely by the additional cost involved, but by questions concerning the relative adaptability of six-year and eight-year students to the economic and social roles which they must realistically be expected to be called on to play. This is a question which should be investigated and kept under review by the proposed Institute of Education (see pp. 311-12).

Even the immediate program of primary and middle expansion, as designed, becomes expensive from its second year, particularly when added to the costs of the planned expansion of secondary facilities and of integration (see p. 319). The Mission believes that, at the present stage of development of the educational system, priority must be given to the expansion of the Standard XII output. It will be necessary to keep under review the financial resources available for education, and to plan the expansion of education from Standard V to Standard VIII accordingly. Teacher training has, of course, to be adjusted in accordance with the intended expansion of the number of school places, and it is therefore essential to plan ahead, even if plans have to be periodically revised.

Standards I - IV

The present provision of places in Standards I - IV appears to be sufficient to take some 55 percent of all African children of the appropriate ages. This is a reasonably high level for a country at Tanganyika's per capita income level, particularly bearing in mind that in many parts of the territory population is very sparse, so that the problem of providing primary education for many of the children at reasonable levels of cost would in any circumstances be very difficult.

In fact, more children receive the beginnings of formal education than are enrolled in the registered primary schools. A large number of children attend "bush schools" and "catechetical schools." The former are partly or wholly religious, and in some cases take the pupils up to or even beyond Standard II. The latter are entirely religious. While the quality of these schools varies, many of them perform a useful service.

Recent increase of the supply of primary facilities has outrun demand in many places, and in 1958 it was estimated that some 20,000 Standard I places remained unfilled; and 1959 enrolments were almost identical in total number. A second feature making for under-utilization of existing primary facilities is the high rate of wastage. Wastage is very much higher among girls than among boys, and is greater between Standards I and II than at subsequent stages. Table 34 shows the degree to which wastage has been cut down since the earlier postwar years.

However, even at the improved rates of wastage occurring from 1958 to 1959, under 70 percent of girls and 85 percent of boys entering

TABLE 34   Wastage in Primary Schools—Average Experience of
1947-50 and 1956-1959 Compared

	Percent Dropping Out between Standards		
	I-II	II-III	III-IV
1947-50			
Boys	28.0	12.4	12.1
Girls	39.9	27.8	33.0
1956-59			
Boys	10.4	6.5	0.9
Girls	15.4	14.0	12.2

SOURCE: Annual Summaries of the Department of Education.

Standard I would survive to Standard IV. There is room for further
improvement, particularly in the case of girls.

Further systematic study is needed to identify the most important
causes of wastage and to determine how they may best be combatted.

Education of Girls

A persistent problem of development of education in Tanganyika
is the education of girls. Not only do fewer girls than boys attend
schools at all levels (see Table 35), but also wastage on all levels is
considerably higher than that of boys. The disparity between the

TABLE 35   Girls as Percentage of All African Pupils in the Various
Standards, 1959

Standard	Percent	Standard	Percent	Standard	Percent
I	38	Vª	17	IX	11
II	36	VIª	18	X	11
III	33	VIIᵇ	18	XI	7
IV	29	VIIIᵇ	17	XII	7

ª Including District School enrolment.
ᵇ Including Pre-Secondary enrolment.

SOURCE: *Annual Summary of the Department of Education, 1959.*

relative number of boys and girls in all schools has been attributed to a multiplicity of factors of which the following have been stated to be the most important:

a. Parents with limited means, when faced with a choice between their sons' and daughters' education, give preference to the education of boys.

b. Parents are reluctant to break with traditional conservative beliefs concerning the education of women. Though considerable progress has been made, nonrecognition of the importance and value of education of girls is still a potent force.

c. Men teachers, especially the older ones, find it difficult to teach girls. This, coupled with a shortage of women teachers, lowers the quality of teaching.

d. The curriculum of the schools is often unrelated to the needs and interests of women.

In addition to these influences, the fact that facilities for further training beyond the primary level are limited seems to influence the parents against sending their daughters to school at all.

These conditions, which explain the disparity between boys' and girls' education, suggest ways for its improvement. Though the disparity might not be eliminated within the foreseeable future, it is of the utmost importance for Tanganyika's future that the education of girls be improved both quantitatively and qualitatively. To accomplish this, practical steps must continue to be taken for the purpose of (a) expanding facilities on all levels, (b) introducing more practical courses for girls in the Middle Schools, and (c) increasing the number and quality of women teachers, and heads of girls' middle schools.

It is difficult at present to find suitable African women to serve as heads of girls' schools, and most of these positions are at present filled by expatriates. To solve this problem, it seems necessary to go back to the earlier levels of girls' education, and to raise the number of girls, particularly from Standard V onwards. This aim is already accepted as desirable by the authorities in Tanganyika.

Institute of Education

The preceding paragraphs have raised points concerning the quality and organization as well as the quantity of African educational facilities. There is a need for further investigation to lay the basis for progressive improvements. It is necessary that education be solidly grounded in a country's own milieu. If attempts are made to introduce into an educational system features which do not take this into account, they will cause tensions and will result in a spurious rather than an authentic kind of education.

The Mission consequently endorses the early establishment of an Institute of Education, which would carry out research aimed at improvement of the quality and organization of education in Tanganyika, in relation to the needs of the territory as it develops.

The research to be carried out at the proposed Institute of Education should serve to improve the quality of teacher training. The Institute should, among other functions, coordinate the work of existing teacher training institutions and supervise in-service training.

Technical and Vocational Education

Present plans for educational expansion in Tanganyika give a prominent place to the expansion of facilities for technical training at various levels. The Mission considers that these plans are well founded.

Technical education in Tanganyika is organized as an alternative form of either "post-intermediate" or "post-secondary" education. There are two trade schools, one at Ifunda and the other at Moshi. They provide a three-year course of trade training in various trades connected with the building and engineering industries. Training in the Moshi Trade School, which started in 1957, is confined to building trades. Admission to both institutions takes place after completion of Standard VIII.

Technical and vocational education is also provided in certain institutions and through various courses. There is the Technical Institute in Dar es Salaam, organized on a nonracial basis for technical and commercial training to technician standard, the College of Commerce at Moshi, and there are full-time residential courses for the training of Engineering Assistants as well as courses for handwork teachers.

In total there are roughly 2,000 students receiving technical and vocational education of one sort or another.

By comparison with highly industrialized societies, technical education in Tanganyika is in its infancy. But as the country expands its industrial enterprises and as it improves its methods of agriculture, more and better trained technologists, craftsmen and technicians will be needed. In seeking ways to meet this demand, however, it is of the utmost importance to take into consideration the experience of other countries that have been engaged in this important task. It has been found that technical education, either narrowly conceived as preparation for specific vocations, or more broadly as training in the principles underlying vocations, must be built on a sound general education. Also technical training, if it is to be effective at all, must be related to the industrial resources and needs of the specific country in question. Finally, as the Five Year Plan pointed out, "it is undesirable that more boys should be produced from trade school courses than can be properly absorbed by industry." All three conditions must be taken into account in future improvement and expansion of facilities for this kind of education. Subject to these observations, the Mission attaches high priority to the expansion of technical training facilities.

Plans for the next three years in Tanganyika call for:

a. The completion of the capital works program at the Ifunda and Moshi trade schools. This would provide facilities for 720 pupils in all in the building sections and 480 in the engineering sections.

b. Completion of planned building at the Technical Institute, Dar es Salaam, and increase of the number of courses given there.

c. The introduction in townships of part-time classes in English, arithmetic, typing, elementary bookkeeping and possibly shorthand in selected centers.

Higher Education

There are at present no facilities for university-level education in Tanganyika. The apex of the Tanganyikan educational system is outside the territory, at the East African University College (Makerere College) in Uganda. In 1958 there were 215 Tanganyikan students at Makerere and 27 at the Royal Technical College in Nairobi. The 1957 statistics show that there were 39 African students studying in the United Kingdom, 3 in Eire, 12 in the U.S.A., 17 in India and Pakistan, 2 in Rome, 2 in Liberia, and 2 in Ceylon. The Government provides bursaries for qualified students who need financial support. In addition, many students avail themselves of the opportunities provided by scholarships offered by other governments.

The possibility of establishing an institution of higher learning in Tanganyika has been thoroughly discussed by two recent working parties, and it is unnecessary to elaborate on what has already been discussed in their reports. The Mission considers that preparations for the establishment of a University College should actively continue. However, given the financial limitations and the small number of potential students at present being produced, it would be premature to start building for a few years to come. The first financial priority for education in the immediate future should undoubtedly be the expansion of the number of African secondary school pupils.

Agricultural Education

The place of agricultural instruction in the general educational system is a matter of some controversy in Tanganyika. Agricultural teaching in the Middle Schools is not well received by many Africans, and is widely held not to lead to any very satisfactory practical results. Nevertheless, the fact remains that the greatest part of the African population will continue to live by agriculture and animal husbandry, and that, as the school population at levels above Standard IV increases, an increasing part will consist of persons destined to make their living from the land. The Mission therefore considers that the link between pupils in Standards V-VIII and the land should be maintained.

We suggest, however, that this should be done not so much by emphasis on the dissemination of modern agricultural techniques as by applying arithmetic, science and even the use of English to topics related to agriculture, animal husbandry, cooperative membership, etc. There is scope for further experiment and for investigation by the proposed Institute of Education.

Adult literacy training within the framework of community development efforts should similarly be given a practical slant. The mere knowledge of how to read and write is of no use to most rural people unless they are given access to reading matter adapted to their interests and needs.

To train potential junior employees on estates, larger farmers and participants in agricultural and irrigation partnership schemes, one year courses following general education to Standard VIII would be of great utility.

INTEGRATION

Present education policy in Tanganyika places major emphasis on the integration of the education systems for the various races, which have hitherto been separate. The ultimate aims are as follows:

a. Any child is to be eligible for admission to any school, subject to appropriate conditions. These conditions include that the primary Standards, whose teaching is in the vernacular, will continue to give preference to pupils of the language groups concerned.

b. The target length for the primary course is eight years.

c. Entry to all secondary courses is to be by competitive examination.

d. Entry to higher secondary courses is to be by selection based on a pupil's results in the School Certificate or General Certificate of Education examinations and on his or her general school record.

e. Entry to Teacher Training Colleges is to be open to students of any race.

At the secondary and higher levels, education is conducted in English, and it is at these levels, in the towns, that integration will effectively begin. The present program for introduction of an integrated system, for which cost estimates will be given below, covers provision of additional facilities in the towns, at secondary level and also between Standards V and VIII. Here, as with African education in general, we raise the question of whether it is desirable without further investigation to plan for an eight-year primary course.

Integration at the secondary level will have a certain impact on the Indian community. Hitherto, secondary education for Indians has been nonselective. As a result of integration, all communities will be obliged to compete for the secondary places available.

This new situation will, in the Mission's opinion, have certain salutary effects for the Indian community and hence for Tanganyika as a whole. To date, Indian secondary education (7th-12th years of education) has been entirely academic in nature. In the Mission's opinion, such an entirely academic conception of secondary education is indefensible. Integration, in its intended final form, will tend to make the Indian community seek more diversified education opportunities after the Standard VIII level.

The extent to which Indian children have made use of their educational opportunities is shown in Table 36. Wastage is fairly high at all stages, and particularly after the tenth year. At the rates of wastage occurring between 1958 and 1959, just over 40 percent of both boys and girls would survive to the 10th year, and roughly 25 percent to the 12th year.

TABLE 36   Enrolment and Wastage in Indian Schools, 1959

	Enrolment			1959 Enrolment as Percentage of Enrolment in Previous Standard in 1958	
Year	Boys	Girls	Total	Boys	Girls
1	1,452	1,356	2,808		
2	1,441	1,244	2,685	90	87
3	1,414	1,226	2,640	96	95
4	1,448	1,351	2,799	107[a]	102[a]
5	1,384	1,271	2,655	69	92
6	1,235	1,050	2,285	95	87
7	1,115	889	2,004	90	76
8	1,003	775	1,778	94	98
9	827	596	1,423	87	91
10	764	501	1,265	91	91
11	445	295	740	72	78
12	348	210	558	82	79

[a] Figures apparently explained by children repeating fourth year course.
SOURCE: Annual Summaries of the Department of Education, 1958 and 1959.

The European community, as was remarked at the beginning of this chapter, is as a whole the least affected by educational policy in the territory, since a high proportion of children from this community is sent outside the territory for education, particularly at the secondary level. However, this community will be somewhat affected by the intended integration of St. Michael's and St. George's School at Iringa, the only European school in the community providing a full secondary course to School and Higher School Certificate level. In 1959 the total enrolment at this school was 273 boys and 227 girls.

A special desire of the European community is for primary schools of standards aligned with those of the more selective schools in Europe. Since available schooling facilities will be an important factor influencing the willingness of Europeans to serve in Tanganyika, and since Tanganyika has need of these Europeans, this desire should be borne in mind by the authorities. The aim of integration should not necessarily be inconsistent with the provision of schools catering to particular scholastic requirements.

COSTS OF EXPANSION

Educational expansion in Tanganyika is limited by three factors in what may roughly be considered ascending order of importance: the willingness of Africans to enter and remain in school; the availability of teachers of suitable standards; and money. The authorities in Tanganyika consider that the expansion plans, outlined above, are realistic in terms of availability of pupils and teachers. It remains to examine whether they are consistent with budgetary considerations as discussed in Chapter 3.

The picture for the finance of current educational expenditures in Tanganyika is rather complicated. Table 37 gives a sketch of the figures for 1959. It shows a total cost to territorial revenue of £ 3,263,000. This may be compared with government current expenditure on education of £ 3,279,000 ("net" basis) allowed for in the 1960/61 budget. These figures, though similar in size, are not quite on all fours. The differences, however, are not important for present purposes.

The increases of current expenditure which the Department of Education estimates would be necessitated by its plans described above are set out in Table 38. It can be seen that, in the years 1961/62 to 1963/64, these plans would absorb around 40 percent of the expected increase of current revenue, estimated by the Mission at around £ 1 million a year. The Mission considers that so great an increase of educational expenditures, if financed from current revenues, would make a greater cut than can be afforded into the resources available for increase of other important types of expenditure. In Chapter 3, a 5 percent annual increase has been allowed for current educational expenditures, by comparison with the 4½ percent increase estimated to be feasible for current expenditures as a whole. The absolute size of this 5 percent increase is shown in the right hand column of Table 38. If these sums only were in fact available, it would be possible to undertake less than half of the increases of current expenditure contemplated by the Department of Education for the next three years. The figures shown indicate a "gap" widening from some £ 230,000 in 1961/62 to just over £ 700,000 in 1963/64. Moreover, these figures do not allow for the fact that integration will presumably involve a drastic reduction of the annual sum of about £ 450,000 at present paid by the non-African communities in Education Taxes and school fees.

TABLE 37   Finance of Current Educational Expenditures in 1959

		(£ '000)
AFRICAN EDUCATION		
Expenditures		
Primary	1,545	
Middle	998	
Secondary	301	
Teacher Training	144	
Technical and Vocational	237	
Post Secondary	209	
Administrative and Non-Allocated	322	
Total	3,757	
Sources of Finance		
Voluntary Agencies		419
Native Authorities		563
Territorial Revenue		2,775
Total		3,757
EUROPEAN EDUCATION		
Total Expenditures (excluding those by Voluntary Agencies)	401	
Sources of Finance		
Education Tax		103
School Fees, etc., at Government Schools		84
Territorial Revenue		217
Total		403
INDIAN EDUCATION		
Total Expenditures (excluding those by Voluntary Agencies)	539	
Sources of Finance		
Education Tax		174
School Fees at Government Schools		74
Territorial Revenue		254
Total		502
OTHER NON-AFRICAN (INCLUDING GOAN)		
Total Expenditures (excluding those by Voluntary Agencies)	37	
Sources of Finance		
Education Tax		15
Territorial Revenue		18
Total		33

NOTE: Where total finance differs from total expenditures, the discrepancy is balanced by a contribution to or a draft on a corresponding "Education Fund."

SOURCE: Annual Summary of the Department of Education, 1958.

TABLE 38 Estimated Annual Increases in Central Government Current Expenditures Involved by Present Plans of the Department of Education

(in £)

Year	Secondary Expansion	Integration	Six-Year Primary Course	Technical	Higher Education	Institute of Education	Total	For Comparison Increases Allowed in Table 12
1961/62	79,200	190,500	39,600	38,000	40,000	6,000	393,300	166,000
1962/63	88,700	187,200	83,450	17,000	33,500	1,000	410,850	170,000
1963/64	56,250	149,800	157,200	8,000	40,000	3,000	414,250	180,000
Later	17,250	200,000	1,594,400	No concrete plans for later periods	113,500	8,000		
		(total further increase to 1967)	(total further increase to 1970/71)		(total further increase to 1965/66)	(total further increase to 1965/66 and subsequent years)		

SOURCE: Government of Tanganyika.

This is not necessarily to say that the plans which have been made are overambitious. There is an increasing realization in the wealthier countries of the pressing problems of raising educational levels in Africa; and Tanganyika can seek outside assistance on the basis of ready-prepared plans which are clearly well adapted to the territory's educational needs. The Mission hopes that Tanganyika will be enabled to proceed with its plans of educational expansion while still keeping increases of the cost to the current budget down to levels consistent with highly desirable increases of other types of current expenditure.

It is none the less necessary to consider what priorities should be given if the full program of expansion is not financially feasible. In the circumstances, the Mission would give high priority to the increase of secondary school places for Africans and of technical training facilities, and the establishment of the Institute of Education. It considers that the lengthening of the primary school course, and planned expansions of urban pre-secondary facilities in the context of integration, will have to be timed according to financial availabilities.

While the current costs of the proposed educational programs are such as to raise potential financial problems, less difficulty arises from the planned capital costs, which are set out in Table 39.

TABLE 39   Estimated Capital Costs to the Central Government Involved by Present Plans of the Department of Education

(in £)

Year	Secondary Expansion	Integration	Six-Year Primary Course	Technical	Total
1961/62	298,100	448,800	48,600	112,500	908,000
1962/63	190,800	176,200	134,000	56,500	557,500
1963/64	113,500	226,200	115,900	37,500	493,100
Later	52,000	350,000 (to 1966/67)	350,000 (to 1970/71)		

SOURCE: Government of Tanganyika.

These estimated capital costs may be compared with annual central government capital expenditures for education of over £ 1 million a year in the three years 1956/57-1958/59, a period when there was widespread building of primary schools. In its provision for future capital expenditures of education (in Table 13), the Mission assumes that it may not be feasible to make quite so rapid a start in 1961/62 as the Department of Education contemplates. Thus we allow for capital expenditures continuing in the neighborhood of £ 600,000 a year, as compared with the sum of £ 677,000 provided in the 1960/61 budget. Capital expenditures of this order seem to us to be both feasible and justified, provided that the associated current expenditures can be accommodated without undue strain.

FISCAL POLICY, FINANCIAL INSTITUTIONS,
PLANNING AND STAFFING

CHAPTER 16 *TAXATION POLICY AND THE MONETARY SYSTEM*

This chapter takes up three topics touched upon but not discussed in Chapters 2 and 3:

A. Taxation policy.

B. Financial arrangements for local government authorities designed to enable them to take an appropriate part in the promotion of development.

C. The future of the monetary system.

A. TAXATION POLICY

Current revenues of central and local governments combined amount, as has been seen, to slightly over 20 percent of estimated total money incomes in Tanganyika. Given the low income level of the territory, the Mission considers that it is hardly possible to contemplate any significant increase of the proportion of total money income taken by tax. The arguments for and against an increase in the basic rate of company tax, in particular, possibly offset to some degree by increased allowances for new enterprises, have been considered in Chapter 12. The Mission there concludes that the authorities in Tanganyika are justified in their preference for the present relatively low basic company tax. In general, indeed, the Mission concludes that greater tax revenues, desirable to make possible increased government developmental expenditures, must be sought not through higher rates of tax but through expansion of taxable economic activity.

While increase of the incidence of tax appears inappropriate, it is by contrast desirable that growth of public revenues should parallel the growth of the monetary economy. The extent to which this will occur depends on the balance between those taxes which tend to be rather sluggish in the face of expanding monetary activities and those taxes which bear more heavily on increases of income than on total incomes.

Present Taxation

It has been remarked in Chapter 3 that increases of African incomes are taxed by the Central Government largely through import and excise duties, the Personal Tax showing little response to income increases although it is in principle on a graduated scale. Increases of incomes of Europeans and of the Asian commercial community are taxed not only through import and excise duties, but also through income tax (including company tax). Table 7 shows that the most rapid increases in central government revenues over the past decade, leaving aside income from provision of goods and services, have been in excise duties, income tax and import duties. Other taxes (including various stamp duties and trade license fees) have increased rather little since 1950, though revenue from vehicle licenses has followed a pronounced rising trend. Personal Tax, in particular, has shown little tendency to increase.

Excise Duties are charged on European-type beer, spirits, cigarettes and tobacco, matches and sugar. Africans, as their incomes rise, and as they move to the towns, tend increasingly to buy these items, and so to incur this variety of indirect tax.

Import Duties are charged on a wide range of items at 22 percent. Many items, however, are charged at higher or lower rates. Thus there are higher rates on a number of items classified as luxuries. It has been seen that imports of various grades of cotton and rayon textiles are taxed in East Africa, for protective reasons, at specific rates ranging from 50 to 75 percent ad valorem. At the other end of the scale, a variety of goods including producers' materials, implements and tools are admitted free of duty.

According to rough estimates by the Mission, the present average incidence of import and excise duties on African money incomes appears to be of the order of 7 percent. The incidence of these taxes on increases of African incomes may well be rather greater.

Personal Tax is in principle charged at the rate of Shs. 12/- per person with chargeable income not in excess of £ 100 a year, Shs. 20/- per person with chargeable income of £100-150, rising to Shs. 180/-

($£$ 9) per person with chargeable income over $£$ 600 a year. In practice, the bulk of the taxable African population is charged at the lowest rate, though in some areas, such as Bukoba District, a majority is charged at the Shs. 20/- level on such evidence of income as the possession of a given area of coffee trees.

Income Tax on individuals is fairly sharply progressive, being charged at the rate of Shs. 2/- in the $£$ (10 percent) on the first $£$ 400 of chargeable income, Shs. 3/- in the $£$ (15 percent) on the next $£$ 400 of chargeable income, and rising to Shs. 15/- in the $£$ (75 percent) on chargeable income in excess of $£$ 9,000. Very few Africans pay income tax. A problem in income tax collection has been to obtain staff of the necessary standards. It is considered that there are now very few cases of major underpayment of income tax, though it appears that there must be widespread petty evasion which is very difficult, in practice, to overcome.

Rates of company tax have been described in Chapter 12 (pp. 244-47).

Native Authority Rates are, together with produce cesses, the main source of revenue for Native Authorities in rural areas. They are a species of poll tax, and range from Shs. 10/- in the Dodoma, Manyoni and Mpwapwa Districts of the Central Province to Shs. 29/- in the Bukoba and Karagwe Districts of the West Lake Province, the Masai District (Northern Province) having the exceptional rate of Shs. 68/-. In some Districts there are cattle taxes.

Produce Cesses are charged, at varying rates on different products and in different areas, on first sales of local produce.

Possible Changes in Taxation

While the Mission did not undertake a detailed investigation of the present tax system, it has certain proposals for the consideration of the Government. These proposals have three parts:

  a. elimination of the Local Government Authority produce cesses;
  b. transfer to the Local Authorities of part of the proceeds of the Personal Tax;
  c. levying by the Central Government of a low and uniform tax on exports.

The produce cesses, at present levied by Native Authorities on sales of a number of agricultural products, appear to have a number of disadvantages. The cost of collection is high in relation to the amount of revenue collected. In many districts evasion appears to be widespread. Such evasion probably also leads to a loss of income tax, traders failing to report transactions which have taken place illegally outside local authority markets. Finally, the incentive to trade illegally outside local authority markets tends to remove cultivators from the protection which these markets are intended to secure for them. (On these points, see Chapter 5, p. 127).

The Native Authorities received £ 600,000 in 1959 from produce cesses. If these cesses were to be abolished, Native Authorities would need some alternative source of revenue. One possible solution would be to transfer to them part of the proceeds of the Personal Tax. In all rural districts the Native Authorities already collect the Personal Tax as an agent for the Central Government. If Native Authorities were authorized to retain a given proportion of Personal Tax collected, this would give them an added incentive to reduce evasion and to attempt to collect tax according to the scales laid down.

The final element in the proposal is the adoption of export taxation. With the exception of minor levies on exports of hides and skins and beeswax, no such tax is at present imposed in Tanganyika. This is in sharp contrast with the many other underdeveloped countries which rely rather heavily on export taxes as a source of revenue. The experience of these countries has on the whole been satisfactory, at least so long as the rates of export tax have been kept rather low. While comprehensive export taxation in Tanganyika would raise certain problems, none of these seem serious. It seems that a tax equivalent to not more than, say, 5 percent ad valorem would have no perceptible tendency to discourage exports or to divert productive effort and sales from export to the home market. In assessing these effects, it must be remembered that the export tax would be compensated in varying degrees for different commodities and in different areas by the abolition of produce cesses. Other possible objections relate to administrative difficulties. An export tax would give to the exporter the incentive to underdeclare; but this difficulty seems no more serious than that which is successfully overcome in relation to import duties. For some exports, the price may be difficult to assess because it fluctuates rapidly; but this difficulty can be met by charging specific rates or applying ad valorem assessments on conventional prices laid down by administrative decision, adjustments being made from time to time to allow for changes in world price levels. One difficulty somewhat peculiar to Tanganyika would be the possibility of avoiding export duty by routing exports by way of Kenya. The cost of overcoming this form of evasion would have to be explored. This possibility may be less serious than it first appears, since the major export crops of the northern part of Tanganyika—cotton, coffee and sisal—are handled by selling organizations which could be made responsible for assuring that the proper export taxes are paid.

A 5 percent tax on all exports would bring in over £2 million. However, the net yield to the Government would in practice probably be considerably less. It might prove impracticable or impolitic to impose the tax on all exports without exception. Moreover, for the estates and industrial enterprises, it might be desirable to allow some remission of income tax in respect of export duty incurred by their produce. For African producers, export duties may be regarded as a substitute for an income tax. Most non-African producers of exports, on the other hand, already pay income tax, and to levy export duty as a net addition to the income tax paid might be thought to raise unduly the total tax burden upon them. Consequently it cannot be thought that the Government could significantly increase its immediate total revenues by imposing an export duty while at the same time relinquishing a substantial part of the Personal Tax. However, in the longer run the proceeds of an export duty might well increase faster than the proceeds of the Personal Tax.

An alternative method of assuring that increase of public revenues parallels that of money incomes, one which is under consideration in Tanganyika, is the effective levying of Personal Tax at progressive rates. It is argued that the Central Government ought to tax Africans to a substantial degree by way of direct taxes, as opposed to indirect taxes such as import, excise and export duties. The difficulty lies in the administrative problem of assessing and collecting a tax on Africans graduated according to income.

As suggested in Chapter 3, the Government should as a general rule attempt to levy fees and taxes on persons and communities to whom it renders specific, recognizable services. An example is the levying of water and other charges in irrigation schemes. However, certain exceptions to this rule must be admitted. For instance, the charging of school fees should not be allowed to keep out of school Africans whose continued education would be to the benefit of the territory as well as of themselves: there may, indeed, be a case for remission of school fees for African girls until a tradition of female education has been more firmly established.

B. LOCAL AUTHORITY FINANCES

Discussions of public finance in this report have been largely concentrated on the finances of the Central Government. The Central
Government spends five to six times as much as do the various local
government bodies. Local Treasuries in rural areas now spend the
rather small sum of £ 4 million a year, and roughly one third of this
is absorbed by the routine tasks of local administration. It has been
mentioned (p. 32) that to some extent the pattern of spending by
local government bodies is shaped by arrangements for matching of
central and local funds.

One peculiar feature of local finance is the tendency of Local Government Authorities to devote a large part of their current revenues
to the finance of expenditures of a capital nature. The proportion of
capital-type expenditures is said to reach 50 percent for several Authorities and to be less than 30 percent for rather few of them.

The Local Councils' Board provides lending facilities for Local
Treasuries, but its lending policies have been rather conservative, and
the Local Government Authorities do not appear to have received
any particular encouragement to borrow to meet capital expenditures.

It was suggested to the Mission that Local Government Authorities
should be encouraged and enabled to borrow more, in order to leave
a greater part of their current revenues for the finance of current
expenditures. This suggestion should receive serious study. While
there are certain advantages in having the bulk of public developmental expenditures concentrated in the hands of the Central Government, in order to allow the planning of activities according to a
territory-wide view, it is also desirable that Local Government Authorities should have a substantial financial stake in activities of importance to local development; and many of these activities involve
expenditures which are to a considerable degree of current nature.

Local Government Authorities could be enabled to increase their
share in current developmental expenditures in two main ways: by
increased provision of loan funds to finance capital expenditures; and
by increasing the share of tax revenues which they collect directly,
e.g., by transferring to them a major part of the proceeds of the
Personal Tax. Further thought should be given to the appropriate
division of financial responsibilities between central and local government, so far as this division can be influenced by the actions and
policies of the Central Government.

C. THE MONETARY SYSTEM

As has been explained in Chapter 2 (pp. 35-36), the currency in circulation in Tanganyika is issued by the East African Currency Board, the chief function of which is to provide East African currency on request against deposits of sterling and to provide sterling on request in exchange for East African currency. It has been pointed out in Chapter 2 that this arrangement has considerable advantages in terms of safety and automatism, but that it also has certain disadvantages in terms of rigidity and of deficiencies in monetary control. Since monetary systems and policies may be capable of exercising effects on economic development, the Mission has had to weigh the relative advantages as between retaining the present currency board system and the major alternative, of establishing a central bank with powers to regulate money supply.

The Mission's conclusion is that the present system should be retained for a few more years. Our reasons for recommending some delay in the establishment of an East African Central Bank are twofold:

a. Although a central bank, provided that it were well run and followed sound policies, would have certain economic advantages, at least in theory, over the present Currency Board, nevertheless the practical balance of advantage at the present time is not so pronounced as to make the establishment of a central bank particularly urgent, given the following argument in favor of some delay.

b. It is desirable to wait to see whether conditions develop which would make possible the effective running of a single central bank for the three East African territories, Tanganyika, Kenya and Uganda (and possibly also for Zanzibar). Such conditions do not fully exist at present.

Economic Advantages of a Central Bank Appraised

The alleged economic disadvantages of the currency board system, which a central bank would be designed to remedy, are twofold:

a. It may be argued that the currency board system leads to an undue part of the savings of the territories going into the reserves of the Currency Board, and so being taken away from the alternative use of productive investment within the territories.

b. Under the currency board system, there is no direct method of controlling the commercial banks' credit policies, which may consequently run counter to the economic needs of the territories.

The Mission considers that in the present circumstances in Tanganyika the first argument has little or no weight, so that the economic argument in favor of establishing a central bank must depend largely on the second point.

Reserve Requirements. Under the traditional currency board system, an increase of issued currency is automatically accompanied by an equal increase of the Board's reserves, since anyone who wishes to obtain a sum in the local currency, if he does not earn it from an existing holder, must pay the equivalent in sterling (plus a small exchange commission) to the Currency Board. Under this system, increase of the Board's reserves is principally a result of the territory's over-all balance of payments, of an excess of external receipts over payments, current and capital,[1] and so means that in a sense the territory is not making full use of its internal savings or of capital inflow. Closer analysis shows that this incomplete use of external receipts must approximately correspond to the accumulation of idle balances of local currency—both working balances and hoards.

Now, while it is necessary for a growing economy to devote part of its resources to the accumulation of an adequate reserve, there is no need for the reserve to increase by as much as do hoards, working balances and other such currency holdings; for it is unlikely that these hoards and balances will ever be by any means fully drawn down, with corresponding calls, direct or indirect, on the reserves.

In fact, in the present practice of the East African Currency Board, the tendency of a currency board system to devote an excessive part of resources to the building up of reserves is mitigated by the "fiduciary issue" provision, whereby the Board is empowered to invest £ 20 million of its reserves in government paper of the territories in which it operates. So long as any part of this £ 20 million remains to be lent to the Governments of the territories, there is an offset to the process whereby an excessive amount of savings is devoted to

[1] Another factor affecting the size of the Currency Board's reserves is the appreciation or depreciation of the value of the securities in which they are invested. The significance of this factor can be seen by comparison of the movements in the first two columns of Table 40.

building up the currency board reserves. When the £ 20 million has been totally lent, it will be desirable to consider whether further enlargement of the fiduciary issue is consistent with safety and with eventual requirements for monetary management.

In these circumstances, the significant factor to be examined is the total size of the reserves, and their adequacy or inadequacy in relation to the calls likely to be made on them. A conventional measure of the size of reserves is the number of months' merchandise imports for which they would pay. It appears that the reserves of the East African Currency Board cover 4-5 months' imports of the territories concerned. This is a fairly large, but by no means exceptional, reserve ratio.

It is relevant to consider what additional flexibility a central bank would give which is not available under the currency board system. It has been seen in Chapter 2 (pp. 35-36) that under present arrangements the East African Governments have to keep their outlays down to the level allowed by the availability of revenue, the proceeds of borrowing, grants from the outside world and accumulated reserves, and that the Governments cannot meet deficits by money creation or by borrowing from a local central bank. The presence of a central bank would make deficit financing possible, but it would not make it safe. The attempt to indulge in deficit financing on any significant scale would lead rapidly to exhaustion of reserves and balance of payments difficulties.

On establishment, an East African central bank would take over the reserves of the East African Currency Board, or a territorial central bank would take over a share of these reserves. It has been seen that these reserves, for East Africa as a whole, are equal to 4-5 months' merchandise imports, and this comparison has not, of course, taken into account the territories' large payments liabilities in respect of services received from the outside world. Thus the reserves are by no means inexhaustible. If an East African Government were to attempt to ease its financial liabilities by printing money or by borrowing from the central bank, the putting of more money into circulation would rapidly lead to an increase of import demand, and this would give the outside world corresponding claims on the (limited) reserves. If depletion of the reserves were countered by restriction of imports, then the additional purchasing power would issue in internal demand. Since it appears that supply in Tanganyika (and in East Africa generally) responds only slowly to increase of money demand, the result would be price inflation, causing inconvenience internally and, by

TABLE 40   Money Supply in Tanganyika

(£ '000)

Year	Currency in Circulation[1] (£ '000)	Currency Reserves[1] (£ '000)	Commercial Banks				Bank Deposits as Percentage of Currency in Circulation		Currency Reserves as Percentage of Currency in Circulation	Commercial Bank Loans, Advances and Bills Discounted as Percentage of Deposits	
			Deposits (£ '000)		Loans, Advances and Bills Discounted (£ '000)						
			Tanganyika and Zanzibar	Tanganyika only	Tanganyika and Zanzibar	Tanganyika only	[2]	[3]		Tanganyika and Zanzibar	Tanganyika only
1938	2,167	1,078	1,799		1,527		83.0		49.8	84.9	
1939	2,167	1,073							49.5		
1948	7,893	7,745	12,941		1,813		164.0		98.1	14.0	
1949	9,080	8,921	13,107		3,429		144.4		98.3	26.2	
1950	9,859	9,980	17,539		4,320		177.9		101.2	24.6	
1951	13,129	13,295	20,064		7,499		152.8		101.3	37.4	
1952	16,116	15,507	21,189	19,416	6,163	5,597	131.5	120.5	96.2	29.1	28.8
1953	16,201	16,783	23,049	21,014	7,638	5,980	142.3	129.7	103.6	33.1	28.5
1954	17,778	19,206	22,965	20,835	10,296	8,596	129.2	117.2	108.0	44.8	41.3
1955	20,137	20,604	23,361	21,198	13,763	10,751	116.0	105.3	102.3	58.9	50.7
1956	20,241	20,440	22,211	20,235	11,595	9,234	109.7	100.0	101.0	52.2	45.6
1957	20,230	21,281		19,321		12,049		95.5	105.2		62.4
1958	19,551	21,143		20,061		10,152		102.6	108.1		50.6

[1] Taken, somewhat arbitrarily, as one third of total for East African Currency Board.
[2] Bank deposits including those in Zanzibar.
[3] Bank deposits in Tanganyika only.

NOTE: Figures for currency in circulation and currency reserves are mid-year figures. Commercial bank figures are end-year.

SOURCE: Tanganyika Statistical Abstracts.

increasing internal money costs, probably jeopardizing the market position of certain of Tanganyika's exports. It cannot be emphasized too strongly that resort to the printing press or to other more sophisticated methods of deficit financing is not merely dangerous in Tanganyikan conditions; it would bring its own refutation so quickly that it would be useless.

The Mission concludes that the apparent increase in flexibility conferred by the institution of a central bank is largely illusory, especially when it is considered that the fiduciary issue provision under the existing currency board system itself introduces a certain degree of flexibility. While it is true that the accumulation of reserves makes a call on the territories' scarce resources, it is equally true that the possession of reasonably large reserves gives benefits by easing external trade and increasing the confidence both of external investors and of internal savers. It is indeed arguable that any excess savings which may be held to have gone into growth of the currency board reserves may have been more than offset by capital inflows which would not have occurred had not the currency board system, with its automatic protection against balance of payments difficulties, been in operation.

Regulation of Commercial Bank Credit. The second main argument for the need to establish a central bank springs from the desirability of regulating the operations of commercial banks. At present, there is no formal mechanism in East Africa for the regulation of commercial banks' credit policy.

Commercial bank credit has played a considerable part in the expansion of purchasing power in the postwar years. While loans, advances and bills discounted in Tanganyika and Zanzibar amounted to £ 1.5 million in 1938 and £1.8 million in 1948, the figure for Tanganyika alone fluctuated around an average of £ 10.5 million in the years 1955-58. This expansion of credit has been accompanied by a striking rise of the ratio of advances to deposits, a ratio to which the banks pay some attention as an indication of the soundness of their position. This ratio increased from 14.0 percent in 1948 and 26.2 percent in 1949 (Tanganyika and Zanzibar) to a peak of 62.4 percent in 1957 (Tanganyika alone; all end-year figures). The average end-year ratio for Tanganyika alone, 1955-58, was a little over 50 percent.

It appears that commercial banks in Tanganyika have followed a rather expansive credit policy. Indeed, some observers claim that there has been excessive credit to merchants and traders, allowing them to carry excessive stocks and to extend excessive credit to lesser traders. However, in a territory developing from subsistence to a monetary economy, this would appear to be a fault on the right side.

If there is an argument against the unregulated credit policy of the commercial banks, it is not so much that the average size or distribution of commercial credits has been inappropriate, as that these credits are subject to fluctuations which are somewhat irrelevant to the requirements of the territories. However, it would be possible to exaggerate the effects on economic development of fluctuations of bank credit. The banks give first priority to loans and advances for trade in the territory's staple crops, and the first credits to be curtailed are in general those least essential to the smooth working of the economy. There remains, nevertheless, the point of principle that it would be desirable for the authorities in Tanganyika, or in East Africa as a whole, to be able to exercise such direct control as they felt necessary over bank credit.

A main question to be asked is whether the establishment of a central bank would give an effective control over commercial bank credit such as does not exist at present.

The commercial banks operating in Tanganyika are expatriate institutions. Their liquid and semi-liquid reserves take the form in part of cash and in part of external assets. The fact that the banks operating in Tanganyika have felt themselves able to extend advances to the amount of 50 percent or more of deposits in the territory reflects their dependence on the backing, in the event of difficulties, of their headquarters outside East Africa.

When a central bank is established in a territory where the commercial banks are expatriate institutions, its effort to exert some degree of control over the policies of the commercial banks is usually exercised by requiring that the commercial banks make with it deposits, the size of which may be varied from time to time. This has been the practice for instance, in the Federation of Rhodesia and Nyasaland. However, while it is undoubtedly possible by making rather large deposit requirements to induce commercial banks to restrict credit, the degree of control which a central bank can exercise over expatriate commercial banks able in the last resort to rely on the financial backing of their headquarters is inevitably somewhat limited.

It is of course usual for central banks to engage not only in direct operations affecting commercial banks' reserves but also in exhortation to commercial banks to follow what are considered to be the proper policies. But, of course, the ability to exhort does not depend on the creation of a central bank, and exists at present. It can in principle be exercised by the Currency Board or by the Governments themselves.

In giving proper weight to the case for establishing a central bank, it has to be remembered that the monetary system in East Africa is still a very rudimentary one. This makes it impossible at this juncture to use open market operations as an instrument of central banking policy. It may be argued that a central bank is needed precisely in order to foster the development of a money market. But this can be done, to some extent at least, by the Currency Board, particularly after its removal to East Africa. For example, part of the backing of the "fiduciary issue" can be used to support the development of the recently instituted markets in treasury bills in the territories.

Regional or Territorial Central Bank

The Mission heard from many quarters the view that it would be impossible to establish a single central bank for East Africa at the present time. The present lack of a general sentiment of solidarity between the three East African territories is a very real factor, which must be taken into account in any consideration of the practical possibilities. An associated and perhaps more fundamental difficulty arises from the present political diversity of the three East African territories, which are at different stages of political development and which have certain divergent interests. While the existence of the de facto customs union necessitates a certain degree of harmonization of economic policies, and there exists a machinery of consultation at various levels to assure that the three territories shall at least act in the knowledge of the effects of their actions on their partners' interests, nevertheless there is no practical assurance of unanimity in matters of economic policy between the three territories. If a single central bank were to be established in present circumstances, it would either have to act independently, making its own policy decisions, or else it would be likely to be exposed to mutually incompatible policy directives from the three territories. Neither alternative would be very satisfactory. In fact, the establishment of a satisfactory central bank appears to demand a single government to which the central bank shall be ultimately answerable.

These present difficulties of establishing a single East African central bank would be avoided if Tanganyika were to establish its own separate central bank. However, this course of action would have the major disadvantage of lessening the ease and freedom of commerce and financial transactions within East Africa. The currencies of Kenya and Uganda would become foreign currencies to Tanganyika, with all that that implies.

Conclusion

Given the advantages of retaining a single currency for the three East African territories, and the absence of urgent economic arguments for the immediate establishment of a central bank, the Mission considers that it would be wise to wait for a few years to see whether political developments in East Africa may be in a direction favoring the establishment of a single East African central bank. The conclusions of the Raisman Commission concerning the future of economic cooperation in East Africa, and actions based on these conclusions, are also likely to have an important bearing on the final decision.

CHAPTER 17 *PLANNING AND STAFFING*

Throughout this report, great emphasis has been put on careful planning. The sums available to public authorities will be extremely small in relation to the tasks, even on the most optimistic assumptions for the future. The administration will inevitably remain small in relation to the population and the physical size of the territory. In these conditions it is necessary to give the closest attention to administrative efficiency; and expenditures on planning staff, far from being a luxury, are a necessity in order to secure the best possible results from scarce resources.

Recommendations for improving the planning process in the Ministry of Natural Resources have been made in Chapter 11. The present chapter deals with the machinery of over-all planning, and with questions of staffing affecting the administration as a whole.

THE ORGANIZATION OF PLANNING

Until recently the administration in Tanganyika was small, and development planning has evolved on a rather informal basis. There has been no separate organization responsible for the planning of economic and social development. Individual projects have been prepared by the relevant ministries and departments. Those involving government expenditures have been subsequently screened by the Treasury and submitted for approval of the Governor, assisted by an Executive Council of ministers. Finally, the expenditures involved have been incorporated in the budget, which, like other territorial laws, has to be enacted by the Governor with the advice and consent of the Legislative Council. Since both the Executive Council and the Legislative Council have had until recently a majority of ex officio members, policies of economic and social development have been shaped by administrative decision. However, with the increase of the number of elected members and of ministers drawn from this group, the budget has increasingly become a document reflecting the political forces in the territory.

In spite of the publication in the postwar period of a rather confusing sequence of development plans, planning in practice has been largely an aspect of the year-to-year budgetary process.

The Development Committee of the Council of Ministers

The system followed in the past has worked reasonably well. Its principal failing has been a certain lack of continuity. At the present stage of development the problems facing the Government do not, in the Mission's view, call for the establishment of a new and elaborate planning organization, which would be costly in relationship to the benefits to be expected from it. Certain changes already made or in hand appear to the Mission to be well adapted to present needs. These changes are:

a. the establishment of a Development Committee of the Council of Ministers;

b. preparation by this Committee of a three-year development plan, to be revised every year;

c. establishment of an Economic Section in the Treasury.

The Development Committee of the Council of Ministers has already been established. It consists of the Ministers in charge of the main "spending departments," meeting under the chairmanship of the Minister for Finance. The Permanent Secretary and the Deputy Permanent Secretary of the Treasury attend meetings, and the head of the Economic Section of the Treasury acts as secretary.

The main function of the Development Committee is to draw up the annually revised three-year development plan.

The Three-Year Development Plans

The intention is to draw up the first of the new Three-Year Plans by December 1960, to cover the period 1961/62-1963/64. This plan will then become the basis for the 1961/62 budget. It is further intended to draw up such a plan in each following year. Thus the second plan will revise the proposals for 1962/63 in preparation for the 1962/63 budget, will revise also the proposals relating to 1963/64, and will look forward one further year to 1964/65.

The Mission has already stated its approval of this procedure, which combines an attempt to secure greater continuity of planning than in the past with flexibility necessary to adapt to changing appreciations of financial resources, changing estimates of the results to be obtained by various programs or policies, and other relevant circumstances.

The intention is to take account in the plan not only of capital expenditures but also of their implications for future current expenditures. The Mission considers, indeed, that in preparing the Plans the Development Committee should in effect make projections for the budget as a whole. We have argued that many current expenditures have as much effect on development as do most capital expenditures, so that a development plan must be a plan for these current expenditures just as much as for expenditures appearing in the capital budget. Moreover, as has been seen in Chapter 3, the feasible level of expenditures on projects and activities of the most direct relevance to development is influenced by the amounts which it is considered necessary to spend on other things of less direct relevance to the developmental process. Thus meaningful planning of government development activities involves planning of the budget as a whole.

For the preparation of the first plan, the various ministries have been invited to prepare lists of investment projects without limit set to the total. The Treasury will not in the first instance suggest allocations or priorities. The ministries are also invited to indicate their own assessments of priority as between the various projects which they propose. It will then be the job of the Development Committee to coordinate the various proposals and to adjust them to the scale of available finances. While the review of all projects which ministries may feel able to prepare is no doubt appropriate for the first planning exercise being carried out by a government consisting for the first time largely of elected ministers, it seems that in future years the planning process should be more a matter of give and take between the Development Committee as a body and the individual ministries: the Development Committee, assisted by the Treasury as a whole and its Economic Section in particular, should form a general idea of the size and shape of the government development effort in order to give the ministries a frame of reference for the preparation of their own plans. At the same time, the ministries will be able to make known their suggestions and criticisms of the outline plan through their ministers, sitting as members of the Development Committee. In practice, of course, the first three-year plan will itself tend to establish a pattern, and subsequent plans will presumably be adjustments, more or less comprehensive, rather than complete reconsiderations based on all the projects which ministries might suggest if left without guidance as to the general shape of the plan.

The Economic Section of the Treasury

The establishment of a specialist Economic Section of the Treasury is now in hand in Tanganyika. The Mission considers that such a section, far from being a luxury, will be of very great value in assuring that scarce resources for development are put to the most effective use.

The new Economic Section would consist of a small number of officials, dealing full-time with problems pertaining to the development of the territory. Under present arrangements, senior officials of the Treasury are in fact dealing with· these matters, but only as part of their total assignments. The proposal is therefore for a small increase of staff, allowing more continuous and specialized attention to certain key matters.

Some of the major functions of the Section would be:

a. To estimate financial resources available for development during the next year or any other period relevant for planning purposes. Such estimates should include not only public revenues but also grants expected to be forthcoming as well as domestic and external loans it is desirable or possible to raise. Since the amount available for development depends in part upon non-developmental and other current expenditures, this particular exercise involves general budgetary forecasting.

b. To appraise new schemes submitted to the Treasury by the various executing ministries and departments. Even assuming that the departments are basing their projects on cost-benefit analysis, the important problem remains of comparing the relative returns of projects put up by different departments, including any indirect effects they may be expected to have.

c. To ensure that the individual parts of the program form a coherent whole. For example, in planning irrigation schemes, account must, of course, be taken of the question whether such schemes are consistent with the existing program for road transport. Similarly, on the demand side there is the problem whether the growth rates for individual commodities or sectors are consistent in the sense that they provide markets for each other.

d. To provide periodic reviews of the actual performance of projects in existence. Planning is a continuous process and, to be successful, requires constant reappraisals in order to achieve maximum flexibility and efficiency. These reviews should not be confined to individual projects: they must necessarily include a study of general trends in the economy, such as foreign trade, public revenues, prices, etc.

To perform the various functions enumerated above would not require any major expansion of the present staff in the Treasury. Assuming that the statistical staff is increased as proposed below, the establishment of a new planning unit could probably be undertaken with an addition of three senior officials, one of whom would be seconded to the Ministry of Natural Resources to assist in planning there (cf. Chapter 11, p. 210). This assumes, however, that the staff of the Economic Section, while being closely integrated with the work of the Treasury as a whole, should be free to specialize in functions related to planning of the kinds outlined above.

The proposed arrangements are of course in no way intended to conflict with the power and responsibility of the Council of Ministers and the Legislative Council to make major planning decisions. The task of the Economic Section is rather to make available the facts and analysis on which decisions should be based, and to point out to the Minister for Finance and the Development Committee the implications of proposed policies or projects. The present intention is that the head of the Economic Section should act as secretary to the Development Committee.

THE STATISTICAL ORGANIZATION

The compilation and analysis of statistics play an indispensable role in the formulation of economic policies and the design of development programs. This is a field of activity in which the present outlay in the territory is small and where the return on some increase of expenditure can be expected to be very high.

Given the limited resources devoted to statistics, the Tanganyika statistical unit is, in the Mission's opinion, doing a remarkable job. During the last decade the amount of statistical information made available has greatly increased. Since the publication in 1958 of a pioneering study on the national income of Tanganyika by Messrs.

Peacock and Dosser, an effort has been made to link a considerable part of statistical work to the improvement of national accounting statistics. As a result it is now possible to describe and analyze the structure of the economy with some degree of statistical accuracy (cf. Chapter 2).

Future Statistical Tasks

Although much progress has been made, some important tasks remain for the future.

In the field of national income statistics, present estimates are based upon the value of annual output of goods and services (gross domestic product). Efforts to improve these estimates should continue. A major task, associated with improvement of gross product figures, is to strengthen information on African agriculture and animal husbandry. For many of the African crops too little is known either about quantities produced or about the proportions which are sold in domestic markets. The Mission understands that a long-term plan for collection of statistics has been prepared jointly by the Tanganyika Statistical Unit and the Agricultural Department and has been approved by the Government. The first stage of this plan, an assessment of reliability of agricultural statistics and consolidation of the existing series, was completed in 1958. The second stage, field experiments and pilot surveys designed to evolve the best sampling methods, was begun in 1959. Stage three, covering several years, will consist of a series of agricultural sample surveys covering gradually, one by one, the typical agricultural areas of the territory.

Estimates of the different categories of expenditure are published—consumption and investment, private and government. Private consumption expenditures, however, are merely derived as a residual. It would be useful to collect direct data on private consumption expenditures—not merely their total size but also their distribution among types of goods, both imported and domestically produced. Some preliminary work has been done on family budgets, but this area of investigation still remains largely unexplored. In relation to policy questions, it is of great interest to explore how such magnitudes as consumption, imports and taxes vary with income. It would be particularly useful to strengthen the factual basis for estimates of the extent to which particular development activities are likely to affect revenue. Estimates of the main types of income—wages, salaries, profits, interest and rent—would also be valuable.

Information is available about the size and composition of private capital formation in the monetary sector. On the other hand, little is known about the ways in which the private sector finances its capital expenditures, that is, whether out of own resources or capital borrowed domestically or supplied from abroad.

At present, national accounting magnitudes are given only at current prices. It would be of interest to produce series at constant prices, in order to show changes of quantities.

In the field of balance of payments statistics, data on commodity trade are reasonably reliable, but statistics on invisibles and capital movements are highly incomplete, especially as concerns movements within East Africa. The Mission is aware of the special difficulties stemming from various East African institutional arrangements such as the common Currency Board and the operations through branches in all three territories of expatriate commercial banks with regional headquarters in Nairobi. But, although Tanganyika has no need to regard its balance of payments as a major consideration in shaping policy, nevertheless more complete knowledge of the structure and development of the territory's individual balance of payments with the outside world, including the remainder of East Africa, would be useful in understanding and following various important aspects of the economic process.

Certain of the gaps in statistical information can be remedied fairly easily over time without any great expansion of the existing establishment. For other tasks, such as agricultural surveys, additional appropriations are unavoidable and, in the Mission's opinion, of vital importance for the efficiency of public policy and administration.

Use of Statistics

Improvement of the quantity and quality of the statistics produced does not in itself guarantee greater efficiency in the conduct of government business (nor, similarly, of private business). Proper use of statistics is as important as proper production of them. It appeared to the Mission that use is in fact lagging considerably behind availability. Government departments and provincial administrations appeared quite frequently to be ignorant of statistical series of relevance to them, and to make insufficient use of such series. It is perhaps not surprising that such a lag exists, considering the very recent development of statistics in the territory. On the other hand, the Statistical Unit has done everything possible to make the figures readily accessible, by gathering together a wide range of the more important figures into an annual *Statistical Abstract,* which is now put out in admirably portable form. The wealth of material to be found in this volume can be gathered by the frequency with which it is cited as the source of statistical tables in this report.

It should be an incidental concern of the members of the Development Committee to ensure that the staffs of their various ministries become adequately statistics-minded.

Organization and Scale of Statistical Work

Until mid-1960, the Statistical Unit in Tanganyika was organized as a branch of the East African Statistical Department, one of the scheduled services of the East Africa High Commission. The balance of advantage between an East African organization and the alternative of separate statistical units answerable solely to the individual territorial Governments has been debated vigorously for several years, there being strong arguments on both sides. In 1960 it was decided to change to the latter arrangement.

The Statistical Unit in Tanganyika is to form part of the Economic Section of the Treasury. The former director of the Statistical Unit becomes head of the Economic Section as a whole, with direct responsibility for the economic side of its work. It is intended to appoint a new man to be in direct charge of the statistical side of the Section. This arrangement has been carefully worked out, and appears satisfactory. The Mission wishes, however, to emphasize one point: the Statistical Unit should be left free to concentrate most of its attention on the building up of basic statistical information; while it can clearly help in *ad hoc* jobs of research and interpretation, these should be primarily the responsibility of the economic side of the Section, and should not be allowed to interfere with longer-range statistical tasks.

Under the former organizational arrangement, Tanganyika's expenditure on statistical services was £ 50,000, of which £ 20,000 went to the East African Statistical Department, while the remaining £ 30,000 went to the Tanganyika Unit. The Mission recommends, as a first step toward augmenting statistical information, increase of the annual allocation for statistical work to £ 70,000. This would enable the Statistical Unit to take on one additional professional officer, and also to carry out various new field investigations and surveys.

FUTURE PROBLEMS IN PUBLIC ADMINISTRATION

Economic planning involves more than top-level decisions about the size and pattern of an investment program. If it is to be more than a declaration of intent, the public services must, of course, be able to implement policy decisions in an effective way. In this respect the territory has been fortunate. Throughout the postwar period the civil service has maintained a high standard of performance, not only in the traditional fields of law and order but also increasingly in the area, new for the central administration of the territory, of planned promotion of economic development. To maintain these standards during the coming period of transfer of political power is a challenging problem.

The Expatriate Official

The Mission is convinced that for several years to come expatriate officials will have to carry a major part of the administrative load in the territory. If finance can be found for the various projects and programs proposed in this report, the civil service would tend to increase, rather than decrease, in size. Since the number of local men qualified to fill the posts is still very small, it follows that dependence on expatriates will continue for many years to come.

To encourage those civil servants already in the territory to stay on, and to attract new overseas personnel, it is necessary to find adequate ways of assuring expatriates that their careers are not going to be abruptly terminated because of political changes.

It should also be emphasized that overseas recruitment is not possible unless salary, tenure and other terms are competitive with those in overseas countries. While expatriate officials are currently well paid by local African standards, their remuneration does not compare favorably with their market value in their own and many other countries. The Mission encountered various cases where the present salary scale in the territory appeared insufficient to attract qualified people and where, in other words, a greater salary differential is perhaps called for. The recent undertaking by the Government of the United Kingdom to take over the cost of inducement pay and allowances of overseas staff (see p. 10) appears to give promise of substantial help in meeting this problem.

Localization

Although for some time to come the dependence on expatriates will remain high, a substantial effort should be, and is in fact being, made to bring about "localization" of the service. A post has been established in the Office of the Chief Minister for a senior and experienced officer whose sole task will be to supervise local recruitment for the civil service, training programs and other steps involved in building up numbers of locally recruited staff.

The day-to-day business of government is carried out by a multiracial civil service of about 33,000 persons, excluding daily paid workers. Of the roughly 4,000 more senior posts enumerated in the annual *Staff List*, 2,418 were held by expatriate Europeans in mid-1960, a number by expatriate Asians, 346 by Africans and 123 by locally recruited personnel of other races. There were in mid-1960 about 500 vacancies, some filled on a temporary basis. The number of Africans in such posts was only five in 1954, jumped to 104 in 1955, reached 139 in 1957 and thereafter has been increasing rather rapidly. The number of African Acting District Officers was brought to eight in December 1959. The 29,000 more subordinate posts are, of course, very largely filled by local Africans and Asians, though it is still necessary to employ mostly European typists.

In recent years some progress has been made toward training Africans for the civil service. Training facilities have been substantially increased, and a government scholarship fund has been established, the resources of which are such that at present the number of scholarships is limited only by the number of students qualified to proceed with higher education.

In spite of this effort, Africanization remains a slow process, primarily because the number of students who annually complete secondary school is low. This illustrates the pressing need to expand African middle and secondary education.

Central and Local Administration

In view of the strategic role of the Treasury in the planning process, it appears to the Mission that closer contact should be established between this ministry and the provincial administrations. Neither the appraisal of new projects nor the periodic review of those already in existence can be fully effective unless members of the central administration have an intimate knowledge of local conditions. Annual meetings in Dar es Salaam of the Provincial Commissioners are only imperfect substitutes for a mechanism establishing close and constant contact between center and provinces. The present intention is that each senior officer of the Treasury should "go on safari" twice a year.

Finally, administrative efficiency at the local level seems to suffer somewhat from frequent transfers of personnel between districts and provinces. "Shifting administration," like shifting cultivation, is inescapably inefficient. It takes time for an official to acquire thorough knowledge of local conditions and vernacular, that is to say, before his usefulness as an administrator in a particular district reaches its peak. Losses due to frequent movement are the greater in those cases, by no means infrequent, where no systematic attempt is made to transmit experience gained by one official to his successor. This problem of shifting administration is encountered in many African territories, and is hard to combat, given the smallness of staff, turnover of personnel and interruptions of service by leave. Nevertheless, close attention should be given to keeping men for a reasonable length of time in posts to which they have shown themselves well suited.

ANNEXES

ANNEX I *GOVERNMENT AND ADMINISTRATION*

This report makes frequent reference to administrative arrangements. Moreover, it has been written during a period of rapid constitutional change in Tanganyika. By way of background information, the present annex describes the recent course of constitutional evolution in the territory and the present administrative framework.

Government and administration in Tanganyika are organized on a dualistic basis: on the one hand there is the Central Government, extending into the Provinces and Districts through the provincial administration; on the other hand there are the Native Authorities, successors to the traditional authorities of African tribal life, and also various councils in urban areas.

THE CENTRAL GOVERNMENT

Constitutional arrangements affecting the Central Government have changed very rapidly over the last five years.

At the beginning of 1957, the Governor, appointed by and responsible to the Government of the United Kingdom as Administering Authortiy under the United Nations trusteeship, was to all practical purposes the Central Government of the territory. Nine officials in charge of the various government departments were directly responsible to the Governor, who was advised by an Executive Council consisting of these nine officials and six unofficial, appointed members. While the laws of the territory were enacted by the Legislative Council, this was an appointed and not an elected body, 31 of its members being appointed specifically as a Government side, and 30 being appointed to represent the various races in the territory and such particular interests as the Governor might think fit. The Legislative Council was thus a consultative and deliberative rather than a true legislative body.

353

Since then, while the Governor still retains his central position in the machinery of government, the spirit of constitutional developments has been to make him increasingly resemble a "constitutional monarch."

In 1957, the officials in charge of government departments were given the title of Ministers. This change, while of no practical importance, foreshadowed other changes to come. At the same time, six non-official Assistant Ministers were appointed.

At the end of 1958 and the beginning of 1959, elections for the Representative side of the Legislative Council were held for the first time, voters in each of ten constituencies having to vote, regardless of their race, for one African, one Asian and one European candidate. A majority of one for the appointed Government side was still maintained.

In July 1959, five of the elected members of the Legislative Council —three Africans, one Asian and one European—were appointed Ministers by the Governor.

In May 1959 a Post-Elections Committee was appointed to consider the next stage of constitutional development. The recommendations of this committee were published in December 1959, and led, with some modification, to the arrangements now in force. The main changes were:

a. The holding of a new election in August 1960, on a larger, though still limited, suffrage.

b. Establishment of an elected majority in the Legislative Council and in the Council of Ministers.

c. Abolition of the requirement that each voter should vote for three candidates, one of each main racial group. Instead, the country was divided into 50 constituencies, each with one seat which could be contested in principle by a member of any race, but which, in view of the predominantly African electorate, could be expected as a general rule to go to an African. In addition, in 11 constituencies in which there was a comparatively large Asian population and in 10 in which there was an appreciable European population, the qualified electors, regardless of race, would also elect Asian and European members respectively. All seats are voted for by qualified voters regardless of race: that is to say, the minority of Asian and European electors may vote for candidates contesting the open seats, and the majority of African electors in constituencies where there are seats reserved for Asian or European candidates may vote for their choice of such candidates, though they are not required to do so. A candidate for a reserved seat had to be nominated by 35 persons of whom at least 25 had to be members of his own racial group.

Voting qualifications were: ability to read and write in English or Swahili; *or* income in cash or in kind estimated at £ 75 a year; *or* present or past occupancy of any of various specified offices. About 885,000 persons registered to vote in the 1960 election. This was only about half of the number of persons estimated to be qualified, but compares with the figure of some 60,000 registered voters under the narrower suffrage in the previous election.

In the 1958-59 election, all of the winning candidates of each racial group were members of, or endorsed by, the Tanganyika African National Union (TANU), a territory-wide party led by Mr. Julius Nyerere. While TANU limited its membership to Africans, the elected Members of the Legislative Council grouped themselves in the Tanganyika Elected Members' Organization with Mr. Nyerere as Chairman. In the 1960 election, only a small number of seats was contested, and TANU or TANU-endorsed candidates won 70 out of the 71 seats.

Following the election, Mr. Nyerere, who had not accepted office in July 1959, was promptly installed in the newly created post of Chief Minister. A new Council of Ministers was formed. Four out of the five elected Ministers who had been in office since the previous year—two of the Africans, the Asian and the European—remained in the Council of Ministers. Four new African Ministers, in addition to the Chief Minister, took up office. The Attorney-General and the Minister for Information Services remain, ex officio, official appointees. The present Minister for Finance, Sir Ernest Vasey, occupies a special position, having been appointed by the Governor earlier in 1960 at the special request of the Representative side.

With the change in the composition of the Government, the place of the Executive Council has increasingly been taken by a Council of Ministers, and the Executive Council has now been abolished.

There has thus been a rapid evolution from a state of affairs in which the territory was, to all intents and purposes, governed by the Governor and a small group of expatriate officials to a situation which is locally described as "representative government." This is a considerable step towards, but still falls somewhat short of, full political independence. Under present arrangements, the Governor retains the power to reject the advice of the Council of Ministers and to

Ministers and Their Responsibilities—Late 1960

CHIEF MINISTER

Leader for Government in Legislative
Council
Provincial Affairs
Staff Matters (including allocation of
accommodation)
Localization of Civil Service (including
Training)
Clerk to Council of Ministers
East Africa Office
East Africa High Commission

MINISTER FOR FINANCE

Financial Policy
Economic Policy
Development Planning
Financial Control (including Estimates)
Accounting Policy and Estimates
Taxation and other Revenue (including Fees)
Statistics and Economic Research
Exchange Control
Economic Relations
Foreign Aid
Land Bank
Post Office Savings Bank
Salary Scales and Establishments
Organization and Methods

ATTORNEY-GENERAL

Legislation
Legal matters
Administrator General

MINISTER FOR AGRICULTURE AND CO-OPERATIVE DEVELOPMENT

Agriculture
Co-operative Development
Veterinary Services (including Tsetse
Control)
Colonial Pesticides Research Unit
Fisheries
Forests
Rural Social Development

MINISTER FOR LANDS, SURVEYS AND WATER

Lands
Surveys
Land Tenure
Water Development and Irrigation
Game
National Parks

MINISTER FOR COMMERCE AND INDUSTRY

Commerce and Industry
Mines
Geological Survey
Export-Import Trade
Development of Secondary Industries
Tourism
Hotels
Weights and Measures
Price Control
African Productivity and Local Development funds
External Trade Relations (including
E.A. Office (Trade))

MINISTER FOR COMMUNICATIONS, POWER AND WORKS

Transport Licensing
Civil Aviation
Posts and Telecommunications
Railways and Harbours
Public Works
Roads
Buildings (including Staff Housing
and Offices)
Urban Water Supplies
Sewerage and Drainage
Electricity
Ferries
Aerodromes (maintenance and construction)
Traffic
Township and Aerodrome Fire Services

MINISTER FOR EDUCATION

Education
Antiquities
Cinematography
Missions
Museums
Languages Board
British Council
E.A. Literature Bureau
U.N.E.S.C.O.
Approved Schools
Probation Service

MINISTER FOR HEALTH AND LABOUR

Health
Hospital Services
World Health Organization
Government Chemist
Labour
International Labour Organization

MINISTER FOR HOME AFFAIRS

Police
Prisons
Immigration
Registrar of Societies
Film Censorship

MINISTER FOR LOCAL GOVERNMENT AND HOUSING

Urban Local Government (Municipalities, Town Councils and Township Authorities)
Rural Local Government
District Councils
Native Authorities
African Housing (including African Housing Loan Fund)
Town Planning
Sociology
Maintenance of Distressed and Destitute Persons
Repatriation of undesirables from Townships
Urban Social Development

MINISTER FOR INFORMATION SERVICES

Information Services
Broadcasting
Printing and Stationery
Public Holidays
Defence
Nationality and Naturalisation
Repatriation
Refugees

---

refuse assent to legislation, though it may be expected that he would exercise these powers only in exceptional circumstances. The Governor, and not the Chief Minister, presides over the meetings of the Council of Ministers. Moreover, the constitution as it now exists has been decided by the Government of the United Kingdom rather than by the Tanganyikans themselves. The Governor retains the right to appoint members to the Legislative Council, though it is expected that he will exercise this right very sparingly. (This provision is used to give the Minister for Finance and the two ex officio appointed Ministers seats in the Legislative Council.)

The Administration

The business of government is carried out by a multi-racial civil service. Most of the senior posts are in practice filled by European expatriates. The progress and problems of "localization" have been described in Chapter 17 (p. 348).

The number of Ministries, and the distribution of responsibilities between them, has changed several times over the past few years. The arrangement following the formation of the new Government in September 1960 is shown on pp. 356-57. The Mission has been particularly interested in the disposition of activities related to agricultural development. This is discussed in Chapter 11 (pp. 211-12).

PROVINCIAL ADMINISTRATION

Activities of the Central Government throughout the territory are organized on a provincial and district basis. The territory is divided into nine Provinces which are in turn subdivided into 57 Districts (see Map 1 at front of report).[1] Each Province is in the charge of a Provincial Commissioner, responsible to the Governor for the general administration of the Province. Each District is in charge of a District Commissioner, who is responsible to the Provincial Commissioner.

The various departments of government—agriculture, veterinary, education, health, etc.—have staff members working at provincial and district levels. Officers of the various departments at provincial level, meeting under the chairmanship of the Provincial Commissioners, form Provincial Teams, and similarly District Teams meet under the chairmanship of the various District Commissioners. For matters of agricultural development and related subjects, meetings are held of Natural Resources Teams, consisting of the officers of the departments concerned. Thus there is both a vertical and a horizontal organization, government officers being responsible to their Ministers in Dar es Salaam but also forming part of the Provincial or District Team. The Mission considers this device of the Provincial or District Team an extremely important one, which should be retained.

LOCAL GOVERNMENT

While the activities and responsibilities of the Central Government extend, in this way, into every part of the territory, a range of functions at the local level is left in the hands of local authorities which,

[1] In 1958, the new Karagwe District, in the northwest of the territory, was formed out of part of Bukoba District, and in 1959 the western part of the Lake Province, consisting of Bukoba, Karagwe, Ngara and Biharamulo Districts, became the West Lake Province.

in rural areas, are the successors to the traditional, tribal African authorities.

Rural Local Government[2]

The functions of rural local government in the territory are mostly exercised by Native Authorities, with jurisdiction over the indigenous inhabitants within their respective areas and with legislative and executive powers conferred by the Native Authority Ordinance (Cap. 72).

Official policy has been "to leave the conduct of local affairs to those who under established indigenous constitutions are the recognised tribal authorities and command the respect of the people, while at the same time taking every possible step to hasten the change over from the traditional to a modern system of administration." Although in some cases the Native Authority is a Chief or a Council of Chiefs, there is an increasing tendency for them to make full use of representative commoners' advice, and almost everywhere, where the Native Authority is not itself a council, there is an active native authority council, usually consisting of representatives of the traditional authorities and elected representatives chosen by the people. These native authority advisory councils frequently co-opt non-African members.

The services for which the Native Authorities are responsible include specific matters in respect of primary education, agriculture, marketing, forestry, veterinary services, health, water supplies and local communications. All rural local authorities have their own treasuries and sources of revenue, and frame their own estimates.

Local authorities and officials of the Central Government working in the Districts naturally perform interrelated functions, and by no means operate in isolation from each other. The nature of their relationships varies with local circumstances.

Urban Local Government

There are in Tanganyika one Municipal Council (Dar es Salaam), 10 Town Councils and 21 Township Authorities.

The Dar es Salaam Municipal Council is now an elected body. It has power both to impose rates and to raise loans.

Town Councils consist in some towns entirely of nominated members, whereas in others varying proportions of the members are

[2] The following account is taken verbatim, though in condensed form, from the Colonial Office Report on Tanganyika for the Year 1959 (Colonial No. 346), q.v.

elected. Mandatory functions include the layout of buildings, the regulation and control of markets and the safeguarding of public health; but the Councils are also given a number of permissive functions. Site rates are levied by all town councils except Tabora, where valuation has not yet been undertaken. Other funds are derived from assigned revenues and from grants from the Central Government.

Township Authorities are not able to impose rates or to make by-laws, but they have the power to enforce rules dealing with various sanitary, building and other matters in their areas. All the larger Township Authorities have their own expenditure budgets but derive their funds from the Central Government. The Chairman of every Township Authority is the District Commissioner, the members being appointed by the Provincial Commissioner.

NON-SELF-CONTAINED SERVICES OF THE EAST AFRICA HIGH COMMISSION

The non-self-contained services of the East Africa High Commission, referred to on p. 34, are the following:

REVENUE COLLECTION
East African Customs and Excise Department
East African Income Tax Department

CIVIL AVIATION AND
METEOROLOGY
East African Directorate of Civil Aviation
East African Meteorological Department

RESEARCH SERVICES
East African Agriculture and Forestry Research Organization
East African Fishery Research Organization
East African Industrial Research Organization
East African Marine Fisheries Research Organization
East African Leprosy Research Centre
East African Institute of Malaria and Vector-Borne Diseases
East African Institute for Medical Research
Medical Research Secretary

East African Trypanosomiasis Research Organization
East African Veterinary Research Organization
East African Virus Research Organization
Desert Locust Survey

ECONOMIC SERVICES
Department of Economic Co-ordination
East African Statistical Department
Lake Victoria Fisheries Service

OTHER
Royal East African Navy
East African Literature Bureau
East African Office in London
Administrator's Office
Legal Secretary's Office
Financial Secretary's Office
Economic Secretary's Office
Public Service Commission
Accountant General
Information Officer
East African Reception Office
East African Central Legislative Assembly

ANNEX II *PROSPECTS AND PROBLEMS OF CERTAIN MAJOR CROPS*

The parts of the main text dealing with agriculture have discussed broad problems and ways in which they can be tackled, bringing in discussions of particular crops or particular areas only by way of illustration. (An exception is sisal, considered in some detail in Chapter 10.) This annex complements the main text, describing the situation of several of the main crops—how much is produced, where and by whom, what are the particular problems of expanding production or improving quality, and how production may be expected to develop in the coming years.

This annex contains various recommendations, some of them of a rather technical nature, for action, public or private, to increase production or to improve quality. While some of these recommendations have been mentioned in the main text, there are others in this annex which do not figure in the main text.

The crops dealt with are:

Coffee

Present Production. In the 1957/58 season Tanganyika produced 21,825 tons of clean coffee, almost as much as the record production of 22,267 tons in the previous season. In 1958 the territory exported 22,225 tons valued at £7.6 million.

Two types of coffee are produced, mild and hard. Mild coffee is obtained from the arabica species. The fruit, or cherry, is put through a pulping machine to remove the outer skins and pulp. The mucilagenous material adhering to the beans is then removed by fermentation and/or washing. Finally, the parchment coffee is dried. Hard coffee, in limited quantities, is likewise obtained from arabica; most, however, comes from the robusta species. The cherry is allowed to dry and is then hulled, removing the parchment from the beans as well as the skin and pulp.

Average annual production in the past three years has been about 12,000 tons of mild coffee and 10,000 tons of hard (see Table 41). Approximately 80 percent of the mild coffee is produced in the Northern Province. Rather less than a quarter of the total comes from non-African estates, mostly in the Northern Province. Almost all of

TABLE 41   Tanganyika Coffee Production by Type and Origin

(in tons, clean coffee)

	1955/56	1956/57	1957/58	1963/64
				(forecast)
Mild (arabica)				
African:				
Northern Province	7,211	6,100	6,347	
Southern Highlands Province	530	1,317	2,189	
Southern Province	490	500	626	
Tanga Province	243	250	464	
Total African Mild	8,474	8,167	9,626	
Non-African:				
Northern Province	2,880	3,250	2,128	
Southern Highlands Province	164	150	278	
Tanga Province	61	50	51	
Total non-African Mild	3,105	3,450	2,457	
Total Mild	11,579	11,617	12,083	17,245
Hard (arabica and robusta)				
Native:				
Lake and West Lake Provinces	9,144	10,200	9,404	
Eastern Province	331	400	255	
Tanga Province	29	50	48	
Western Province	—	—	35	
Total Hard	9,504	10,650	9,742	13,050
Total, Mild and Hard	21,083	22,267	21,825	30,295

the hard coffee comes from African producers in the West Lake Province; only 4 percent is produced by non-Africans.

The Policy of Expanding Production. Coffee production has increased by well over 25 percent since 1953 and considerable efforts are being made to secure further increase of production by Africans. Sixteen of the 28 "Increased Productivity Schemes" assisted from Colonial Development and Welfare funds are concerned with coffee production. Efforts to promote or improve coffee production in a further 15 areas are carried on through normal, unassisted extension work. These efforts aim at expanding production both by increasing efficiency and yields per acre in existing coffee plantations and by planting of new areas, but they are in fact more successful in extending acreages than in improving yields. On the basis of present progress, the Agricultural Department estimates that coffee production in the 1963/64 season will be about 30,000 tons, 17,000 tons of mild and 13,000 tons of hard.

The Need to Increase Yields Per Acre and Improve Quality. It seems inevitable that the present world overproduction of coffee will bring about a further fall of price. Although Tanganyika may be able to continue to sell the bulk of its crop, the benefit of increased production to the African's standard of living and to the territorial economy as a whole is likely to be less than was formerly expected. Hard coffee is particularly vulnerable, and its price may fall to a low level; and not only does hard coffee account for nearly half of Tanganyika's production, but there are several schemes in operation further to increase production of this type.

In view of the world coffee situation, and especially because good quality is very important if Tanganyika coffees are to compete with those from Central and South America, the Mission recommends that much more emphasis should be placed on efforts to increase cultural efficiency and yields per acre and to improve quality, and less on expansion of acreage.

Present standards of culture and yields per acre are low. For example, African growers on Kilimanjaro, under good conditions of soil and rainfall, average about 3 cwt. of clean coffee per acre, whereas African growers under similar conditions in the Embu and Meru districts of Kenya are averaging 8-10 cwt. per acre. Quality in Tanganyika is also too low. In the 1958/59 season the Kilimanjaro Native Co-operative Union (KNCU), which gets the best prices for African-grown mild coffees in Tanganyika, obtained an average price of £ 315 per ton for the top three classes; the average paid for all Kenya coffee sold in the top three classes was £ 461, a difference of £ 146. As this Kenya price is an average for both African- and European-produced coffee, the figures are not strictly comparable. But a comparison with the Embu-Meru African growers, who sold over 70 percent of their crop in the top three classes, would be even less favorable to the KNCU. The KNCU sold only 53 percent in the top three classes, and it seems that it must have received at least £ 150 per ton less for its coffee than did the Africans of Embu and Meru.[1] In the main hard coffee producing area of Bukoba (West Lake Province) the standards of cultivation and preparation have remained low despite continued efforts to improve them.

For either type of coffee, but especially for mild arabica, quality depends to a considerable extent on good field culture as well as on good preparation: it is impossible to prepare good quality coffee with cherry from trees which are in poor condition.

The Mission recommends that the planting of coffee on new land should be encouraged only in areas where soil and climatic conditions are really well suited to the crop and where high yields per acre can be expected. Remote areas, without adequate communications, should be disregarded even if growing conditions appear favorable; in such places supervision and extension work are difficult and costly, and the returns to the growers are reduced by high transport costs.

In existing plantations, the quality of trees and fruit could be considerably improved if growers could be persuaded to pay more attention to shade, pruning, mulching, regeneration of old coffee trees, and the preparation of the beans.

The Wachagga, and many people in other parts of Tanganyika, grow coffee and bananas in mixed culture. Since the bananas form their staple food, they probably regard them as the more important crop. This is understandable, but it does not make for efficient coffee production. Yields are reduced by excessive shade and competition for soil nutrients from the banana trees. It is argued that the mixed stand gives a greater total return per acre than could be obtained from pure stands of the same crops. However, although there is no firm evidence to refute this argument, it is probable that greater total

[1] The comparison may be affected by some difference in the definition of the top three classes on either side of the border. Also, Kenya coffee commands a premium because of its established reputation.

returns could be obtained from pure stand coffee, with only limited banana or other shade and on the multiple stem pruning system (see below), the bananas being also planted in pure stand, as windbreaks. This system should be tried and, if successful, should be widely demonstrated. In any case, efforts should be made to reduce the excessively heavy shade of bananas found in many plantations, since there is no doubt that this is greatly reducing coffee yields.

All the Chagga coffee is pruned on the single stem system, even though it has been demonstrated that the multiple stem system normally gives higher yields and is easier and cheaper to carry out. The multiple stem system is said to be unsatisfactory under heavy banana shade, resulting in long, whippy stems. If this is so, it is an added argument for gradually switching to pure stand coffee, or at least for having lighter shade. The existing standard of pruning on the single stem system is extremely poor. If, and where, this method is retained, efforts should be made to improve the technique employed. In some other areas, where the multiple stem system is used, the standard of pruning could be much improved.

The mulching of coffee with banana trash or grass has been shown to give a considerable increase in yields. Efforts to get this practice much more widely and efficiently adopted should be continued.

A high proportion of the coffee bushes on Kilimanjaro are old, debilitated and low-yielding. Since the plants have been grown from unselected seedlings, they are in any case of inherently low yield potential. It is therefore desirable that there be a long-term program of progressively replanting old coffee gardens with seedlings of the Lyamungu Coffee Research Station. As an interim measure, a proportion of the old coffee bushes might be rejuvenated by cutting them back and converting them to multiple stem.

Although the low quality of the Kilimanjaro coffee as compared with that from the better Kenya African areas may be due in part to differences in climate or environment, it is mainly due to the poor condition of many of the bushes, and also to poor preparation of the beans. On Kilimanjaro, and in many other parts of Tanganyika, each grower pulps and ferments his own coffee, some doing it well, but many poorly. Even a few poorly prepared parcels will lower the quality of a large quantity of coffee when it is bulked for sale. In Kenya the African-grown coffee is prepared in central cooperative pulperies, where the work can be done efficiently by trained personnel. It would be a great advantage if this system were introduced wherever feasible in Tanganyika. The opinion was expressed to the Mission that, while central pulperies undoubtedly produce better quality coffee, nevertheless the premium obtainable would not recompense the growers for the extra cost of having their coffee prepared by paid labor instead of by family labor. This opinion is almost certainly erroneous. The cost of erecting a central factory to handle 150 tons of clean coffee is about £ 2,500. Factory costs per ton in Kenya vary widely, from Shs. 373/- to Shs. 900/-; available figures suggest the average to be about Shs. 600/- (£ 30). Allowing for a 20-year amortization of £ 2,500 borrowed at 6 percent, the pulpery cost per ton would not exceed £ 32, while, as already mentioned, the difference in price between Kilimanjaro and Kenya African-grown coffee in the 1958/59 season was at least £ 150 per ton. The Mission recognizes that central pulperies are not practicable everywhere. We suggest, however, that the experience of the Meru Co-operative Union, Ltd., which has just installed a central pulpery, should be followed with care. If this proves profitable, some of the other cooperative unions or larger societies should erect such factories at suitable sites in their areas. The Mission considers that cooperative pulperies would be of greater benefit to the Southern Highlands Province than the coffee curing plant which it is proposed to establish there.

Cotton and Cotton Seed

The Postwar Increase in Production. Cotton in Tanganyika is grown solely by African peasant farmers. This cotton is of the American upland type of 1-inch to 1 3/16-inch staple. Production has increased rapidly since the second World War. The crop of 1958 set a record of 171,433 bales of 400 lbs. (lint); the value of exports of lint, seed, oil and cake, at some £ 8 million, was rather greater than that of coffee exports. Nearly 90 percent of the cotton is grown in the Lake Province, where production has increased from 36,000 bales in 1949 to 151,000 bales in 1957 and 1958. The following paragraphs refer to conditions in the Lake Province. Discussion of cotton growing in other areas is deferred to p. 370.

Several factors account for the postwar growth of production. In the first place, the grower has been able to sell his cotton at good prices, fixed in advance by the Government. He has obtained a greater share in the profits of the industry, as a result of the rapid growth of marketing cooperatives and, more recently, the establishment of ginneries owned by the cooperatives. The existence of a cotton price stabilization fund has aided in securing these advantages. This fund, established by the Government, was built up by withholding from the grower a part of the value of his cotton in the period of high prices during, and for several years after, the war. Money from this fund, which is now administered by the statutory Lint and Seed Marketing Board, has been used to support the price to the growers in the last few years, to make loans to help cooperatives through their early years and to finance the creation of ginneries. The fund is also used by the Board to provide its working capital and for various other purposes, including grants for cotton research and for the construction of roads and bridges in cotton growing areas. Recently the policy has been to restrict the making of grants from the fund.

Another factor in the increase of production has been the work of the Empire Cotton Growing Corporation at the Ukiriguru Research Centre. Specialists at the Centre have bred varieties of cotton which give higher yields and improved ginning outturn, pest resistance and quality. Seed of improved varieties is distributed by the Department of Agriculture through the ginneries.

More than to any other factor, however, the increase of production has been due to the greatly increased acreage planted to cotton. Government activity in tsetse clearing and the provision of water supplies in the formerly uninhabited, or very sparsely populated, areas of Geita, Maswa and Biharamulo Districts has played a major part in making possible this expansion of area. Large numbers of people from the overcrowded and worn-out land of central Sukumaland have moved into these districts with their livestock. Unfortunately, the opening up of these new areas has not been accompanied by any improvement in methods of land use, and the fertility of the new lands is threatened as a result of poor methods of cultivation and overstocking. Overstocking is aggravated by the fact that money obtained by growing more cotton has been used mainly to buy more stock. Increased cotton production has thus been mainly achieved at the expense of soil fertility in the new areas, which are steadily deteriorating towards the overcrowded and worn-out condition of central Sukumaland. Since the amount of new land still available for further settlement is limited, a serious problem is being built up for the future.

Methods of Increasing Yields. Practicable and economic measures are known which would greatly aid in maintaining fertility in cultivated land and would considerably increase yields of cotton per acre.

Tanganyika's average yield of 450 lbs. of seed cotton per acre is low. It has been clearly demonstrated that yields can be approximately doubled by early planting, tie-ridging to conserve soil and rainfall, and the application of cattle manure and/or fertilizer. On the worn-out soils, where yields are very low, the effect of tie-ridging and the application of a single dressing of cattle manure is spectacular and leaves a beneficial residual effect for as long as five years. But it has so far proved impossible to persuade the majority of farmers to adopt these measures. The use of manure has been resisted, partly because it is against native customs, and also requires a good deal of labor. The use of fertilizer has not caught on despite widespread demonstrations and the issue of free fertilizer for trial. Tie-ridging is of prime importance for prevention of soil erosion, and attempts were made to enforce it by Native Authority rules. These attempts failed because the matter became a political issue, and the rules were rescinded. Recently, however, the leaders of the cooperative movement have shown signs of appreciating the need for adopting these measures to increase yields and maintain fertility. In 1959, for example, they borrowed money from the Lint and Seed Marketing Board to finance a pilot scheme for the issue of 100 tons of fertilizer to about 2,000 growers, the cost of the fertilizer to be recovered when the cotton growers sold their cotton. Although only 20 tons of fertilizer were in fact distributed in 1959, the experiment appears worth repeating.

There is already a considerable concentration of the extension staff of the Department of Agriculture in the cotton-growing areas of the Lake Province. The Mission attaches great importance to continued collaboration between the agricultural department and the cooperatives in an effort to promote improved techniques of cotton growing designed both to increase production per acre and to aid in maintaining soil fertility.

Production Prospects. Prospects for further expansion in the Lake Province are on the whole good. Provided that the cotton is well processed, graded and marketed, it should be possible to sell considerably more Tanganyika cotton in the Far East and on the continent of Europe. In 1959 about 160,000 bales were produced on approximately 420,000 acres. The Department of Agriculture estimates that by 1963/64 production will increase to 250,000 bales, grown on 500,000 acres, provided the market remains satisfactory. This estimate assumes a continuation of existing unsatisfactory methods of cultivation and the achievement of increased production by expansion of acreage, 500,000 acres being considered the maximum area likely to be brought under cultivation during the period.

As stated above, the Mission recommends that every effort be made to increase production through higher yields per acre. While considerable improvement should be possible, it is difficult to predict how rapidly increase of yields can be secured.

Two major factors affecting prospects for expansion are quality and price to the grower. The former, of course, influences the latter. The quality of Tanganyika cotton is not as good as it should be, and steps should be taken to improve it. What is required is more efficient ginning and better handling of the seed cotton. Present handling methods allow excessive extraneous matter, such as twine and pieces of sacking, to become mixed with the lint. The larger bags with special fastenings, recently tried experimentally in one zone, would reduce this admixture of foreign matter.

Some rise of the world price of cotton above the levels of 1958 and 1959 may be hoped for, and it seems likely that the price will remain at a level satisfactory for Tanganyikan growers. In case of low prices in particular years, it will be appropriate to draw on the Price Assistance Fund to maintain the price to the grower. It follows that the Price Assistance Fund should not be allowed to become exhausted by making miscellaneous grants from it and by subsidizing the price to the grower for seed cotton while the world market price allows an unsubsidized price to the grower of, say, at least 45 cents per lb. In other words, the Price Assistance Fund should be used primarily as a genuine stabilizing device, and should not be deliberately drawn down to subsidize the price to the grower at present world price levels. These remarks are intended as a guide for future action rather than as a criticism of present policy. Of course, so long as the policy is followed of fixing in advance of each season the price at which the Lint and Seed Marketing Board will buy cotton, there are liable to be losses to be met from the Price Assistance Fund in some years, which may be offset by profits in other years.

A program affecting the price receivable by the grower is the construction and improvement of roads in the cotton-growing areas. Road development, especially construction of feeder roads, has not kept pace with the expansion of the cotton-growing areas. Existing roads should be improved and new ones built to reduce transport costs on seed cotton. In areas where cotton growers are dispersed rather widely, it will be desirable to investigate whether the problem of preventing damage to harvested cotton during the rainy season may not be most economically solved by constructing storage facilities rather than by improving or building roads so as to facilitate evacuation of the cotton before or during the rains. This comparison should, of course, take into account the wider effects of road building and improvement in opening up the areas concerned.

The steps recommended above to increase yields per acre would, of course, themselves have the effect of considerably increasing the return per grower.

Other Cotton-Growing Areas. The cotton-growing areas in the Eastern Province, together with small areas in the Northern and Tanga Provinces, produce rather less than 20,000 bales a year. Production in these areas suffers several disadvantages. Cotton growing is scattered over a wide area and, since roads are often non-existent or in poor condition, the transport of seed cotton is frequently difficult and costly. On occasions the onset of the rains makes the roads impassable and cotton cannot be transported to the ginnery until the season following its production, with consequent deterioration of quality. There are far too many ginneries for the size of the crop, and most of them are old, inefficient and of low capacity. As in the Lake Province, ginnery charges are too high. Pests of cotton are much more troublesome than in the Lake Province, although measures for their control are known.

Because of these factors, and also because of the attitude of the growers, who receive a lower return than those of the Lake Province, no great increase in cotton production outside the Lake Province can be expected in the near future. It seems unlikely that this production will exceed 25,000 bales by 1964. Expansion would, however, be encouraged by:

a. the formation of cooperatives to strengthen the grower's position vis-a-vis the ginners, to aid in organizing pest control and to assist in promoting better methods of cultivation and higher yields per acre;

b. reduction in the number and increase in the efficiency of ginneries;

c. more concentrated development of cotton growing in certain areas, coupled with increased provision of feeder roads.

Possibilities for increasing cotton production by irrigation schemes are discussed in Annex VII.

Cotton Seed. In 1958 there were about 55,000 tons of cotton seed over and above requirements for planting. Some 11,000 tons were exported, at a value of £ 182,510. Exports of cottonseed oil averaged 1,800 tons in the years 1956-58, while exports of cottonseed cake averaged 17,600 tons. During these three years, the total value of exports of cotton seed and cottonseed products ran at an annual level of about £ 750,000. At present exports take rather more than half the available cotton seed. There is a considerable production of oil for domestic use, mainly in the manufacture of soap.

The amount of cotton seed will of course increase with the increase of production of seed cotton. It will be desirable to take such steps as are necessary—for instance, provision of loans—to ensure that processing capacity keeps pace with the supply of cotton seed.

Cashew Nuts

Cashew trees are grown mainly in the Southern Province, which is likely to remain the principal center of production, although there have been plantings on a fairly large scale in Eastern Province and the coastal districts of Tanga. Exports of cashew nuts have increased rapidly, from 4,000-5,000 tons a year 10 years ago to the present level of 30,000-35,000 tons a year. Since the tree is drought resistant and does not require very fertile soil, there are very large areas suitable for its cultivation. Because of the recent, and continuing, planting of trees, a further increase in exports, up to about 45,000 tons by 1964, may be expected.

Almost all the nuts have been exported unshelled. Shelling before export could almost double the contribution to the economy, partly through savings on ocean transport and partly by way of the additional value added. There are successful hand-shelling establishments on the coast of Kenya and in Portuguese East Africa. The failure of an enterprise of this kind set up in Tanganyika was attributable to a number of reasons, but was probably chiefly due to its situation close to the port of Mtwara, where there was a shortage of suitable labor. Several projects for hand-shelling at more favorable locations are being discussed. The Mission recommends that suitable ventures be encouraged and, if necessary, given financial backing.

Some research has been conducted both in Tanganyika and in the United Kingdom with the object of developing mechanical shelling equipment which would also make possible the production of cashew shell oil as a by-product. This research seems to have lost impetus. Since it appears to have prospects of success, the Mission recommends that arrangements for its continuation should be made, probably with the National Institute of Agricultural Engineering and the National Research and Development Corporation in the U. K. It should be possible for Tanganyika to share the cost of financing this work with the several other British territories which produce cashew nuts, or the project might appear to justify a Colonial Development and Welfare grant.

Cocoa

To date only a very small amount of cocoa has been produced in Tanganyika, on a single estate. Possibilities for growing cocoa in Tanganyika were recently examined by Mr. D. H. Urquhart. His main conclusions were as follows:

a. Soil and climate in certain areas of Tanga Province are suitable for the economic production of cocoa. The extent of these areas is not known, but indications are that it is large enough to make cocoa a worthwhile crop in the Province. (Three estates are already planting cocoa in Tanga, a soil scientist is making a survey to map suitable soils, and the Department of Agriculture has established trial plots in the Tanga, Handeni and Lushoto Districts.)

b. Possibilities of growing cocoa, worth investigating by the establishment of trial plots, exist in parts of Morogoro District, in the Rungwe area and in the foothills of the Livingstone Range in Njombe District. (The Department of Agriculture has established trial plots in most of these areas, but some of the plots are unsatisfactory on account of inadequate shade or neglect.)

c. Amelonado and Upper Amazon (i.e., Forastero) types of cocoa are the most likely to succeed in Tanganyika, whereas the bulk of the cocoa now growing there is probably of the Nacional (Trinitario) type.

The scale and profitability of cocoa growing in West Africa show how well the crop is adapted to cultivation by Africans. Market prospects appear favorable. Consequently the Mission recommends that every effort should be made to develop it in Tanganyika on both estate and peasant lines. As a first step the survey and mapping of soils suitable for cocoa in the Tanga Province, already in hand, should be completed. If the survey shows that a worthwhile development is possible, the Mission recommends that an agronomist with considerable experience of cocoa should be recruited to the Department of Agriculture, to assist in planning and executing a development program for this crop. Much time and effort may be wasted unless expert assistance is obtained, there being no one locally available with sufficient knowledge of cocoa.

Until the nature and extent of suitable areas have been determined, and the methods of development decided upon, it is impossible to indicate what finance is likely to be required or what returns may be expected.

In due course trials in other possible areas should be pressed forward.

Oil Seeds

Coconuts are grown mainly on the coast north of Dar es Salaam and in Mafia Island. Part of the crop is sold locally or over the Kenya border as fresh nuts, part is used for the production of copra, some of which is crushed locally. Both the copra and the coconut oil are divided between local consumption and export. There is also a small production of coir fiber. The total value of production considerably exceeds the value of exports, which amounted to £ 465,000 in 1958.

The average yield of nuts is very low, partly because the rainfall is below the optimum for coconuts, partly because of pest damage, but largely because the palms receive very little cultural attention. A government bonus scheme, aimed at encouraging proper planting and maintenance of plantations, met with very little response. No great increase in production or exports is envisaged.

Annual Oil Seeds; Soya Beans. In the past, three factors have seriously affected the volume of oil seed production: pests and diseases; a lack of varieties suitable to the Tanganyika lowlands; and periodic lack of interest on the part of merchants and exporters. Production has fluctuated in ways which cannot be fully explained by fluctuations of price.

Groundnuts and castor have always been the most important oil seeds, and in the Mission's opinion will remain so. Following in importance are sesame and sunflower.

Recent research at the agricultural research station at Nachingwea has resulted in the production of locally adapted and high yielding strains of both sesame and soya beans. There seem to be good prospects for expansion of both these crops as soon as seed of the new types can be bulked up. This bulking can readily be done on the TAC farms at Nachingwea, and the introduction of these new varieties may well increase the profitability of the Nachingwea tenant farming schemes. The Mission recommends that research be extended to sunflower and castor seed.

A considerable increase of production of annual oil seeds appears likely, based on the evolution of improved varieties, the effect of better roads and more trading posts, and also the probable development of cooperative marketing. The value of production might well rise from £ 3 million in 1958 to £ 5 million in 1964 and £ 7 million in 1969. This development should not involve any great investment, either in extending cultivation or in processing.

Pyrethrum

The production of pyrethrum increased steadily from 275 tons of dried flowers in 1953 to 737 tons in 1957. The fall of production to 625 tons in 1958 is attributed largely to an unfavorable season. Production is confined almost entirely to the Northern Province and Southern Highlands Province, and to date is very largely by non-Africans. In 1958 the Northern Province produced 376 tons, of which only a negligible amount came from Africans, who had only 20-25 acres under this crop, while the Southern Highlands Province produced 249 tons, of which African growers contributed 26 tons.

In the Southern Highlands Province, European production increased only from 150 to 291 tons during the period 1953 to 1957 and fell to 223 tons in 1958. No rapid or spectacular increase is likely in the near future, since a good deal of the alienated land is not highly suitable for pyrethrum and there has been an over-all decline in yields per acre. The use of lime and fertilizers, and the rotation of pyrethrum with other crops and grass, would almost certainly improve yields; but the cost of lime and fertilizers is high and it is not certain that their use would be economic. In the Northern Province, European production has declined over the past three years from 479 tons in 1956 to approximately 376 tons in 1958. In the past a good deal of the pyrethrum was produced from forest glade lands, which were leased to farmers for 10 years on the condition that at the end of this period all the land would be left planted with softwood trees. Conditions in these glades are excellent for pyrethrum growing, but it now appears to be the policy of the Forest Department to establish softwoods in them directly, possibly using mechanical equipment for land preparation and cultivation. The Mission considers that the glades should continue to be leased for pyrethrum where this can be done without detriment to water conservation and where any land tenure problems involved can be suitably adjusted. The country can ill afford to lose the revenue from growing pyrethrum on this land. With a yield of 800 lbs. per acre, a conservative estimate for this good land, one acre leased for 10 years would produce a gross return of £ 960. Provided that the leasing of glades continues, a moderate increase in European production might be expected.

The main increase in production is, however, to be expected from the expansion of pyrethrum growing by the African farmers. It is the present policy to encourage them to grow the crop in suitable areas, and special extension effort is being directed to this end in the Arusha, Moshi and Mbulu districts of the Northern Province and in the Njombe and Mbeya districts of the Southern Highlands Province. In the Southern Highlands, fair progress is being made, and 436 acres had been planted by 1958. In the Northern Province, the African pyrethrum acreage is so far very small. In both provinces the standard of cultivation and the condition of much of the pyrethrum leaves a good deal to be desired and certain insect pests, particularly red spider and thrips, are already causing a good deal of trouble, with prospects of more severe damage in the future.

There is always a possibility that pyrethrum may be displaced from some or all of its uses by the production of new synthetic insecticides. So far as is known, this is not an imminent danger. Tanganyika has an opportunity of making a valuable increase in pyrethrum production, but this opportunity must be seized quickly. There is every reason to believe that during the next three to five years a firm market will exist for at least 2,000 tons of dried flowers from their territory, i.e., an increase over 1958 production of 1,375 tons, which at the present average price of approximately £ 280 per ton would be worth £ 385,000 a year.

There is ample land suitable for pyrethrum: in the Southern Highlands Province there are at least 10,000 acres, and in the Northern Province at least 7,000 acres. The crop gives a good return. A yield of 500 lbs. per acre should be readily obtainable on the good land available, and at the present price to the producer of Shs. 2/40 per lb.

the gross annual return is £ 60 per acre. The crop has so far proved popular among African farmers. The Mission therefore urges that every effort be made to increase the production of this high-priced crop as quickly as possible up to a level of 2,000 tons per annum. This will require the planting of a further area of about 7,000 acres. The following action is recommended:

a. Increased extension effort in order to obtain a more rapid expansion of the African acreage.

b. The maintenance of a higher standard of field culture by the African farmers, without which yields will be well below those potentially obtainable. This will demand close supervision and hence, again, increased extension effort. It also requires experimental work, which is mentioned below.

c. The control of the insect pests, particularly thrips and red spider, which threaten to cause considerable losses. The Department of Agriculture already has an entomologist working on this.

d. The production of improved planting material suitable for both the northern and the southern areas. The material now in use is variable in yield and generally low in pyrethrins content. There is need for a program of selection and breeding to produce good strains suitable for the local conditions, particularly since the Kenya strains are unsuitable. The Department of Agriculture is making a start on this work. However, such a program will take some years to yield results, and in the meantime there is an urgent need to use the best material possible for the new plantings. The Mission therefore suggests that a survey be made of the material being grown on European farms, and that arrangements be concluded with one or two farmers, who are found to have the best strains, for the production of seed from selected areas.

e. Agronomic experimental work is needed, especially in the Southern Highlands Province, particularly on the use of fertilizer, manure and rotational cropping in order to maintain yields.

The cost of these increased efforts has not been estimated, as the majority of it can be met from the funds already available to the Agricultural Department.

Seed Beans and Peas

Seed beans are produced in the Arusha District of the Northern Province, mainly by Europeans, but also to a limited extent by African farmers. Other producing areas are Mbulu (Northern Province) and Mbeya (Southern Highlands Province). In these areas a considerable part of production is by Africans. In 1957/58, 3,420 tons were exported. Output has been on the increase. Since it is probable that a market could readily be found for 6,000 tons, African farmers should be encouraged to develop this crop.

Seed peas are grown by European farmers in the West Kilimanjaro area of the Northern Province and in the Iringa, Mbeya and Njombe Districts of the Southern Highlands Province. Here, African farmers grew about 100 tons out of the total 230 tons produced in 1958.

Seed peas, mainly for the United Kingdom and the Netherlands, were formerly produced largely in North Africa and Central European countries. Since the supply from these countries became unsatisfactory, production has been developed in South Africa, Southern Rhodesia, Australia, New Zealand and Canada. Conditions in the Tanganyika highlands are well suited to seed pea production, particularly as the low temperatures during the growing season appear to prevent the occurrence of bacterial blight—a great advantage since the United Kingdom only allows import of seed peas accompanied by a blight-free certificate. There is a very good demand for seed peas at present, and Tanganyika should endeavor to increase production rapidly before this demand is met by other suppliers.

Seed peas are a popular crop among Africans in the Southern Highlands Province and there is a good opportunity for increasing their production. Hitherto the cultivation of the crop has largely resulted from the commendable efforts of one European who has made contact with the buyers, imported seed and issued it to the growers. To encourage further rapid and satisfactory growth of production by Africans one or two men should be employed to encourage and supervise production (cost about £5,000 a year), and a further £5,000 should be invested in vehicles and equipment. If this can be arranged —and it seems probable that a local firm could be interested in the enterprise—then it is thought that the African production in the Province could be raised in about three years from the 1958 level of 100 tons, valued at £7,000, to 2,000 tons, worth £140,000.

Sugar

White sugar is at present produced in Tanganyika by one large company and several smaller ones. Total production in 1958 was approximately 21,500 tons. In addition, production of jaggery by small enterprises operating a simple open pan process totaled about 1,500 tons in 1958.

Consumption of all types of sugar was about 40,600 tons in 1958, imports totaling 20,000 tons. The Government is the sole importer, fixes maximum prices, ex factory, for locally produced sugar, and controls the price of sugar on first sales on the basis of the average of the prices of local and imported sugar. This is considered to result in a relatively high price for sugar, thus restricting consumption. The Government's policy is that sugar should be produced in Tanganyika ". . . to the fullest extent to which it can be marketed at prices representing reasonable remuneration to efficient producers, and that consumers should have available to them all the sugar they want and are able to buy at the lowest price consistent with the same criterion." To encourage local production, the Government proposes to continue the present price fixing and controls until self-sufficiency is within sight, and subsequently to afford some measure of tariff protection to the local industry.

Provided wholesale prices do not increase and the distribution system is improved, the Mission estimates that consumption of white sugar will gradually increase, from 40,000 tons in 1958 to about 73,000 tons in 1969. It is unlikely that the present producers will increase their annual production to more than 35,000 tons, and there should therefore be room for one more enterprise with a factory of economic size, i.e., producing 20,000 tons, rising to 30,000 tons at a later stage.

Plans have now reached an advanced stage to establish a sugar estate and factory of this capacity in the Kilombero Valley. Management will be brought in from the outside and the total capital required, estimated at £ 3 million to £ 3½ million, is being raised partly outside and partly by local issue of shares. On the basis of extensive investigations, the location envisaged appears to present sufficient good land, which could be amply served by irrigation water. Trials have already demonstrated that cane grows well there.

Including the output of this enterprise, the Mission estimates that territorial sugar production will be 50,000 tons by 1964 and 65,000 tons by 1969. Both figures are somewhat below estimated consumption at the same dates. On this basis, the value of production would increase from £ 1 million in 1959 to £ 2.3 million in 1964 and £ 3.1 million in 1969.

Tea

Tea is produced entirely on non-African estates, which are situated in the Usambaras in Tanga Province and in the Mufindi, Tukuyu and Njombe districts of the Southern Highlands Province. In 1958, the total area under tea was 15,334 acres, of which 7,475 acres was mature, 3,575 acres semi-mature, (4-10 years of age), and 4,284 acres immature (1-3 years of age). In the past few years the area under tea has been increasing at the rate of about 1,250 acres a year. The most rapid expansion has been in the Usambaras, and any future increase in estate acreage is likely to be mainly in this area, where most of the alienated land suitable for tea is situated. In the Mufindi and Tukuyu districts only a limited area of alienated land suitable for further tea planting is available. In the Uwemba and Lupembe areas of the Njombe District, tea is a new venture, and it is too early to say with certainty what the prospects for the crop are. In each of the two latter localities some 300-400 acres of tea have been planted, but none of this is in full production. Rainfall is probably just adequate, but owing to the high altitude, growth is slow. The soils of the area are variable, but mostly not of high fertility. Decisions on further planting in this district are likely to depend greatly on the yields and the fertilizer requirements of the tea recently planted.

Since the war there has been a big increase in tea planting in East Africa, particularly in Kenya. According to a recent FAO projection,[2] by 1965 world supply of tea might well exceed consumption by about 5 percent, assuming continuation of the present price level, so that in practice there may be downward pressure on the prices of the cheaper grades. While the outlook for tea cannot be called gloomy, neither is it particularly bright. The proportion of plain, or common, tea to quality tea has been increasing. This trend is likely to continue, so that unless Asian or African consumption expands to absorb increased production of the lower quality product, the outlook for common tea will be less favorable. All East African teas are strong, common teas. Nevertheless, it is thought that the large estate companies in East Africa will have no difficulty in disposing of increased production and that expansion of tea acreage is likely to continue at the present rate. On this assumption, the estate acreage would increase to about 21,500 by 1964 and to about 27,500 by 1969, and production would probably

[2] FAO, *Tea—Trends and Prospects,* Commodity Bulletin Series 30, 1960.

increase somewhat faster than acreage. The total area of alienated land suitable for tea is probably of the order of 30,000 acres to 35,000 acres.

So far there is no tea growing by Africans in Tanganyika, although suitable land is available in the existing tea areas, particularly in the Southern Highlands Province. In Kenya, Africans are already growing tea on a small scale, and are obtaining good yields and quality. The tea, processed in a factory financed by a government loan, is selling well on the London market. These promising results, however, have only been obtained by rather heavy government expenditure on close supervision of the growers. Plans are now being discussed for the expansion of African tea growing in Kenya on the basis that one or more tea companies and the Colonial Development Corporation (CDC) will jointly finance and erect factories which will buy green leaf from the African growers and process and market it. It is envisaged that at a later stage the Africans would be able to acquire some of the shares in the factory enterprise held by the CDC. There is also a possibility that the CDC may provide funds for developing the tea plantations, but how this is to be arranged is not known.

It would be advantageous if African tea growing could be developed on some similar partnership basis in Tanganyika. Representatives of tea companies and government officials in Tukuyu informed the Mission that estates would be prepared to increase their factory capacity to enable them to process African tea, provided the supply of that tea was guaranteed for a period of years, but that Africans were not prepared to give that guarantee, since they would wish to own and operate their own factories as soon as their production justified it. A further difficulty is the probable opposition to the alienation of an area of land on which the TAC or some similar organization could establish a nucleus tea estate with a factory, which would also process green leaf from African tea gardens in the area. Little progress can be made while these attitudes persist. However, it seems possible that, if the matter were fully discussed and explained, Africans would see the advantage of some form of partnership scheme for tea production and would be prepared to accept it. The Mission does not consider that the Government should invest in this enterprise, or that the limited staff of the Agriculture Department should be involved; rather, finance, management and supervision should be obtained from another source, perhaps by an arrangement similar to that in Kenya. Provided that this can be arranged, the Mission recommends that an

effort be made to encourage tea growing by Africans and to obtain
their agreement for the provision of land to the TAC or some similar
organization for a nucleus tea plantation and for a factory which
would process green leaf from tea gardens to be established by
Africans on their own land nearby.

Tobacco

Production of tobacco in recent years has been:

	1954	1955	1956	1957	1958	Value 1958
	(lbs. '000 (cured leaf))					(£ '000)
Flue-cured	3,572	3,387	3,423	3,644	3,694	592
Fire-cured	1,917	1,344	1,193	1,071	1,792	75
Total	5,490	4,731	4,616	4,715	5,486	667

The main production of *flue-cured tobacco* is from European estates
in the Iringa District, which in 1958 produced 2.7 million lbs. of cured
leaf and in 1959 were expected to produce nearly 3 million lbs. If
the land suitable for tobacco in the alienated areas held by existing
growers were efficiently used, it could produce about 7 million lbs.
of cured leaf per annum. Thus, land is not a factor limiting increase
of production. On the other hand, the limited availability of trained
labor might at least retard expansion.

The East African Tobacco Co. is prepared to buy between 2 million
and 2¼ million lbs. of this leaf at a price which is in a sense subsidized in relation to the world price, due to a duty of Shs. 14/- per lb.
on unmanufactured tobacco imported into East Africa. The company's present view is that it is unlikely to be able to accept any
appreciably greater quantity of tobacco from this area. For any production in excess of 2¼ million lbs., therefore, a market must be
found overseas. However, the main overseas buyers of Tanganyika
tobacco are of the opinion that an overseas market for tobacco in
excess of the requirements of the East African Tobacco Company can
be guaranteed only if the quality is somewhat improved, and that
quality standards will be maintained at a satisfactory level only if the
increase in production does not exceed about 10 percent a year. This
view is probably sound, since the quality of the leaf is certainly not

high and tobacco production is not at present highly efficient. It seems that farmers should aim at improving yields per acre and quality, thus increasing profits, and should expand their acreage only slowly. There is also a need for the growers to invest in improvements to their factory and its facilities, in order to raise the quality of export leaf. They should come to agreement on marketing policy and for a territorial pool under a marketing agency.

Flue-cured tobacco is produced also by European and African tenants of the Tanganyika Agricultural Corporation at Urambo in the Western Province, and by its African tenants in a new scheme recently started at Lupa Tingatinga in the Chunya district of the Southern Highlands Province. In both areas tobacco growing is so far on a relatively small scale, but it is proving profitable, and suitable land is available for considerable expansion, especially in the Chunya district. However, the Corporation's quota from the East African Tobacco Co. is 1½ million lbs., and increased production above this level would have to be marketed overseas. Finally, at Tumbi in the Western Province, the East African Tobacco Co. has itself sponsored tobacco growing on a limited scale.

The prospects for flue-cured tobacco may thus be summarized as follows. Plenty of land suitable for this crop is available in various parts of Tanganyika. The crop lends itself to partnership schemes between African farmers and European capital, supervision and management: on the one hand, flue-cured tobacco needs careful cultivation and curing, and on the other it is a relatively high-priced crop which pays for the cost of supervision. However, the market position is such that large and rapid extension of production would not be justified. The East African Tobacco Co. cannot at present indicate any prospect of purchasing more than 3.76 million lbs. of cured leaf a year from Tanganyika, although it would be reasonable to suppose that its requirements would increase slowly with rising consumption. The overseas market could probably absorb an increase of 10 percent a year, provided that quality is well maintained. It might therefore be assumed that a market will be found, in East Africa and overseas, for a certain increase above present production.

Fire-cured tobacco is produced in the Kibondo, Biharamulo and Ngara districts by Africans, who sell to the East African Tobacco Co. in Kampala, and in the Songea district of the Southern Province also by Africans, who sell both to the company and to overseas buyers. In both areas a good deal of tobacco is sold for local consumption, and the producers in the northwestern districts sell to Ruanda-Urundi; but these sales are not recorded. The East African Tobacco Co. at present takes 1 million lbs. of leaf, and will not commit itself to any increase of its purchases. Since a considerable proportion of fire-cured tobacco is exported and the external market is more flexible, the position regarding expansion is the same as for flue-cured.

ANNEX III *THE SCOPE FOR WATER DEVELOPMENT*

This annex considers the nature, amount and development potential of water resources in the various parts of Tanganyika, and ends with a preliminary calculation of the total area which could potentially be developed by suitable combinations of irrigation and flood control.

The river basins of Tanganyika are conveniently classified into four main groups (cf. Map 7). The largest group drains into the Indian Ocean. Two small groups border upon and drain into, respectively: Lake Tanganyika, and thus ultimately into the Atlantic Ocean; and Lake Victoria, and thus ultimately into the Mediterranean. A fourth group has no outlet to the sea: the seasonal excess of water is absorbed in a number of internal drainage basins, some covering large areas.

The river basins bordering on the Indian Ocean are characterized by the perennial character of their main streams. In the other areas, even most of the main streams are dry at certain seasons. In considering the ultimate possibilities for water development in Tanganyika, therefore, it is convenient to distinguish between two broad regions: that lying to the southeast of a line from Mbeya to Tanga, about a third of the total area of Tanganyika; and that to the northwest of this line, about two thirds of the total area.

While hydrological data are still somewhat scanty for Tanganyika as a whole, systematic surveys have been made in recent years, with the help of experts provided by the FAO, of three of the principal eastern river basins, those of the Pangani, the Ruvu and the Rufiji. The Rufiji basin in fact covers almost one fifth of the total area of the territory, an area reputed to be of high potential for agricultural development, but one which is only thinly populated at the moment.

THE EASTERN REGION

Pangani River Basin

One of the main basins is that of the Pangani River in the northeast of the territory. This basin extends from Arusha and Moshi southeast to the ocean. It covers 11,200 sq. miles, or roughly 7,200,000 acres. The Pangani basin has been studied in recent years by an expert from the FAO, and a number of data and recommendations for its development have been put forward.

Geography. In the upper part of the basin, on the slopes of Mount Kilimanjaro and of Mount Meru, the highest population density in Tanganyika is found. The high rainfall, from 30 to over 70 inches per annum, and the very good soil conditions, have favored the development of intensive land use, especially for the cultivation of coffee. Great concentrations of population are also found in the high rainfall area of the Usambara Mountains and to a lesser extent in the Pare Mountains. Both mountain ranges border on the northern side of the middle part of the basin. The rest of the basin consists mainly of large, rather flat plains divided by narrows, through which the main river, the Pangani, finds its way southeastward, before passing through a last narrow east of Korogwe. The plains southeast of Nyumba ya Mungu are severely flooded in periods of heavy rain. Ground water for domestic and livestock supply is scarcely available in the plains, and if found is mostly of bad quality. Humans and cattle have to rely on the Pangani River for their supplies.

Flow. The average yield of the catchment area is estimated at some 1,200 cusecs. Due to the rather constant flow of a number of springs on the fringe of the volcanic area, the Pangani River has as its main characteristic over large reaches a relatively high minimum flow. Above Nyumba ya Mungu the annual yield of the catchment is 10-15 percent of the rainfall. This figure appears to be low, if only the high rainfall and the effect of the slopes are taken into account; but the high intake rate of the volcanic soils, irrigation on the slopes and in the area south of Moshi, and probably subsoil losses in the complex hydrological conditions of this area account for the relatively low yield percentage.

Quality of Water. The quality of water has been investigated and appears to be, in terms of the classification system used in the irrigated areas of the U.S.A., C_2-S_1, and in some periods even C_3-S_1. This indicates a low and favorable sodium content, but a medium to sometimes high salinity hazard in applying the water for irrigation purposes.

Soils. Investigations have shown that the valley soils around the mountains and between Kilimanjaro and Nyumba ya Mungu are generally speaking of good quality. In an area of 230,000 acres below Nyumba ya Mungu a soil survey has been made by an FAO soil expert.[1] The results here were very disappointing from the point of view of agricultural development. Half the land is unsuitable for agricultural use, due to shallowness and impermeability of the soil. Only 5 percent has promising features. The remaining 45 percent is heavily saline and alkaline, and will require further investigations to decide on the possibilities for development, which will in any case certainly involve high reclamation costs. For the remainder of the flat plains and of the coastal belt, insufficient data are available.

Scope for Irrigation and Power Development. Irrigation is practiced on an estate at Arusha-Chini near Moshi, and on numerous furrows on and around Kilimanjaro and Meru.

Though an average annual discharge of over 800,000 acre-feet has been measured, there is no certainty that a corresponding further irrigation development of, roughly speaking, 150,000-200,000 acres could take place. Engineering and soil conditions are not favorable. Furthermore it is necessary to take account of another aspect of the river basin, one which up to now has been the most important: its high potential for hydro power development. The successive rapids offer, generally speaking, excellent opportunities for the installation of hydro power plants. The high minimum flow is another favorable characteristic. As early as 1936 a power station was established at the lower rapids immediately above the coastal belt. This has since been expanded to 17,500 kw. installed capacity, the maximum attainable at this site with the present minimum flow of 450 cusecs. Studies are in hand for the installation of a power plant at another rapids in the immediate future (See Chapter 12, pp. 250-51). It would be possible to increase the flow available for power generation by building a storage dam at Nyumba ya Mungu; and, with expansion of irrigation, it may become necessary in time to build this dam even to assure a continued minimum flow of 450 cusecs.

The cost of hydroelectricity goes down as the size of the generating plant increases. Thus within certain limits there is competition between the reservation of water to meet the needs of large generating plants on the one hand and future demands for water for irrigation on the other (see again Chapter 12, *loc. cit.*).

[1] T. W. G. Dames, *The Soils of the Pangani Valley,* FAO Report No. 970, 1959.

Wami River Basin

South of the Pangani Basin, the large basin of the Wami River covers 18,000 sq. miles,[2] comprising a large mountainous upper catchment and a rather extended plain east of the escarpment of the Nguru Mountains. Not much is known in detail of this large river basin. The mean annual rainfall on the upper part can be considered to be high only over a relatively small area. Nevertheless, the upper catchment is large enough to provide water which, if stored, could irrigate large areas in the plain. There are indications that soil and topographical conditions would favor such a development. Until a comprehensive general study of the basin has been made, no specific recommendations for its development can be considered. As, however, some of the major improvements of communications recommended in the near future are in this area (see Chapter 14), an investigation of its hydrological and agricultural potential should, in the Mission's opinion, receive thorough attention.

Ruvu River Basin

The Ruvu River discussed here lies south of the Wami, and enters the ocean just north of Bagamoyo. Some confusion is possible because the Pangani River is also alternatively named the Ruvu.

A comprehensive study has been made of the Ruvu Basin by an FAO expert who completed his investigations and recommendations in 1959.

Geography. The basin, immediately west of Dar es Salaam, covers some 6,800 sq. miles or 4,350,000 acres. It is traversed by the main road and the railroad between Dar es Salaam and Morogoro. It includes the densely populated area of the Uluguru Mountains, which receives 50-90 inches mean annual rainfall and covers 7 percent of the basin. The major part of the basin receives 25-40 inches rainfall per annum and consists mainly of undulating woodland. A number of sisal estates are found in this area. Three flood plains occur as an exception in the topography. One of 170,000 acres is found immediately south of the Ulugurus; it is traversed by the Mgeta River, the main tributary of the Ruvu. A second plain lies on the southern

[2] This description does not cover the linked Kinyasungwe catchment.

border of the basin on both sides of the Ruvu, and covers 235,000 acres. A third, of 30,000 acres, stretches alongside the lower part of the Ruvu. These plains are, with the exception of the upper part of the first-mentioned plain, generally speaking uncultivated due to heavy flooding, uninhabited and quite inaccessible. Though they cover nearly 10 percent of the basin, it is thought that the acreage to be recommended for development could be put at only about 290,000 acres, by reason of irregularities in the soil conditions.

Flow. On the mountain slopes the annual runoff will be 20-50 percent, in the rolling country 10-20 percent. Most of the streams and rivers are dry in the rainless season, though the Mgeta and the Ruvu flow throughout the year. It is said that the Ngerengere used also to maintain a certain flow in the dry season. This river winds in a narrow valley around the Ulugurus at the northern and western sides. The several sisal estates in this valley have become dependent, for the supply of water to their processing plants, on special provisions. In some cases water is pumped into reservoirs; in other cases boreholes have been sunk to reach the ground water, sometimes with good, sometimes however with meager yields. Consideration has been given to improving the situation by building a dam in the Ngerengere in order to provide a regular flow. However, many conflicting interests are involved, including those of estates and African farms in the prospective reservoir areas. A further attempt should be made to solve this water supply problem.

The Ngerengere probably lost its perennial character because of the denuding of the slopes of the Ulugurus and of agricultural practices which are not adapted to water and soil conservation on steep slopes: for example the burning in every dry season of the natural cover even on the steep slopes. Here a striking example is found of the relationship between high rainfall, high pressure on the land, unsuitable land use practices, lack of water conservation and the consequent detrimental effects not only for the area itself but also for areas downstream. These effects have also been felt in a small irrigation scheme which has been developed in the same part of the valley. In the design and construction of the main works, a minimum flow of 5 cusecs was taken into account. There is considerable annual variation of flow, which has in fact been recorded as dropping to as little as 1 cusec.

Water Quality. As far as data are known about the quality of the water, they indicate with one exception of probably minor importance a favorable salt content for irrigation purposes, classification C_1-S_1. Also the silt load of the rivers and streams does not indicate any particular hazards, so far as data are available.

Irrigation Potential. There are some minor irrigation developments in the flood plains and at some other places in the more narrow parts of the Ruvu valley. These do not exceed 1,000 acres. They are mainly on estates, and further development is halted partly by lack of capital and partly by the risk of floods. In some of these areas, irrigation water is brought onto the land by pumping from the river.

There is scope for future development by harnessing the waters of the basin in reservoirs so far as is needed to free the plains from flooding. Available data suggest that the upper plain has good soil qualities. For the middle plain, insufficient data are available. The lower plain is of good soil quality in the upper part, but the lower part near the sea is saline. The rolling topography, and, to a lesser extent, the soil conditions, seem to prevent large-scale reclamation and irrigation of the rolling woodlands, at least in the near future.

By constructing storage reservoirs, it would probably be possible to realize at the same time adequate flood control for those parts of the upper plain which are now subject to flooding. Water for irrigation purposes could be either released from the reservoirs by gravity or secured by pumping from the regulated flow of the river.

To provide for flood control in the second plain, additional reservoirs would be necessary on the upper Ruvu and its tributaries. While annual yield of the catchment area and water requirements for irrigation are more or less in balance for the first plain, for the second plain emphasis has to be laid in the first place on storage for flood control. If this were completed, sufficient water would at the same time be made available for irrigation purposes. In the third, lower plain, provision of irrigation water does not offer any difficulties, but first of all flood control has to be realized. This means that, for the specific purpose of flood control in this relatively small area, another series of conservation reservoirs would have to be built.

Possibilities for Hydro Power. Since the Ruvu Basin both includes and lies near densely populated areas with considerable industrial development, the possibilities of hydro power development have been investigated. However, these investigations, completed in general outline, do not indicate any major possibilities for power development such as would justify the construction of transmission lines over long distances to areas of consumption.

Rufiji River Basin

The largest river basin of Tanganyika is that of the Rufiji River and its tributaries, covering 68,000 sq. miles or 43,500,000 acres. In 1952 the Government of Tanganyika asked the FAO to make a general preliminary reconnaissance of the basin, parts of which were reported to be of high potentiality. After a preliminary survey the FAO sent out a team of experts, the largest ever assigned by the FAO to a single job. The survey investigated the feasibility of development projects, and included topographical surveys, soils reconnaissance, hydrology, geology and other relevant topics. The reports of the survey are to be completed in 1960.

The Rufiji Basin has a peculiar geography, to a certain extent similar to that of the Ruvu Basin. The basin is characterized by: (a) a large plain in its upper reaches, the Great Ruaha Plains; (b) a large valley in its middle part, the Kilombero Valley; and (c) a narrow lower valley near its outflow into the Indian Ocean, the Lower Rufiji Valley. In the case of the Rufiji Basin this configuration has the important consequences that not enough water is available for irrigation development in the upper part, while the high incidence of heavy floodings in the lower part makes water control for that region an expensive undertaking.

The Great Ruaha Plains. The upper plain, 3,000 to 4,000 feet above sea level, lies north and west of the highlands stretching from Mbeya to Iringa and from there to Dodoma. It is essentially a dry area, with an average rainfall of 20-25 inches per annum, even less in some arid parts. Some 20-25 percent, or 15,000 sq. miles, of the river basin is made up of this huge plain, through the southern part of which runs its main river, the Great Ruaha. Here development seems feasible only in the stretch of flat land, of the order of magnitude of 1 million acres, between the Great Ruaha and the highlands from Mbeya to Iringa. In this area an appreciable runoff is available, and some development is already taking place. The area north of the

Great Ruaha is practically uninhabited and inaccessible. Not much is known of this region, but by comparison with other parts of the basin its development possibilities appear negligible, mainly due to scarcity of water.

The annual yield in the form of runoff from the rainfall of the highlands draining into the Great Ruaha may be put at 35-45 percent. Peak floods occur, and, because of the small gradient in the Great Ruaha, the plains are often flooded and there are a number of more or less permanent marshes. The marshes, with their impeded runoff, lose much water by evaporation. At Mtera, where the Great Ruaha leaves the upper plain and enters a gorge in the highlands roughly halfway between Iringa and Dodoma, the annual runoff is stated to be only 6-7 percent of the rainfall over the catchment area (26,000 sq. miles) above this point.

As stated above, only in the area between the Great Ruaha and the highlands is some use made of the land. This area falls in two parts, the Bohoro Flats in the western part and the Pawaga Flats north of Iringa. Soil conditions and topography seem, so far as data are available, to favor irrigation development. Sandy patches occur, and, in part of the Pawaga Flats, there are saline-alkaline soils. In the dry season arid conditions prevail, while in the wet season surface runoff and overflow from the rivers cause floodings. A few villages are found on the higher sites. The perennial character of the main rivers coming from the highlands provides for rural water supplies and also for take-off of water into furrows for irrigation purposes. The number of such irrigation schemes is however small and their size restricted. The African farmers apparently feel no very strong desire to expand this traditional irrigation.

On the basis of the FAO recommendations, the Government has established an irrigation trial farm of some 100 acres in this area, near Rujewa. The results are promising from the point of view of crop growth. Recently the construction was started of a further scheme using water derived from the Mbarali River. In its first stage the scheme will be of 500 acres, to be extended gradually to a maximum of 5,000 acres.

The difficulties of water resources development in this region are sufficiently illustrated by the low flow in the Mbarali River, which drops to 60-80 cusecs. It appears that 40 cusecs have to be left in the river for domestic purposes in areas downstream. The amount of water remaining available for use is thus only 20-40 cusecs. Irrigation of 5,000 acres can only take place if additional water is made available. In the long run, storage would be necessary to make water available for irrigation.

Preliminary data indicate that for the Bohoro and Pawaga Flats a quantity of water of the order of magnitude of one million acre-feet will become available for irrigation, if storage reservoirs are constructed. This is a relatively small quantity in relation to the land area of nearly one million acres, and will make irrigation possible on only some 200,000 acres. Thus it appears that development should be primarily directed towards the most promising soils.

Water quality problems do not seem to exist. Precautions against flooding of irrigated areas would be necessary. Flooding and the consequent sheet erosion could be impeded by bunding.

Bordering on the area just described are the highlands between Mbeya and Iringa. This is a relatively highly developed region extending to Njombe. There is some risk of overcultivation and overgrazing. Projects for water conservation are being studied and are considered essential for the future of this region. The Bohoro and Pawaga Flats might offer a valuable outlet for the population.

The Kilombero Valley. After the Great Ruaha leaves the upper plains, the river traverses mountainous country over a considerable distance. At Kidatu it starts its flow towards the Rufiji near Stiegler's Gorge, traversing the lower part of the second largest flat area of the Rufiji Basin, the Kilombero Valley.

The Kilombero Valley, 500-1,000 feet above sea level, comprises at a rough estimate 1,500,000 acres of partly fertile, partly sandy flat land. The valley is surrounded on the northwestern side by the highlands between Njombe and Iringa, on the southeastern side by the Mahenge Plateau. In both areas a rather high rainfall (up to 80 inches annual average) occurs in the mountainous areas of the headwaters. The annual yield of these catchment areas surrounding the valley is 35-40 percent.

The valley itself receives an average rainfall of 30-50 inches, and somewhat more at the immediate fringes of the bordering escarpments. Due to its topographical situation and its small gradient, the Kilombero Valley is frequently and heavily flooded. Land occupation is rather intensive on the fringes of the valley, where a number of alluvial fans from tributaries of the Kilombero River provide somewhat higher lands.

Development of the valley is severely impeded by flooding. A trial irrigation farm of 120 acres has been set up near Ifakara, but so far water control on the farm has not been successfully achieved. It was hoped that the farm could come into operation with a new layout in the year 1959/60.

The most important development at present envisaged in this area is the projected plantation of the Kilombero Sugar Company, Ltd., which plans to clear about 7,000 acres on a strip of land near Kidatu bordering the Great Ruaha and to irrigate from this river.

Development of water resources in the Kilombero Valley depends in the first place on the provision of flood control. The necessity for irrigation depends on rainfall conditions and on the crops to be grown. To give an idea of the problem, an area of 290,000 acres between the Kilombero River and the escarpment stretching northeast from Ifakara has been classified according to combinations of rainfall and soil conditions. Information received indicates 28.5 percent of this area as alluvial clay in the rainfall zone with 40-50 inches average per annum, and 22 percent of the same soils group with 35-40 inches mean annual rainfall. From this an indication could be derived as to the possibilities of water resources development consisting only of flood control and drainage or of a combination of flood control and irrigation.

In some areas soil conditions will definitely not favor development because of alkalinity. A rough estimate puts the area which could be developed once water control is realized at 400,000-600,000 acres. Water resources are amply available for the irrigation of such an area.

The Lower Rufiji Valley. East and south of the Kilombero Valley and the Mahenge Plateau lies a huge empty part of the river basin, traversed by the Luwegu and its tributaries. The Luwegu and Kilombero Rivers flow into the Rufiji River, which is then joined by the Great Ruaha shortly before the waters forge their way through a narrow gorge known as Stiegler's Gorge and enter the lower part of the basin, the Rufiji Valley.

This valley is some 100 miles long from west to east and some 5 to 20 miles wide, bordered by higher areas. It has already been pointed out that the valley is subject to frequent flooding. The valley receives some 25-45 inches of rainfall average per annum. A breakdown of soil groups and rainfall indicates that 175,000 acres of alluvial clays are found, of which 10 percent receive 25-30 inches, 25 percent receive 30-40 inches and 65 percent receive 40 inches or slightly more mean annual rainfall.

This valley has a relatively dense population by comparison with the other valleys and plains of the Rufiji Basin, the permanent settlements being on the higher grounds. The superior attractiveness of the more fertile valley floor as against the poorer soil surrounding it, even in the present conditions of lack of flood control, is clearly demonstrated: of a population in the Rufiji District of slightly over 100,000, 75 percent has settled on the valley floor and its immediate neighboring slopes, that is, on 16 percent of the district.

The type of land use is largely influenced by the hydrographic conditions. The major crop is paddy planted on receding floods. Maize is grown both in the valley and outside it (where cassava is the other food crop). In the valley the third crop is cotton. If the paddy planting is successful, no cotton will be planted. But there are years when paddy cannot be planted because of lack of floods or is washed

Year	Flood or Rainfall Conditions	Total Yield (tons)	
		Paddy	Cotton
1947	Ideal floods	3,000	600
1948	Heavy irregular floods	300	100
1949	No floods, failing rainfall	200	350
1950	Favorable floods	3,500	900
1951	Good rainfall	7,000	100
1952	Heavy floods	1,000	300
1953	Good rainfall	4,300	100
1954	Moderate floods	6,300	250
1955	Ideal floods	9,600	200
1956	Short heavy floods	600	1,900

away by severe floods. Then cotton is planted, sometimes successfully. An idea of the situation is given by the accompanying table (approximate figures).

Once out of three years the hazards of this land use system bring about failure in yields. It is interesting to note that over the favorable years 1947, 1950 and 1955 crop production shows an increase, reflecting a continuous increase in agricultural output which has in fact continued over the last 30 years.

It is very difficult to decide how improvement should be approached. Complete flood control deprives the farmers of the good chance of planting paddy on receding floods or of planting cotton in the wet soil if the paddy fails or is washed out. Flood control is possible but expensive, as the whole of the excees of water of the large basin has to find its way through the lower valley. Irrigation of perhaps 250,000 acres would be possible once flood control could be realized. Irrigation and flood control would have to be linked in any water resources development program for this lower valley, at least for the parts which do not receive sufficient rainfall. In the lower part near the ocean, where the rainfall is higher, development by stages could perhaps take place on the basis of flood control by bunding, if at the same time contour ridging were applied so that as much as possible of the rainfall would penetrate into the soil. Additional drainage might then be necessary to control the ground water table. In this way it might be possible to realize more stable production conditions.

Irrigation development has not taken place to date, but trials have been undertaken. However, the two trial farms have both been abandoned because of flooding difficulties. Thus progress in investigating the future potential and the desirable systems of water control and land use have been blocked.

Hydro Power and Navigation. In the whole Rufiji Basin, the most favorable site for a major hydro power installation is Stiegler's Gorge, 110 miles from Dar es Salaam. Here an average annual flow of over 15 million acre-feet is available, with a drop of 150 feet at a possible dam site which has been investigated. There are also other possible sites for power development. However, at present it is more advantageous to develop hydro power in the Pangani Basin rather than in the Rufiji Basin, since the Pangani Basin is conveniently located in relation to the Tanga area as well as to Dar es Salaam.

Ruvuma Basin

It has been possible to give fairly detailed information on the water resources in three of the group of river basins bordering upon and draining into the Indian Ocean. It may be assumed that the Ruvu and the Rufiji Basins are representative of the eastern part of Tanganyika. No comprehensive data on water resources are available for the large part lying in Tanganyika of the basin of the Ruvuma River, the river forming the border with Portuguese East Africa. Possibilities for water development in this basin have nevertheless been indicated by officers of the Water Development and Irrigation

Department. In the narrow valley, a start has been made with the construction of embankments to control the floods. This work might, with due response of the population, lead to irrigation development, especially for the cultivation of paddy.

A major project executed in this area is the Makonde water scheme, a large-scale scheme for the supply of water to a rural population over an area of some 900 sq. miles on an almost waterless plateau by pumping water up a vertical distance of over 2,000 feet.[3]

THE WESTERN REGION

For the other groups of river basins—those draining into Lake Tanganyika and Lake Victoria, and the various internal drainage basins—no comprehensive and detailed surveys have been carried out. The following description is based on impressions and information received during field visits to the Northern, Lake, Central and Western Provinces. In the circumstances, it is only possible to describe conditions in this large area (175,000 square miles) in rather general terms.

Throughout much of the Central Province, Western Province, Lake Province and the southern part of the Northern Province, the streams and rivers are dry for a considerable part of the year. Some perennial streams are, of course, found in the areas of higher rainfall in the extreme northwest, and around the lakes it is technically possible to draw upon lake water. But huge areas have no natural supply of water in much of the year, except for that provided by a number of very small streams trickling down escarpments from patches of higher land which receive rather more rainfall than the surrounding areas. Many of these streams disappear at a certain distance from the

[3] This scheme has provided a striking and painful illustration of the need in water development for a thorough appreciation of all relevant factors, human as well as technical. The intention was to secure a return on the investment by selling the water. In 1958, only 16 million gallons were in fact sold, against the forecast of 43 million gallons which the financial estimates had assumed. It was therefore necessary to ask the Legislative Council to make an interest-free loan of £125,000 to tide the Corporation over its immediate commitments, including interest charges. Shortfalls in sales of water are said to have been due in part to an unforeseen decline in money incomes from agricultural produce; but in addition there seems to have been some resistance to purchase of water, and women have continued to climb up and down the escarpment to fetch water without payment.

escarpment, as the water evaporates, seeps into the sandy river bed or is lost in ground faults of geological origin.

This area consists largely of rolling or flat country, with a number of high plateaus, surrounded by steep escarpments dropping to lower areas around. The aspect of the land changes markedly with the seasons. In the dry season, it becomes increasingly arid. During the rains, growing conditions are favorable, and the rivers and streams begin to flow. They discharge their water either into the larger rivers draining into Lake Tanganyika and Lake Victoria or into the large valleys of the internal drainage basins, which become gradually swampy and flooded. When heavy rainfall occurs, the rivers and streams overflow, and flooding occurs in valleys. The Wembere Mbuga and the flood plains of the Malagarasi are examples of large flooded areas, but there are many smaller valleys of only a few hundreds or thousands of acres which are temporarily inundated by floodwaters. Such flooding disrupts communications, not only minor roads and tracks, but also major arteries. There is virtually no connection between the western and central parts of the territory for many months of the year except by the Central railway line; and even this line is not free from the hazards of floods, as was proved in 1955/56, when the flood waters of the Kinyasungwe River were very high.

The heavy rainfall also has another impact. In many areas the ground surface cannot absorb the water quickly enough and surface runoff occurs, causing on the one hand flash floods, on the other hand erosion, especially if the vegetational cover of the soil has been partly or wholly destroyed by overgrazing or if cultivation practices do not have due regard to soil and water conservation. The existence of heavy soil erosion in some areas is well known, for instance in Kondoa District. In its travels through the northern part of the Lake Province with its great cattle density, the Mission saw appalling examples of increasing erosion even on land with only rather gentle slopes.

Conditions of life are shaped to a great degree by seasonal shortages of water (and, in places, by seasonal excess). Settlement is restricted to areas where water can be obtained throughout the year, even if this involves hauling of water in the dry season over distances of over ten miles.

In many of these drier parts of the territory, cattle are kept on a large scale. In the rainy season the herds are grazed in the drier parts, from which they are moved, often over long distances, to the areas where grazing is only possible in the dry season due to floodings in the wet months. In Masailand, for example, the herds follow in the dry season the waters as they recede from the center of Masailand to the bordering escarpments. In the Igunda Swamps in Lake Province 3,000 head of cattle are found in the wet season, 20,000 in the dry season. The Isunga Valley gives the reverse picture: wet season 20,000-25,000 head of cattle, dry season 8,000-10,000.[4]

In many localities, there is a constant threat of famine following failure of the rains.

GROUND WATER RESOURCES

No complete survey of availability of ground water has yet been made. However, prospecting by geophysical survey methods is being carried out in some areas at a rate sufficient to keep ahead of the drilling program of some 50 boreholes a year. This work is making a valuable contribution to knowledge concerning the availability of ground water.

Generally speaking no large aquifers containing large amounts of readily available ground water of good quality are found. The many granitic, basement and other rock formations with only a shallow weathered surface provide conditions far from ideal for the retention of ground water. In the volcanic areas, ground water is more readily available; but prospecting is difficult due to the type of geological formation, and the quality of the water may often be unfavorable. The fact that the volcanic regions have more ground water available is reflected in the fact that only in those regions of Tanganyika do springs of any importance occur. There are only two springs of more than 100 cusecs and as far as is known only three to four springs of 10 to 100 cusecs. These are all found in volcanic areas. Springs occurring in other regions all have a smaller yield.

Recently an important aquifer seems to have been struck in a region between Kilosa and Morogoro, a valley floor of sand and gravels yielding very large amounts of water. There might be more similar sites in areas where ground water development has not so far been considered because surface waters were amply available.

A rough idea of conditions in the regions of ground water development is given by the following data. The footage to be drilled varies

[4] Data for 1954 from Report on Smith Sound Scheme, Sir Alexander Gibb & Partners, 1955/56.

from 100 to 500 feet, and averages 200 to 250 feet. This means in general high-cost development. The average yield obtained is between 100 and 3,000 gallons per hour, too little to provide for irrigation development on pumped ground water. Occasionally high yields of the order of magnitude of 10,000 gallons occur, for instance in the aforementioned valley floor. Total solids may range from roughly 100 to 2,000 parts per million, with exceptions, when the salt content is too high for drinking purposes. Difficulties are met with the fluorine content. In a number of cases the fluorine content is too high for human consumption and even for livestock supply. Roughly 20 percent of the boreholes drilled have had to be abandoned due to too low yields, too high salinity and/or fluorine content. All water has to be pumped, the static water level being mostly between 10 and 70 feet, occasionally 100-200 feet or even more, below land surface.

THE SCOPE FOR DEVELOPMENT BY IRRIGATION AND FLOOD CONTROL

The Eastern Region

The studies made of irrigation possibilities in the basins of the Ruvu and Rufiji Rivers indicate that, in the part of these river basins lying southeast of the line Mbeya-Tanga, there is roughly 1.3 million acres of flood plains and valleys which could be turned into valuable cultivable land by various combinations of flood control and irrigation. This figure is based on a combined appraisal of water resources and of readily irrigable land, although the data on soil conditions remain rather general up to the present.

1.3 million acres is nearly 4 percent of the total areas of the two river basins insofar as they lie southeast of the Mbeya-Tanga line. If it is assumed that a similar proportion would apply to the other, less thoroughly surveyed river basins of this region, the conclusion is that 3-4 percent of the southeastern one third of the territory could benefit from some combination of irrigation and flood control.

The Western Region

A calculation of the availability of irrigation water northwest of the Mbeya-Tanga line has to be based on an estimate of average runoff. The average yield of the smaller catchment areas can be put at 4 percent of the annual rainfall. Available data do not allow differentiation of this figure according to size of area, rainfall or topographical and other conditions. It is further assumed that:

    a. irrigation will require 3-4 acre-feet of water per acre per annum;
    b. transmission losses from reservoir to field are 20-40 percent;
    c. reservoir losses, given the fact that reservoirs will mostly be shallow and the rate of evaporation is high, may be put at 30-50 percent.

According to these assumptions, storage of roughly 8 acre-feet of water would be required for each acre to be irrigated. As the average annual rainfall in the area is 30 inches, and the average yield of catchment areas 4 percent, it follows that a catchment area of roughly 80 acres is required to provide sufficient water to irrigate one acre. On this basis, it would appear that roughly 1 percent of the northwestern two thirds of Tanganyika could be irrigated.

The application of this simple calculation model to an area of over 200,000 sq. miles will meet with many objections. There are large plains such as Masailand, the Wembere Mbuga and the Malagarasi Valley where this type of calculation will not hold. There are large uninhabited areas in Western Province, covered with miombo, where conditions might differ from those assumed in the calculation. There are the mountainous areas in the extreme northwest where runoff will undoubtedly be much larger than the average assumed.

A further complication is introduced by the restriction which the Nile Waters Agreement places on the use of water in the Lake Victoria drainage basin. The catchment area of Lake Victoria in Tanganyika covers over 20 million acres. Assuming that in this area one acre can be irrigated for every 80 acres of catchment area, then the potentially irrigable area would be 250,000 acres. This leaves out of consideration the possibility of deriving water from Lake Victoria or of utilizing water flowing into this part of Tanganyika from neighboring countries. The technical feasibility of using this water has still to be determined. Moreover, complex international implications are involved in the development of irrigation around Lake Victoria. The Mission is not in a position to give its opinion on these implications.

In spite of differences of local conditions, it is felt that for many regions which were visited by the Mission the conclusion that available water resources would permit irrigation of roughly 1 percent of the land in the northwestern two thirds of the territory is a fair initial estimate.

No appraisal of availability of suitable land for irrigation development has been included in the calculation for the northwestern part of the territory. On the basis of such data as are available on soil and topographical conditions, it is felt that generally speaking enough land of good quality will be available for irrigation schemes covering one percent of the countryside.

From this calculation and from the topographical conditions generally prevailing in these parts of Tanganyika, it may be concluded that irrigation there will probably be a widespread enterprise of a large number of small areas each under the command of a small to medium-sized reservoir.

Summary for the Territory as a Whole

The above considerations suggest the possibility of development by irrigation, combined where necessary with flood control, of 2 million —3 million acres southeast of the line Mbeya-Tanga, and of nearly 1.5 million acres northwest of this line, or of around 4 million acres for the territory as a whole. This area, while two percent or less of the total area of the territory, is large both in absolute terms and in relation to the present cultivated area (cf. Chapter 4, p. 82). It must be stressed that this calculation is only of a very approximate nature, but it probably gives a fair idea of the orders of magnitude.

ANNEX IV *EXISTING OPERATIONS OF THE TANGANYIKA AGRICULTURAL CORPORATION*

The Tanganyika Agricultural Corporation (TAC) is at present responsible for the following schemes and investigations:

A. THE "TRANSFERRED UNDERTAKING"
  (areas originally cleared under the Groundnut Scheme):
  a. Nachingwea (Southern Province)—TAC-run farms and farming settlement scheme;
  b. Urambo (Western Province)—partnership tobacco farms and farming settlement scheme;
  c. Kongwa (Central Province)—breeding ranch and farming settlement scheme.
B. RUVU RANCHING SCHEME (Eastern Province)—fattening of immatures.
C. LUPA TINGATINGA TOBACCO FARM (Southern Highlands Province).
D. RUFIJI BASIN SURVEY SCHEME.
E. MBARALI IRRIGATION SCHEME.

A. THE TRANSFERRED UNDERTAKING

In 1951 the original design of the Groundnut Scheme was abandoned, and the body responsible for it, the United Kingdom Overseas Food Corporation, was charged with ". . . a scheme of large scale experimental development to establish the economics of clearing and mechanized, or partly mechanized, agriculture under tropical conditions." In 1955, this scheme was transferred to the newly established Tanganyika Agricultural Corporation.

a. *Nachingwea*

In 1957/58 the TAC operated at Nachingwea 14 "production farms" totaling some 11,500 acres, and a farming settlement scheme taking in some 1,500 acres.

402

The production farms have been operating at a loss. However, it is now believed that success achieved in breeding varieties of soya and groundnuts adapted to the somewhat unfavorable climatic conditions of the area will make these farms financially self-supporting in the near future.

Of more interest from the point of view of this report is the farming settlement scheme.[1] In each year from 1952/53 a number of African peasants have been given between about 10 and 50 acres to cultivate under a tenancy formula. Mechanical operations, supervision and marketing services have been provided at cost by the TAC.

The scheme has been a success to the extent that crop yields per acre have been equal to, or in some instances have surpassed, yields on European-managed large farms in the same area. Published figures understate gross yields, and consequently net returns, since some of the produce is sold on markets outside the scheme or is eaten directly from the field.

However, the scheme has not been very successful in attracting and retaining tenants. The lack of continuity of tenure is shown by the following:

Nachingwea Farming Settlement Scheme—Number of
Tenants Remaining from Each Year's Arrivals[2]

Year of arrival	Remaining in:					
	1st year	2nd year	3rd year	4th year	5th year	6th year
1952/53	28	12	9	8	7	5
1953/54	42	31	16	14	11	
1954/55	62	29	13	9		
1955/56	68	27	13			
1956/57	38	15				
1957/58	35					

With the exception of the 1953/54 group, which was financially the most successful, more than half of the tenants have left after one year, and after two years less than one third remain. This ratio has not improved over the years. The total number of tenants reached 121 in 1955/56, but had fallen off to 88 in 1957/58.

[1] This has been examined in more detail in W. P. Cocking and R. F. Lord, "The Tanganyika Agricultural Corporation's Farming Settlement Scheme," *Tropical Agriculture,* Vol. 35, April 1958.

[2] Tanganyika Agricultural Corporation figures.

While sociological explanations of various kinds have been advanced, it would seem that economic reasons are at least as important. Although a falling trend of recorded gross income per farmer may be illusory, resulting from the increasing tendency to make (unrecorded) sales to outside traders, there has on the other hand been a marked rise of the charges on tenants for the common services provided by the Corporation.

There is a pressing need to find means of reducing the charges on the tenants for common services. At their present level, these charges absorb too high a proportion of the obtainable gross return, and thus prevent participation on attractive terms. Africans in the neighborhood told Mission members that they would rather work as manual laborers. And, while the return to the tenants is unsatisfactory, at the same time the Corporation has incurred losses in respect of the settlement scheme.

The Mission considers that the most desirable solution of present difficulties, if feasible, would be to enlarge the settlement scheme in order to spread certain overhead costs more widely. To facilitate this expansion, the charges on the tenants should be reduced. At present, the scheme provides an opportunity to experiment in agricultural techniques and also in the organization of planned settlement. In this period of experiment, costs are inevitably high in relation to returns. It is inappropriate to burden the tenants with what are, in effect, costs of experiment. The Mission therefore recommends that the Government should reimburse TAC for part of the costs of the scheme. The payment would not have to be large in order to make a substantial difference to the financial position of the average tenant.

The TAC is proposing that its future responsibilities for the settlement farms should be largely limited to the provision of mechanical cultivation services, water and bulk supplies of sacks and fertilizer. It proposes that the marketing services at present provided by the Corporation should be taken over by a cooperative of the tenants.

The future of the whole area, settlement scheme and production farms alike, is closely bound up with the future of the Southern Province railway. Closing of the railway would increase costs of fuel and other supplies, and would imperil the establishment of financial viability. However, the present policy is to keep the railway running, if this can be done without excessive losses. If the railway can indeed be kept open, then there would be further advantages in increasing the scale of operations at Nachingwea, provided that the resulting improvement of the finances of the railway and the port of Mtwara would not be offset by additional losses at Nachingwea. This points to an expansion of the production farms as well as of the settlement scheme. The management of the TAC estimates that the output of the production farms could be doubled at the cost of a capital outlay of £ 100,000-150,000, and that this operation should be financially viable. Such an expansion would increase the west-east traffic of the railway by about 650,000 ton-miles, and would presumably lead to some increase of the east-west traffic. However, when it is considered that an increase of traffic from about 3 million ton-miles in 1958 to something of the order of 10 million ton-miles is needed for the railway to break even, it can be seen that the impact of extension of the production farms on the viability of the railway would in any case be rather small.

b. *Urambo*

At Urambo, the TAC operates a multi-racial settlement scheme. The main crop is tobacco (which is flue-cured), generally grown in fallow rotation. Groundnuts and maize are grown further up the catena from the sandy tobacco zone.

An interesting feature of the scheme is that it allows tenants to enter at a level of operations suited to their knowledge and ability, with an opportunity to graduate to larger and more profitable operations as and when they are ready. The operation is divided into a farming settlement scheme, medium farms and large farms.

The *farming settlement scheme* originally consisted of one large unit of 70 tenants, growing 200 acres of tobacco. This unit was found unwieldy, and has been broken down into three separate units with 41, 17 and 15 tenants respectively, growing 250 acres of tobacco in all. The Corporation grows the seedlings and cures the tobacco, the tenants' contribution being limited to transport, cultivation and harvesting. On this basis, the remuneration to the tenant cannot be large. However, the experience gained may enable the tenant to move to a medium farm. In the three years 1955/56-1957/58, five tenants moved to medium farms. By contrast with the situation at Nachingwea, the number of farmers in the settlement scheme has gradually increased, in spite of wastage.

The number of *medium farms* has recently been increased from three to six. These farms are from 150 to 200 acres each, designed for an annual tobacco crop of 15 acres. The medium farmers are on year-to-year tenancy, and have their mechanical operations carried out for them against repayment either by the Corporation or by neighboring large farmers. They grow their own seedlings and cure their own crop. The medium farmers hire an average of 16 laborers each. The medium farmers have shown skill and enterprise in overcoming various difficulties, and in 1957/58 the three made money profits ranging from £ 223 to £ 422.

The *large farms* average 1,200 acres of cleared land, designed to provide an annual tobacco crop of 60 acres. The present plan is for 28 large farms: in 1957/58, 22 were leased to individual growers, five were vacant and one was under construction. The large farms are self-contained units, carrying out their own mechanical operations. Several of the farms have had satisfactory financial results, but a few have been tending to lose money.

The operation at Urambo has on the whole developed satisfactorily. Further experimentation and expansion are highly recommended.

c. *Kongwa*

At Kongwa there are 90,000 acres of land which were fully cleared for arable farming under the Groundnut Scheme and subsequently allowed to tumble down. The two main enterprises at present are the ranching by the Corporation itself of Zebu-Boran cattle for meat production and a settlement scheme for African tenant farmers.

Ranching is going very well, and has already demonstrated the viability of such an operation at Kongwa. The farming settlement scheme, by contrast, appears to be barely economic at best, and suffers from several disadvantages. In the first place the rainfall is frequently insufficient to give economic crop yields. Secondly, largely because of the equipment needed for mechanical cultivation, capitalization is high—at least £ 30,000 for only about 1,600 acres under crop, even excluding the original clearing costs. Thirdly, and again mainly because of mechanization but also because of the need for keeping detailed records for individual farmers, the charges for administration, supervision and depreciation are high.

The Corporation is therefore proposing to alter this scheme so that the tenants will chiefly rely on ranching cattle and will cultivate not more than five acres, mainly to provide their own food, and without costly mechanization. This shift of the emphasis to cattle should have the following advantages;

a. It will give a better return to the tenant in an area where the rainfall is too low and unreliable for economic crop production.

b. Capitalization and overheads will be much reduced by eliminating mechanical cultivation, and because one European will be able to supervise a larger number of farmers and a greater area of land.

c. The cattle owned by the tenants will form an asset from which the Corporation can readily recover debts if the tenant cannot discharge such debts in any other way.

The Mission recommends that this ranch should be developed to its full carrying capacity, and that operations should be progressively concentrated on the breeding and rearing of stock from the herds on the ranch, the buying and fattening of immatures being reduced in scale as the breeding herd is developed to full capacity.

B. RUVU RANCHING SCHEME

Ruvu is a ranch of 78,000 acres, situated only 50 miles from Dar es Salaam, and operated by the Tanganyika Agricultural Corporation. Finance was obtained by a loan of up to £ 75,000, bearing interest at 5 percent, negotiated by the Tanganyika Government with the Standard Bank of South Africa.

The ranch is at present only partly developed and carries about 6,000 head of stock. The policy has been to concentrate on purchase and fattening of immatures, and the present intention is to use the ranch largely as a fattening and holding ground near to the final market for steers bred at Kongwa and Mkata. Since conditions are rather less suitable than at Kongwa for the breeding of improved cattle, it would seem wise to continue the present policy for the time being; but it may be desirable to consider a partial switch to breeding activities when the ranch is fully developed.

C. LUPA TINGATINGA TOBACCO FARM

The experimental tobacco growing scheme at Lupa Tingatinga was transferred from the Department of Agriculture to the TAC in 1957. The Corporation has been developing a central farm of 5,000 acres to prove the area and the project to be suitable and commercially viable for the production of flue-cured tobacco. The intention for the next stage is to develop a planned settlement scheme on an area of over 8,000 acres adjoining the central farm.

D. RUFIJI BASIN SURVEY SCHEME

The Corporation has been responsible for the management and administration of the Rufiji Basin survey, in which it has been assisted by experts from the Food and Agriculture Organization of the United Nations. In connection with this scheme, the Corporation has been operating three trial farms at Beta, Lumemo and Rujewa (formerly called Mbarali). In 1958, management of the Beta farm was transferred to the Department of Agriculture.

E. MBARALI IRRIGATION SCHEME

The Mbarali irrigation scheme, adjacent to the Rujewa trial farm, is intended as the first step in the practical application of the findings of the Rufiji Basin survey. Its main purpose is to determine the organizational implications of irrigation on a large scale. The ultimate aim is to establish supervised irrigation farming of 5,000 acres by African farmers. The Corporation was authorized, in 1958, to undertake the scheme as managing agents for the Government.

ANNEX **V** *FOOD CROP PRODUCTION*

There are as yet no accurate, comprehensive statistics on production of food crops in Tanganyika. The following estimates of food crop production, by province, were made by the Mission on the basis of discussions with agricultural officers and observations in the field, and in consultation with the Tanganyika Unit of the East African Statistical Department. They present some revisions by comparison with the figures used in the estimates of the product of the agricultural sector published by the East African Statistical Department.[1] These revisions are necessarily extremely tentative. We would not recommend any adjustment to the official series until more reliable information becomes available, in particular from the projected agricultural sample surveys (cf. Chapter 17, p. 344).

Quantities Produced

Table 42 sets out estimates of total annual production of food crops in each province and Table 43 gives the same information in per capita terms.

Valuation of Production

Much of the food production covered by Tables 42 and 43 is unmarketed, subsistence production. In order to reduce the quantity figures to homogeneous, money terms, it has been necessary to decide between various alternative methods of valuation. In the first place,

[1] See: *The Gross Domestic Product of Tanganyika, 1954-57;* Tanganyika *Statistical Abstract, 1959.*

TABLE 42 Estimated Annual Production of Major Food Crops in Recent Years, by Province

('000 tons)

Crop	Southern Highlands	Southern	Eastern	Central	Western	Lake and W. Lake	Northern	Tanga	Tanganyika Total
Cassava (dried root equiv.)	15	120	45	70	90	150	80	50	620
Other root crops	20	10	20	10	5	25	15	15	120
Maize	120	40	80	50	60	120	80	50	600
Millet	60	80	30	80	100	130	30	30	540
Sorghum	20	50	50	60	40	130	40	40	430
Beans and peas	20	20	20	20	20	60	30	20	210
Bananas	80	80	80	50	60	150	100	70	670
Fruits	10	10	20	20	50	40	40	50	240
Vegetables	5	5	20	5	10	20	15	10	90

SOURCE: Mission estimates.

TABLE 43 Estimated Annual Per Capita Production of Major Categories of Food Crops in Recent Years, by Province

(Kgs. per head of population)

Crop	Southern Highlands	Southern	Eastern	Central	Western	Lake and W. Lake	Northern	Tanga	Tanganyika Total
Root crops	34	128	60	90	89	78	123	94	84
Grains	194	168	148	214	188	169	194	174	179
Pulses	19	20	18	23	19	27	39	29	24
Bananas	78	79	74	56	56	67	129	102	76
Fruits and vegetables	15	15	37	28	56	27	71	87	38

SOURCE: Mission estimates.

TABLE 44   Valuation of Food Crop Production as at Nearest Market Prices, 1958

(£'000)

Crop	Southern Highlands	Southern	Eastern	Central	Western	Lake and W. Lake	Northern	Tanga	Tanganyika Total
Cassava	210	1,200	630	490	990	2,250	960	550	7,280
Other root crops	120	120	460	110	60	300	240	180	1,590
Maize	1,320	480	1,280	550	720	2,280	1,440	850	8,920
Millet	1,200	1,040	570	1,600	1,700	3,510	630	600	10,850
Sorghum	440	950	1,050	780	760	2,600	600	640	7,820
Beans and peas	420	540	560	440	480	1,680	720	520	5,360
Bananas	800	800	800	500	600	1,500	1,000	700	6,700
Fruits	150	150	300	300	750	600	600	750	3,600
Vegetables	80	80	320	80	160	320	240	160	1,440
Total	4,740	5,360	5,970	4,850	6,220	15,040	6,430	4,950	53,560

SOURCES: Tables 42 and 46.

such production may be alternatively valued at "ex-farm" or at "nearest market" prices. Since producers in Tanganyika as a rule carry their surplus product to a nearby Native Authority Market or to a merchant living close to that market, it has seemed appropriate to apply "nearest market" prices. In Table 44, production has been valued according to provincial average price levels: that is to say, the production has been recorded as nearly as possible at the price it would in fact have fetched if sold at the nearest market, on the assumption that the hypothetical sales would not have affected prices. This last assumption shows the necessarily somewhat arbitrary nature of the calculations. Table 45, showing per capita values, implies a comparison between the level of production in the various provinces, and so the same prices have been used for each province in order to eliminate the influence of different provincial price levels. The weighted average of provincial prices for the various commodities has been used. Prices applied are shown in Table 46.

TABLE 45   Estimated Per Capita Value of Food Crop Production by Province, Based on Weighted Averages of Provincial Prices, 1958

Province	Shillings per Head of Population
Northern	162
Tanga	145
Central	130
Western	127
Southern	122
Lake and W. Lake	114
Southern Highlands	104
Eastern	100
Tanganyika	122

SOURCES: Tables 42 and 46; population figures from Tanganyika *Statistical Abstract, 1959.*

TABLE 46 Average Prices for Food Crops, in 1958, by Province

(£ per ton)

Crop	Southern Highlands	Southern	Eastern	Central	Western	Lake and W. Lake	Northern	Tanga	Weighted Average for Territory
Cassava (dried root)	14	10	14	7	11	15	[12]	11	11.7
Other root crops	6	12	23	11	12	12	16	12	13.3
(Potatoes)	(10)	(21)	(33)	(22)	(25)	(18)	(17)	(18)	
(Sweet potatoes)	(6)	(n.a.)	(23)	(n.a.)	(26)	(12)	(n.a.)	(12)	
Maize	11	12	16	11	12	19	18	17	14.9
Millet	20	13	19	20	17	27	21	[20]	20.1
Sorghum	22	19	21	13	19	20	15	16	18.2
Beans and peas	21	27	28	22	24	28	24	26	25.5
Bananas	[10]	[10]	[10]	[10]	[10]	[10]	[10]	[10]	[10.0]
Fruits	[15]	[15]	[15]	[15]	[15]	[15]	[15]	[15]	[15.0]
Vegetables	[16]	[16]	[16]	[16]	[16]	[16]	[16]	[16]	[16.0]

SOURCE: East African Statistical Department.

TABLE 47   Estimates of Values of Sales of Food Crops, 1958

Crop	Value Produced	Percentage Sold	Value of Sales
	(£ '000)		(£ '000)
Cassava	7,280	10	730
Other root crops	1,590	10	160
Maize	8,920	25	2,230
Millet	10,850	10	1,085
Sorghum	7,820	15	1,175
Beans and peas	5,360	30	1,610
Bananas	6,700	10	670
Fruits	3,600	30	1,080
Vegetables	1,440	20	290
Total	53,560	17	9,030

SOURCE: Mission estimates.

Food Crop Production and Standards of Living

As indications of standards of nutrition, the figures in this annex are incomplete, in particular in that they make no allowance for the high degree of dependence on animal products of certain pastoral tribes. However, available knowledge of local consumption and internal trade in livestock products is extremely fragmentary.

Another factor affecting the interpretation of the figures is the existence of interprovincial trade in foods. For example, the fact that the Eastern Province is in last place in terms of value of food production per head (at weighted average prices) reflects the influence of the large urban, non-food-producing population of Dar es Salaam. Similarly the Lake and West Lake Provinces show below average per capita food crop production, by reason of their relatively high degree of dependence on cash crop production, associated with imports of food from other provinces.

Apart from the question of trade, provincial figures conceal differences in food supply as between particular areas. Some areas enjoy relatively safe food supplies, whereas others are subject in varying degrees to malnutrition and hunger. Many root crops, notably cassava, introduced by a missionary less than a century ago, are grown in many areas largely as famine reserves. With the introduction of crops adapted to local conditions and the opening up of transport routes to remote areas of the territory, the risks of disastrous famines have been progressively reduced over the years; but local standards of nutrition still vary considerably from the patterns indicated by the above figures.

In many parts of the territory, diets have been observably improving in quantity and quality over the years. There is a broad tendency for a shift away from root crops via sorghum to maize and thence to rice. In some crop-growing areas, meat, milk and sugar are coming to be regarded as necessities of daily life.

Sales of Food

Food crops are still predominantly grown for domestic consumption. Only a limited proportion of the major foodstuffs is at present sold or exchanged, except in a very narrow circle of relatives or neighbors. However, sales of food have developed with the growth of non-agricultural employment; and in some agricultural areas farmers are prepared to concentrate to a considerable degree on cash crop production, to the extent of relaxing their traditional preoccupation with self-sufficiency in food.

There are no comprehensive statistics on sales of food crops. Records of sales in Native Authority Markets inevitably understate total sales, one reason being the volume of illegal transactions made outside the markets in order to evade produce cesses. The estimates of sales set out in Table 47, made in consultation with the Statistical Department, are based on impressions of the percentage of the various crops which are sold. On this basis, sales of food crops are very roughly estimated at about £ 9 million, or some 17 percent of the total, by value.

ANNEX VI   *STRUCTURE OF THE GROSS DOMESTIC PRODUCT*

The official estimates of the gross domestic product of Tanganyika, prepared by the Tanganyika Unit of the East African Statistical Department,[1] are based on the pioneer study made in 1956 by Professor A. T. Peacock and Mr. D. G. M. Dosser.[2]

The approach used and the problems encountered are described rather fully in the works cited in the footnotes to this page. It is the aim of the Tanganyika Statistical Unit to refine the estimates progressively as additional and improved data are collected.

The official figures are based, for the most part, on recorded magnitudes: that is, to all intents and purposes, on magnitudes the year-to-year changes of which are known to some degree. The desire to rely on figures having an adequate empirical foundation is in itself praiseworthy. However, it leads to certain obvious distortions when the figures are used in an examination of the structure of the economy. In particular, while the figures distinguish between the "monetary economy" and the "subsistence economy," the figures for the monetary economy are in fact for recorded money transactions only, and the remainder of the estimated product is attributed to the subsistence economy. This leads to some underrepresentation of the extent to which goods and services are exchanged among Africans for money.

Since the Mission wished to use the domestic product figures more in order to study the structure of the economy than to investigate rates of growth, it felt the need to attempt certain rough adjustments.[3] It

[1] *The Gross Domestic Product of Tanganyika, 1954-57* (Dar es Salaam, 1959); other figures are given in Tanganyika *Statistical Abstract, 1959.*

[2] Peacock and Dosser, *The National Income of Tanganyika, 1952-54,* Colonial Research Study No. 26.

[3] It could be argued that the domestic product figures are not in fact very useful as indications of rates of growth, even though they are mostly based on magnitudes for the year-to-year changes of which there is a fair degree of evidence. In the first place, the official estimates extend only from 1954 to 1958. It is not possible to extend the series back to 1952 by using the Peacock and Dosser estimates, since the

417

is not suggested that the particular adjustments made here should be incorporated into the official series. On the other hand, it would be highly desirable to have fuller knowledge of the amount and nature of money transactions in the economy (cf. Chapter 17, p. 344) ; and fuller knowledge may make possible useful adjustments in the official product statistics.

Amendments Suggested to Show the Structure of the Domestic Product

Table 48 shows the differences between the estimates of the gross domestic product used by the Mission in Chapter 2 and the official, published figures.

It can be seen that the adjustments affect only the agriculture, handicraft and miscellaneous services sectors, and that their general effect is slightly to increase the estimate of the total product, and to increase the importance attributed to monetary as against subsistence activities.

The changes made for agriculture are based on the estimates of production and sales of food crops set out in Annex V.

For "craft industries," the official estimates give figures attributed entirely to the subsistence sector. These are based on the Peacock and Dosser figures, which cover largely the brewing of *pombe*, other arts and crafts having been considered of relatively minor magnitude. The amendments proposed by the Mission reflect the known fact that there has been a considerable growth of monetary transactions in pombe, plus a small allowance for some additional African sales of goods not allowed for in the official figures.

A small allowance has been made in "miscellaneous services" for African monetary transactions in services, such as haircuts, not fully covered in the official statistics.

Neither the official statistics, nor the figures suggested by the Mission, include any valuation of services in the subsistence sector. That is to say, the imputed value of subsistence activities covers the value of goods only. This treatment can be justified by analogy with the treatment used in more highly developed countries, where services

official figures contain certain unexplained differences as against the Peacock and Dosser figures. Secondly, the Statistical Unit has not found it possible to give estimates in terms of constant prices. Since, in particular, the export unit value index fell by over 15 percent from 1954 to 1958, it is difficult to interpret changes over time of product figures expressed only in current prices.

TABLE 48　Tanganyika Gross Domestic Product at Factor Cost, 1958—Estimates of the East African Statistical Department and of the Mission Compared

(£'000)

	Mission Estimates			East African Statistical Department Figures			Revision Suggested by Mission		
	Monetary Sector	Subsistence Sector	Total	Monetary Sector	Subsistence Sector	Total	Monetary Sector	Subsistence Sector	Total
Agriculture	36,273	44,900	81,173	32,236	42,812	75,048	+4,037	+2,088	+6,125
Livestock	3,502	11,525	15,027	3,502	11,525	15,027	—	—	—
Forestry	3,135	2,150	5,285	3,135	2,150	5,285	—	—	—
Hunting and fishing	347	2,581	2,928	347	2,581	2,928	—	—	—
Mining	6,186	—	6,186	6,186	—	6,186	—	—	—
Manufacturing ..	6,750	—	6,750	6,750	—	6,750	—	—	—
Handicraft	1,500	4,698	6,198	—	5,698	5,698	+1,500	−1,000	+ 500
Construction	6,089	4,381	10,470	6,089	4,381	10,470	—	—	—
Public utilities ...	955	n.a.	955	955	n.a.	955	—	—	—
Transport and distribution	19,251	n.a.	19,251	19,251	n.a.	19,251	—	—	—
Ownership of dwellings	3,334	n.a.	3,334	3,334	n.a.	3,334	—	—	—
Public Administration	11,326	n.a.	11,326	11,326	n.a.	11,326	—	—	—
Misc. services	5,334	n.a.	5,334	4,834	n.a.	4,834	+ 500	—	+ 500
Total	103,982	70,235	174,217	97,945	69,147	167,092	+6,037	+1,088	+7,125

SOURCES:　Tanganyika *Statistical Abstract, 1960*; Mission estimates.

TABLE 49   Supply and Use of Resources in Tanganyika, 1958,
Estimates of the East African Statistical Department and
Modifications Suggested by the Mission

(£ '000)

	Mission Figures	E.A. Statistical Department Figures	Modification Suggested by Mission
Gross domestic product at			
factor cost	174,217	167,092	+ 7,125
Commodity imports	40,677	40,677	—
Invisibles (net)	[4,000]	—	+ 4,000
Taxes on expenditure	9,206	9,206	—
Less subsidies	217	217	—
Available resources at			
market prices	227,883	216,758	+11,125
Exports	46,420	46,420	—
General government			
consumption expenditure	17,556	17,556	—
Gross capital expenditure			
of general government	6,963	6,963	—
Gross capital expenditure			
of private enterprises	18,918	18,918	—
Gross capital expenditure			
of government enterprises	1,520	1,520	—
Private consumption expenditure	136,506	125,381	+11,125
Use of resources	227,883	216,758	+11,125

SOURCES: Tanganyika *Statistical Abstract, 1960;* Mission estimates.

not performed for money are not included in the reckoning of the national product. However, in interpreting the figures for Tanganyika, it has to be borne in mind that such services are likely to be relatively more important there than in more advanced economies. For this reason, and because of a necessarily arbitrary element in the valuation of non-marketed production, no very exact meaning can be attached to the suggestion, conveyed by the table, that subsistence activities constitute roughly 40 percent of the total product of Tanganyika.

Supply and Use of Resources

To the figures for supply and use of resources published by the Statistical Unit, the Mission proposes three amendments.

In the first place, Table 49 substitutes the Mission's adjusted figure in place of the official estimate of the gross domestic product.

Secondly, the official statistics include under imports and exports only merchandise trade. This leads to a probable underestimate of the total supply of resources, since theoretical considerations and such factual evidence as is available suggest a considerable import of services, outweighing the export of services. In Table 49, an allowance of £ 4 million for the net deficit in respect of external service transactions (invisibles) is inserted on the side of available resources. The figure is based on such rudimentary estimates as have been made of the balance of payments of Tanganyika with the outside world, including Kenya and Uganda. However, the figure is very rough.

The third change is a consequential increase of the figure for private consumption expenditure. This figure is not directly estimated in the official statistics, but is the residual in the table. "Private consumption expenditure" thus reflects all errors and omissions, and also covers any changes in stocks in the private sector.

ANNEX VII ECONOMIC AND FINANCIAL EVALUATION (with Special Reference to Irrigation Projects and Cattle Ranches)

This annex considers the net effect on the public finances of development projects financed by borrowing. The cases of irrigation projects and cattle ranching schemes are considered by way of example. The annex has two purposes:

a. to consider what financial returns to public authorities may in fact be expected from different types of irrigation and ranching schemes;

b. to demonstrate types of calculation which should be carried out in greater detail in evaluating projects.

The calculations set out below are preliminary approximations only: not only are they based on rough estimates of costs and physical returns, but also they depend on rather crude assumptions of the financial returns likely to accrue to public authorities as a result of given increase of physical production in particular circumstances. However, they provide a *prima facie* case of the financial feasibility of certain development operations, and they also give a model which should be elaborated by further work in Tanganyika.

THE MEASURING ROD

In order to expand public expenditures in Tanganyika, it will become necessary beyond a certain point to seek loans on "hard" terms. The service charges on "hard" loans can therefore be regarded as representing the ultimate cost of expanding public development activities in Tanganyika, and thus as providing a standard against which to measure the returns to be expected from particular projects.

Since the amount which the Government can spend, now and in future years, is of central importance for the rate of economic and social development in Tanganyika (as explained at the beginning of Chapter 3) the discussion here is conducted in terms of the net budgetary effect of borrowing—the balance between service obligations and the total fiscal returns resulting from the expenditures made possible by borrowing.

The following service terms will be taken as representative for "hard" loans: 6 percent interest and commission, with repayment over 20 years on the basis of constant service annuities. These terms result in an annual service charge of roughly 8.7 percent.

This assumed cost of obtaining funds has two implications:

a. To the extent that government expenditures can be found which will yield total returns to revenue on the original capital sum (net of depreciation of the assets installed), at least equal to the interest rate on borrowing (here put at 6 percent), there is a *prima facie* case that it is worth borrowing in order to make possible such expenditures. Government borrowing is the surrender of a stream of future revenue for the sake of being able to spend more now. If the rate of net return on spending now is more than equal to the rate of interest, then the quickest expansion of productive capacity installed by government expenditures will be secured by borrowing. If, on the other hand, total returns in terms of revenue (after allowing for depreciation), are less than the rate of interest on borrowing, then from the point of view of the long-run budgetary situation it is better to finance expenditures directly from revenue rather than by borrowing.

b. If borrowing involves fixed amortization obligations (and if these amortization obligations cannot be effectively postponed by further borrowing to cover them), then it is necessary to take into account the budgetary effect of total service payments—interest and amortization. According to the yardstick used, if Tanganyika borrows it has to pay not 6 percent extending into the indefinite future, but some 8¾ percent for 20 years. If borrowing is incurred to finance expenditures which yield total revenue returns of less than 8¾ percent, then there is a net burden on the budget. Less remains for the finance of other expenditures. This does not mean that the Government is not justified in borrowing to finance expenditures which (according to the figures being used) bring in a (net) return of more than 6 percent but a (gross) return of less than 8¾ percent. To some extent, it may be worthwhile tying up revenue to meet the net burden of service charges in such cases; for on a long view it may be better to have a project with a long productive life financed by borrowing, even if at some net cost to revenue over 20 years, rather than to spend the revenue in an alternative use. However, it is clear that there is a limit to the sums which Tanganyika can afford to borrow at 8¾ percent (total service) to finance expenditures giving smaller (gross) returns to the government finances: for borrowing in such cases encroaches on the sums remaining for other government expenditures, including those which, for institutional reasons, do not qualify for finance by borrowing. Thus the criterion of an 8¾ percent return to the government finances[1] can be used as a first measure. Any expenditures which give a fairly certain prospect of a return of at least 8¾ percent can be adopted without further thought, at least insofar as their budgetary effects are concerned. For expenditures in the range of prospective return 6 percent net to 8¾ percent gross, it is necessary to consider whether they justify the net burden on revenue for 20 years involved in borrowing to make them possible.

The implications of the measuring rod may be illustrated by means of a numerical example. The average incidence of central government taxation on increases of income in Tanganyika appears to be of the order of 17 percent. Therefore a government expenditure of £ 1,000, in order to give rise to an increase of revenue of £ 87 (8.7 percent) must lead to an increase of annual incomes of £ 512 (£ 87 = 17 percent of £ 512). In order to give rise to an increase of revenue of £ 60 (6 percent), it must lead to an increase of annual incomes of £ 353 (£ 60 = 17 percent of £ 353). If the government borrows £ 1,000 on the terms assumed, and the additional government expenditure thus made possible increases incomes by £ 353 a year, then revenues (in the representative case) will rise by £ 60, as against the 20 years' service obligation of £ 87. Thus the government will be incurring a net budgetary burden of £ 27 a year for 20 years, in order to secure a once and for all increase of incomes of £ 353 a year. This may, of course, well be the best way of spending the £ 27 a year.

Two further points must be made in connection with this calculation. First, it does not follow that, with a tax incidence of 17 percent, the annual incomes of the original beneficiaries of the government expenditure have to be raised by as much as half of the amount of the expenditure in order to secure a revenue return on the operation of 8.7 percent. It is the total return to public authorities which is relevant, and, hence the total effect on tax-bearing incomes. A pri-

---

[1] Gross of depreciation, provided that the asset does not totally depreciate within the life of the loan—in which case, of course, the gross return would not be maintained over the whole period of amortization of the loan.

mary increase of agricultural production for export, for example, will normally give rise to increased activity in transport and commerce as the produce is brought to market. People whose incomes are increased will normally increase their spending on internally produced goods and services, possibly thus provoking additional production and a consequent secondary increase of incomes.

Second, the government can increase its return from a given expenditure by levying a direct charge on the original beneficiaries: for, by so doing, it takes back 100 percent of some part of the increased incomes, instead of a smaller fraction by way of the normal incidence of tax. The importance of this consideration will be illustrated below, in relation to water charges in irrigation schemes.

IRRIGATION SCHEMES

Construction Costs

The construction cost in Tanganyika of small dams allowing irrigation of some 5-50 acres has been about £ 2,500-7,500. If some of the construction cost is imputed to supply of water to livestock, then the capital cost of small dams may be put at between £ 60 and £ 80 per irrigable acre. For larger dams no experience of construction costs has been gained in Tanganyika, and costs have to be estimated on the basis of experience elsewhere. It seems that dams for large schemes, such as will be feasible in flat valleys in the eastern part of the territory, will cost about £ 15-20 per irrigable acre. However, dams on escarpment sites may well cost up to £ 40-50 per irrigable acre.

The costs of the system of irrigation channels and of the necessary drainage ditches can be estimated to be £ 20 per acre for very small irrigation schemes and £ 35 for larger schemes.

Some £ 30-50 per acre should further be allowed for land clearing and lay-out and leveling of fields. So far costs of leveling have not been included in irrigation estimates in Tanganyika; but, as indicated in Chapter 8, it appears highly desirable to include leveling in the original project: otherwise the irregular topography of the fields will prevent an even distribution of water and thus result in low yields.

For ancillary works, including roads within the areas covered by larger schemes, some £ 10-25 per acre has to be allowed.

On the basis of these estimates, the over-all cost for construction of irrigation schemes may be put at £ 150 per acre for smaller schemes and £ 100 per acre for larger schemes. Costs will be somewhat higher if the reservoir dams have to be constructed on the edge of escarpments.

Required Gross Output

It is now possible to apply the proposed measuring rod of an 8¾ percent annual return to public authorities on original capital costs incurred. To secure this return, public authorities would need to secure £ 8.7 a year, net,[2] for each acre of schemes with capital cost of £ 100 per acre and £ 13 a year, net, for each acre of schemes with capital cost of £ 150 per acre. Additional public expenditures to be taken into account are maintenance costs and costs of supervising cultivation practices. These costs may perhaps be put at £ 2-3 per acre per year. Thus the required gross return to public authorities may be put in the range of roughly £ 11-16 per acre per year, or at roughly 11 percent of construction costs.

The financial return to public authorities from irrigation schemes may take three forms:

a. increase in taxes, direct and indirect, paid by the cultivators;

b. water rates paid by the cultivators;

c. increase in taxes due to increased incomes generated elsewhere as a result of increase of production and increase of income in the irrigation scheme.

A model of the required rate of return might then be set out as shown on following page. According to this model, gross annual output per acre must amount to just over 30 percent of the original construction cost in order to secure the "required return" to public authorities.

This calculation, however, depends on a number of assumptions of a somewhat arbitrary nature:

a. An allowance has been made for output "elsewhere foregone" at 10 percent of the gross output on the irrigation scheme. That is to say, it is assumed that the net addition to territorial agricultural

---

[2] Net, that is, of associated costs other than depreciation.

Required return to the public authorities as
percentage of original construction costs   11

Required gross output (percent)		31.4
Yield elsewhere foregone		3.14
Net primary increase of agricultural output and incomes	(i)	28.26
Water rate charged		6.28
Increase of cultivators' incomes net of water charge	(ii)	21.98
Tax from increased cultivators' incomes, at 12 percent		2.64
Additional incomes in commerce and transport from (i)	(iii)	5.65
Tax on above at 20 percent		1.13
Primary generation of disposable incomes .....(ii) + (iii)[a]		27.63
Secondary generation of incomes		5.53
Tax on secondary income increase at 17 percent		0.94

[a] The water rate charged has been deducted to arrive at disposable incomes generated in the first round. On the other hand, disposable incomes are stated before tax. It is assumed throughout this annex that the additional tax receipts are used for the service of external debt, so that they constitute a leak in the multiplier process.

output is only 90 percent of the output on the irrigation scheme itself. When the irrigated plots are on newly cultivated land, and are cultivated by farmers who have moved from overcrowded areas, then there may well be no deduction to make for decrease of production elsewhere, since the old land will be taken up by land-hungry farmers and its production maintained. But when cultivators move from more empty areas onto irrigation schemes, then the product of their former plots may be lost. Moreover, some of the irrigated areas in the northwestern two thirds of the territory may be expected to take in land which is already cultivated. In a "representative" calculation of this kind, it seems prudent to make some deduction for alternative production foregone. For calculations relating to actual schemes, it would be necessary to consider how great this item should be.

b. It has been assumed that a water rate[3] can be charged equivalent to 20 percent of gross output. In fact the size of the water rate makes a great difference to the outcome of the calculations. In the model shown, if the water rate were 30 percent of gross output, the "required gross output" would be only 25.3 percent of original construction costs, whereas if the water rate were 10 percent of gross output, then required gross output would be 41.5 percent.

c. The incidence of tax on the primary increase of agricultural incomes is put at 12 percent. It is assumed that the relevant increases of African incomes have no effect on direct tax receipts (personal tax, local rates, etc.), but that the increase of disposable incomes leads to increased receipts from indirect taxes, notably import and excise duties. On this basis, the assumed incidence of 12 percent seems reasonable. The average incidence of import and excise duties on African money incomes appears to be of the order of 7 percent at present. The marginal incidence may be expected to be somewhat higher. For comparison, it is assumed that Africans will spend about a third of additional incomes on imports, recorded net of duty: i.e. they will spend over one third of additional incomes on imported goods as they are priced in the shops with duty included in the prices.

d. No allowance has been made for cultivation costs. These cultivation costs, of course, represent expenditures by the cultivators just as do consumption outlays. It may well be that the effective incidence of tax on cultivation expenditures is substantially different from that on consumption outlays, but no attempt was made to allow for this in the above calculation.

e. It is assumed that an increase of agricultural production gives rise to an increase of incomes of a further 20 percent in commerce and transport, as the goods are moved to market.

f. It is assumed that the additional incomes in commerce and transport are taxed at an average rate of 20 percent. This figure is selected as being somewhat higher than the 17 percent incidence of central government taxation on all money incomes in the territory.

g. The primary increase of disposable income of cultivators and in commerce and transport may be considered to lead to additional expenditures on domestically produced goods, and so to additional generation of income and so of taxes (multiplier effect). This additional generation of domestic incomes has been assumed to be small—

[3] "Water rate" is used as a convenient expression to cover all charges on cultivators, possibly including such elements as land rent and payments for supervisory and other services.

20 percent of the "primary" increases of income. The reasons for this assumption will be discussed below.

h. It is assumed that incomes generated by way of the multiplier effect will be taxed at 17 percent, that is to say at a rate equal to the average incidence of central government taxes on all money incomes in the territory.

As has been indicated, the multiplier effect has been taken as rather small for the purposes of a "representative" calculation. The multiplier is set in action by an increase of domestic incomes unaccompanied by a corresponding increased supply of consumers' goods on the domestic market, as occurs when there is an increase of exports. The size of the multiplier in Tanganyika is indicated by the following consideration. Central government revenues have increased over recent years by about 40 percent of the increase in export earnings, while the average incidence of tax on money incomes is about 17 percent. This and other indications are consistent with a Keynesian multiplier for the territory of the order of 2.5. If it were assumed that the whole of the increase of output due to irrigation projects would be exported, then the model for the "required gross output" might be something as follows:

Required gross output (percent)		20.2	
Yield elsewhere foregone		2.02	
Net primary increase of agricultural output and incomes	(i)	18.18	
Water rate charged			4.04
Increase of cultivators' incomes net of water charge		14.14	
Tax from increased cultivators' incomes at 12 percent			1.70
Additional incomes in commerce and transport from (i)		3.64	
Tax on above at 20 percent			0.73
Primary generation of disposable incomes		17.78	
Secondary generation of incomes (multiplier 2.5)		26.67	
Tax on secondary income increase at 17 percent			4.53
			11.0

In this model, increase of exports (f.o.b.) = 21.82 (= 18.18 + 3.64). Increase of revenue including water charge comes to more than 40 percent of increase of exports, because of high incidence of water charge.

If, by contrast, all of the increased production on "irrigation" schemes were offered for domestic consumption, the multiplier would operate in a downward direction. This is illustrated by the following example:

Net increase of agricultural output .... (i)	100	
Water rate charged		22
Increase of cultivators' incomes		
net of water charge .... (ii)	78	
Additional incomes in commerce		
and transport .... (iii)	20	
Increase of disposable incomes .... (ii) + (iii)	98	
Of which, expenditure on imports (say)	33	
Increased demand for home-produced		
goods and services	65	
Increased supply of home-produced		
goods and services .... (i) + (iii)	120	

In this case, the initial effect is to increase supply on the domestic market more than demand. The part of additional incomes spent on imports and also the water rate charged (assumed to be used to service external debt) are "leaks" of purchasing power.

In any given program of irrigation works, the two cases of production for export and production for home consumption will be in some sort of balance. Part of the increase of internal demand due to increased production for export will be offset by increased production for domestic consumption in other irrigation projects. Some increase of production in irrigation projects may be looked on as instigating the multiplier process, and some as being its consummation. The actual strength of the multiplier effect to be taken into account in estimating tax returns will depend on the balance between production for export and production for home consumption. It is because a considerable part of production in a program of irrigation development may be expected to be for domestic consumption that the multiplier effect in the representative calculation has been shown as small.[4]

[4] In this annex, no attention is paid to the multiplier effect consequent on the original investment. This multiplier effect only operates if there is an increase of investment, and is inoperative if investment is constant, at whatever level. Moreover, if investment is financed by external borrowing, it can be shown that the rate

Another consideration to be borne in mind is that other forms of increased production, outside irrigation schemes, in response to increase of demand, may be dependent on government expenditures. However, we have assumed that existing government expenditures, both capital and current, are creating a certain "slack" of capacity in the economy, so that it is possible for output to respond to increase of domestic demand without the necessity for supplementary government expenditures.

It is an accepted rule of thumb that the initial construction cost of irrigation projects should not exceed 3-4 times the expected value of gross output in the irrigated areas. The above model calculation shows the relevance of this rule in the conditions of Tanganyika. Projects giving prospects of gross output below 20 percent of initial construction costs should probably be undertaken only in very exceptional circumstances, such as the relief of acute local hardship. Over a large-scale irrigation program as a whole, it will probably be desirable to look for gross output of 30 percent or more of construction costs.

The discussion has shown, however, that the "required gross output" will vary considerably according to the particular circumstances of individual projects. It depends on such features as the amount of the product destined for export, the rate of water charge which can be levied on the cultivators, and the amount of additional incomes generated in commerce and transport as the produce is brought to market. In order to put the planning of irrigation development in Tanganyika onto a sound financial basis, an economist seconded to the Ministry of Natural Resources should carry out more refined calculations of the type indicated, in relation to the various particular types of irrigation project.

In the above calculations, no allowance has been made for the fact that some considerable period may elapse between the time when construction costs are incurred and the time when the full return to public authorities begins to come in. Depending on the terms on which loans are available, it might be appropriate to take account of this delay by capitalizing interest obligations in the interim period. This would have the effect of raising the "required gross output." The problem of delayed returns to the initial investment will be illustrated below in the example of cattle ranching schemes.

Another set of considerations which may have to be allowed for is

---

of increase of investment must be somewhat higher than the rate of total service payable on the borrowing if the multiplier is to operate in an upwards direction.

costs of settlement such as provision of access roads, hospitals, schools, etc.

Prospective Gross Products

The above discussion of "required gross output" gives a rough standard of comparison for the size of the product which may in fact be expected from various types of irrigation schemes.

Cultivation on some of the larger dams should probably be on a partnership basis and under strict supervision. Such strict supervision would be likely to assure larger yields than can be expected in irrigated areas where there is only moderate supervision carried out by extension workers. Table 50 shows the yields of irrigated crops which might be expected alternatively under strict supervision and under moderate supervision.

TABLE 50   Prospective Crop Yields Under Irrigation

Crop	Yields in lbs. per acre		Assumed Price, £ per ton	Yields in £ per acre	
	Strict Super-vision	Moderate Super-vision		Strict Super-vision	Moderate Super-vision
Cotton					
(seed cotton)	1,800	1,250	49	39	28
Paddy	3,500	2,250	30	47	30
Onions	2,500	2,000	33	37	29
Groundnuts					
(decorticated)	1,400	800	46	29	16
Maize	3,750	2,250	14	23	14
Beans	1,250	1,000	25	14	11
Castor seed	1,250	750	28	16	9

SOURCE: Mission estimates.

Crop patterns. To calculate the output of irrigated areas, assumptions have to be made with regard to the crop pattern. If in these paragraphs well-defined patterns are given, it should be borne in mind that these should be looked upon as examples.

Three categories of crop patterns are foreseen; each category is sub-divided according to degree of supervision.

A. Paddy schemes such as have been developed, for instance, in the Western Province, around Tabora. Here a number of small areas, 25-100 acres each, with rather heavy, mbuga-type soils, have been brought under cultivation. The African farmers grow exclusively paddy, with onions and vegetables in the dry season on an estimated 10 percent of the area.

There is scope for an increased number of these schemes: first of all to provide a high-valued (and, perhaps, too high-priced) food crop sold within Tanganyika; secondly, to replace rice imports; and in the third place to develop gradually an export crop for markets nearby, notably Uganda, Madagascar and Zanzibar.

A*. If these schemes were to be developed as schemes organized on the "strictly supervised" basis, crop yields would be higher, and perhaps on 10 percent of the area beans would be added as a second crop in the dry season.

B. Irrigation schemes in areas where soil and/or climate are unfavorable for paddy growing. Irrigation will then be applied to both food and cash crops. Some of these schemes are developing slowly and under great difficulties in Central Province. A scheme, large in size for Tanganyika circumstances, is under construction in the Bohoro Flats, the Mbarali scheme (first stage 500 acres, ultimately some 5,000 acres).

For this type of scheme the cropping pattern will probably be: $\frac{1}{3}$ cotton, $\frac{1}{3}$ maize, $\frac{1}{6}$ groundnuts, $\frac{1}{6}$ castor. In the dry season perhaps $\frac{1}{10}$ will be planted with onions and vegetables. Schemes of this kind will be applied to somewhat lighter soils in Central Province and to a number of lightish areas in development areas of the Kilombero Valley, the Rufiji Valley, the flood plains of the Ruvu Basin, the upper Pangani River Basin, etc.

B*. If strict supervision is applied, crop yields will be on a higher level and probably $\frac{1}{3}$ will be planted in the dry season with beans.

C. On irrigated heavier soils a more intensive type of irrigation farming is possible with $\frac{1}{3}$ cotton, $\frac{1}{3}$ paddy, $\frac{1}{6}$ maize, $\frac{1}{6}$ groundnuts and in the dry season $\frac{1}{10}$ onions and vegetables. There is scope for this type of scheme, once irrigation development is undertaken, in the heavier parts of the development areas mentioned under B.

C*. If strict supervision in well organized irrigation schemes is applied, again crop yield will be higher, and it is assumed that then in the dry season $\frac{1}{6}$ will be planted with beans.

TABLE 51   Gross Output of Irrigation

Category of irrigation scheme (A*, B*, C* with strict supervision)	A	A*	B	B*	C	C*
Gross output in lbs. averaged per irrigated acre per year						
Paddy	2,240	3,470	—	—	750	1,155
Cotton (seed cotton)	—	—	420	600	420	600
Maize	—	—	750	1,235	375	615
Beans	—	120	—	420	—	210
Groundnuts	—	—	130	230	130	230
Castor (seed)	—	—	120	210	—	—
Onions	200	245	200	245	200	245
Gross output in £ averaged per irrigated acre per year ..	33	51	21	36	27	43
Gross output as percentage return on original construction cost reckoned at:						
(i) £ 100 per acre	33	51	21	36	27	43
(ii) £ 150 per acre	22	34	14	24	18	29

SOURCES: Mission estimates.

Gross output by type of scheme. Table 51 shows estimated production figures for each type of scheme, in quantity and value.

It is suggested in Chapter 8 that a balanced program for the period 1965-70 might aim at irrigation development of 90,000 acres, which would be distributed between the different types of scheme as follows:

| A | 18,000 acres | B | 6,000 acres | C | 6,000 acres |
| A* | 6,000 acres | B* | 24,000 acres | C* | 30,000 acres |

It will be noticed that the areas proposed for the lower-yielding types of schemes have been kept down, so that the weighted average gross output over the whole 90,000 acres works out, on the assumptions used, to £ 37 per acre. The average construction costs for this collection of schemes may be estimated at about £ 120 per acre, so that the average gross product works out at roughly 30 percent of construction costs. A ratio of output to costs of this order might well be sufficient to secure financial returns to public authorities adequate to service debt on borrowing to finance construction. However, it would be highly desirable to test this conclusion by more meticulous calculations.

Double cropping. The above estimates of yields are based on the assumption of one crop a year, except for some limited cultivation of onions, beans and other vegetables in the dry season.

It is not clear whether cultivation of a second crop during the dry season is feasible in Tanganyikan conditions, especially in the more arid areas and areas with great changes of temperature over the twenty-four hours. Initially, too, double cropping is likely to prove beyond the scope of African cultivators. However, experiments with double cropping may be worthwhile on the more highly supervised schemes.

CATTLE RANCHES

The following calculations apply to two types of ranch, the first specializing in the fattening of immatures and the second operating with a breeding herd.

Fattening of Immatures

A ranch of 80,000 acres would carry about 8,000 head when fully stocked. Immatures would be held for three years. When in full operation, the ranch would sell an average of 2,500 fattened beasts in each year, allowance being made for mortality, and buy, say, 2,800 immatures. Its receipts and purely operating costs would then be as follows:

	(in £)
Receipts from sale of 2,500 fattened beasts at £ 15	37,500
Cost of 2,800 immatures at £ 5	14,000
Operating costs at £ 2¼ per head	18,000
Receipts less operating costs	5,500

On the estimate that fixed capital costs would be of the order of £ 30,000, receipts less purely operating costs would thus yield a rate of return of about 18 percent on the original fixed capital alone.

However, the total capitalization to be taken into account is considerably greater than the fixed capital. For the first three years of operation, stock must be bought and operating expenses incurred, while no receipts are yet coming in.

It will be assumed that the government or the authority responsible for the ranch can secure a loan sufficient to cover all outlays incurred before the ranch comes into operation, and that there is a period of grace such that service payments do not fall due until the ranch has reached full operation in the fourth year. Then, on the assumption that there is an obligation to make a deferred interest payment on the loan disbursements of the first three years at 6 percent, and that the size of the loan also covers this liability, the total capitalization would be as follows:

(in £)

	First Year	Second Year	Third Year
a. Liability carried forward	—	56,180	87,429
b. Fixed capital	30,000	—	—
c. Purchase of immatures	14,000	14,000	14,000
d. Operating costs	9,000	12,300	18,000
Total, a.-d.	53,000	82,480	119,429
Plus 6 percent interest	3,180	4,949	7,166
			126,595

On these assumptions, the debt on which service would be due from the fourth year would be rather over £ 125,000, made up as follows:

(in £)

Fixed capital	30,000
Three years' purchase of immatures	42,000
Three years' operating costs	39,300
Cumulative interest	15,295
Total	126,595

Reckoning the full annual service charge, as elsewhere in this annex, at some 8¾ percent over 20 years, then the annual service obligation would be roughly £ 11,000 against a purely operating surplus of £ 5,500. The rate of direct return on the initial capitalization through the third year would be under 4½ percent, on the assumptions used.

This calculation suggests that fattening ranches could not be run by the Tanganyika Agricultural Corporation (TAC) or any other financially autonomous public body, borrowing for its capital costs on commercial terms, without the necessity for a subsidy. It also suggests that if the Government were to run fattening ranches, or were to take financial responsibility for them, their operation might well involve a charge on revenue. However, in estimating the net effect on government finances, it is necessary also to take into account indirect returns to the Government by way of:

a. taxes directly generated by the wages and expenditures entering into the operating costs of the scheme;

b. taxes generated by the increase of incomes of cattle keepers from whom the immatures are purchased;

c. taxes generated by increase of incomes in transport, commerce and processing in the course of handling the increased supply of fattened beasts;

d. (possibly) export tax on increased exports of beef products (cf. suggestion for a general export tax in Chapter 16) ;

e. (possibly) increased dividend receipts from Tanganyika Packers, Ltd., in which the Government has a part interest;

f. taxes generated by secondary increase of incomes as a result of the multiplier process.

The annual deficit of the ranching operation on the basis of hard loan finance has been estimated at £ 5,500 a year. Assuming that the average incidence of tax on incomes generated by the ranching operation is 17 percent (the same as the average incidence on all money incomes), then the increase of annual incomes due to the ranching operation would have to be of the order of £ 32,000 in order to assure to the public sector as a whole a financial return sufficient to cover the cost of servicing borrowing to finance the establishment of the ranch. This figure of £ 32,000 may be compared with the following annual figures reached at full operation of the ranch:

purchases of immatures	£ 14,000
operating costs	£ 18,000
value (ex ranch) of fattened beasts sold	£ 37,500

The size of these figures suggests considerable doubt whether the generation of additional incomes, and hence of taxes, would indeed amount to as much as £ 32,000 a year.

It thus seems that the establishment of fattening ranches is likely to impose a certain charge on public revenue, though one which will be rather small in absolute terms. The Mission considers that it is probably worth accepting this charge, since the provision of an improved market for immatures should benefit the improvement of the African livestock industry. However, the first fattening ranch or ranches will have to be regarded as trial projects, and it will be necessary to keep a careful watch on the net charge on revenue and on the benefits.

If the fattening ranches are to be run by the TAC or another financially autonomous public body, the question arises of how to spare the public body from the necessity of financial loss in operating the scheme. One method which might be appropriate, given the returns which will accrue to the government as opposed to the body running the scheme, would be some kind of subsidy. This might well take the form of relieving the TAC or other body of part or the whole of the service charge on debt accumulated before the ranch begins to sell fattened cattle.

The above calculations have been made on the basis of the ranch being run as a straightforward public enterprise. However, for social or political reasons it may be desirable to run all ranches as partnership enterprises, yielding a remuneration to the partners considerably in excess of the payment which would have to be made to have the same work done by paid employees. This would, of course, reduce the amount of debt service which the body responsible for the ranches could afford to pay and would thus increase the charge on revenue.

Ranch with Breeding Herd

The type of ranch operating with a breeding herd is also assumed to be of 80,000 acres, carrying about 8,000 beasts. At full operation, there would be 2,400 breeding cows producing 1,900 weaned calves a year (80 percent) with 1,800 beasts reaching 3 years of age, after allowance for mortality.

The mature animals would fetch a higher price than fattened immatures, say £ 17.5 a head,[5] so that sales would reach about £ 31,500 by the ninth year.[6] Operating costs would be rather higher than in ranches fattening immatures—say £ 2.5 per head, or £ 20,000 when the ranch reaches full operation. Thus by the stage of full operation,

[5] Based on a price of 50 c. a pound for three-year-old beasts of 700 lbs. live weight.
[6] It is assumed that the cost of rearing replacements for the breeding herd would be offset by sales of old cows.

receipts less operating costs would be of the order of £ 11,500 a year, roughly twice as great as in the ranch fattening immatures.

However, the initial capitalization would also be greater. With the pattern of build-up assumed, only in the seventh year would sales exceed operating costs. It is assumed that the ranch would begin operations with 30 bulls and 1,250 3-year-old in-calf heifers bought from the TAC ranch at Kongwa for £ 20 each (their value in the alternative use of sale for slaughter). In the second, third and fourth years, enough female calves would be reserved to bring the breeding herd up to the full 2,400 by the seventh year. On this basis, the physical build-up would proceed as follows:

Year	1		2		3	
	(a)	(b)	(a)	(b)	(a)	(b)
Cows		1,250		1,250		1,250
1-year immatures	—	—	550	450	550	450
2-year immatures	—	—	—	—	530	435
3-year immatures	—	—	—	—	—	—
Bulls		30		30		30
Total stock	1,280		2,280		3,245	

Year	4		5		6	
	(a)	(b)	(a)	(b)	(a)	(b)
Cows		1,250		1,670		2,090
1-year immatures	670	330	1,330	—	1,670	—
2-year immatures	530	435	650	320	1,290	—
3-year immatures	510	420	510	420	630	310
Bulls		30		45		55
Total stock	4,175		4,945		6,045	

Year	7		8		9	
	(a)	(b)	(a)	(b)	(a)	(b)
Cows		2,400		2,400		2,400
1-year immatures	1,920	—	1,920	—	1,920	—
2-year immatures	1,620	—	1,860	—	1,860	—
3-year immatures	1,250	—	1,570	—	1,800	—
Bulls		60		60		60
Total stock	7,250		7,810		8,040	

NOTE: Animals in column (a) are for sale, those in column (b) for breeding.

To simplify presentation, the need to reserve immatures for replacement, as opposed to the original building up, of the breeding herd is ignored. It is assumed, as mentioned above, that purchase or reservation of beasts for purposes of replacement is balanced by the sale of old cows.

To assess total capitalization, it is necessary to make a further assumption concerning the terms on which finance will be available. It is assumed that the ranch is financed by a loan with a grace period of seven years during which no repayment is due, but during which interest liability accrues at 6 percent of the debt outstanding at the end of each year. Then the growth of indebtedness over the first six years would be as follows:

(in £)

Year	1	2	3	4	5	6	7
a. Liability carried forward	—	48,230	68,084	86,055	92,782	102,827	113,846
b. Fixed capital	15,000	10,000	5,000	—	—	—	—
c. Purchase of in-calf heifers	25,000	—	—	—	—	—	—
d. Purchase of bulls ...	1,500	—	—	—	750	500	250
e. Operating costs	4,000	6,000	8,100	10,400	12,400	15,100	18,100
Total, a. to e.	45,500	64,230	81,184	96,455	105,932	118,427	132,196
Less: Sales	—	—	—	8,925	8,925	11,025	21,875
Cumulative liability ..	45,500	64,230	81,184	87,530	97,007	107,402	110,321
Plus 6 percent interest	2,730	3,854	4,871	5,252	5,820	6,444	6,619
							116,940

Thus total capitalization would build up to some £ 120,000 after seven years, made up as follows:

(in £)

Fixed capital	30,000
Purchase of breeding stock	28,000
Operating costs	74,100
Accrued interest liability	35,590
Less: Sales	50,750
	116,940

Service on £ 120,000 at 8¾ percent (including repayment over 20 years) would require roughly £ 10,200. The position in the eighth and following years would then be something as follows:

(in £)

Year	8	9 - 28	29 and following
Sales	27,475	31,500	31,500
Operating costs	18,800	20,000	20,000
Interest and repayment on capitalization	10,200	10,200	—
Surplus	−1,525[a]	1,300	11,500

[a] Deficit.

From the surpluses shown, it would be necessary to make some allowance for depreciation of buildings, equipment and vehicles.

It is clear that the breeding ranch gives financial results superior to those of the ranch for fattening immatures. Indeed, providing that an appropriate way can be found of financing the deficits of the years of build-up, it may be possible to run breeding ranches as self-contained, self-liquidating ventures.

However, the financial results of the 9th to the 28th years do not allow any significant margin for increasing the remuneration of tenants under a "partnership" arrangement. If such an arrangement is considered desirable, it may well be necessary for the government to return to the ranching enterprise all or part of the indirect revenue returns resulting from it.

ANNEX VIII *NOTES ON PRESENTATION OF FUTURE GOVERNMENT CURRENT EXPENDITURES*

The pattern for future government current expenditures set out in Table 12 is arranged according to the economic significance of the various expenditures. The presentation thus differs from that of the budget, in which expenditures are arranged according to the department of government concerned. The main purpose of this annex is to show the correspondence between the items in Table 12 and the heads in the Tanganyika *Estimates of Expenditure, 1960/61.*

The annex also explains certain discrepancies between the presentation of the current budget figures for the future, as set out in the table mentioned, and that of the current expenditures of the past, as set out in Table 8. These discrepancies are due, first and foremost, to the new "net" basis of presentation used in Table 12: as explained in the footnote on p. 54, Table 12 records expenditures net of certain hypothecated revenues, while Table 8 records them without subtraction of these revenue items. Further, in Table 12 some rearrangement has been made of certain items, as against the grouping employed in the *Statistical Abstract* figures used for Table 8. In particular:

a. urban water supplies are classified in Unallocated Public Works in Table 12, instead of in water development (Other Economic Services) as in Table 8;

b. commerce and industry are included in Mines and Commerce in Table 12, whereas in Table 8 they are included in General Administrative Services;

c. the charge on the current budget for railway losses is put in Miscellaneous in Table 12.

The following notes show the content of each item in Table 12 in terms of the related heads from the *Estimates of Expenditure, 1960/61.* The figures against each head give the sum allowed in the 1960/61 Estimates, in £'000. The gross figures recorded are true gross figures —expenditure estimates with no deductions whatsoever.

442

Under some items, supplementary notes give an explanation of the Mission's projections fuller than could be conveniently inserted in Chapter 3.

COVERAGE OF ITEMS IN TABLE 12

General Administrative Services

This item corresponds with the following heads of the Tanganyika *Estimates of Expenditure, 1960/61.*

		Gross	Net
Head 2:	Pensions and Gratuities	1,011	1,011
Head 3:	Widows' and Orphans' Pensions	86	86
Head 4:	Governor	36	36
Head 5:	Judiciary	193	128
Head 6:	Legislative Council	74	69
Head 7:	Audit	81	71
Head 8:	Public Service Commission	18	18
Head 11:	Office of the Chief Secretary	269	266
Head 12:	Printing and Stationery	145	57
Head 13:	Information Services	87	72
Head 14:	Miscellaneous Services—Chief Secretary	107	107
Head 16:	Attorney General	51	51
Head 17:	Administrator General	16	16
Head 21:	Treasury	218	171
Head 23:			
Subhead 28:	East African Customs and Excise Department	279	279
Subhead 29:	East African Income Tax Department	178	178
Head 28:	Miscellaneous Services—Treasury	355	321
Head 55:	Transport Licensing Authority	13	5
Head 71:	Ministry of Provincial Affairs	65	65
Head 72:	Provincial Administration	1,244	1,131
Head 76:	Ministry of Security and Administration	28	28
Head 77:	Defense	48	48
Head 78:	Immigration	40	—
Head 79:	Police	1,957	1,867
Head 80:	Prisons	675	639

Agriculture
Head 62:	Agriculture	983	832

Veterinary
Head 66:	Veterinary	628	502

Rural Water Supplies
Head 67;	Water Development and Irrigation	488	359

The figures in Table 12 for future years are made up as follows (in £ '000):

Year	Personal Emoluments[a]	Other Expenditures	Less: Sums Charged to Capital Works	Net Total	For Comparison: Capital Expenditures Assumed[b]
1960/61	317	171	129	359	534
1961/62	352	195	147	400	610
1962/63	496	239	180	555	745
1963/64	647	298	225	720	930
1964/65	768	375	283	860	1,170
1965/66	900	484	364	1,020	1,505
1966/67	900	600	477	1,023	1,975
1967/68	900	650	646	904	2,675
1968/69	900	700	815	785	3,375
1969/70	900	750	993	657	4,110

[a] Subhead A, Personal Emoluments and Subhead H, Passages.

[b] Total of Irrigation, Flood Control and Small Water Supplies, as in Table 13.

In accordance with the recommendations made in Chapter 8, allowance is made for the building up of staff to some three times the present size by 1965/66. It is assumed that other expenditures will at first increase in the same proportion as expenditures on capital works, but thereafter somewhat more slowly. Sums charged to capital works and deducted to arrive at the net total are increased in proportion to the increase of capital works.

	Gross	Net

Forests

	Gross	Net
Head 63: Forest	345	333

Mines and Commerce

	Gross	Net
Head 51: Ministry of Mines and Commerce less Subhead N, Loss on Railways	37	37
Head 52: Commerce and Industry	56	45
Head 54: Mines Department	49	48

In the figures set out against Mines and Commerce for future years in Table 12, allowance is made for the annual payment of £ 15,000 towards the cost of a company to investigate and publicize prospects for particular industrial developments (see Chapter 12, pp. 242-44.) The remaining increase is intended to cover, amongst other things, the running costs of an increasing number of field units for training Africans in the running of commercial enterprises.

	Gross	Net

Lands and Surveys

	Gross	Net
Head 46: Ministry of Lands and Surveys	331	284
Head 47: Topographical Surveys	39	17

	Gross	Net

Geological Survey

Head 53: Geological Survey 135   135

Road and Bridge Maintenance

Head 92: Public Works Recurrent,
Subhead C: Roads and Ferries 1,119   1,091

In the net total, account is taken of receipt item Z 93, Receipts, Ferries.

	Gross	Net

Aviation

Head 23:
Subhead S-24: East African Directorate of Civil Aviation 160   160
Head 92: Public Works Recurrent,
Subhead D: Maintenance of Aerodromes 41   13

In the net total, account is taken of receipt item Z 90, Fees, Aircraft Landing, Passenger and Parking.

	Gross	Net

Other Economic Services

Head 61:	Ministry of Natural Resources	197	161
Head 64:	Game	112	110
Head 65:	Pesticides Research	103	—
Head 87:	Cooperative Development	113	111

Education

Head 31:	Ministry of Education and Labour (half of)	32	32
Head 33:	Contribution to Non-Native Education Funds	440	440
Head 34:	Education, Administration and General (includes, notably, post-secondary bursaries and contributions to Makerere College and to the Royal Technical College of East Africa)	351	294
Head 34/263:	African Education	2,556	2,060
Head 34/264:	Technical Training	176	165
Head 34/266:	European Education	446	—
Head 34/267:	Indian Education	566	—
Head 34/268:	Other Non-Native (including Goan) Education	31	—
Head 26:			
Subhead D:	Transfer of Non-Native Education Tax to European Education Authority	100	100
Subhead E:	Transfer of Non-Native Education Tax to Indian Education Authority	173	173
Subhead F:	Transfer of Non-Native Education Tax to Other Non-Native Education Authority	15	15

Medical

| Head 41: | Ministry of Health .... | 2,114 | 1,931 |

TABLE 52:   Derivation of Public Debt Service Figures for 1962/63–1965/66, as Shown in Table 12

(£ '000)

Year	Figures from Table 14			Service on (A) + (B) Reckoned at 6 per cent	Service on (C) Reckoned at 7 per cent	Total Service	For Comparison: Increases of Public Debt Service as Shown in Table 12	
	"Tap" Issues of Local Development Bonds (A)	Internal Long-Term Borrowing (B)	Balance to be Met from External Borrowing, etc. (C)					
1961/62	105	365	3,500	28	245	273	1961/62-1962/63	275
1962/63	110	380	3,650	29	256	285	1962/63-1963/64	285
1963/64	110	395	4,195	30	294	324	1963/64-1964/65	325 [a]
1964/65	115	410	5,525	32	387	419	1964/65-1965/66	240

[a] Increase shown in Table 12 is in fact £225,000. However, this allows £325,000 of additional debt service, since repayment of the 3 percent loans from Imperial Funds, 1964, will be completed in 1963/64, thus relieving the budget of a service burden of £100,000 a year.

Other Social Services

		Gross	Net
Head 31:	Ministry of Education and Labour (half of)	31	31
Head 35:	Film Censorship	2	—
Head 36:	Labour Department	130	110
Head 86:	Ministry of Social and Co-operative Development ..	21	21
Head 88:	Social Development	115	108

Unallocated Public Works

		Gross	Net
Head 91:	Ministry of Urban Local Government and Works less Subheads 98-114, Town Planning and Architectural Division and Head 91/275, Township and Airport Fire Services	843	840
Head 92:			
Subhead A:	Maintenance of Public Buildings	234	234
Subhead B:	Urban Water Supplies	196	−210
Head 92:			
Subhead E:	Maintenance and Replacement of Tools, Plant and Transport	161	161
Subhead F:	Maintenance of Electricity Supply Installations, of African Urban Housing Scheme Buildings, etc.	48	26

It will be noted that the net figure for Urban Water Supplies is negative. This is because expenditures are outweighed by receipts. Urban water receipts can be expected to increase fairly rapidly over the coming years. Hence the rather slow increase of net expenditures on Unallocated Public Works shown in Table 12 is consistent with a somewhat more rapid increase of gross expenditures.

Local Government

		Gross	Net
Head 95:	Grants and Contributions to Town Councils	537	537
Head 96:	Salaries and Expenses of Township Authorities	80	78
Head 91:			
Subheads 98-114:	Town Planning and Architectural Division	38	38
Head 91/275:	Township and Airport Fire Services	35	35

Public Debt Service

		Gross	Net
Head 1:	Public Debt	1,734	1,594

It is possible to make a rough estimate of the debt service charge to be expected in 1961/62 on the basis of borrowing plans for 1960/61. The figures in Table 12 for prospective debt service charges in the years 1962/63 to 1965/66 have been derived as shown in Table 52.

		Gross	Net

Miscellaneous

Head 23:	Contributions to the Cost of East African High Commission Services, less Subheads S-24, East African Directorate of Civil Aviation, V-28, East African Customs and Excise Department, and W-29, East African Income Tax Department	426	426
Head 24:	Loans from Territorial Funds	—	—
Head 26:	Revenue Transfers, less Subheads, D, E, F, Transfers of Non-Native Education Tax	76	76
Head 32:	Antiquities	7	7
Head 51:			
Subhead N:	Loss on Railways and Mtwara Port	187	187

For the purposes of Table 12, it is assumed that the Government will find a way of reducing the annual liability for losses of the Southern Province Railway and the Port of Mtwara. Such reduction is likely to be somewhat offset, in the next few years, by losses of the Mpanda Branch line resulting from the closing of Uruwira Minerals Ltd.

		Gross	Net

Contributions to Development

Head 22:	Contribution to Development Fund	250	250

COMPARISON BETWEEN 1960/61 ESTIMATES AND 1958/59 ACTUALS

The comparison between future budgetary expenditures as suggested in Table 12 and the actual expenditures of the past is most readily established by comparing the estimates of expenditure for 1960/61 with the last available set of actual expenditures, that for 1958/59 (Table 53). This comparison is most readily made on a "true gross" basis, that is to say, on the basis of expenditure items with no deductions whatsoever. This gives figures for 1958/59 somewhat higher than those recorded in Table 8, since expenditures in this table are already net of CD&W contributions and various other receipts.

Gross budgeted expenditures for 1960/61 are larger than actual expenditures in 1958/59 for all items except Geological Survey, Aviation and Miscellaneous. Thus, when Chapter 3 suggests increase in net expenditures in the years following 1960/61, it similarly envisages increase of gross expenditures in all categories except Geological Survey and Miscellaneous above the levels of actual expenditures in 1958/59.

Table 54 shows the difference of layout between Table 12 and the *Statistical Abstract* figures used in Table 8.

TABLE 53   Tanganyika Central Government Current Expenditures of 1958/59 and Estimates for 1960/61 Compared on "True Gross" Basis

(£ '000)

	1958/59 Actuals	1960/61 Estimates
General Administrative Services	6,522	7,275
Economic Services		
Agriculture	797	983
Veterinary	484	628
Rural Water Supplies	391	488
Forests	309	345
Mines and Commerce	99	142
Lands and Surveys	361	369
Geological Surveys	139	135
Road and Bridge Maintenance	970	1,119
Aviation	204	202
Other Economic Services	283	525
Social Services		
Education	4,347	4,884
Medical	1,822	2,114
Other Social Services	205	300
Unallocated Public Works	1,383	1,483
Local Government	578	691
Public Debt Service	1,326	1,734
Miscellaneous	821	696
Contribution to Development	—	250
Total:	21,040	24,363

SOURCE: *Estimates of Expenditure, 1960/61.*

TABLE 54 Subject Arrangement in Tables 8 and 12 Compared—Current Expenditure Estimates of the Government of Tanganyika for 1960/61 (£ '000)

Items Arranged as in Table 12	Figures comparable with those used in Table 8	Difference	Explanation
General Administrative			
Services 6,720	6,877	−157	*Stat. Abst.* includes Head 52, Commerce and Industry, and half of Head 51, Min. of Mines and Commerce. Table 12 does not.
Economic Services			
Agriculture 832	832	—	
Veterinary 502	502	—	
Rural Water Supplies 359	149	+210	Table 12, omits Head 92 s/hB, Urban Water Supplies. Net figure for this item is negative, because of large receipts.
Forests 333	332	+ 1	Rounding.
Mines, Industry and Commerce 130	160	− 30	Table 12 includes Head 51, Ministry of Mines and Commerce, *less* Railway Losses; also Head 52, Commerce and Industry.
Lands and Surveys .. 301	301	—	
Geological Surveys .. 135	135	—	
Road and Bridge Maintenance 1,091	1,091	—	
Aviation 174	174	—	
Other 382	382	—	
Social Services			
Education 3,279	3,279	—	
Medical 1,931	1,931	—	
Other Social Services. 271	271	—	
Unallocated Public			
Works 1,052	1,261	−209	Table 12 includes Head 92, s/hB, Urban Water Supplies (negative net).
Local Government 688	693	− 5[a]	
Public Debt Service ... 1,594	1,594	—	
Miscellaneous 696	504	+192	Table 12 includes Railway Losses from Head 51.
Contribution to			
Development 250	250	—	
Total 20,718	20,718	—	

[a] This figure is compensated by a residual discrepancy of +5 in the Miscellaneous Item.

ANNEX IX *PROSPECTS FOR PRODUCTION, EXPORTS AND REVENUE*

The Mission considers that Tanganyika's export earnings might well increase from £ 44.3 million in 1958 to about £ 60 million in 1964 and roughly £ 73 million in 1969. These forecasts assume continuation of present public policies and about the present level of public development expenditures. It should therefore be the aim of public policy to improve on this performance.

According to this forecast, export earnings would increase by some 5 percent a year in the next few years but slightly less rapidly thereafter. It is on the basis of this forecast that the Mission maintains that an increase of central government revenues of about 4½ percent a year should be possible over the next few years.

The forecast increase of value corresponds roughly to an increase in volume. The Mission assumes that the average price level of Tanganyika's exports will remain at about the 1958 level in the coming years. While we make allowance for a further fall in the price of coffee, we assume some rise of the price of sisal above the 1958 level. The price increases and decreases assumed for other products roughly cancel out.

Over the past few years, the volume of exports appears to have been increasing at an average annual rate of 6 percent. The forecast of a 5-5½ percent annual increase to 1964 and a rather slower increase thereafter thus conforms with the Mission's thesis that some modification of present measures and policy is needed to prevent a slowing down of the rate of growth of the economy.

EXPORT FORECASTS

The following export forecasts cover exports to Kenya and Uganda as well as to the world outside East Africa.

TABLE 55   Forecasts of Export Volume of Agricultural Products

Commodity	Percentage of total exports by value in 1958	Volume index—1958 = 100				1964		1969	
		1955	1956	1957	1958	min.	max.	min.	max.
Sisal	23.4	86.9	92.7	91.2	100.0	114.0	120.6	120.6	187.0
Cotton	16.4	63.5	87.0	84.9	100.0	148.2	187.1	177.8	249.5
Coffee—arabica	13.4	77.0	97.9	76.5	100.0	106.6	138.0	138.0	175.6
robusta	3.7	101.5	95.4	99.9	100.0	112.6	160.8	128.7	160.8
Other commodities [a]	19.1	73.8	109.4	92.4	100.0	140.0	172.9	179.9	238.4
Total of above	75.9	77.5	96.7	88.0	100.0	126.5	153.1	151.3	194.7
For comparison—5 percent annual increase		86.4	90.7	95.2	100.0	134.0		171.0	

[a] Cashew nuts; groundnuts; groundnut oil; sesame seed; castor seed; sunflower seed; cotton seed; cotton seed cake; copra; coconut oil; coconut cake; palm kernels; cassava; vegetable flour, flakes and starches; maize; maize meal and flour; rice and paddy; millet; beans, peas and pulses; soya beans; onions; bran, pollard and sharps; tea; cocoa beans; tobacco; pyrethrum; kapok; papain. Other crops, not covered by the above estimates, contributed about 7 percent of export earnings in 1958.

SOURCES: *Annual Trade Reports*; Mission estimates.

Crops

The Mission considered in detail the production and export prospects of a wide range of agricultural products. It was in fact necessary to make a broad survey, since exports of several of the minor crops may be expected to increase more rapidly than those, notably, of sisal and coffee.

Table 55 presents the forecasts for the agricultural products considered, in the form of a volume index. Table 56 shows the price assumptions used.

TABLE 56   Agricultural Unit Value Indices, 1955-58 and Forecasts

(1958 = 100)

	1955	1956	1957	1958	1964 and 1969 min.	max.
Sisal	110.5	112.5	100.4	100.0	113.0	131.8
Cotton	120.4	118.6	107.1	100.0	99.6	106.2
Coffee—arabica	116.6	133.0	122.8	100.0	64.3	75.1
—robusta	99.2	96.6	96.9	100.0	61.1	76.3
Other crops[a]	106.7	114.8	111.8	100.0	98.0	108.7
Total	112.2	117.2	108.5	100.0	95.2	107.8

[a] As in Table 55.

SOURCES: *Annual Trade Reports*; Mission estimates.

On the basis of the quantities and unit values set out in Tables 55 and 56, and on the assumption that exports of agricultural products not specifically considered will evolve parallel to those of the large group of "other commodities," then the value of agricultural exports would increase from £ 34 million in 1958 to around £ 48 million in 1964 and around £ 59 million in 1969. The figures would, of course, be considerably lower if all the minimum price and quantity estimates were realized, and considerably higher if all the maximum price and quantity estimates were realized. However, it is unlikely in practice that all the prices and quantities will be simultaneously at either the upper or lower limits assumed. Nevertheless, the average value forecasts given must be recognized as subject to fairly wide margins of error.

Livestock Products

While there is scope for Tanganyika to increase its exports of live-stock products (£ 2.3 million in 1958), it is difficult to predict what increase may be expected in practice. Nevertheless, it is not to be ruled out that exports might increase at more than 5 percent a year in the coming years.

Forestry

These forecasts do not assume any substantial increase of timber exports over the next ten years. Beeswax may well increase its con-tribution to export earnings (just over £ 240,000 in 1957 and 1958). The value of exports of wattle bark may well be considerably raised by increased local processing into wattle bark extract, provided that a market can be found.

Hunting and Fishing

No great increase of exports of hunting and fishing products is expected. An increase of exports of dried fish (dagaa) may well be offset by a further decrease in exports of crocodile skins, as crocodiles become progressively more rare.

Mining

The margin of error in predicting mineral production and exports is inescapably large. A major new discovery could transform the situation.

While exports of diamonds and gold may be expected at a mini-mum to remain at the 1958 level of £ 5 million combined, it seems by no means unreasonable to assume an alternative of a 5 percent annual increase in value.

Against this possible increase for diamonds and gold, it is necessary to allow for the disappearance of exports of lead ore and concen-trates, and of certain associated minerals, consequent upon the closing of the Mpanda mine (cf. Chapter 13, p. 260). These exports averaged just over £ 1 million a year in 1956-58.

TABLE 57   Forecasts of Export Value by Main Commodity Groups

(£'000)

Commodity Group	Actual		Forecast			
	1957	1958	1964		1969	
			min.	max.	min.	max.
Agriculture	32,345	34,006	45,610	50,285	53,380	64,590
Livestock	1,948	2,291	3,785	4,595	3,975	5,865
Forestry	1,232	1,059	1,570	1,970	1,830	2,230
Hunting and Fishing ..	411	252	405	445	405	470
Mining	5,276	6,160	5,200	6,900	5,200	8,760
Other	296	542	690	760	840	1,020
Total	41,508	44,310	57,260	64,955	65,630	82,935

NOTE: The division of exports into commodity groups has been made by the Mission, and evidently differs in some respects from the sector classifications used for the national accounts of Tanganyika.

SOURCES: *Annual Trade Reports*; Mission estimates.

Manufactures and Miscellaneous

The remaining exports are only small, amounting to roughly £500,000 in 1958. These exports are a heterogeneous collection, including both some minor local manufactures and exports of second-hand items of imported equipment. It seems reasonable to expect an increase of the order of 5 percent a year, roughly paralleling the development of activity in Tanganyika and the neighboring territories.

REVENUE FORECAST

In forecasting the increase of central government current revenue to be expected over the next few years, the Mission has preferred to make the transition direct from export earnings to revenue, rather than to attempt to make estimates based on the increase of domestic incomes. In fact, given that exports amount to about 40 percent of total money incomes in the territory, the development of money incomes may be expected to be determined to a major degree by the growth of export earnings. A more detailed revenue forecast, based on the probable development of yields of the individual taxes or on the incidence of tax on various sectors of the economy, does not seem justified for the present purpose: the apparent refinements would be offset by crudities in the data and assumptions used. The judgment that it should be possible to secure increase of revenue roughly proportionate to the increase of export earnings is supported by past experience, as shown in Diagram 2: from 1947 to the present, total revenue has increased by a proportion slightly smaller than that of the increase of export earnings. It is true that this result has been achieved in part by raising the rates of various taxes. On the other hand, at the end of the period certain factors were at work which temporarily lowered the proceeds of income tax. These included a new provision for the carry-forward of losses, new initial allowances in respect of capital expenditure and allowances based on more rapid rates of depreciation. Quite apart from the evidence of the past, we would argue that it should be one aim of taxation policy in Tanganyika to assure that the growth of revenue keeps pace with the growth of the monetary economy. The question of possible tax changes has been discussed in Chapter 16.

Given the forecast of an average annual increase of export earn-

TABLE 58   Central Government Current Revenue (Net Basis) as a Percentage of Export Earnings with 18-Month Lag— Actual and Projected

Year	Current Revenue (Net Basis)	Domestic Exports in Period 18 Months Previous	Revenue as Percentage of Exports with 18-month Lag
	(Actual)	(Actual)	
1958/59	18,087	41,462	43.6
1959/60	[20,666][a]	44,333	46.6
	(Projected)		
1960/61	20,800	47,861	43.5
		(Projected)	
1961/62	21,735	49,985	43.5
1962/63	22,715	52,291	43.4
1963/64	23,735	54,733	43.4
1964/65	24,805	57,289	43.3
1965/66	25,920	60,000	43.2

[a] Near-final figure for outturn, as estimated in September 1960.

SOURCES: Tanganyika *Statistical Abstract; Financial Statements and Estimates of Revenue, 1960/61;* Tanganyika Treasury; Mission estimates.

ings of the order of 5 percent, it seems reasonably conservative to assume that it should be possible to secure average annual increase of central government current revenue of the order of 4½ percent.

A particular problem is to select the base figure to which a 4½ percent increase of revenue should be related. Revenue in 1959/60, at nearly £ 22.1 million (gross basis),[1] was nearly 14 percent greater than revenue in 1958/59, and represented an annual increase of over 8 percent by comparison with 1957/58. It seems likely that revenue in 1959/60 was somewhat above the trend. On the other hand, the official forecast for revenue in 1960/61, as published in the spring of 1960, appears low. This estimate was for £ 21.7 million, gross basis. At that time, the estimate for the 1959/60 outturn was £ 20.9 million. Thus revenue was expected to increase from 1959/60 to 1960/61 by about £ 800,000 (gross basis). In the light of the outturn of over £ 22 million in 1959/60, the Mission suggests a revised revenue estimate for 1960/61 of £ 22.25 million (gross basis), corresponding to a revenue of about £ 20.8 million on the new "net" basis of presentation (cf. footnote on p. 54). Such revenue would amount to some 46.5 percent of exports in 1959 (gross basis, 18-month lag) or to 44.5 percent of the value of exports projected by the Mission for 1960 (six-month lag). On the basis of past experience, these ratios appear to be not unreasonable.

The projection of revenue ("net" basis) has been derived by applying the 4½ percent rate of annual increase to the "net" figure of £ 20.8 million in 1960/61. Table 58 shows the evolution, actual and projected, of revenue (net basis) as a percentage of exports 18 months previously.

[1] Near-final figure, communicated to the Mission in September 1960.

SUPPLEMENTARY STATISTICAL TABLES

NOTE: The source of all the following tables, unless otherwise stated, is the Tanganyika *Statistical Abstract*.

TABLE 59 Tanganyika—Vegetation Types, Over-all and by Province[a]

	Total Tanganyika	Lake and West Lake Provinces	Central Province	Tanga Province	Southern Province	Eastern Province	Western Province	Southern Highlands Province	Northern Province
Total land area (thousand square miles)	342.7	38.8	35.3	14.0	56.1	41.6	78.7	45.0	33.3
Vegetation actively induced by man (thousand square miles)	30.0	8.2	4.9	1.5	4.7	2.9	4.2	2.3	1.3
Percentage of total									
Vegetation actively induced by man	9	21	14	11	8	7	5	5	4
Grassland and wooded grassland	37	56	32	21	30	47	27	39	45
Miombo	35	8	21	12	51	31	60	38	2
Woodland bushland intermediate, bushland and thicket	16	11	33	45	8	12	4	14	42
Closed forest and forest woodland intermediate	2	1	—	6	2	2	—	3	4
Swamp	1	2	1	1	—	1	2	1	1
Desert and semi-desert	1	—	1	4	—	—	1	1	1

[a] Provinces are arranged in descending order of the percentage of total area covered by vegetation actively induced by man.

TABLE 60   Population by Province and by Origin, 1957, and
Population Density by Province

| Province | Population (thousands) | | | | | | Density per Square Mile |
	Total	African	European	Indian and Pakistani	Arab	Goan and Other	
Lake and West Lake	2,246.2	2,228.5	2.3	10.0	4.3	1.1	59.3
Tanga	688.3	671.4	2.4	8.5	4.0	1.9	49.4
Eastern	1,084.6	1,039.8	6.2	29.5	5.2	3.9	26.3
Central	887.0	879.4	1.3	3.5	1.8	0.9	25.3
Northern	772.4	759.0	3.6	7.7	0.2	1.9	23.5
Southern Highlands	1,030.3	1,023.8	2.3	3.4	0.3	0.5	23.0
Southern	1,014.3	1,008.0	1.1	4.6	0.2	0.3	18.2
Western	1,062.6	1,052.8	1.3	4.4	3.1	1.0	13.8
Total Tanganyika..	8,785.6	8,662.7	20.5	71.7	19.1	11.6	26.0

TABLE 61   Population of Fourteen Principal Towns, 1957

(number of persons)

	Total	African	European	Others
Dar es Salaam	128,742	93,363	4,479	30,900
Tanga	38,053	27,973	768	9,312
Mwanza	19,877	15,241	366	4,270
Tabora	15,361	12,005	340	3,016
Morogoro	14,507	12,440	281	1,786
Moshi	13,726	9,399	441	3,886
Dodoma	13,435	10,386	350	2,699
Ujiji	12,011	11,739	11	261
Mtwara	10,459	9,617	207	635
Lindi	10,315	8,370	100	1,845
Arusha	10,038	5,161	878	3,999
Iringa	9,587	7,792	304	1,491
Mbeya	6,932	5,641	266	1,025
Mikindani	4,807	4,383	2	422
Total, fourteen towns	307,850	233,510	8,793	65,547
Percentage of total for the whole of Tanganyika	4%	3%	43%	64%

TABLE 62   Industrial Distribution of African Employees in
Tanganyika, 1958

(number of persons)[a]

Industry	Total	Adult males	Adult females	Young persons & children[b]
Agriculture, forestry & fishing ...	213,092	169,719	20,935	22,438
Mining and quarrying	12,182	11,787	135	260
Manufacturing and electricity ...	21,326	19,919	603	804
Construction	10,438	10,221	52	165
Transport and communications ..	7,891	7,878	—	13
Commerce	11,800	11,146	483	171
Miscellaneous services	15,559	13,708	1,116	735
Public service	97,170	94,810	1,979	381
Total of above	389,458	339,188	25,303	24,967
Domestic service	[40,000]	[36,000]	n.a.	n.a.
Unclassified	1,089	n.a.	n.a.	n.a.
Total, all African employees ..	430,547	n.a.	n.a.	n.a.

[a] Reported employees only.
[b] Includes all workers whose apparent age does not exceed 18 years.

TABLE 63   Occupational Status of African Adult Male Employees in
Tanganyika, 1958

Occupation	Number of persons[a]
Clerical	11,031
Shop, office and store hands	8,750
Drivers, mechanics and fitters	15,522
Carpenters and joiners	5,986
Masons and bricklayers	7,078
Teachers	5,783
Other services (excluding domestic service in private households)	4,443
Headmen (foremen)	14,388
Other skilled workers	39,551
Unskilled laborers	226,656
Total of above	339,188
Plus: Domestic service	[36,000]
Unclassified	n.a.

[a] Reported employees only.

TABLE 64   Gross Domestic Capital Formation in Tanganyika by
Sector, Industrial Use and Type of Asset—1954-58

(£ million)

	1954	1955	1956	1957	1958
					(pre-liminary estimate)
BY SECTOR					
Monetary economy					
Private	11.5	13.7	14.0	14.3	13.2
(of which: building & construction	(5.4)	(4.3)	(4.9)	(5.0)	(4.6)
machinery & equipment)	(6.1)	(9.4)	(9.1)	(9.3)	(8.6)
Public: general government	5.1	5.5	6.4	7.0	7.7
government enterprises	5.1	5.4	3.0	2.8	1.9
(of which: building & construction	(6.8)	(7.1)	(7.4)	(7.8)	(8.1)
machinery & equipment)	(3.4)	(3.8)	(1.9)	(2.0)	(1.5)
Subsistence sector—private building & construction[a]	4.2	4.3	4.3	5.4	5.5
Total[a]	26.0	28.9	27.6	29.5	28.3
BY INDUSTRIAL USE					
Agriculture	2.1	2.1	2.3	2.3	1.9
Livestock and forestry	—	—	—	—	—
Hunting and Fishing	—	—	0.1	0.2	0.2
Mining and quarrying	1.1	0.9	1.1	1.2	1.1
Manufacturing	1.0	2.0	1.9	1.7	1.7
Construction	1.2	1.8	1.5	1.5	1.5
Public utilities	0.6	0.2	0.4	0.7	0.5
Transport, storage & communications	5.6	6.5	4.0	3.8	3.1
Distribution	1.1	2.0	1.9	2.0	1.8
Ownership of dwellings	8.0	7.8	8.3	9.1	9.0
Public administration & defense[b]	4.7	5.0	5.7	6.1	6.7
Miscellaneous services	0.5	0.5	0.6	0.8	0.7
Total gross domestic capital formation	26.0	28.9	27.6	29.5	28.3

	1954	1955	1956	1957	1958
					(£ million)
					(pre-liminary estimate)

BY TYPE OF ASSET

Building

Dwellings	8.0	7.8	8.3	9.1	9.0
Non-residential buildings	3.3	3.1	3.8	4.7	5.2

Construction

Water supply	0.5	0.8	1.2	1.4	1.4
Communications	2.1	1.6	1.4	1.1	1.1
Railways and harbors	1.8	1.8	1.1	1.1	0.8
Other construction and works	0.7	0.7	0.8	0.8	0.7

Equipment

Transport equipment	5.2	8.5	6.2	5.6	5.5
Machinery and other equipment	4.4	4.7	4.8	5.8	4.7
Total gross domestic capital formation	26.0	28.9	27.6	29.5	28.3

ᵃ Estimates of capital formation outside the monetary economy, as used in the principal national accounting tables, cover only a relatively small amount of building and construction. No effort is made in the official national accounts to evaluate any other investment, or disinvestment, which may take place outside the monetary economy.

ᵇ Covering the bulk of government capital formation, regardless of industrial use (cf. Table 5).

TABLE 65   Percentage Distribution of Gross Domestic Capital
Formation in Tanganyika by Sector, Industrial Use and Type of
Asset, 1954-58

	Percentage of total gross domestic capital formation at market prices				
	1954	1955	1956	1957	1958
					(preliminary estimate)
BY SECTOR					
Private enterprises	60.7	62.3	66.2	66.7	66.0
General government	19.7	19.1	23.0	23.8	27.3
Government enterprises	19.6	18.6	10.8	9.5	6.7
Total gross domestic capital formation.	100.0	100.0	100.0	100.0	100.0
BY INDUSTRIAL USE					
Agriculture	8.1	7.4	8.2	7.8	6.6
Livestock and forestry	—	—	—	—	—
Hunting and fishing	0.1	0.2	0.5	0.8	0.8
Mining and quarrying	4.3	3.2	3.9	4.0	4.0
Manufacturing	3.9	7.0	6.9	5.8	6.0
Construction	4.5	6.1	5.5	5.2	5.4
Public utilities	2.3	0.8	1.3	2.5	1.8
Transport, storage and communications	21.6	22.4	14.5	12.9	10.9
Distribution	4.4	7.0	6.8	6.8	6.5
Ownership of dwellings	30.7	26.9	29.9	30.8	31.7
Public administration & defense	18.2	17.3	20.5	20.7	23.6
Miscellaneous services	1.8	1.8	2.1	2.6	2.6
Total gross domestic capital formation.	100.0	100.0	100.0	100.0	100.0
BY TYPE OF ASSET					
Building					
Dwellings	30.7	26.9	29.9	30.8	31.7
Non-residential buildings	12.8	10.6	13.9	16.0	18.4
Construction					
Water supply	2.1	2.7	4.2	4.8	4.9
Communications	8.0	5.6	5.1	3.7	3.8
Railways and harbors	6.8	6.1	4.1	3.8	2.9
Other construction & works	2.8	2.4	3.1	2.5	2.5
Equipment					
Transport equipment	19.9	29.3	22.4	18.8	19.3
Machinery & other equipment	16.9	16.2	17.4	19.5	16.5
Total gross domestic capital formation.	100.0	100.0	100.0	100.0	100.0

NOTE: Figures cover limited part only of capital formation outside the monetary
economy. See notes to Table 64.

TABLE 66 Total External and Interterritorial Trade of Tanganyika, Value, Volume, and Price, 1948-1958

	1948	1949	1950	1951	1952	1953	1954	1955	1956	1957	1958
VALUE (£ million)											
Exports	16.6	21.4	25.3	41.5	48.3	36.8	38.8	39.1	48.4	43.1	46.4
(of which: external	(15.1)	(19.9)	(23.1)	(39.3)	(46.5)	(34.2)	(36.2)	(36.2)	(44.9)	(39.4)	(41.7)
interterritorial	(1.2)	(0.9)	(0.9)	(1.2)	(0.9)	(1.2)	(1.1)	(1.7)	(2.1)	(2.0)	(2.6)
re-exports)	(0.3)	(0.6)	(1.3)	(1.0)	(1.0)	(1.4)	(1.5)	(1.2)	(1.4)	(1.6)	(2.1)
Imports (c.i.f.)	22.2	28.8	27.9	31.7	41.9	33.9	37.8	49.1	42.2	47.0	42.6
(of which: external	(20.1)	(25.5)	(24.0)	(28.1)	(37.5)	(28.4)	(32.0)	(43.5)	(35.9)	(39.3)	(33.6)
interterritorial)[a]	(2.1)	(3.2)	(3.9)	(3.6)	(4.5)	(5.5)	(5.9)	(5.6)	(6.3)	(7.7)	(9.0)
Trade balance (imports c.i.f.)[a]	−5.7	−7.4	−2.6	+9.8	+6.4	+2.9	+1.0	−10.0	+6.2	−3.9	+3.8
INDICES (1956-58 = 100)											
Domestic Exports											
Value	87	47	55	90	105	80	84	85	105	94	101
Volume	40	n.a.	52	58	77	73	78	86	100	94	106
Price (unit value)	81	n.a.	110	167	148	114	113	102	108	99	93
Imports											
Value	51	65	64	72	95	77	86	112	96	107	97
Volume[b]	n.a.	n.a.	70	64	79	70	88	113	93	108	99
Price (unit value)[c]	n.a.	n.a.	91	112	121	110	98	99	103	99	98
Terms of trade	n.a.	n.a.	121	148	123	104	115	103	105	100	95

[a] Interterritorial imports are recorded gross of certain excise duties charged at the place of origin but which are repayable to Tanganyika.

[b] Obtained by dividing value index by the average value index for the imports of the three East African territories. This method, while unsatisfactory, is the only feasible one.

[c] For the three East African territories combined.

TABLE 67 Changes in Quantity of Principal Exports from Tanganyika to Destinations Outside East Africa

Commodity	Average annual value, 1956-58 (£ million)	Average quantity, 1956-58 ('000 tons unless otherwise stated)	1925	1935	1938	1947	1948	1949	1950	1951	1952	1953	1954	1955	1956	1957	1958	1959
							(Index: average quantity 1956-58 = 100)											
Sisal	10.2	188.5	10	44	54	51	62	70	64	75	84	91	89	92	98	96	105	111
Coffee, hulled	8.0	20.8	29	89	66	67	54	58	72	80	90	73	93	89	104	89	107	94
Cotton	7.1	29.1	15	34	31	24	34	37	24	29	38	51	42	70	96	94	110	106
Diamonds	3.5	415,391 carats	—	—	1	22	36	32	32	2	80	41	79	78	86	90	124	134
Lead ore and concentrates	1.1	13.7							8	22	35	45	36	60	110	92	98	
Hides, skins and furskins	1.2	4.7	57				71	86	116	85	83	118	121	105	98	100	103	125
Cashew nuts	1.2	27.2			3a	5	20	13	24	30	42	42	60	67	61	124	115	122
Groundnuts	1.0	14.6	62	112	24	24	21	6	1	24	65	7	17	38	104	110	86	83
Castor seed	0.8	14.6					17	12	23	52	84	81	66	54	82	95	122	
Tea	0.6	2.2		—	7	21	21	20	22	38	47	52	72	78	91	101	108	124
For comparison:																		
Export volume index							40	52	52	58	77	73	78	86	100	94	106	

a 1959.

SOURCES: Annual Trade Reports; *Digest of Colonial Statistics.*

TABLE 68   Tanganyika's Principal Exports, 1956 and 1958

(£ '000)

	To destinations Outside East Africa		To Kenya and Uganda		Total	
	1956	1958	1956	1958	1956	1958
Sisal	10,823	10,349	—	7	10,824	10,356
Coffee—arabica	7,725	5,942	5	1	7,730	5,943
—robusta	1,499	1,631	—	—	1,499	1,631
Cotton fibre	7,486	7,249	1	—	7,487	7,249
Cotton seed	92	139	14	43	106	183
Cotton seed oil	155	117	51	17	206	135
Cotton seed cake	443	422	1	—	444	422
Diamonds	2,865	4,415	—	—	2,865	4,415
Hides and skins	1,111	1,133	145	—	1,256	1,133
Cashew nuts	881	1,087	2	6	883	1,092
Lead ore and concentrates.	1,352	895	—	—	1,352	895
Groundnuts	1,017	779	8	19	1,025	799
Canned meat and						
meat extracts	329	906	36	76	365	982
Castor seed	721	812	6	—	727	812
Gold	742	705	—	—	742	705
Wood, lumber and cork ..	474	489	[172]	[98]	[646]	[587]
Sesame seed	668	592	1	—	669	592
Tea	543	632	49	44	591	675
Beans, peas, pulses	562	561	178	114	741	675
Tobacco, unmanufactured .	26	44	269	440	295	484
Vegetable flour, flakes,						
edible starches	483	303	5	2	488	305
Sunflower seed	483	277	3	—	485	277
Maize—unmilled	2,063	24	6	298	2,069	322
—flour	30	82	29	110	58	192
Beeswax	171	243	—	—	171	243
Coconut oil	6	1	189	255	195	256
Copra	204	135	63	61	267	196
Coconut cake	64	67	[—]	[—]	64	67
Papain	39	190	—	—	39	190
Gum arabic	152	44	[—]	—	152	44
Millet	105	50	42	98	147	148
Metal containers	44	131	15	49	59	180
Pyrethrum	89	62	82	71	170	133
Rice and paddy	78	39	71	76	149	114
Kapok	133	107	1	3	133	109
Exports not shown above—						
Total	1,228	1,076	643	715	1,872	1,792

SOURCE: Annual Trade Reports.

TABLE 69   Tanganyika: Composition of Imports, 1958

(£ '000)

Class and Principal Commodities	From Overseas	From Kenya	From Uganda	Total
Food	2,108	1,987	446	4,541
(Sugar, refined)	(488)	(—)	(360)	(848)
(Wheat flour)	(1)	(565)	(—)	(566)
(Butter)	(3)	(200)	(—)	(203)
(Tea)	(—)	(356)	(15)	(371)
Beverages and Tobacco	288	2,162	1,536	3,986
(Beer)	(35)	(468)	(88)	(592)
(Cigarettes)	(15)	(1,653)	(1,436)	(3,105)
Crude Materials, Inedible Except Fuel	108	98	15	221
Mineral Fuels, Lubricants and Related Materials	4,125	—	—	4,125
Animal and Vegetable Oils and Fats	154	56	169	379
Chemicals	1,871	301	54	2,226
Manufactured Goods, Classified Chiefly by Material	12,491	1,247	105	13,843
(Rubber tires and tubes)	(786)	(8)	(—)	(794)
(Cotton fabrics)	(2,897)	(7)	(80)	(2,984)
(Fabrics of synthetic fibers)	(1,028)	(—)	(—)	(1,028)
(Bags and sacks)	(537)	(44)	(1)	(582)
(Blankets)	(330)	(2)	(—)	(332)
(Other textiles)	(824)	(39)	(2)	(865)
(Aluminum household utensils)	(20)	(120)	(—)	(140)
(Cement)	(580)	(561)	(4)	(1,145)
(Iron and steel manufactures)	(2,497)			
(Miscellaneous manufactures of metals)	(1,644)			
Machinery and Transport Equipment	8,629	85	9	8,723
Miscellaneous Manufactured Articles	2,530	686	21	3,237
(Clothing)	(763)	(198)	(11)	(972)
(Footwear)	(222)	(361)	(—)	(583)
Miscellaneous and Commodities N.E.S	1,264	58	1	1,323
Total	33,568	6,681	2,357	42,606

Note: Certain articles traded interterritorially, notably beer and cigarettes, are recorded gross of excise duties which are charged at source but are subsequently repaid to the importing territory.

SOURCE: Annual Trade Report.

TABLE 70   Geographical Distribution of Tanganyika's External Trade

(Percent of total)

	1950	1952	1954	1956	1958
Destination of Exports					
(excluding re-exports)					
United Kingdom	39.1	40.3	34.1	29.9	31.9
Kenya and Uganda	3.7	2.0	2.8	4.4	5.8
Other sterling countries	19.9	14.3	16.0	17.5	17.0
Total, sterling area	62.8	56.6	52.9	51.8	54.8
United States and Canada	11.5	22.7	15.8	9.3	8.2
Non-sterling O.E.E.C. countries ...	20.1	18.3	26.8	33.6	30.4
Others	5.6	2.4	4.4	5.2	6.7
Total	100.0	100.0	100.0	100.0	100.0
Origin of Imports					
United Kingdom	48.3	42.1	36.3	[38.0][1]	[30.3][1]
Kenya and Uganda	14.0	10.6	15.5	15.0	21.2
Other sterling countries	14.2	18.2	23.9	[14.7]	[11.4]
Total, sterling area	76.5	70.9	75.6	[67.7]	[62.9]
United States and Canada	5.7	4.2	2.8	[2.3]	[2.3]
Non-sterling O.E.E.C. countries ...	7.6	15.0	14.8	[16.0]	[13.2]
Others	10.1	8.3	3.3	[11.1]	[18.8]
Unallocated	—	1.6	3.5	[2.9]	[2.7]
Total	100.0	100.0	100.0	100.0	100.0

[1] Figures for imports originating outside East Africa in 1956 and 1958 ("external imports"), which appear in the column below, cover "direct imports" only: this is to say, they exclude imports arriving by way of Kenya or Uganda. For these two years, direct imports were 92 percent and 85 percent of total external imports. In this table, it has been assumed that the ratio of direct imports to total external imports is the same for imports from each source. This is unlikely to be the case in practice.

SOURCES: East African Statistical Department and Annual Trade Reports.

TABLE 71   Principal Destinations of Tanganyika's Exports in 1957-58 and Principal Commodities Exported to These Destinations

(Figures are average exports in 1957-58, in £'000)

Destination	Total Exports	Of which					
United Kingdom	13,121	Diamonds	3,828	Sisal	3,187	Coffee	1,657
Germany	4,332	Coffee	1,471	Cotton	1,437	Sisal	684
United States	3,186	Coffee	2,182	Sisal	539		
Japan	2,304	Cotton	1,076				
Hong Kong	2,252	Cotton	2,052				
Belgium	2,252	Lead ore and concentrates	1,012	Sisal	874		
India	2,243	Cashew nuts	1,293	Cotton	657		
Netherlands	2,163	Sisal	1,014	Coffee	320		

SOURCE: Annual Trade Reports.

TABLE 72   Principal Destinations of Tanganyika's Main Exports, 1957-58

(Figures following countries are percentage of
total exports of commodity in 1957 and 1958)

Commodity	Average value of total exports 1957-58 (£'000)	Destinations					
Sisal	9,925	United Kingdom.	32%	Belgium	9%	Germany	7%	Australia	6%
Coffee	7,377	United States ...	30%	United Kingdom.	22%	Germany	20%	
Cotton	6,913	Hong Kong	30%	Germany	21%	Japan	16%	
Diamonds	3,828	United Kingdom.	100%				
Hides, skins and furskins	1,321	United Kingdom.	33%	Italy	14%	United States ..	14%	Netherlands	11%
Cashew nuts	1,304	India	99%				
Groundnuts	938	Japan	31%	United Kingdom.	29%	Hong Kong	17%	

SOURCE: Annual Trade Reports.

TABLE 73   Major Items in Tanganyika's Trade with
Kenya and Uganda

(£ '000)

Exports	1951	1952	1953	1954	1955	1956	1957	1958
Tobacco, unmanufactured .	123	113	72	43	329	269	450	440
Coconut oil	119	113	183	147	169	189	159	255
Wood lumber and cork ...	142	114	78	139	165	172	152	[98]
Beans and peas, etc.	60	90	140	98	221	178	136	114
Hides, skins and fur skins.	89	42	80	34	70	157	45	5
Electric energy	n.a.	n.a.	n.a.	42	73	81	68	70
Sugar and sugar preparations	—	1	88	34	45	117	10	4
Other	618	463	586	516	629	924	1,011	1,618
Total	1,151	935	1,227	1,053	1,701	2,087	2,031	2,603
Imports								
Cigarettes	1,288	1,815	2,138	2,362	2,685	2,939	3,147	3,089
Beer	111	300	344	424	500	517	488	556
Wheat flour	349	517	582	581	612	385	506	565
Clothing and footwear ...	285	249	185	274	314	354	347	570
Manufactures of metals ..	n.a.	n.a.	n.a.	181	194	317	283	
Tea	144	199	175	242	61	204	387	371
Sugar and sugar preparations	216	185	287	46	55	140	356	457
Cement	—	4	3	23	33	146	312	565
Other	1,232	1,183	1,805	1,723	1,159	1,347	1,900	
Total	3,625	4,452	5,519	5,856	5,613	6,349	7,726	9,038

NOTE: Exports are for use in Kenya and Uganda and imports for use in Tanganyika.
See also note to Table 69.

SOURCES: East African Statistical Department and Annual Trade Reports.

TABLE 74   Miscellaneous Indicators of the Growth of the Tanganyika Economy in Recent Years

(Index, average 1956-58 = 100)

Item	Average quantity, 1956-58	1948	1949	1950	1951	1952	1953	1954	1955	1956	1957	1958
Cement consumption ...	122,775 tons	41	68	90	92	88	104	91	131	95	103	102
Licensed private motor vehicles	29,302						65	75	83	89	101	109
Total electricity sales[a] ...	114.6 million kwh.	21	28	35	48	56	64	74	84	93	99	107
Cotton piece goods[b] and artificial textile fabrics —retained imports	77.3 million sq. yds.			63	62	80	66	101[c]	125[c]	89[c]	131[c]	80[c]
Estimated consumption of:												
Sugar	40,518 tons		35	52	58	62	77	91	88	99	102	99
Beer	2 million Imperial gallons		46	44	53	61	71	81	96	109	118	73
Cigarettes	1,169 tons		46	56	58	69	81	86	87	93	104	104
African primary education —number of pupils enrolled in Standard I ...	109,263	51	49	53	61	70	78	85	95	101	101	98

[a] Including exports to Mombasa.
[b] Excluding blankets.
[c] Including artificial silk piece goods.

TABLE 75   Industrial and Agricultural Processing Establishments and Employment, December 31, 1958

	Number of Establishments	Number of Employees
I. INDUSTRIAL ESTABLISHMENTS		
Food, Drink, Tobacco, Milling, etc.	1,208	8,538
Aerated water manufacture	58	475
Bread and other bakery products	87	624
Breweries	2	312
Dairy produce	6	86
Edible oil refining	5	73
Fish curing	2	98
Flour milling	846	3,453
Food canning	6	1,061
Fruit cordial manufacture	2	57
Milk pasteurizing	5	55
Rice mills and hulleries	100	944
Soap manufacturing	61	574
Sugar confectionery	9	123
Sugar manufacture	6	495
Other	13	108
Carpentry, Furniture and Sawmilling	475	8,078
Sawmilling	105	3,581
Woodworking, general	370	4,497
Clothing and Footwear	990	2,374
Shoemaking and repairing	121	341
Tailoring and dressmaking	860	1,954
Other	9	79
Motor Vehicle Repair and General Engineering *and Repair*	547	11,034
Agricultural plant maintenance and repair ..	39	480
Bicycle assembly and repairs	32	80
Boat building and repairing	5	408
Electrical repairs	19	147
Engineering, general	105	2,270
Locomotive and rolling stock repairs	14	2,228
Marine engineering	3	53
Motor vehicle repairing	246	4,172
Petrol, oil and lubricants, packing and servicing of motor vehicles	40	974
Sheet metal work	25	132
Other	19	90
Brick, Block and Tile Making	25	1,211
Brick and tile manufacture	16	741
Precast concrete works	9	470

TABLE 75—continued

	Number of Establishments	Number of Employees
Other	336	3,143
Can manufacture	2	244
Chemical products manufacture	4	91
Electrical power generation	32	581
Jewellers and goldsmiths	28	107
Laundering	8	56
Letterpress printing	30	811
Mica cutting and grading	2	174
Paint manufacture	1	51
Photographic developing and printing	12	74
Stone grading and crushing	9	82
Tire retreading	6	72
Water supply	176	599
Other	26	201
Total Industrial Establishments	3,581	34,378
II. AGRICULTURAL PROCESSING ESTABLISHMENTS		
Cashew nut processing	2	256
Coffee curing	11	638
Coffee pulping	133	1,576
Coir fibre processing	5	159
Cotton ginning	38	4,066
Crop processing	14	1,025
Hides and skins processing and baling	42	467
Jaggery manufacture	56	734
Kapok ginning	14	179
Pyrethrum drying	32	133
Sisal processing	236	27,210
Tea manufacture	16	887
Tobacco processing	49	1,468
Vegetable oil extraction	85	1,130
Other	13	131
Total Agricultural Processing Establishments	746	40,059

TABLE 76   Central Government Current Revenues and Expenditures
and Balance of Current Budget

(£ '000)

	Current Revenue	Current Expenditure	Balance of Current Budget
1947	5,624	5,368	+ 256
1948	6,711	5,842	+ 869
1949	8,586	7,062	+1,524
1950	10,397	8,127	+2,270
1951	11,931	10,808	+1,123
1952	16,430	13,334	+3,096
1953	14,728	14,318	+ 410
1954 (1st half)	9,133	7,481	+1,652
1954/55	19,277	16,469	+2,808
1955/56	18,680	18,491	+ 189
1956/57	17,492	17,847	− 355
1957/58	18,834	18,694	+ 140
1958/59	19,412	19,527	− 115
1959/60	[22,066][a]		

[a] Estimate supplied by the Government of Tanganyika.

TABLE 77   Government of Tanganyika Current Revenues by
Category, 1957/58 and 1958/59   (£ '000)

	1957/58	1958/59
Direct Taxation		
Income tax	4,283	3,525
Estate duty	50	252 [a]
Personal tax	1,381	1,288
Native house tax, etc.	32	18
Non-native education taxes	289	287
Municipal tax	26	24
Total, direct taxation	6,061	5,394
Indirect Taxation		
Import duties	5,312	6,691
Export duties	25	24
Excise duties	2,095	2,059
Stamp duties	192	180
Vehicle licenses	458	493
Trade licenses	102	100
Other indirect taxes, cesses, etc.	419	312
Total, indirect taxation	8,603	9,859
Provision of Goods and Services by Government Departments		
Medical and dental	157	155
Medical stores and drugs	1	—
School fees:		
Non-native	176	167
Other	36	42
Dairies	19	19
Water	337	380
Printing and stationery	88	82
Other earnings	489	479
Total, provision goods and services	1,303	1,324
Government Property Income		
Land rents	271	274
Premia on leases	86	82
Rent of buildings	234	242
Mining rents and royalties	659	601
Forest royalties	167	142
Other property income	18	42
Interest and dividends	404	358
Sales of assets and loan repayments	133	112
Total, property income	1,972	1,853
Miscellaneous Revenue		
Pensions and Provident Fund	193	189
Other	701	792
Total, miscellaneous	894	981
Total Current Revenue	18,834	19,412

[a] Exceptionally high figure.

TABLE 78 Government of Tanganyika Current Revenues, 1950-1958/59

(£ '000)

Year	Total	Import Duties	Excise Duties	Income Tax	Personal Tax, Etc.[a]	Other Taxes	Provision of Goods and Services	Government Property Income	Miscellaneous Revenue
1950	10,397	2,984	713	1,884	1,052	1,524	402	1,244	595
1951	11,931	3,469	756	1,973	1,198	2,336	511	1,176	511
1952	16,430	4,303	957	3,887	1,608	2,305	681	2,117	571
1953	14,728	3,258	1,011	4,209	1,796	1,247	770	1,503	934
1954 (1st half)	9,133	1,881	599	2,974	1,318	832	407	907	217
1954/55	19,277	4,820	1,346	4,601	1,946	1,707	888	1,768	2,201[b]
1955/56	18,680	5,527	1,604	4,507	1,537	1,276	995	1,839	1,397
1956/57	17,492	4,999	1,824	4,066	1,163	1,476	1,104	1,786	1,074
1957/58	18,834	5,312	2,095	4,283	1,413	1,561	1,303	1,972	894
1958/59	19,412	6,691	2,059	3,525	1,306	1,672	1,324	1,853	981

[a] For the years to 1950, native house and poll tax *plus* non-native poll tax.
[b] Increased by Custodian of Enemy Property receipts.

TABLE 79   Government of Tanganyika Current Expenditure, by Category, 1957/58 and 1958/59

(£ '000)

	1957/58	1958/59
Administration		
Central	181	318
Provincial	1,083	1,086
Sundry services[a]	312	308
Total, administration	1,576	1,712
Law and Order		
Judicial and legal	222	218
Police	1,264	1,418
Prisons	565	594
Total, law and order	2,051	2,230
Revenue Collection and Financial Control		
Accountant General and Audit	205	475
Customs and excise	229	252
Income tax	186	192
Total, revenue collection and financial control	620	919
Pensions and Gratuities	938	963
Defense	662	675
Economic Services		
Agriculture	633	630
Forests	300	292
Veterinary	456	440
Mines	49	44
Lands and surveys	331	340
Geological survey	144	130
Water supplies	487	491
Road and bridge maintenance	908	970
Aviation	240	216
Sundry services[b]	271	293
Total, economic services	3,819	3,846
Local Government		
Municipalities and Townships	617	603
Town planning	20	21
Native administration	10	2
Total, local government	647	626

TABLE 79—continued

	(£ '000)	
	1957/58	1958/59
Social Services		
Education:		
Contribution to Non-Native Education Funds	387	426
Revenue assigned to non-native education	465	455
Other	2,272	2,422
Medical	1,723	1,785
Labor	120	137
Social development	82	81
Total, social services	5,049	5,306
Miscellaneous		
Other public works	903	1,470
Other subventions and subsidies	164	122
Loans from revenue	20	25
Miscellaneous services	805	72
East Africa High Commission services n.e.s.[c]	435	310
Total, miscellaneous	2,327	1,999
Public Debt	1,005	1,251
Total Current Expenditures	18,694	19,527

[a] Includes Administrator General, Custodian of Enemy Property, Immigration and Passports, Public Relations, Printing and Stationery, Commerce and Industry and Transport Licensing Authority.

[b] Includes Cooperative Societies, Game, Tsetse, Government Chemist, Grain Storage.

[c] All items except Civil Aviation, Customs and Excise, Income Tax, and East African Naval Force.

TABLE 80   Government of Tanganyika Current Expenditures, 1950-1958/59

(£'000)

| Year | Total | General Administrative Services and Local Government | Economic Services | | | | Social Services | | | Unallocated Public Works | Public Debt Service | Miscellaneous |
			Agriculture	Veterinary	Road and Bridge Maintenance	Other	Education	Medical	Other			
1950	8,127	3,006	279	211	281	519	709	683	130	701	131	1,477
1951	10,808	3,547	255	250	293	784	1,071	993	86	1,468	179	1,882
1952	13,334	4,157	290	299	338	784	1,333	1,036	111	2,203	229	2,558
1953	14,318	4,913	408	381	454	1,082	1,914	1,126	157	1,440	309	2,132
1954 (1st half)	7,481	2,928	221	207	261	667	1,064	592	76	321	241	903
1954/55	16,469	6,421	482	386	664	1,367	2,455	1,288	169	918	561	1,759
1955/56	18,491	6,034	566	359	785	1,684	2,669	1,669	200	1,447	543	2,537
1956/57	17,847	6,291	647	466	826	1,743	2,915	1,665	194	1,201	715	1,182
1957/58	18,694	6,494	633	456	908	1,822	3,124	1,723	202	903	1,005	1,424
1958/59	19,527	7,125	630	440	970	1,806	3,303	1,785	218	1,470	1,251	529

TABLE 81   Government of Tanganyika Capital Expenditures, 1950-1958/59

(£'000)

| Year | Total | Economic | | | Communications | | Social Services | | Township Development |
		Agriculture and Animal Husbandry	Water Supplies	Other	Roads	Aerodromes	Education	Other	Public Buildings and Works, Etc.
1950	3,438	359	168	100	1,094	14	292	44	1,369
1951	3,830	396	123	112	1,237	153	109	75	1,624
1952	4,989	252	209	291	1,880	331	211	176	1,640
1953	3,726	209	129	198	1,669	296	108	119	998
1954 (1st half)	1,601	96	67	104	689	187	50	69	388
1954/55	3,337	130	294	216	1,210	175	388	206	718
1955/56	4,084	90	311	183	1,172	25	674	346	1,283
1956/57	5,282	72	470	58	939	27	1,026	419	2,272
1957/58	5,454	147	492	68	906	22	1,196	309	2,314
1958/59	5,159	247	634	124	849	16	1,135	291	1,863

TABLE 82   Composition of the Public Funded Debt of Tanganyika at June 30, 1960

Issue	Sum Outstanding[a] (£)	Repayment, Sinking Fund Provisions, Etc.
3% Loans from Imperial Funds, 1964	371,906	Equated annuities: Government £ 35,939; Railway Administration £ 64,113; terminating March 1964.
4% Tanganyika Guaranteed Loan, 1952-72	500,000	Sinking fund: Government £ 7,817; Railway Account £ 1,533.
3½% Inscribed Stock 1970-73	4,030,000	Sinking funds at 1% on £ 1,750,000 and at 1¼% on £ 2,280,000.
4½% Inscribed Stock 1967-72	4,410,000	Sinking fund at 1%.
5¾% Inscribed Stock 1978-82	4,000,000	Sinking fund at 1%.
5½% Registered Stock 1975-79	1,500,000	Sinking fund at 1%.
6¼% Registered Stock 1966-67	817,600	Sinking fund at 1¼%.
6¼% Registered Stock 1980-83	182,400	Sinking fund at 1%.
6½% Tanganyika Stock 1967-68	1,367,800	Sinking fund at 1¼%.
6½% Tanganyika Stock 1981-84	132,200	Sinking fund at 1%.
5½% Exchequer Loan	1,500,000	To be serviced by constant annuities with repayment over 25 years.
3% Barclays Overseas Development Corporation Loan 1963	210,000	A reserve of £ 210,000 has been created to meet the repayment of the loan outstanding.
4% Lint and Seed Marketing Board Loan 1974	1,000,000	Sinking fund of £ 40,583 a year.
Loan of £ 1,317,272 from De Beers Consolidated Mines Ltd.	1,059,006	Repayable with interest at 6% a year within twenty years from August 13, 1958. The dividend from the shares, purchase of which was financed by the loan, will be applied to pay interest due, and up to two-thirds of any balance will be paid towards reduction of the principal sum.

[a] Accumulated sinking fund provisions have not been subtracted.
SOURCE: *Estimates of the Revenue and Expenditure of Tanganyika,* 1960/61.

TABLE 83   Commercial Banks in Tanganyika, Liabilities and Assets

(£'000)

LIABILITIES

As at 31st December	Deposits				Balances due to Banks		Other Liabilities	Total
	Demand	Time	Saving	Total	In the Territory	Abroad and E.A. Branches		
1952	16,673	2,144	599	19,416	63	1,631	378	21,488
1953	17,190	3,030	794	21,014	36	2,352	442	23,844
1954	17,353	2,443	1,039	20,835	4	2,849	548	24,236
1955	16,942	2,735	1,521	21,198	98	5,820	1,235	28,352
1956	14,608	3,791	1,836	20,235	111	4,944	1,294	26,585
1957[a]	13,798	3,514	2,010	19,321	123	5,492	1,129	26,066
1958[a]	14,457	3,360	2,244	20,061	392	5,342	1,229	27,024

ASSETS

As at 31st December	Cash	Balances due from Banks		Loans and Advances and Bills Discounted				Investments in East Africa	Other Assets	Total
		In the Territory	Abroad and E.A. Branches	Industry	Agriculture	Other	Total[b]			
1952	1,780	66	13,548	1,073	1,604	2,593	5,597	—	497	21,488
1953	1,560	36	15,840	1,565	1,877	2,093	5,980	49	879	23,844
1954	2,064	48	12,909	2,152	2,652	3,143	8,596	50	568	24,236
1955	1,690	125	14,302	1,499	2,625	5,572	10,751	50	1,434	28,352
1956	1,499	136	14,249	2,175	2,047	3,549	9,234	50	1,417	26,585
1957[a]	1,290	80	11,305	4,173	2,445	4,116	12,049	57	1,285	26,066
1958[a]	1,583	365	12,769	1,982	2,637	4,224	10,152	58	2,097	27,024

[a] Provisional.
[b] Including total bills discounted. These are not distributed among the categories shown.

TABLE 84   Tanganyika: Evolution of Prices

(1958 = 100)

Year	Import Unit Values (East Africa)	Cost of Living Index (Dar es Salaam)[a]	Retail Price Index of African Consumer Goods (Dar es Salaam) (June figures)
1950	93	70	
1951	115	80	
1952	123	86	84
1953	112	87	101
1954	100	90	98
1955	101	92	93
1956	105	94	92
1957	101	98	98
1958	100	100	100

[a] Excluding rent.

RECOMMENDATIONS

LIST OF RECOMMENDATIONS

The following summary sets out the Mission's recommendations, not in the order in which they appear in the report, but according to the following classification:

A. Policy Outlines.
B. Institutional Arrangements.
C. Projects and Programs.
D. Research and Investigations.
E. Budgetary and Financial Policies.
F. Recommendations of a More Detailed or Technical Nature.

A. POLICY OUTLINES

Central Points

The following four groups of points to some extent form a nucleus about which many of the Mission's other recommendations are grouped:

1. a. The task of securing widespread income increase is to a major degree one of agricultural and livestock development (p. 13).

b. In the next few years, the main increase of agricultural production will have to be looked for in "improvement" within the general framework of existing African methods (pp. 5, 90, and Chapter 5).

c. Policy must pay increased attention to maintaining the fertility of the soil (pp. 6, 77, 84, 90, 131, 146-47).

d. "Improvement" activities, designed to secure piece-by-piece improvement of methods within the general framework of existing patterns of African land use, should be progressively supplemented by a "transformation" approach, designed to make more productive use of land, sustainable without loss of fertility, by efficiently run, planned farms of economic size, justifying the injection of capital (pp. 6, 91, 129).

2. a. A considerable proportion of public expenditures should be

491

so directed as to secure the maximum feasible increase of revenue-yielding economic activity. This cannot be an exclusive or over-riding aim, but it must be a very important aim (pp. 70-72).

b. This point is to some degree related to (1. d). The preliminary investigations, trials and experiments on which a successful "transformation" approach must depend will place an additional burden on the public finances in the initial phase. This reinforces the need so to organize "improvement" activities that they shall bring about the greatest possible increase of marketable production and hence of revenue (pp. 7-8, 72-73).

c. Consequently, a major part of the "improvement" effort in the near future should be concentrated on crops and areas which promise the greatest returns to public expenditure in terms of increase of marketed production (pp. 8, 71, 73, 102-04).

3. a. Many construction projects and useful activities, which would be out of the question if they had to be financed from the central budget, could be undertaken with great benefit on the basis of locally organized contributions of labor, materials or money. The new political climate appears to give great opportunities to turn the energies of the people towards constructive achievement (pp. 3, 5, 72, 87, 109-11, 151, 213-14).

b. However, it is important to avoid, so far as possible, projects which have harmful or disappointing results (pp. 110-11).

4. Careful attention must be given to the organization and methods of planning:

a. planning to secure that public activities result in adequate returns, and to avoid damage, as, for example, by destruction of soil fertility (pp. 89-90, 102, 104, 110, 111, 143, 146, 150-51, 153, 154-55);

b. planning to ensure that the scarce financial resources available to government are so deployed as to secure the greatest and most favorable development results (pp. 4, 9, 38, 47, 69, 339).

Sector Programs

5. The agricultural "improvement" effort should be continued by means of: extension work (with some changes of organization and methods); a revitalized program of agricultural credit; and measures to improve the market outlets for African crops and to increase cash incentives (Ch. 5, passim).

6. a. Continued measures should be taken to encourage and facili-

tate increased production by African pastoralists of meat animals for sale.

b. Policy towards African cattle keepers should, however, aim as much at prevention of overgrazing as at increase of production.

c. Expenditures designed to improve animal husbandry within the framework of present African practice should be scrutinized very critically, in order to avoid outlays the returns on which are smaller than the economy can afford (pp. 146-159).

7. Immediate steps should be taken to prepare a program of "transformation" activities in agriculture, largely in the form of planned settlement schemes and partnership schemes. A continuous production line should be established leading from the initial collection of basic data through trials and pilot projects to the institution of improved farming systems (Ch. 6 passim).

8. Preparations should be made for an expanded program of irrigation and flood control works, to reach a suggested scale of 25,000 acres a year by 1969/70 (Ch. 8 passim).

9. The existing ranching schemes under skilled management, at Kongwa, Ruvu and Mkata, should be developed to full capacity. Subsequently, the feasibility should be investigated of establishing further partnership ranches, some operating breeding herds and some fattening immatures purchased from African cattle keepers (pp. 160-63).

10. The possibilities of development of dairying should be systematically investigated (pp. 166-73).

11. The Mission considers that estates run by non-Africans make a valuable contribution to the economy of the territory, and that they should receive assistance from the Government according to the same criteria applied to the rest of the agricultural sector (Ch. 10 passim).

12. Investment in afforestation is recommended, though on a slightly smaller scale than that planned by the Forestry Department. However, the scale of this activity should be revised following an F.A.O. study of prospective timber requirements (pp. 194-95).

13. A general study of the fishing industry should be made as a basis for increased government efforts to stimulate development of production and marketing of fish (pp. 199-200).

14. Development of mining should be assisted and encouraged by the acceleration of basic geological mapping, by further measures to encourage prospecting by private firms and by government mineral reconnaissance surveys on a more systematic and sustained basis than in the past (pp. 266-71).

15. A policy of forced-draft industrialization would not be appropriate. However, the Government should continue to provide a favorable climate for private industrial enterprise. A company to investigate and publicize industrial and commercial opportunities would be useful provided that it could draw on the assistance of the Colonial Development Corporation or some suitably qualified outside body. A final decision on the establishment of an investment company could well be left until the work of the exploratory company has thrown more light on the nature of the opportunities (pp. 13, 232-33, 240-44).

16. Certain works to extend or improve the main transport network of roads and railways should be completed or undertaken. However, investment in transport facilities should now be increasingly devoted to construction and improvement of feeder roads in rural areas (pp. 274-78, 287).

17. Means should be found of accelerating topographical mapping (p. 185).

18. A priority program of expanding secondary school places and technical training facilities for Africans should be undertaken (Ch. 15 passim).

B.   INSTITUTIONAL ARRANGEMENTS

Planning and Administration

19. The Mission approves the present intention to draw up three-year development plans, with annual revisions, to be undertaken by the Development Committee of the Council of Ministers. These plans should cover current as well as capital expenditures (pp. 40, 340-41).

20. The Economic Section of the Treasury should be brought up to a strength of two or three senior officials with assistants. Its function should be to make available to the Minister for Finance and the Development Committee of the Council of Ministers the facts and analysis on which policy decisions should be based. While being closely integrated with the work of the Treasury as a whole, the Economic Section should be free to specialize in functions related to economic and budgetary planning (pp. 342-43).

21. The Land Use Committee should continue as the final arbiter of the feasibility and priority of natural resources development projects, and should direct the common effort of the various departments

concerned with a development project. It should remain as at present a committee of heads of departments within the Ministry of Natural Resources, unless the Water Development and Irrigation Department is in another ministry, in which case the Land Use Committee will have to become an interministerial body (pp. 209-10).

22. A small specialist staff, under the direction of a Chief Technical Officer, should be built up to assist the Land Use Committee, in particular by preparing appraisals of projects (p. 210).

23. An economist from the Economic Section of the Treasury should be seconded to the Land Use Committee, with the task of ensuring that economic reasoning and information receive sufficient weight in agricultural planning, and also of teaching officers in the field to give proper attention to the economics of programs and projects and to collect the data required for proper economic evaluation. This officer should be a member of the Land Use Committee (pp. 210, 343).

24. The device of "teams" to coordinate the operations of officers of the various departments of the central government, working at Provincial or District level, should be maintained. There is need for some improvement of coordination between various ministries and departments (pp. 115, 117, 188, 218, 358).

25. a. It is desirable that all the departments concerned with agriculture, animal husbandry, forestry and fisheries should so far as possible be combined in a single ministry (p. 209).

b. If the choice must be made, it would be preferable to have responsibility for water development and irrigation in the ministry responsible for agriculture, even if this involves having cooperative development and community development in another ministry (p. 212).

26. A study should be made with a view to recommending some reorganization of the ministry responsible for agricultural development and related matters (p. 210).

27. A single extension department should be established within this ministry, covering crop husbandry, irrigation agronomy, elementary animal hygiene and health, and establishment of tree plantations on farms (p. 113).

28. The present Social Development Department should be converted into a Department of Community Development. This Department should be mainly concerned with the organization of intensive community development schemes, at first on a pilot basis and in one or two limited areas. However, it should also provide a certain amount of technical guidance and specialized services to the wider,

less intensive community development efforts to be carried out through local authorities and other existing bodies. An effort should be made to recruit a nucleus of skilled senior officials with experience in the practical execution of community development schemes (pp. 212-13).

29. New land tenure legislation should be enacted, providing for the recognition of various categories of rights and interests (see p. 96). The Mission endorses the adoption of enabling legislation to permit the establishment of area land boards, and laying down their powers and responsibilities. The area covered by any single land board should be decided according to local circumstances: in some places it would be advisable to make the jurisdiction of the land boards coterminous with existing tribal or administrative boundaries; however, the geographical coverage of the various land boards should eventually come to correspond with ecological areas. The boards should be appointed rather than elected, and should contain effective representatives of the traditional land authorities, of progressive land owners, and a limited number of officers of the technical departments most concerned (pp. 96-98).

30. Local Government Authorities should be encouraged and helped to take an extremely important part in the organization and execution of local development programs and projects (pp. 110-11, 213-14).

31. An expert consultant should be called in to study the future organization of the Local Development Loan Fund, the African Productivity Loan Fund, the Urban Housing Loan Scheme, the Land Bank, and, in general, institutional arrangements for the provision of credit for small-scale agricultural, industrial or commercial ventures, African or non-African (pp. 220-21).

32. It is essential that the territory should maintain the efficiency of its civil service (pp. 9-10, 347-49).

33. The pace of "localization" of the civil service depends on the expansion of middle and secondary education (p. 348).

34. It is necessary to find adequate ways of assuring expatriate government servants that their careers will not be abruptly terminated because of political changes. Remuneration of expatriates should be kept in line with the remuneration which they could obtain in alternative employment elsewhere (pp. 10, 347).

35. Closer contact should be established between the Treasury and the provincial administrations (pp. 348-49).

36. Attention should be given to keeping men for a reasonable length of time in posts to which they have shown themselves well suited (p. 349).

The Tanganyika Agricultural Corporation

37. The Tanganyika Agricultural Corporation (TAC), should be established on a permanent basis to take over responsibility for agricultural partnership schemes, cattle ranches under skilled management and various other agrarian operations (pp. 133, 160, 223).

38. The terms on which the present financial arrangements between the TAC and the Government of the United Kingdom will be wound up will have to be discussed between the Governments of Tanganyika and of the U.K. (p. 224).

39. Ownership of the assets used by the TAC should be vested in the Government of Tanganyika. The TAC should have an obligation to pay service to the Government, whether on fixed or some variety of equity terms (p. 224).

40. An effort should be made to distinguish between the experimental and commercial aspects of the Corporation's operations. Experimental operations should be carried out against direct remuneration by the Government, while commercial operations should be expected to yield reasonable rates of return on the capital employed (p. 225).

41. For commercial-type operations, it should be the general rule that the Corporation should borrow to finance new investments at the full commercial rate. Nevertheless, there may be a case for some degree of subsidization by the Government for certain projects of importance to the development of the territory. One factor to be taken into account is the indirect returns which the Government may expect to receive by way of increased revenue as a result of the operations in question. While it is in general desirable that subsidies should be clearly recognizable in nature and amount, it may be appropriate in some cases for the Government to lend to the TAC on service terms "softer" than those which the Government has to pay on its own marginal borrowing (p. 225).

42. It is essential that the working relationships between the TAC and the Government should be clearly defined (pp. 225-26).

a. TAC should be given considerable independence in its day-to-day operations. However, the Minister for Natural Resources should have power to decide what operations the TAC should undertake and to issue directives on broad matters of policy, and should be answerable for the Corporation's broad policies, but not for the details of its operations (p. 226).

b. It should be considered whether the Directors of Agriculture and of Veterinary Services should be on the Board of the Corporation, or whether this would tend to confuse the constitutional relationship (p. 226).

c. The Government should be given full facilities to investigate costs and returns on TAC projects, not merely in order to keep a check on the Corporation's commercial efficiency in cases where government subsidy is involved, but also in order to obtain data of relevance to the selection and planning of future development projects, whether to be executed by the TAC or by the Government itself (p. 226).

d. The respective responsibilities of the Government and of the TAC in the design of projects should be clearly laid down. The Mission considers that initial surveys and the investigation of projects up to the stage of drawing up the master design should be in the hands of the specialist staff of the Ministry of Natural Resources. The Corporation should become involved at the stage of detailed design, and should be able to express an opinion on the technical and commercial feasibility of proposed projects. For its participation in detailed design of projects, the TAC could call in consultants as needed (p. 226).

Development Company or Companies

43. The establishment of a small company to investigate and publicize opportunities for the establishment of new enterprises, preferably with the collaboration of the United Kingdom Colonial Development Corporation or some other suitable external body, warrants further exploration (pp. 242, 244).

44. A final decision on the establishment of an investment company, and on the organization and functions of such a company, could well be left until the work of the exploratory company has thrown more light on the nature of the opportunities (p. 244).

45. A danger to be guarded against in establishing an investigatory company and, as a possible second step, an investment company is that overheads may be too large in relation to the amount of additional development which the institutions would promote. Another danger in the case of an investment company is that it may be inclined to make a show of its worth by rapidly committing the funds provided to it, without due regard to the soundness of the enterprises

financed. This risk would be reduced by the participation of an experienced outside body (p. 243).

The Monetary System

46. The Mission considers that the East African Currency Board should be retained for the immediate future in its present form (pp. 36, 331, 338).

47. It would be advantageous to retain a single currency for Tanganyika, Kenya and Uganda (pp. 337-38).

Regulation, Organization and Staffing of Cooperative Bodies

48. The cooperatives can play a useful part in many aspects of agricultural development (pp. 114-15, 120-21, 121-27, 148, 214).

49. The Mission approves the principle that reasonably high standards must be maintained in the requirements for the registration of cooperative societies, and also in auditing and in the general conduct of the societies' business (p. 218).

50. A delicate balance has to be struck in assisting the formation and successful operation of cooperatives without endangering their vitality and self-reliance (p. 218).

51. While there are strong practical reasons for the establishment of single-channel marketing for certain agricultural products in certain areas, every effort should be made to avoid serious infringement of the voluntary and democratic character of the cooperatives (pp. 126-27).

52. The Mission believes that the proposed central cooperative body to perform common services for the cooperatives would be useful (p. 218).

53. There is a need for expanded training facilities for staff for cooperatives (p. 219).

54. Thought might be given to using the facilities of the K.N.C.U. College of Commerce in Moshi specifically for training staff for the cooperative societies and unions, for the proposed new central body and also for the Department of Co-operative Development (p. 219).

55. The idea of establishing a cooperative bank deserves further exploration (pp. 123, 219).

a. This cooperative bank should attempt to pool the liquid re-sources of cooperative societies, thus securing economies to the extent that different societies have different seasonal liquidity requirements (p. 219).

b. The attempt should be made to attract savings from individual members of the cooperatives (pp. 123, 220).

c. However, the main function of a cooperative bank would be to act as an intermediary between individual societies on the one hand and commercial banks and other potential lenders on the other hand (pp. 123, 220).

d. A cooperative bank should not only make medium- and long-term loans to cooperative societies to finance buildings and equipment, but should also help cooperatives to obtain the necessary working capital (p. 220).

e. A cooperative bank might also play a part in channelling credit to individual cultivators (p. 120).

56. To the extent that a cooperative bank was successful in attract-ing savings from individual cooperative members, it would need to hold a considerable part of its assets in a secure and liquid form, such as Treasury Bills (p. 220).

57. A cooperative bank would require management of a high cali-ber. It might be possible to combine it under the same management as a government small loans institution. In this case, the cooperative bank would still publish its own separate accounts, and it would be important that it should be felt by the cooperatives to be a separate institution belonging to the cooperative movement (p. 220).

Other Institutional Recommendations

58. No major reorganization of the East African Railways and Har-bours Administration should be contemplated. However, certain measures of decentralization might help to increase the responsiveness of the system to local requirements (pp. 283-84).

59. An Institute of Education should be established in the near future to carry out research aimed at improvement of the quality and organization of education in Tanganyika, in relation to the needs of the territory as it develops (pp. 311-12).

60. Preparations for the establishment of a University College in Tanganyika should be actively continued. However, it would be pre-mature to start building for a few years to come (p. 314).

C. PROJECTS AND PROGRAMS

Agricultural Improvement

61. The efforts of the Department of Agriculture should be even more highly concentrated than at present on areas and crops likely to give high returns in terms of increased money income (p. 102).

62. While certain public efforts and works designed to encourage and facilitate the growth of internal trade may be thoroughly justified, it remains the case that favorable opportunities to bring about expansion of monetary activity will continue for several years to come to be largely in export production (p. 103.)

63. The Mission attaches great importance to continued collaboration between the agricultural department and the cooperatives in an effort to promote improved techniques of cotton growing designed both to increase production per acre and to aid in maintaining soil fertility (pp. 102, 368).

64. Existing roads in the cotton growing areas of the Lake Province should be improved and new ones built to reduce transport costs on seed cotton. In areas where cotton growers are dispersed rather widely, it will be desirable to investigate whether the problem of preventing damage to harvested cotton during the rainy season may not be most economically solved by constructing storage facilities rather than by improving or building roads so as to facilitate evacuation of the cotton before or during the rains. This comparison should, of course, take into account the wider effects of road building and improvement in opening up the areas concerned (pp. 369-70).

65. In relation to coffee, much more emphasis should be placed on efforts to increase cultural efficiency and yields per acre and to improve quality and less on expansion of acreage, particularly in areas remote from the main transport routes (pp. 102, 363-66).

66. Every effort should be made to develop cocoa growing in Tanganyika on both estate and peasant lines (pp. 372-73).

67. A considerable increase of annual oil seed production appears possible, helped by breeding of improved varieties, better roads, more trading posts and the development of cooperative marketing (pp. 103, 373-74).

68. Increased extension effort should be undertaken to encourage the planting of about 7,000 additional acres of pyrethrum by Africans,

and to improve methods of cultivation (pp. 103, 376).

69. Increased production of seed beans and seed peas by African farmers should be encouraged and assisted (pp. 102-3, 377).

70. There is scope for some increase of tobacco growing by Africans. Flue cured tobacco lends itself to partnership schemes between African cultivators and European capital, supervision and management (pp. 103, 381-83).

71. Provided that finance can be obtained from a source other than the Government of Tanganyika, further efforts should be made to encourage tea-growing by Africans in the Tukuyu area, and to obtain their agreement for the provision of land to the TAC or some similar organization for a nucleus tea plantation and for a factory which would process green leaf from tea gardens to be established by Africans on their own land nearby (pp. 380-81).

(Certain of these recommendations are supplemented by more detailed or technical recommendations below).

72. Factors to be taken into account in the planning of agricultural improvement activities include not only suitability of soil and rainfall, and interest and ability of the cultivators, but also market prospects for the crops under consideration, accessibility of markets or the cost of providing the requisite transport facilities, and the spending habits of those whose incomes will be increased (p. 104).

73. There should be a switch from the present, specialized agricultural extension workers to multi-purpose workers at the village level. These workers should receive elementary training in crop husbandry, irrigation agronomy, animal husbandry, elementary animal hygiene and health, and forestry insofar as it concerns the establishment of tree plantations on farms. They should also receive training in extension methods and principles, community development, and the principles and practice of cooperative societies, insofar as this is needed to help them to work with and through cooperatives. These village level workers would refer particular problems, beyond their competence, to more highly trained or specialized officers of their own or another department (pp. 109, 113).

74. Training of Africans for extension work is of the greatest importance. As funds allow, and as the number of candidates of suitable educational level increases, it will be desirable to establish perhaps two new "natural resources schools" preferably in ecological environments differing from that of the present school at Tengeru (p. 114).

75. At present, the limited number of local candidates does not

justify the establishment of an agricultural diploma course in Tanganyika. It may, however, become desirable to establish one at some later date (p. 114).

76. The cooperatives should be increasingly used as a channel of communication and information between individual growers and extension officers (pp. 114-15).

77. A dual community development approach should be instituted:

a. Community development as a skilled operation carried out by carefully chosen and highly trained experts should be started on a pilot scale in one or two limited areas, and only after experience has been gained should the attempt be made to spread this effort to other areas. This program should incorporate efforts to secure objective measurement of achievement (p. 111).

b. The desire to make a widespread appeal to the energies and enthusiasm of the people should be organized not through the creation of a large new organization, but through existing bodies such as local authorities, cooperatives and the provincial administration, with the support and cooperation of the dominant political party. Technical guidance and specialized skills should be provided largely by officers of the existing departments of government. Efforts should be made to steer activities into useful projects, capable of being carried through without great risk of disappointment, and not involving dangers of serious damage due to inadequate technical planning. To maintain control and direction of this program, it would be desirable to build up a small body of skilled "trouble shooters" directly answerable to the Chief Minister but working in collaboration with technical staff of the relevant government departments (pp. 110-11).

78. These two approaches should be kept distinct. They would nevertheless cross-fertilize each other. Intensive, skilled community development work would perfect techniques which can be applied more widely over the territory; and experience gained in the less intensive but more widespread effort would reveal problems to be tackled by the specialist approach and would point to areas where intensive effort would be likely to secure large returns (p. 111).

79. The essence of the community development approach is to win the confidence of the people and to stimulate and organize their energies to work for the improvement of their conditions of life. It is based on the premise that an all-embracing approach to rural betterment is more likely to succeed than a number of piecemeal attacks on individual problems (p. 109).

80. Community development can also be regarded as a means of teaching the farmers that the community has a right to ensure that individuals carry out certain duties, notably the duty to assist in the preservation of land and natural resources (p. 110).

81. Agricultural credit needs to be linked to extension work to assist producers to select suitable types of equipment and to put it to good use. There should be the closest possible collaboration between extension workers and the credit-providing agencies (p. 117).

82. The requirement appears to be for a rather large number of small loans, of tens of pounds rather than of hundreds, for fairly simple articles of equipment or improvements such as ox-plows, ox-carts, wheelbarrows, groundnut shellers, improved livestock, fertilizers or spraying and dusting equipment (p. 117).

83. There are limits to the extent to which the risk of defaults on agricultural loans can be met by progressive tightening up of repayment terms. Beyond a certain point, loans would cease to be worthwhile and potential borrowers would be forced back on financing improvements from their own funds (p. 119).

84. The possibilities of having the cooperatives act as agents for the Loan Funds should be further investigated (pp. 120-21).

85. Specialist Loan Funds Officers should be established in the main agricultural areas, perhaps six in all. The cost of these officers could probably not be met out of interest on loans, and they would have to be subsidized to some degree (p. 121).

86. The experiment of the Victoria Federation of Co-operative Unions in issuing fertilizer against payment from the proceeds of the ensuing crop should be repeated. The reasons for the poor response in the first year should be carefully examined, and any indicated adjustments made (p. 122).

87. The credit scheme of the Bukoba Native Co-operative Union is also recommended for careful follow-up and for study by other cooperatives (pp. 122-23).

88. The economic section in the Treasury should keep a watch on the development of marketing problems and suggest such measures as they may appear to require. Policy should be kept flexible (pp. 123-24).

89. Compulsory grading and marking of exports may be highly desirable in order to preserve the reputation of Tanganyika's products by preventing the export of low quality, adulterated or dirty lots (p. 126).

Agricultural Transformation

90. To a major degree, the hope for better land use lies in African leaders becoming convinced of the urgency of the need and in their convincing the farmers. It may be hoped that the new Government, with an elected majority, will be able to carry the people with it in action to improve land use, and even to back that action, where necessary, by legislation to ensure soil conservation measures (p. 129).

91. At the same time, in order to promote more productive farming methods, making more intensive use of the land on a sustainable basis (cf. Recommendation (1. d.)) there is a need to establish a continuous production line leading from the initial collection of basic data to the institution of improved farming schemes (p. 134).

92. The final stages of "transformation" programs may take the form of intensive campaigns in settled areas, involving a variety of coordinated measures, or of planned and supervised settlement of areas which are at present uninhabited or thinly inhabited (p. 129).

93. Reorganization of farming in settled areas, as undertaken in parts of Kenya, would involve:

a. replacement of customary land tenure by a system under which everyone so entitled obtains a consolidated holding of economic size;

b. provision to the farmers of farm plans, indicating the soil conservation layout to be adopted and showing how the holdings can be efficiently operated on an improved and intensive farming system;

c. close supervision and advice, continued over a long period, to enable the farmer to understand the farm plan, gradually to implement it and eventually to develop his holding to a high standard;

d. provision of loans to farmers in order to enable them to develop their holdings by putting up buildings for stock, erecting fencing, providing water supplies, buying fertilizers etc. (p. 130).

94. It is quite unlikely that any such reorganization of farming could be achieved on a large scale in the settled areas of Tanganyika in the near future. Nevertheless, agricultural extension work and the other parts of the improvement program should aim at increasing production on planned holdings; at improving yields per acre rather than at expanding acreage under methods which deplete the fertility of the soil; and at promoting methods which safeguard soil fertility and guard against erosion (pp. 130-31).

95. For considerable areas possessing reasonably good soil and rain-

fall it is possible to recommend with some confidence a mixed farming system, in which crops would be rotated with grass utilized by productive stock (pp. 131, 138, 159).

96. In general, quicker progress is likely to be made towards the desired ends of improved land use by planned settlement of empty areas rather than through exclusive concentration on improvement of methods in settled areas (pp. 7, 131).

97. Settlement of new areas should, so far as possible, be undertaken on a planned basis, designed to give higher yields than are secured in traditional African agriculture while at the same time safeguarding or building up the fertility of the soil (pp. 90, 132).

98. Compliance with rules of good husbandry should, where possible, be made a condition of settlement. Agreement should be secured from those who have rights over land to be settled that settlement should be made conditional on the observance of certain rules (pp. 90, 132).

99. Supervised settlement schemes should involve:

a. laying out of holdings of economic size;

b. working out of suitable farming systems and prescription of the necessary rules of soil conservation and good husbandry;

c. helping and persuading the settlers to farm efficiently and to follow the rules (p. 132).

100. Preliminary vocational training of a rather elementary nature for potential settlers should be experimented with, only the most responsive trainees being accepted for settlement in the early stages of each settlement scheme. Such training might well give good returns by increasing and accelerating improvement of yields (p. 132).

101. The immediate need is for further pilot projects to explore the inducements and financial arrangements required to make a success of planned settlement schemes (p. 132).

102. Partnership schemes should also be developed, in which an effort is made to increase the productivity of the holdings by provision by government, or some other agency, of management, supervision and capital for the acquisition of stock and equipment, or installation of irrigation or other facilities (p. 133).

103. Partnership schemes should as a general rule be run by the Tanganyika Agricultural Corporation (p. 133).

104. Further experience of agricultural partnership schemes should be secured at Nachingwea and Urambo. Further experimentation and expansion should be carried out at Urambo. At Nachingwea, the farming settlement scheme should, if possible, be enlarged, in order

to spread the overhead costs more widely. The Government should reimburse the Corporation for part of the costs of this scheme, in consideration of its value as a pilot project, thus enabling the charges on the cultivators to be reduced (pp. 133, 225, 404, 406).

Land Tenure

105. Reform in the field of land tenure is desirable not only on account of the difficulties which communal tenure places in the way of agricultural improvement and development but also to restore order in land tenure arrangements (p. 94).

106. The central problem is to reconcile initiative for change, which may well have to come largely from the center, with the due consultation of local interests and the securing of local consent, on which successful reform must depend (p. 96).

107. The area land boards (see Recommendation 29) should be consulted if and when the central government wishes to increase or decrease the area designated as "government lands" or "reserved land". The boards' main function, however, would lie with "local government lands" and with land available for African agriculture and animal husbandry (p. 97; for the classifications of types of land use, see p. 96).

108. In many areas, a major task of the area land boards would be the development of rules for the proper use of communal grazing grounds, designed to secure full advantage from provision of water, flood and tsetse control, etc. In performing these functions, the boards would have to consider the technical advice of the natural resources team (including the land utilization officer) (p. 97).

109. Where permanent improvements are proposed involving large public investments, it might well be made the responsibility of the land board to set rules for the use of the improved land or of water, under leasehold rights of tenure. The board might also be charged with drawing up financial arrangements designed to secure a return on the public investment directly from land and water users (pp. 97-98).

110. The right to confer individual title to land need not necessarily continue to be vested in the Crown, Governor or Central Government. Registration of individual title by an area land board might well help to increase its acceptability (p. 98).

111. The term "freehold" should be reserved for the existing land

held in freehold, perhaps with the addition of land in urban areas for business or residential purposes. It seems possible to devise a suitable alternative term, in Swahili or with an acceptable Swahili counterpart. In English this might be "individual tenure" (p. 98).

112. While individual tenure can only be satisfactorily instituted where there is a fair measure of local consent, in certain areas it will be desirable for the central government to support the case of progressive individuals who desire, and would benefit from, individual tenure, and to bring about more rapid change than would occur solely on the basis of uninfluenced local public opinion (pp. 98-99).

113. The recognition of individual tenure could in many cases be usefully registered, with a simple situation map, by the area land board (p. 99).

114. Security for borrowing would be enhanced by a simple procedure for pledging of land and tree crops, with the requirement of making the pledge official by an annotation in the local ledger of registration (p. 99).

115. In order to assure the institution of a reasonably stable market for land under individual tenure, it may be desirable to set up a government agency which will be willing on occasion to buy land and to hold it until a qualified private buyer is found who is willing to offer a fair price (p. 99).

116. Where land is needed for irrigation projects, planned settlement schemes and cattle ranches, it would be for the area land boards to concur in putting aside land for these uses, taking into account existing rights (p. 100).

Livestock

117. The Mission considers that demand, within the territory and for export, justifies the aim of increasing annual production of beef animals by 100,000 head. It would be time enough to reappraise the situation when such a figure had been attained (pp. 144, 146).

118. The object of policy should be to persuade African cattle keepers of the great advantages of systematic management of stock and pasture and to induce them to adopt the requisite methods. Measures to increase calving rates, decrease calf mortality, improve the quality and condition of the animals and increase the carrying capacity of pasture land are best presented as a coherent whole, capable of converting cattle into a valuable cash crop (p. 147).

119. Government provision of water or tsetse clearing should be used to the greatest possible degree as an inducement to secure improved management of cattle and pasture. Effort should be concentrated in particular places in the main cattle areas, where there is the best chance of securing adoption of a range of improvements allowing higher calving rates, lower calf mortality, better quality of stock, better condition of the animals and improved pasture. If a few communities in different parts of the territory can be thoroughly convinced of the benefit of the necessary combinations of measures and practices, then these communities can be used as demonstrations to others (p. 159).

120. Efforts to develop a commercial attitude amongst the pastoralists will have to continue for some time (p. 148).

121. The program to increase and improve markets and stock routes, worked out by the Veterinary Department and estimated to cost £ 28,000 a year over the next five years, should be carried through (p. 148).

122. At least one mobile meat-processing plant should be put into operation in one of the more remote areas of comparatively dense cattle population, and its results checked to see whether more may not be justified (p. 148).

123. It is to be hoped that the three cattle cooperatives, recently registered in the Lake Province, will increase appreciation of cattle as a cash crop in their areas, and will show the way for useful development of similar institutions in other areas (p. 148).

124. To secure improvement of pasture, the primary needs are usually for the introduction of simple systems of rotational grazing and for the provision of grazing reserves, and for doing away with indiscriminate burning and its replacement with a controlled use of fire in those areas where this is needed to deal with bush regeneration. In some places a further desirable step would be the rehabilitation of denuded areas by sowing or planting of suitable grasses after a minimum of preparatory cultivation (p. 150).

125. Bush clearing and elimination of tsetse by the Central Government should be limited to areas of high potential for ranching or mixed farming and to localities where only limited future clearing is needed to safeguard existing fly-free areas, or to extend them considerably. The task of opening up areas for use should be left to a considerable degree to local effort. A reasonable central government program would cost £ 10,000 a year, enough to clear about 25,000 acres annually (p. 151).

126. There should be no great acceleration of the program of provision of water supplies for livestock until further investigations and planning have been undertaken to assure that this form of investment shall indeed make an adequate contribution to the economy of the territory (p. 153). Possible rates of investment are shown in Table 19, p. 157.

127. The provision of additional water supplies should form part of a planned program in which watering points are sited with regard to the pasturage available and arrangements are made for the control of stock numbers and for pasture management (p. 156). (Cf. Recommendation 119).

128. In order to avoid erosion in the neighborhood of watering points, it will be desirable to aim at not more than 1,250 head of cattle to each watering point, or 1,500 at the utmost. If the water supply takes the form of a running river or of a pipeline with a number of cattle troughs, then calculations of allowable stock numbers should be made on the basis of the carrying capacity within a range of two or three miles (p. 154. See also Recommendation 273).

129. In order to promote direct contributions to the cost of cattle water supplies by the beneficiaries, the Mission recommends return to a 50/50 sharing of costs of cattle water supplies between the Central Government and Local Government Authorities (p. 155).

130. Local Authorities should not necessarily be allowed to "buy" water development, unless such development meets adequate criteria of economic justification (p. 155).

131. While it is desirable to increase facilities for control of diseases of livestock, the prime task is to promote increased use and appreciation of these facilities (p. 157. See also Recommendation 275).

132. The production and distribution of earlier maturing and more productive stock will only be effective as adequate progress is secured in pasture management, animal husbandry and disease control. However, it will be important in the longer run. The Veterinary Department should continue its work of selection and breeding. Partnership breeding ranches can be of great value as cattle improvement centers (pp. 158-59).

133. The Tanganyika Agricultural Corporation should be instructed and enabled to complete the development of the ranches at Kongwa and Ruvu. The Mkata ranch should be transferred from the Veterinary Department to the TAC, which would become responsible for building it up to full capacity (pp. 160-61).

a. Operations at Kongwa should be progressively concentrated on the breeding and rearing of stock from the herds on the ranch, and buying and fattening of immatures should be tapered off as breeding activities are developed to full capacity (pp. 161, 407).

b. Ruvu should for the time being continue to concentrate on purchase and fattening of immatures, but a partial switch to breeding activities should be considered when the ranch is fully developed (pp. 161, 407).

c. Initially, at any rate, it may be considered desirable to continue to run Mkata partly with improved cattle bred on the ranch and partly with immatures for fattening (pp. 161-62).

134. a. It would be wise to await some results from this experiment before attempting the further development of partnership ranches. Thus for the next five years at least, effort should be concentrated on building up the ranches at Kongwa, Mkata and Ruvu (p. 162).

b. Subsequently, provided that demand for beef appears adequate, it will be advantageous to set up further breeding ranches as adequate supplies of breeding stock become available (p. 162).

c. The economics of ranches for fattening immatures should be further investigated (pp. 162-63, 437-38).

d. Both types of ranch should probably be run on a partnership basis, the whole or part of the herds being managed by African tenants or partners, but with central provision of capital, services and skilled management (p. 163).

Dairying

135. An investigation by dairy experts should be made of the means by which an increased, improved and cheaper supply of milk could be secured for Dar es Salaam. It might be possible to secure help from FAO-UNICEF (p. 173).

136. For suggested technical methods of improving the supply of milk to the towns, see Recommendation 278.

137. The FAO-UNICEF plan for improvement of dairying and milk supply in the Arusha-Moshi area appears workable, but certain points require further consideration (pp. 167-69).

138. A study of the economics of African milk production is needed before it can be decided whether, and where, an expansion of this activity is desirable. In the meantime effort should be made to make the most economic use of available milk supplies from African farmers, particularly those in the neighborhood of some of the towns, where some encouragement of increased production might also be given (p. 170. See also Recommendation 279).

Irrigation and Flood Control

139. Preparations should be put in hand forthwith for a program of irrigation and flood control works to reach an annual development of 25,000 acres a year from about 1969/70. To undertake irrigation and flood control works on this scale, it will be necessary to build up a considerably increased staff and to make extensive preparations. While this is being done, the extent of properly designed capital works which can be executed will necessarily be somewhat limited. Thus there should be a cautious expansion in the first years, reaching not more than 7,500 acres per year in 1965/66. If preparations proceed satisfactorily, and finances allow, the acreage under construction should be increased from 7,500 in 1965/66 to the full 25,000 acres a year by about 1969/70 (p. 175).

140. Planning of irrigation and flood control works should pay attention to such aims as:

a. improvement or diversification of food supply in areas where the present supply is inadequate in quantity or variety;

b. relief of overcrowding;

c. demonstration at points distributed throughout the territory of irrigation methods and the advantages to be secured by their adoption (p. 176).

141. A skeleton plan for the development of 100,000 acres by irrigation and flood control, between 1965/66 and 1970/71, is set out in Table 21, p. 177 (see also pp. 88-89, 177-78).

142. Within this framework, development should be directed towards areas of high potential (p. 176).

143. It is estimated that the program of irrigation and flood control works contemplated for 1969/70 and subsequent years could be managed by a staff of some three times the present size. It will be necessary to increase staff well in advance of any considerable enlargement of capital expenditures, in order to be able to undertake the preparatory work required before each phase of construction. An additional allowance should be made for special investigations and surveys. Provision has also to be made for agricultural officers to carry on extension work on the development schemes (pp. 179-80).

144. In a territorial program of irrigation and flood control development, it will be necessary to look for gross output on the projects of the order of 30 percent of the original total capital costs. Only for exceptional reasons, such as relief of acute local hardship, should

irrigation or flood control projects be carried out in which the expected annual value of the gross product is less than 20 percent of the original construction costs. The validity of these rule-of-thumb ratios should, however, be further examined (see Recommendation 244) (pp. 180-81).

145. Charges on the cultivators for water, land rent and any special services provided should be at the highest levels consistent with attracting a sufficient number of cultivators. However, a period of, say, three years should elapse on schemes before charges are assessed at the full rate (p. 182).

146. Several more irrigation trial farms should be set up, avoiding so far as possible the difficulties encountered in the past (p. 187).

147. Trial farms and pilot projects should be used to train skilled irrigation men of all classes from laborer to manager (p. 188).

148. Completion of the Mbarali pilot project should receive the full attention of the Government (pp. 187-88).

149. Integrated design of irrigation projects should be promoted by establishing planning groups consisting of members of the design staff of the Water Development and Irrigation Department together with agronomists specially assigned by the Department of Agriculture (p. 188).

150. On the basis of preliminary investigations of projects, master plans should be designed and presented to the Land Use Committee. This Committee should ascertain that preliminary investigations have been sufficient to warrant a decision. The ultimate decision on the priority of the project should depend on firm criteria concerning the relationship of prospective benefits to costs. It may often be desirable to investigate the costs and potential effects of alternative projects of different sizes and types. The objectives of schemes should be clearly defined. These objectives should include, within reasonable limits, the expectation that the population in the development area will react favorably to the execution of the project and be willing to cooperate (pp. 188-89).

151. Future participants should be prepared for the fact that they will be starting on a completely new type of land use. The economic consequences, including the necessity of paying water charges, should be made clear. Groups of farmers should be taken to visit other irrigation areas. It may be appropriate to direct preliminary extension work to the preparation of cooperative ridging and plowing schemes, cooperative marketing etc. (p. 189).

152. Development of irrigation farming on a partnership basis may

well be feasible on the larger projects, whereas a more limited type of supervision of independent cultivators will probably be appropriate in smaller schemes (p. 190).

153. The control of use of water would probably best be left to a local body. Firm water rights should be established under the new Water Ordinance. In the future, water laws will be necessary, providing the framework for regulation of water distribution, construction and maintenance of works, and assessment of water rates (p. 190).

154. Pilot projects of flood control should be carried out, both coupled with irrigation and also in high rainfall areas where irrigation is unnecessary, to give experience of the technical problems and economics of such schemes (p. 191).

Forestry

155. The Mission proposes capital expenditures for afforestation amounting to £ 180,000 in 1961/62 and 1962/63, and falling off to £ 140,000 in 1965/66 (p. 195).

156. The scale of expenditure should be reconsidered in the light of the findings of the FAO survey of potential demand for wood and timber in Tanganyika (p. 195).

157. Afforestation should be mechanized only to the degree absolutely necessary, and careful experiments should be made with various mixtures of mechanization and hand labor (p. 195).

158. Forestry policy should pay careful regard to location (pp. 195-96).

159. The Land Use Committee should assure that forestry policy pays proper regard to the value of land in alternative uses (p. 196).

160. Extension work related to production of beeswax and honey should be further increased (p. 196).

Fisheries

161. There is little doubt that a fair degree of priority should be given to expanding government effort to promote development of fishing (p. 199).

162. A general survey should be made of the fishing industry, covering potential production and potential markets in the various parts of the country (pp. 199-200).

163. The further development of Lake Victoria Fisheries requires a combined approach through improved marketing arrangements and

better methods of fishing in the more remote areas offshore (pp. 197-98).

164. Further attention should be given to the problems of increasing markets for dagaa from Lake Tanganyika (p. 198).

165. If further interest is shown by private interests in developing deep-water fisheries in Lake Tanganyika, means should be explored of working out an arrangement which will win local assent (p. 199).

166. Agricultural extension workers, particularly those working in areas of irrigation development, should have at least a minimum training in matters of fishery development (p. 199).

Estate Agriculture

167. In the reorganization of lending institutions, attention should be given to the capital needs of (non-sisal) estates (p. 207).

169. Advisory services should continue to be provided in areas where occupants of alienated agricultural land have sufficient knowledge and experience to enable them to farm the land efficiently (p. 207).

169. Advisory services should continue to be provided in areas where there are concentrations of non-African farms (p. 207).

170. The Government should assist in the solution of estates' marketing problems, along lines which serve the interests of the economy as a whole. Marketing arrangements should as a rule be financed by the producers themselves, with the aid of borrowing from commercial banks (p. 208).

171. The Tanganyika Agricultural Corporation should be prepared as a temporary measure to bid for estates which are offered for sale. Estates bought by the Government or by a public body might be run as partnership operations or as demonstration farms. Alternatively the TAC might act as an agency house, taking over estates and installing paid managers to run them, the present owners being compensated by the device of issuing shares to them (p. 206).

Manufacturing

172. The circumstances of Tanganyika are such as to call for no more than a moderate application of protection as a measure for encouraging secondary industry. However, protection of particular products—e.g. cement—may be justified (pp. 13, 232-33, 236).

173. The Mission believes that economic cooperation between Tanganyika, Kenya and Uganda, and the prevention of the growth of economic barriers between these territories, is in the best interests of

the long-run development of the area. However, it is desirable that efforts should be made to promote a satisfactory distribution of industrial development and of its fruits between the three territories (pp. 33-35, 238-39).

174. Consideration should be given to abolishing the system of industrial licensing. At the least, no addition should be made to the list of scheduled industries (p. 241).

175. The establishment of a development company or companies has been covered by Recommendations 43-45.

176. Concerning industrial research, see Recommendation 246.

Mining

177. Basic work by the Government in surveying potentialities of mineral development should be expanded (see Recommendations 227 and 228).

178. Government courses for African prospectors and for staff of mining and prospecting companies should be continued or even increased, according to the response encountered (p. 268).

179. The present regulations which provide for granting of special or exclusive prospecting licenses are usually necessary to attract concerns willing to make substantial exploration expenditures. However, such rights should be granted only for short periods and should be renewed on the basis of performance rather than of stated intentions. As a first step in attracting fresh mining capital, the territory should be opened to diamond prospecting by any reputable group (pp. 269-70).

180. Additional tax incentives to mining, possibly on the Canadian model, should be considered (pp. 270-71).

181. A highly qualified, full-time resident Mining Consultant should be installed. He should maintain contact with foreign enterprises and development groups, draw their attention to possibilities for mineral exploration and development as revealed by various surveys, and advise the Government on general policies relating to mineral exploration and development and on specific projects (p. 271).

Transport

182. Priorities in main road development are:
a. upgrading of the link Segera - Mkata - Chalinze;

b. completion of the link from Singida to Nzega;

c. improvement of sections of the road from Dar es Salaam to Nzega and the southwest.

d. further development of link and branch roads such as from Mpwapwa to the Dodoma-Dar es Salaam road, Tabora-Nzega, Songea-Lake Nyasa and Mbeya-Lake Nyasa (p. 275).

183. Extension of the railway line from Mikumi to the site of the Kilombero Sugar Company plant is to be considered. However, careful attention will have to be given to the relative merits of road and rail communications in the Kilombero Valley and beyond (p. 287).

184. Ocean port facilities are adequate for the traffic to be expected for several years to come. However, a project for one or two additional deep water wharves at Dar es Salaam should be worked out in sufficient detail to be ready for construction at short notice should the need arise (pp. 288-89).

185. In planning road and rail development, attention must be given to avoidance of superfluous expenditures by duplication of routes (pp. 272, 276).

186. In the coming years, expenditures on construction and improvement of feeder roads should be increased, while capital expenditures on main roads can be somewhat reduced. Feeder road development should be related to plans for agricultural development programs, irrigation and flood control schemes etc. (p. 277).

187. Funds should be allowed for some improvement of standards of road maintenance (p. 278).

188. The traffic density considered to justify bitumenization should be carefully examined (p. 279).

189. The number of licenses issued to public road carriers to operate along any portion of the main routes should be limited. The issue of public carriers' licenses should be conditional on the demonstration of some proof of understanding of the cost, obligations and requirements of the intended operations, as well as compliance with safety regulations governing vehicle, passengers, load and crew and the observance of appropriate published timetables and tariffs and insurance requirements (p. 281).

190. However, licensing conditions should be administered with a considerable measure of flexibility. Greater competition should be allowed in rural areas, and standards of service there need not necessarily conform to those applied on the main routes. Where large numbers of small operators are now licensed to cover the same route, they should be encouraged to pool their resources and also to shift

their business off the main routes to the feeder roads as they are developed (p. 281).

191. Steps should be taken to strengthen the Transport Licensing Authority, including the appointment of officers with power to charge and prosecute offenders. This should be accompanied by a campaign to inform the public of the reasons for the licensing policy and its specific regulations (p. 282).

192. Motor schooners of all sizes, and sailing schooners of 125 tons and over, should be made subject to regulations governing seaworthiness of vessel, safety and comfort of passengers, safety of cargo, and qualifications and conditions of service of crew. Motor vessels should be surcharged appropriate rates for use of dhow wharves (p. 290).

193. When these steps have been taken, it will be necessary to consider whether any further measures are required to maintain or secure adequate coastal shipping services (p. 290).

194. Some degrees of regulation of private mechanized lake craft should be instituted, to prevent them from undermining the regular scheduled services. However, such regulation should be administered flexibly to avoid suppression of desirable initiative and excessive protection of the regular shippers (p. 291).

195. The possibilities of securing economies in the staffing of the smaller internal airports should be examined (p. 292).

196. Internal air services provide an essential passenger and freight service to remote places, and must be maintained (p. 292).

197. Recommended development expenditures for the Tanganyika Directorate of the East African Posts and Telecommunciations Administration are set out in Table 32, p. 294.

198. A telephone link from Dar es Salaam to the Lake Province via Singida should await the completion of the road link (p. 294).

199. The possibility of a VHF radio link from Dar es Salaam to the Southern Province should be explored, as construction of feeder roads makes accessible suitable sites for sub-stations (pp. 294-95).

Tourist Trade and Game Reserves

200. Policy in promoting tourism should attempt to increase the volume of middle-income tourists rather than of the luxury trade or big-game hunting safaris (p. 297).

201. Joint East African efforts for international publicity of tourist attractions and facilities, and organization of tours by groups, should be continued (pp. 295-96).

202. Promotion by the East African Railways and Harbours Administration of low-cost package tours should be further developed. Continuing efforts should be made to secure reduction of air fares from Europe (p. 297).

203. Public efforts to build and improve roads in areas of interest to tourists and to promote provision of improved hotel accommodation should be continued (p. 296).

204. Investigation of the methods and economics of systematic game-cropping in game reserves should be continued, if possible with the aid of outside technical assistance (p. 297).

Education

205. First priority in educational development should be given to increasing the annual number of African school certificate candidates to 2,000 or 2,500 (pp. 305-06).

206. Every effort should be made to avoid the dilution of teaching standards (p. 307).

207. The Mission is in sympathy with the immediate aim of lengthening African primary education to a six-year course, though at such a pace as financial considerations may permit. The further aim of an eight-year primary course should be subjected to further investigation (pp. 308, 315, 320).

208. Further study is needed to identify the most important causes of wastage, particularly in the Primary Schools, and to determine how they may best be combatted (p. 310).

209. Special efforts should be made to improve and increase the education of girls by:

a. expanding facilities at all levels;

b. introducing more practical courses for girls in the middle schools;

c. increasing the number and quality of women teachers, and heads of girls' middle schools (p. 311).

There may be a case for remission of school fees for African girls until a tradition of female education has been more firmly established (p. 329).

210. High priority should be given to the expansion of technical training facilities (pp. 312-13).

211. The development of education should be planned on the basis of a view of the balance of requirements for those emerging from the educational pipeline (pp. 306-07, 308, 313).

212. Continuing research into the theory and practice of education suited to Tanganyikan conditions should be carried out as a basis for educational planning and teacher training in the territory. This research should include investigation of the appropriate length of the primary course in relation to economic and social conditions in the territory (pp. 306, 308, 311-12. See also Recommendation 59).

213. The link between African pupils in Standard V-VIII and the land should be maintained, not so much by emphasis on the dissemination of modern agricultural techniques as by applying arithmetic, science and even the use of English to topics related to agriculture, animal husbandry, cooperative membership etc. There is scope for further experiment and investigation relating to agricultural education (p. 314).

214. Adult literacy training should similarly be given a practical slant (p. 314).

215. One-year courses following general education to Standard VIII could usefully be employed to train potential junior employees on estates, larger farmers and participants in agricultural and irrigation partnership schemes (p. 314).

216. It is desirable that, within the context of the intended racial integration of the educational system, the Indian community should abandon its exclusively academic concept of secondary education (p. 315).

217. The aim of integration should not necessarily be inconsistent with the provision of schools catering to particular scholastic requirements. Thus attention should be paid to the desire of the European community for primary schools of standards aligned with those of the more selective schools in Europe (p. 316).

Miscellaneous

218. A more positive attitude should be taken towards non-African traders. The interests of the African consumer are best served by the maximum of competition between traders, and the growth of the economy is benefited by the greatest possible availability of consumer goods and small implements. The desire to facilitate entry of Africans into trade should be met not by restricting others, but by such measures as training and provision of appropriate credit facilities (p. 128).

219. The proposal to establish field units, under the Ministry of Mines and Commerce, to assist Africans to operate commercial projects

and small-scale industrial enterprises and to give courses to African traders should be implemented. These units might also administer small-scale loans, though with due precautions against the growth of favoritism (p. 222).

220. The Government should encourage to the maximum possible extent the entry of technicians, professional persons and businessmen (p. 232).

D. RESEARCH AND INVESTIGATIONS

Physical Investigations

221. Means should be found of accelerating progress in topographical mapping (p. 185).

222. Statistical analysis of rainfall in various parts of the territory should be continued, with emphasis on the reliability of annual amounts both of 25 inches and of 30 inches (p. 136).

223. Expanded analysis of rainfall data should be related to more comprehensive studies of water requirements of various crops in Tanganyikan conditions (pp. 136-37).

224. Efforts should be made to accelerate soil survey work by obtaining from some outside organization the services of four experienced soil classifiers and an experienced soil chemist for a period of three years. The soil classifiers, one of whom at least should be knowledgeable in land classification for irrigation purposes, should carry out detailed surveys in selected areas believed to be of good potential, in conjunction with the local land utilization officers. They might also endeavor to obtain something of an over-all picture of the soils of Tanganyika by carrying out in certain areas reconnaissance or transient surveys which would serve as a basis for more detailed surveys later. The soil chemist should carry out laboratory examination of soil samples and, in particular, should develop the laboratory organization and training of junior staff necessary for the routine examination of large numbers of soil samples by modern methods (pp. 137-38, 187).

225. Increased investigation should be made of trace element deficiencies (pp. 138-39).

226. Training of hydrometrists deserves continued high priority. Study should be progressively accelerated of silt loads in rivers and

streams, the quality of available water for domestic and irrigation purposes, availability of ground water and the water balances of reservoirs. General hydrological surveys of the river basins of the east of the territory should be continued (p. 186).

227. Means should be found of speeding up basic geological mapping (p. 267).

228. Mineral reconnaissance surveys should be undertaken by the Geological Survey Department on a more systematic and sustained basis than in the past (p. 268).

Agricultural and Livestock Research

229. There is a need for further research and experiment to discover what methods are in fact required to protect or to build up fertility in the conditions found in many parts of Tanganyika (p. 81).

230. Further investigations are required of the response of different soils to fertilizers and on the economics of their use with the various crops grown in Tanganyika (pp. 81, 138).

231. Field trials should be made on an increased scale of crops to be grown under irrigation and of appropriate cultivation methods (p. 184).

232. Technical assistance should be sought for the work on water requirements of crops and for related work on crop breeding. Such work might appropriately be placed on an interterritorial basis and administered by the East African Agricultural and Forestry Research Organization (p. 137).

233. As examples of work to be undertaken:

a. Agronomic experimental work is needed in the growing of pyrethrum, especially in the Southern Highlands Province and particularly in the use of fertilizers, manure and rotational cropping in order to maintain yields (p. 376).

b. The program of breeding strains of pyrethrum adapted to conditions in Tanganyika and with good pyrethrins content should be actively continued (p. 376).

c. Research in breeding new varieties of sunflower and castor seed, adapted to Tanganyikan conditions, should be undertaken (p. 374).

234. Suitable cropping patterns for various areas should be determined by field trials (p. 138).

235. More trial farms and pilot projects should be maintained to develop methods of irrigation agriculture (pp. 187-88).

236. Pilot projects should investigate the methods of organizing planned settlement, irrigation and partnership schemes (pp. 140, 187-88).

237. Work on pasture improvement and management should be expanded. The TAC pasture research station at Kongwa should be taken over by the Government (pp. 163-64).

238. Estimates of the size and composition of African cattle herds, calving rates, mortality rates and rates of take-off should be checked for internal consistency and plausibility, and veterinary officers should be encouraged to improve upon their present estimates (p. 164).

239. The research division of the Department of Agriculture should draw all possible advantage from cooperation with the East African Agricultural and Forestry Research Organization and by collaboration and exchange of visits with staff of the research divisions of the agricultural departments in Kenya, Uganda and the Federation of Rhodesia and Nyasaland. More adequate provision of funds should be made to cover traveling costs of Tanganyikan research officers visiting these other territories (pp. 135-36).

240. Arrangements should be made for the continuation of research into the mechanical shelling of cashew nuts, perhaps in cooperation with the National Institute of Agricultural Engineering and the National Research Development Corporation in the U.K. It should be possible for Tanganyika to share the cost of financing this work with the several other British territories which produce cashew nuts, or the project might appear to justify a Colonial Development and Welfare grant (pp. 371-72).

Agricultural Economics

241. As improved systems of farming are developed by research, additional trial holdings should be established to study their economic and management aspects (p. 139).

242. Studies should be made of the economics of various types and sizes of holdings, including holdings in irrigation schemes, with different crop patterns (pp. 139, 182).

243. Outside assistance should be sought for the provision of an agricultural economist experienced in these types of work. With the aid of one or two local agricultural officers (preferably Africans) this agricultural economist should initiate economic studies (p. 139).

244. Further studies should be made of the economic and financial

aspects of breeding ranches, fattening ranches, irrigation schemes and flood control works (pp. 162-63, 181, Annex VII).

245. Factual data should be accumulated on the economics of watering points. Developments at new watering points of various kinds in various parts of the territory should be studied over a period of several years (p. 155).

Industrial Investigations

246. Tanganyika should make the most effective possible use of the East African Industrial Research Organization as well as of other available sources of technical and industrial advice. Particular attention should be paid to research leading to new uses for agricultural materials now produced or capable of being produced in Tanganyika, and to their further processing in the territory (p. 248).

Investigations Related to General Economic Planning

247. The work of the statistical unit should continue to be linked very largely to a national accounting framework (p. 344).

248. The program of improving knowledge of African agricultural production should be carried on (p. 344).

249. It would be useful to collect direct data on private consumption expenditures—not merely their total size but also their distribution among types of goods, both imported and domestically produced. It is of relevance to planning to explore how consumption, imports and taxes vary with income (p. 344).

250. Estimates of the main types of income—wages, salaries, profits, interest and rent—would be valuable (pp. 344-45).

251. It would be of interest to investigate sources of finance for private capital formation (p. 345).

252. The effort should be made to produce national accounting series at constant prices (p. 345).

253. More complete knowledge of the structure and development of the territory's individual balance of payments with the outside world, including the remainder of East Africa, would be useful in understanding and following various important aspects of the economic process (p. 345).

254. Studies should be made of complementarity and competitive-

ness between various development projects. Examples are:

a. The relations between power development at Hale, a dam at Nyumba ya Mungu, irrigation in the middle Pangani basin, power development for the Moshi-Arusha area and (possibly) the development of the phosphate deposit at Minjingu Hill (pp. 251-52, 263).

b. The relations between development at Nachingwea and the future of the Southern Province railway and the port of Mtwara (pp. 404-05).

E. BUDGETARY AND FINANCIAL POLICIES

255. The implications of the Mission's recommendations for future budgetary expenditures are described in pp. 51-62.

256. Changes in the appreciation of financial resources available, refinement and revision of costings, revised assessments of technical feasibility and of returns may all give the Development Committee reason to make adjustments to the size and pattern of expenditures shown (pp. 41, 68-69).

257. It is important to make the best possible assessment of future financial resources, and particularly of the prospective development of current revenue (pp. 47, 342).

258. The Mission considers that the Government of Tanganyika would be justified in borrowing the sums required to support expenditures on the scale suggested by this report, provided that loans are available on reasonably favorable terms; and that it should shape its present policies on the assumption that such loans will in fact be available (pp. 67-68).

259. Development in Tanganyika could benefit greatly from continued and expanded inflow of grants and technical assistance and from the availability of loans on soft terms (pp. 4, 38, 39, 59, 66, 68).

260. It is hardly possible to contemplate any significant increase of the over-all ratio of tax to money incomes. Greater tax revenues, desirable to make possible increased government developmental expenditure, must be sought through expansion of taxable economic activity (pp. 70, 71, 325).

261. It should nevertheless be an aim of fiscal policy to secure that growth of public revenues should parallel the growth of the monetary economy (pp. 325-26, 456).

262. The Mission proposes for consideration a combination of three changes in the tax structure:

a. elimination of Local Government Authority produce cesses (pp. 127, 327-28);

b. transfer to the Local Authorities of part of the proceeds of the Personal Tax (pp. 327, 328);

c. levying by the Central Government of export tax at a low rate (pp. 327, 328-29).

263. The Government should as a general rule attempt to levy fees and taxes on persons and communities to whom it renders specific, recognizable services (cf. Recommendations 129 and 145). However, this policy, should not be allowed to interfere with other important aims of public policy (cf. Recommendation 209) (p. 329).

264. Attention should be given to the extent to which, and ways in which, Local Government bodies should be enabled to increase their financial stake in activities of importance to local development (p. 32). Possible measures are:

a. increased provision of loan funds to finance Local Authorities' capital expenditures;

b. increase of the share of tax revenues directly collected by Local Authorities (p. 330).

F. RECOMMENDATIONS OF A MORE DETAILED OR TECHNICAL NATURE

Agricultural Production

265. *Sisal:* a. No special public action to help the sisal industry appears to be needed. Various technical changes, calling for private action, are listed for the sake of completeness (p. 202).

b. Practicable and economic means are required of increasing yields per acre and, at the same time, maintaining or improving soil fertility. Appropriate methods have already been shown by research, to a considerable degree, but the economics of applying them on estates require further investigation (pp. 202-04).

c. Means of economizing labor require further investigation (pp. 202, 204-05):

i. There is scope for further labor-saving in land preparation and cultivation, particularly in weeding (pp. 204-05).

ii. An appreciable economy could probably be affected by switching from a system of paying on the basis of a task based on the number of leaves to piece rates, based on weight, for handling between field and decorticator (p. 205).

iii. There are possibilities of finding means of mechanizing, or partially mechanizing, the collection and transport of leaf from the field to the rail trucks or lorries, of mechanizing loading and unloading of the trucks, and in the evolution of a satisfactory automatic leaf-feed through the decorticator (p. 205).

iv. Handling of the fiber after it leaves the decorticator could also probably be mechanized with benefit (p. 205).

266. *Cotton:* a. Continued extension work is required to encourage early planting, tie-ridging, timely weeding and the application of cattle manure and/or fertilizer (pp. 105, 368).

b. More effective ginning and better handling of seed cotton are required (p. 369).

c. The Cotton Price Assistance Fund should not be allowed to become exhausted by making miscellaneous grants from it and by subsidizing the price to the grower for seed cotton while the world market price allows an unsubsidized price to the grower of, say, at least 45 cents per lb. (p. 369).

d. Cotton growing outside the Lake Province should be encouraged by:

i. formation of cooperatives to strengthen the grower's position vis-a-vis the ginners, to aid in organizing pest control and to assist in promoting better methods of cultivation and higher yields;

ii. reduction in the number and increase in the efficiency of ginneries;

iii. more concentrated development of cotton growing in certain areas, coupled with increased provision of feeder roads (p. 370).

e. It will be desirable to take such steps as are necessary—for instance, provision of loans—to ensure that processing capacity keeps pace with the supply of cotton seed (p. 371).

267. *Coffee:* a. In existing coffee plantations, the quality of trees and fruit could be considerably improved if growers could be persuaded to pay more attention to shade, pruning, mulching, regeneration of old coffee trees, and the preparation of the beans (p. 364).

b. In Uchagga, experiments should be made in planting coffee in pure stand, with only limited banana or other shade and on the multiple stem pruning system, the bananas also being planted in pure stand, as wind breaks. If successful, this system should be widely demonstrated. In any case, efforts should be made to reduce the excessively heavy shade of bananas found in many plantations, and to improve pruning methods (pp. 364-65).

c. Efforts should be continued to get the mulching of coffee with banana trash or grass more widely and efficiently adopted (p. 365).

d. A long-term program is desirable of progressively replanting old coffee gardens on Kilimanjaro with seedlings of the Lyamungu Coffee Research Station. As an interim measure, a proportion of the old coffee bushes might be rejuvenated by cutting them back and converting them to multiple stem (p. 365).

e. The experience of the Meru Co-operative Union Ltd., which has just installed a central pulpery, should be followed with care by other cooperatives. If this proves profitable, some of the other cooperative unions or larger societies should erect such factories at suitable sites in their areas (p. 366).

f. The Mission considers that cooperative pulperies would be of greater benefit to the Southern Highlands Province than the coffee curing plant which it is proposed to establish there (p. 366).

g. Specialist coffee advisory officers should be maintained in areas where there are coffee-growing estates (p. 207).

268. *Cashew Nuts:* Suitable ventures in the hand-shelling of cashew nuts should be encouraged and, if necessary, given financial backing from public funds (p. 371).

269. *Cocoa:* a. The survey and mapping of soils suitable for cocoa in the Tanga Province should be completed (pp. 372-73).

b. If this survey shows that a worthwhile development is possible, an agronomist with considerable experience of cocoa should be recruited to the Department of Agriculture, to assist in planning and executing a development program for this crop (p. 373).

c. In due course trials in other possible areas should be pressed forward (p. 373).

270. *Pyrethrum:* a. Forest glades in the Northern Province should continue to be leased for pyrethrum where this can be done without detriment to water conservation and where any land tenure problems involved can be suitably adjusted (p. 375).

b. Extension effort should be increased to promote more rapid expansion of the acreage of pyrethrum grown by Africans (p. 376).

c. African cultivation should be closely supervised to secure higher standards of field culture (p. 376).

d. Work should continue on the control of insect pests attacking pyrethrum, particularly thrips and red spider (p. 376).

e. A survey should be made of the pyrethrum strains being grown on European farms, and arrangements concluded with one or two farmers, who are found to have the best strains, for the production of seed from selected areas (p. 376).

271. *Seed Peas:* To encourage further rapid and satisfactory growth of production by Africans in the Southern Highlands Province, one or two men should be employed to promote and supervise production, and a further £ 5,000 should be invested in vehicles and equipment. It might be possible to interest a local firm in this enterprise (p. 377).

272. *Catchment areas:* Where irrigation is developed on a large scale, special attention should be given to the catchment areas above the reservoirs. It may be desirable to control grazing in these areas. In places the eventual aim should be to establish forest reserves to prevent the deterioration of soil cover and resulting erosion (p. 190).

Livestock

273. Steps should be taken to prevent overgrazing round watering points (cf. Recommendation 128) (p. 153):

a. One possible solution might be to erect fences to prevent the approach of cattle near to the reservoir. Water should then be provided in cattle troughs supplied by pipes from the reservoir. However fencing of reservoirs is impracticable unless the collaboration of the people can be obtained (p. 153).

b. Another solution may be to construct fairly large dams from which water can be released steadily over the dry period of the year to provide a steady flow of water in the river bed downstream for a considerable distance. This solution however is applicable only under conditions where the water does not seep into the soil and where the river traverses an area which is not susceptible to erosion (p. 153).

c. Where water is made available by boreholes or by pipeline systems, it may be possible to restrict the amount of water made available at a particular place. However, it will be necessary to guard against efforts to circumvent such restriction (p. 153).

d. Reservoir schemes should only be installed if there is reasonable assurance of adequate grazing control. Only in a very small number of severe hardship cases should exceptions be made to this rule (p. 156).

274. In certain circumstances, the control of water supplies could be directly used to bring about improved pasture management (p. 156).

275. The following operations for the control of livestock diseases deserve early attention:

a. Expansion of the existing scheme whereby financial assistance to cover the cost of dipping or spraying facilities to control tickborne diseases is given to the Native Authorities in districts where stock owners apply for such assistance. £ 15,000 a year will be required over ten years for the partial finance of 100 dipping centers.

b. The construction of a further 100 crushes a year over the next ten years, for the accommodation of cattle receiving innoculations against such diseases as rinderpest, anthrax and blackquarter, or antry-cide treatment against trypanosomiasis.

c. The eventual provision of about ten quarantine stations at strategic points on the stock trade routes. The most urgent requirement is for three stations on the routes by which cattle enter the Northern and Tanga Provinces from Kenya, primarily for the control of foot-and-mouth disease (pp. 157-58).

276. There is a general need for improvement in the present low standards of animal husbandry, particularly in the matter of provision of dry season feed, the correction of mineral imbalance or deficiencies by the provision of licks, the better housing of stock and the provision of bedding for calves (p. 158).

277. For cattle ranches with skilled management, 80,000 acres appear to be the minimum unit which would support the overheads entailed in expert supervision and management (p. 163).

Dairying

278. A means of making cheaper milk available to Africans in the towns would be the preparation of a toned or standardized milk of, say, not more than 3 percent butter fat but with its original content of non-fat solids, or possibly an enhanced content. Such a standardized milk would be produced by:

a. separating from whole milk a part of the cream for manufacture into butter or ghee; or

b. adding to whole milk a preparation of fluid skim milk derived from the manufacture of butter or ghee at another center; or

c. reconstituting dried skim milk and adding to whole milk.

Method (c) would be the most effective means of using the present surplus of skim milk. Dried skim milk resulting from processing surplus milk during the rainy season at, say, Iringa, could be stored and transported to Dar es Salaam for toning purposes. This would augment the inadequate supplies available during the dry season. This method, however, would necessitate the installation of suitable drying plants (pp. 171-72).

279. Measures to increase and improve milk supplies from African cattle keepers near the towns are:

a. The development of the fresh milk market, which would give a greater return to the farmer than ghee production and would result in his having a greater interest in dairying.

b. The improvement of milk collection and marketing facilities, notably by provision of milk collecting and pasteurizing centers to which the milk is delivered by the producer or to which it is brought by vehicles which pick it up from the producers at collection points on the roads.

c. Improvement in simple dairy hygiene, in order to avoid wastage of milk which goes bad before reaching the collecting center, or the delivery of poor quality milk to the consumers. This is mainly a matter of avoiding contamination of the milk during milking, and of ensuring the provision of suitable containers, their cleanliness and their protection against dirt and flies until they reach the collection center. It would require an increase in simple extension activities among the producers. Subsidiary and longer term requirements for the improvement of African dairying would be the provision of more water supplies, better disease control, and breeding stock of improved milk-producing capacity (p. 171).

Miscellaneous

280. The customs authorities should invite the shipping companies to consider together with them the simplification of customs formalities for coastwise shipping (p. 290).

281. A long range Sferics network for the detection of thunderstorms should be established, with centers in Tanganyika at Dar es Salaam and Tabora, and storm-detecting radar should be installed at Tabora and Mwanza. Financial provision should be made for the operation of the wind-finding equipment at Tabora (p. 293).

282. Establishment of public call boxes along the main roads is not justified (p. 295).

INDEX

For special terms *see* Currency, Weights, Statistical Conventions
and Glossary, pp. x-xiii.